Editorial
A Promise of Freedom

Melissa Makele, Anh-Linh Ngo

Freedom. Hardly any other word is invoked more frequently than this one in recent societal debates, for example on racism, gender, ecology, or even the Covid-19 pandemic. Curiously enough, it has mutated into a rallying cry for those who want to preserve the status quo by any means. "Free speech" is the mantra invoked by racists, anti-feminists, or homophobes, right-wing Covid-19 deniers and so-called climate skeptics who lament the supposed threats to their freedom of expression. Often enough, their arguments revolve around a concept of freedom based on sovereignty, autonomy, and consumption.

But one's own freedom cannot be considered in isolation from social, economic, infrastructural, and natural dependencies; the pandemic and its consequences have reminded us of this, as do the effects of global warming. "We are always in the midst of it." That is how the feminist theorist Donna Haraway put it in 1995, speaking about the subjective interconnectedness of all knowledge, in which those on the outside are never independent;[01] it is also why she has called for "embodied, and therefore accountable, objectivity."[02] This insight is at the base of this issue, in which we consider how forms of social injustice are entangled at different spatial levels. How can architecture, a discipline still strongly influenced by patriarchal hierarchies of power and exploitative relations, fulfill a new promise of freedom based on a transformative notion of justice?

Looking back

Over forty years ago, in December 1981, under the editorial direction of Sabine Kraft and Sibylla Hege, the first and so far only issue of *ARCH+* with a feminist stance was published under the title *Kein Ort, nirgends: Auf der Suche nach Frauenräumen* (No Place, Nowhere: In Search of Women's Spaces). The issue builds upon the struggles of second-wave feminism, which in Germany emerged from the student protests of 1968. The feminist discourse around architecture and urbanism that was developed in the 1970s in West Germany negotiated issues of gender equality and women's emancipation at the level of space and the various disciplines of spatial design. Structural change was demanded, focusing on the equal participation of female architects and spatial planners in design and planning processes, as well as the reduction of gendered discrimination in the heavily male-dominated profession of architecture.

On a systemic level, the discourse was centered on a fundamental critique of the built environment as a product of the patriarchal hegemony caused by capitalism's gendered division of labor into a "public sphere" of production and a "private sphere" of reproduction (of labor power). In the decades following World War II, this paradigm was spatially cemented, literally cast in concrete, revolving around the model of the bourgeois nuclear family and its prescribed roles: the father as the breadwinner and the mother in charge of housekeeping and rearing children. One of the main contributions in that *ARCH+* issue—an essay by the US architect and urban historian Dolores Hayden that continues to be widely cited—asked: "What would a non-sexist city be like?" How might an egalitarian reorganization of private space succeed? How can the associated gendered divisions of labor, dependencies, and conventions be eliminated by expanding collective infrastructures for reproductive activities (washing, cooking, raising children, etc.)?

In the context of these questions, the German feminist slogan *Wohnen ist Arbeiten* (dwelling is working), analogous to the "Wages for Housework" campaign, was formulated as a deliberate provocation against the established idea of modernity that being at home was only about leisure and recreation. This idea was criticized as representing only a *male* point of view, reflected in the "androcentric" design of housing and residential environments, in the location and furnishings of housing developments, and in their one-sided designation as "dormitory towns"—accompanied by considerable restrictions on women's and girls' mobility and their ability to appropriate space for themselves. Building upon this critique, the feminist demands of the 1980s in the fields of architecture and spatial planning were accordingly diverse.

The *ARCH+* publication from 1981 took a differentiated approach to these issues. On the one hand, it politicized housing to highlight women's needs in housing design, from more flexible, non-hierarchical floor plans to new community-oriented typologies. On the other hand, it took on urban planning, calling for the recognition of the realities of daily life, for mixed-use planning, spatial bundling of family-oriented infrastructure, a reduction of so-called *Angsträume* (places of insecurity) in public space, and decelerating traffic in the sense of a "compact city" as a counter-model to the car-centric city. This was accompanied by a feminist critique of prevailing structures such as top-down planning, "master" plans, and deference to "experts," as well as a call for broader participation and the involvement of residents in planning processes. Last but not least, *Kein Ort, nirgends: Auf der Suche nach Frauenräumen* underscored the need to create women-only spaces and projects, such as women's cafés, women's centers, women's counseling offices, women's bookstores, autonomous women's shelters, and women's housing projects. These would create spaces of protection, networking, and action for women in an otherwise patriarchal society. The editorial concludes: "In search of an environment that offers women room to develop instead of imprisoning them in roles, in search of ways out of the dead end of male-dominated planning and prescribed aesthetics. [...] Where is this place? There are only contours; nothing measured out. But what is clear is the need for a new start—with no turning back. Never."

CONTEMPORARY FEMINIST SPATIAL PRACTICE

Looking back at that issue of *ARCH+* today, many of the topics and demands it addressed are still relevant. At the same time, from today's perspective, what stands out is a conceptual narrow-mindedness and gaps related to the complexities revealed by feminist theory and insights in recent decades. On the one hand, in the wake of the post-structuralist debate in the 1990s, the concept of gender has become increasingly differentiated, going beyond the binary logic of woman/man, queering our understanding of sex, gender, and political subjectivation. On the other hand, as Niloufar Tajeri points out in her contribution to this issue—on the planning history of the international building exhibition (IBA Alt) in Berlin in 1984–87 from a migrant and feminist perspective—there are "perspectives, needs, problems, aspirations, and hopes [that] were entirely absent from discourse at that time, and have only been made visible in recent years. This was because the feminist planning discourse had emerged from the critique of power articulated by the second women's rights movement, but reduced this critique to the single aspect of gender injustice." The term "intersectional" in the subtitle of Tajeri's essay, "Why We Need Intersectional Knowledge Production and a Culture of Memory in Architecture," refers to the intertwining and interdependence of different forms of social oppression, which, in addition to gender injustice and sexism, include racialization or racism and discrimination based on social origin (classism), among others. This phenomenon of multiple discrimination in terms of "race, class, and gender" was described by Black feminists as early as the 1950s and more broadly discussed in the 1970s, until the Black American lawyer Kimberlé Crenshaw coined the term "intersectionality" in the late 1980s.

The fact that we are only now discussing this feminist perspective—which forms the conceptual basis of this issue—despite longstanding critiques of feminism's focus on problems of the white middle class, reveals the entrenchment of power relations and the dominance of Western, white reasoning and epistemic assumptions, especially regarding our systems of knowledge production, which are in urgent need of revision. As Niloufar Tajeri states, "capitalism is crisis. This can be seen in various forms: climate catastrophe, displacement and distribution struggles within our cities, and racism and forced migration around the world. Given this, our answers and approaches must be developed in a way that is intersectional and critically anti-racist. Anti-racist because many problems are structurally racist and more strongly affect Black people, Indigenous people, and people of color (BIPOC). Intersectional because inequalities are intertwined between sexism, racism, and classism."

In her introductory essay, architect and gender researcher Yvonne P. Doderer makes it unmistakably clear that analyzing and fighting against social and spatial injustice cannot be a matter of "pitting issues of recognition and redistribution against one another." Not only is a material redistribution required but also "all those social, cultural and legal norms and codes must be challenged which situate and devalue women as well as LGBTQ+ and people of color as Other."

The broad feminist movements of the 20th century successfully expanded (mainly white) women's social participation and recognition as well as their access to education, professionalization, and (gainful) employment. However, it needs to be said that their social equality is still not in sight. These achievements have also led to additional labor for women because housekeeping, childrearing, and care work must still be done, either on the side or outsourced—often entailing new (and old) exploitative relationships. The market for domestic and care work, including the increase in gig-based care work through online platforms, enables wealthier income groups to externalize these activities as low-wage jobs held by economically weaker and structurally disadvantaged groups, often immigrants or minoritized ethnic people and women of color.

In their conversation in this issue, Silvia Federici and Lilian Chee lay out the consequences of these shifts from unpaid to paid reproductive services on a global scale, and how they affect political strategies, political subjects, and feminist struggles—particularly in terms of spatial politics and design—in the 21st century. In her contribution to the issue, Elke Krasny shows how deeply the politics of space are enmeshed with questions of labor, especially the organization of reproductive labor. With her conceptual groundwork for a "critical theory of architecture and care work," she argues against making "the built environment complicit in maintaining systems of injustice and perpetuating unjust local and global relations." According to Krasny, "an architecture that actively contributes to preserving the habitability of planet Earth and sets standards against gendered, racial, and classist discrimination will have to build up care work differently in order to repair the future."

Toward the back of this issue, the topic of repair opens the feminist discourse to decolonial and postcolonial questions: "How do we repair a world that seems irreparably broken?" asks architectural historian Irene Cheng against the backdrop of ongoing debates about structural racism and the continuities of colonial violence, spurred by the

May 2020 murder of George Floyd and exacerbated by a global pandemic that claimed over six million lives worldwide and exposed significant social inequalities. Drawing on architect and historian Mabel O. Wilson, Cheng outlines various "dimensions of repair" which do not aim to recreate what came before, but rather, informed by a feminist ethics of care, target more radical forms of redress and repair "that are explicitly unfinished, bridging historical research with contemporary design and activism." Cheng and Wilson call for a response to the violent actions that have led to disruption and social division: "The task of repair, at once impossible and imperative, calls for new techniques of discovering, revealing, and writing the past, as well as for linking history to actions that call forth a different future."

AN OUTLOOK FOR ARCHITECTURE

In our 2017 anniversary issue, *Am Ende: Architektur – 50 Jahre ARCH+ Projekt und Utopie* (In the End: Architecture – 50 Years of the ARCH+ Project and Utopia), longtime co-publisher Nikolaus Kuhnert concludes the lead interview by outlining what distinguished the ARCH+ project from the onset: "We have always advocated for the argument that architecture is a political medium. As a magazine, we have highlighted topics that support the practical political work of architecture to this effect. In doing so, we must engage concretely with life and ask what contribution architecture can make in order to fulfill the promise of freedom." Interestingly, he concludes with the observation that the architectural concepts of the last 50 years have failed to project new models of living beyond the nuclear family, which is increasingly losing its normative power. Thus, it is "the project of the current generation [...] to show, under the transformed social conditions, how we can and want to live, produce, and work together."

At its core, this call to action reflects an argument that has characterized the field of feminist spatial practice and theory for decades. In recent years, the editorial team has recognized the need to catch up, steering the discourse back to topics such as property and housing, ecological urban renewal, processes of commoning, bottom-up urbanism, and the question of "real" participation, including feminist struggles and issues. Nevertheless, we must acknowledge how much ARCH+ as an institution has failed in terms of discourse and the possibility of feminist positioning since its last feminist issue was published over 40 years ago. This is reflected not least in the editorial direction taken over the years: of the more than 20 predominantly theoretical ARCH+ monographs published since 1968, not a single one was devoted to women's work. This status quo testifies to the undeniable patriarchal structures that still shape the profession and the dominant architectural discourse, which we significantly contribute to with our journalistic work.

Yet, as the range of topics in this issue makes clear, these structures, as well as the strategies to combat them, have an impact far beyond questions of representation and formal equality. How can the foundations of a white, male, Eurocentric canon be intersectionalized and decolonized? How can queer perspectives and marginalized bodies of knowledge, practices, and values not yet part of the dominant spatial planning paradigm find their way into the discipline and practice? How can exploitative work structures in terms of workload and hours be abolished? How can more family-friendly workplace policies be established?

It is a good sign that the Scottish-Ghanaian architect Lesley Lokko has recently been appointed chief curator of the 18th Venice Architecture Biennale—as the third woman after Kazuyo Sejima and architect duo Yvonne Farrell and Shelley McNamara, and as the first Black person. In this issue, she speaks with Tom Emerson about the need to "decarbonize, decolonize, and deinstitutionalize" architectural institutions. Her appointment must not remain a one-off symbolic political statement, but signal the start of a structural confrontation that establishes transformative justice on a larger scale and holds all of us responsible.

Against this backdrop, this issue is intended not least as a long-overdue provocation of the discipline as a whole. Not only do we ask the compelling question formulated by Nikolaus Kuhnert above, but we must also expand it: What contribution can—indeed, *must*—architecture make in order to fulfill the promise of freedom *for all*?

Thanks

We would like to thank our guest editors, Torsten Lange, Charlotte Malterre-Barthes, Daniela Ortiz dos Santos, and Gabrielle Schaad, who helped us to finally make good on the promise made five years ago to produce an issue on the issues of gender and feminism. With their support and expertise, we were able to expand the discourse and fill this issue with a diversity of voices. We warmly thank all the contributors who have changed—and are changing—the discipline, as well as us, with their knowledge, commitment, and passion.

We would also like to thank the ARCH+ team, especially Nora Dünser and Max Kaldenhoff, Franziska Gödicke, Anna-Maria Mayerhofer, Vera Krimmer, Paul Barth, Mirko Gatti, Markus Krieger, Daniel Kuhnert, and Victor Lortie, as well as our copy editor Alisa Kotmair. And last but not least, we would like to thank the Swiss Arts Council Pro Helvetia and the Harvard University Graduate School of Design, who helped to realize this English publication with their generous financial support.

01 **Donna Haraway, "Wir sind immer mittendrin. Ein Interview mit Donna Haraway," in Donna Haraway, *Die Neuerfindung der Natur: Primaten, Cyborgs und Frauen* (1991), eds. Carmen Hammer and Immanuel Stiess (Campus: Frankfurt a. M. 1995), 98–122.**

02 **Donna Haraway, "Situated Knowledges: The Science Question in Feminism and the Privilege of Partial Perspective," *Feminist Studies* 14, no. 3 (Autumn 1988): 575–99, 588.**

Torsten Lange, Charlotte Malterre-Barthes, Daniela Ortiz dos Santos, Gabrielle Schaad

Introduction

Calls for equity and parity in the hierarchically organized and economically driven field of conventional architecture have never been louder than today. While not everyone may hear these with the same urgency, a new generation of young practitioners is actively working across all areas of the discipline to transform architecture into an ethical practice that protects resources and society. This is even more urgent given the current global challenges, from the climate catastrophe and environmental destruction to resource scarcity, digitalization, decolonization, and the exacerbation of social inequality. Creating more equitable ecological and social conditions is also a matter of good design. Who looks after the children, cares for relatives, and cleans the apartment while others work overtime in the office to meet a competition deadline? Which ideal user groups are we building and planning for in the first place? Hasn't strong authorship always consisted of collaboration rather than the supposed "genius" of individuals? Looking beyond the usual canon of architecture, how can more culturally diverse concepts and solutions be implemented into the discipline and its knowledge repository? Beyond a separation between theory, practice, and education, how can projects address the experiences of marginalized and invisibilized groups? After all, an essential prerequisite to do so is greater participation and inclusion of these same groups in the planning process. However, access to education and jobs is still determined by numerous barriers and the highly selective Western European–North American (academic) value system prevalent in our latitudes. At the same time, as the collective of guest editors for this issue, we do not want to hide the fact that we ourselves are products of this system, of the knowledge and values we have internalized. From 2014 to 2019, we worked (sometimes together) in various positions at the Department of Architecture at ETH Zurich. We called for strengthening queer feminist perspectives in teaching and transforming higher education towards greater diversity and equity. When ARCH+ invited us to work on this issue, we saw it as an opportunity to broaden our horizons, create spaces for our role models, and learn from them to uncover our blind spots.

It could be argued that the general conditions for social balance are better today than they were 20 or 30 years ago. Isn't gender equality, inclusive language, political correctness, etc., already a reality in everyday life? What does all this have to do with architecture, anyway? Isn't architecture *the* "neutral" discipline par excellence? If so, why should you pick up this journal at all?

Forty years ago, ARCH+ published issue no. 60 under the title *Kein Ort, nirgends – Auf der Suche nach Frauenräumen* (No Place, Nowhere: In Search of Women's Spaces). For the first time, a spectrum of feminist spatial practices and other forms of action was laid out within its pages. Unlike perhaps in the 1980s, however, we don't consider feminist perspectives on architecture and spatial planning to be a niche topic that should be separated into a special issue of *ARCH+*. With this issue, which will hopefully be followed by numerous other contributions in future issues of the journal, we are instead making a case for an ethics of care. Far more people need to be involved in architectural discourse and in the processes of spatial production than are doing so today.

This issue of *ARCH+* asks how intersectional feminist practices shape contemporary architecture and spatial disciplines. Convergences between the active struggle for gender equality in the built environment and other forms of social justice engagement are discussed, including anti-racism, anti-colonialism, and the fight against trans- and homophobia. It synthesizes critical, reflective, speculative, embodied, and performative practices—from design, activism, craft, and education to theory and writing—across different scales, media, locations, and forms of expression. This includes names, practices, and places/situations outside of Europe within a web of translocal actors. We combine a variety of formats, from conversations to architectural and spatial interventions to essays and theoretical positions. Our central focus is the work of those who champion social causes in the built environment. We aim to eliminate the separation of theory and practice—the distinction between those who do and do not build—which continues to characterize contemporary building culture. To effectively counter all forms of discrimination in architecture, this issue of *ARCH+* maps the complex web of practices that deconstruct the power relations and barriers that continue to determine architectural discourse—from norms to work cultures, from archival policies to academic curricula.

From the beginning, we were aware that we were not speaking from one position but bringing very different perspectives to the table—forming the framework that enables us to critically examine spatial and intersectional injustices in the first place. Recognizing our positions was the starting point for us to show the complex cultural, social, economic, and political contexts gathered here. Working on such an issue in this constellation, with many mainly collectively organized contributors, almost inevitably means getting one's hands dirty. Nevertheless, this issue was born from passionate collaboration. At the same time, we knew early on that the positions represented in this issue would be far from exhaustive. The fact that the last *ARCH+* issue with an explicitly feminist agenda appeared more than 40 years ago was already a sound basis for discussion. In this respect, compiling a thematic issue like this one can only document a learning process on the part of the guest editors and the ARCH+ editorial team.

It was important for us that the contributions at least attempt to convey what is going on in much of the world—instead of merely reproducing the Northern Hemisphere's discourse. With each working session, the collection of feminist practices from recent years grew in our "carrier bag," to borrow a motif from the science fiction author Ursula K. Le Guin. And yet, the topics addressed identify missing points in the current discussion, particularly in the German-speaking area, where, even now, the professional world often retreats to narrow notions of professionalism and perspective. Nevertheless, the contributions that have made it into this issue comprise neither a "best of" nor a compendium, or even an atlas, but instead, starting points that envision the future—be it new forms of working or living, architectures of care, or queer, resistant, and activist spatial practices.

Critical international voices within the discourse on architecture and intersectional feminism have penned new *essays* for this issue, and key texts have been reprinted. Various *conversations* bring together experts from the broader field of architecture and feminist engagement to share and update perspectives—revealing frictions between different approaches, generations, and institutional functions. Similar to the conversations, our email-based *correspondence* format sees itself as an alternative to conventional forms of knowledge production by replacing an omniscient narrator's voice with a polyphony that bespeaks events and objects. Looking at architecture from a feminist standpoint is a political act, and foundational texts often serve to develop and substantiate one's positions. To what extent have texts by theorists such as Sara Ahmed, Frantz Fanon, Donna Haraway, and Audre Lorde shaped how we approach architecture—even without dealing explicitly with design? In our *positions* format, contributors reflect on their engagement with a specific text and discuss its impact on their practice. The various formats in this issue foreground collective knowledge production and are complemented by recent examples of feminist (spatial) *practices* and *interventions*.

This issue does not contain an exhaustive inventory of the myriad ways feminist practices shape or at least give glimpses of a better future. From the presented works—written, spoken, drawn, collaged, coded, sewn together, lived, and built—emerges a generous, hopeful, and composite body of possibilities for transforming current conditions. These contributions show what can and must change to keep architecture and planning relevant in the face of the ongoing social and ecological crisis. Constellations of queer, anti-racist, anti-colonial, solidarity-based, intersectional, and eco-feminist actors reject profit-oriented, destructive, and extractivist modes of operation that persist in architecture and the construction industry. They are depatriarchalizing, decolonizing, and decarbonizing the profession. They are producing the resistant and emancipated spatial practices we urgently need today and tomorrow. Committed to past as well as current forms of feminist engagement, the kaleidoscopic collection we present here—of tech-savvy activists and politicized students, queer thinkers, intersectional historians, critical theorists, committed designers, radical archivists, uncompromising educators, design cooperatives, repair collectives, and risk-taking spatial practitioners—offers paths out of the crisis toward a truly sustainable future that is rooted in gender equity and social and spatial justice. It is high time for architecture to introspect and open itself up to this discourse.

A Section of Now:
Social Norms and Rituals as Sites for Architectural Intervention
What will you do if you live to 100? How many parents do you have? We ask these and other questions in our upcoming book, published as part of our one-year investigation Catching Up with Life. Co-published by the CCA and Spector Books, available in January 2022.
CCA
cca.qc.ca/catchingupwithlife

Contents

Page 34

Page 44

ARCH+ features

Page 28

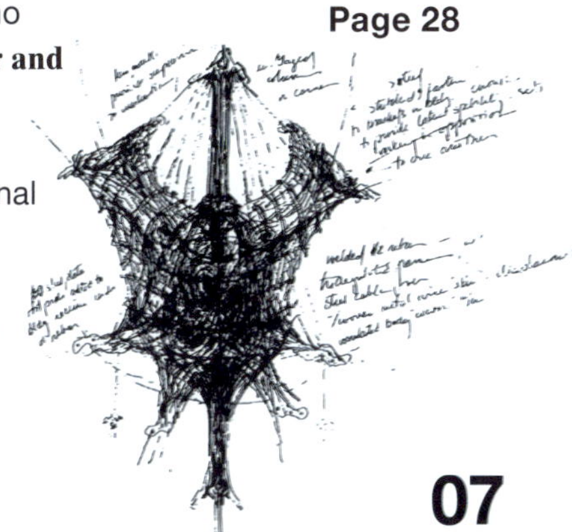

Contents

"So many women who played key roles have been systematically thrown out with the bathwater. Every work of architecture is a deeply collaborative enterprise, but we work so hard to deny it."
– **Beatriz Colomina,** **Page 110**

Page 107

Page 121

Page 100

Page 94

Page 207

ARCH+ TEAM FOR THIS ISSUE:
Nora Dünser (managing editor), Max Kaldenhoff (creative direction), Melissa Makele (project leader) (MAK), Anh-Linh Ngo (editor-in-chief), Paul Barth, Mirko Gatti, Franziska Gödicke (FG), Markus Krieger (MUK), Vera Krimmer (VK), Daniel Kuhnert, Victor Lortie, Anna-Maria Mayerhofer (AM)

GUEST EDITORS:
Torsten Lange, Charlotte Malterre-Barthes (CMB), Daniela Ortiz dos Santos (DOS), Gabrielle Schaad (GS)

COVER: © African Futures Institute, Design: Fred Swart, Director of Visual Identity, AFI.

Essay

Queer Feminist Cities for a Different Way of Living

TEXT
Yvonne P. Doderer

Photo: Yvonne P. Doderer.

The urban history(s) and struggles of the feminist movement(s) and the lesbian, gay, bisexual, transgender, and queer (LGBTQ+) activism(s), with their performative forms of protest and manifold projects, are expressions of difference made productive, contributing to the modernization of (urban) societies. Urban space favors the formation of these emancipatory movements with its various forms of community building and strategies of spatialization, both *in* and *as* urban spaces. As the philosopher and sociologist Henri Lefebvre noted in his seminal work, *The Production of Space*, "Moreover—and more importantly—groups, classes, or fractions of classes cannot constitute themselves, or recognize one another, as 'subjects' unless they generate (or produce) a space."[01] Today, however, we must ask to what extent this observation still holds.

HISTORICAL LINES

As demonstrated in my study of feminist discourse and community building in five (West) German cities between 1976 and 2000, many women's projects covering a broad spectrum of topics were spatialized during that period.[02] The culture of women's projects grew out of autonomous women's centers—the first central common spaces of German second-wave feminism (also called the new women's movement) after 1968. In its early days, the women's rights movement was radically feminist in its orientation, especially in the United States, directing much of its criticism toward the Western, white, male hegemonic order for being sexist and patriarchal. Women were seen as a class whose oppression formed the basis of all other forms of domination, class formation, and the exercise of power. Over time, however, the focus visibly shifted to a more differentiated view of feminism. Autonomous women's projects, joined later by lesbian projects, created space for the development of female subjectivity, self-determination, and sexuality, connecting everyday life with feminist political activism.

In terms of architecture and urban planning, a feminist line of questioning was formulated early on: how do architecture and urban planning influence women's lives? "What would a non-sexist city be like?"[03] The critique of the built reality around them was directed against the relegation of domestic reproductive labor to women, as well as their exclusion from planning decisions ("dormitory towns"), the separation of functions, hierarchized housing floor plans, and the "architectural-spatial rule by men" (German: *baulich-räumliche HERRschaft*), which limited women's and girls' opportunities to appropriate space for their own needs and mobility.[04] As it evolved, discourse around feminist planning increasingly focused on transforming practices in architecture and urban planning. Participatory models were developed and "women-suitable" and "women-friendly" housing was designed, resulting in a significant number of women's housing projects across Germany.[05] Such concepts were grounded in the demand to recognize the needs of everyday life in the sense of a *compact city*, to facilitate the domestic and care work performed by women, decelerate traffic, and make public spaces safer for women. They also called for effective civic participation, urban ecological renewal from a female perspective, and consideration of the needs of single women and mothers in housing policy.

The city tended to have negative connotations in feminist planning discourses; "female just" (German: *frauengerecht*) urban planning aimed primarily at "reducing spaces of fear so that women's mobility and their access to public spaces are not further hindered by planning that ignores their interests."[06] While this demand remains justified today, it neglects the fact that femicide and sexual violence against women continue to occur mainly in the domestic sphere. Given this context, many women campaigned to establish women's shelters as places of refuge and protection. While the Protection Against Domestic Violence Act was introduced in Germany in 2002 after years of campaigning, women's shelters are still far from becoming superfluous.[07] This issue also elucidates the importance of housing as a means of enabling emancipation and self-determined ways of living. Particularly in Germany, with its high proportion of rental housing, drastically rising rents are making it increasingly difficult for many to find housing that meets their aspirations, affecting especially low-income single women and members of the LGBTQ+ community. German housing policy and construction continue to be geared toward the heterosexual nuclear family, offering few options to accommodate alternative lifestyles and people's changing needs throughout the course of their life.

GAYBORHOODS

In the United States, against the backdrop of the civil rights movement, the student movement, and the protests against the Vietnam War, a gay liberation movement formed alongside the women's movement. The 1970s and 1980s saw the emergence of a process that US researchers have referred to as the "great gay migration": the influx of young men, in particular, into major East and West Coast cities.[08] The Stonewall Uprising in June 1969 on Christopher Street in Greenwich Village, New York City, was the first climax of a defiant appropriation of urban space. This uprising had already been preceded by smaller revolts, such as those by trans women and drag queens in San Francisco, which historian and trans activist Susan Stryker has pointed out in her work.[09] The Stonewall Riots, as will be recalled, gained attention well beyond the United States as the beacon of a collective coming out. It also marked the emergence of feminist lesbian separatists who set themselves apart not only from gay men but also from the heterosexism of early feminists; many manifested this separation spatially by establishing their own rural communities.

Inspired by the gay movement in the United States, the West German (and, to a lesser extent, the East German) gay scene also began to assert itself and become more spatialized. In addition to the existing cruising areas in urban parks and public toilet facilities, there were now openly gay bars, clubs and other hot spots, gay bookstores, projects for counseling and recreation, political initiatives, and networks. Similar to the women's and lesbian scenes, these places were concentrated in specific urban districts, making them attractive places to live. In English-speaking countries, such neighborhoods have been referred to as "gay villages" or "gayborhoods." One of the most internationally well-known examples is the Castro in San Francisco. In the United States, however, gayborhoods, like most neighborhoods, remain

Christopher Street Liberation Day, New York 1972 © Leonard Fink Photographs, The LGBT Community Center National History Archive.

In 1981, seven women planners and architects stormed an all-male expert hearing with about 300 participants, held in Berlin in the run-up to the 1984–87 International Building Exhibition (IBA). In addition to calling for staffing women in IBA planning positions, they also demanded a stronger consideration of programmatic aspects of gender sensitive planning within the building exhibition's framework. Following what they self-mockingly called a faux pas, they founded the Feminist Organization of Women Planners and Architects (its German tongue-in-cheek acronym being FOPA). After an all-male jury again judged "women's housing" designs by men in a design seminar during the IBA in 1986, FOPA again protested. As a result, Zaha Hadid, Christine Jachmann, and Myra Warhaftig were commissioned to design one building each. The latter designed the apartment building at Dessauer Strasse 39 (pictured) in Berlin-Kreuzberg. View from the courtyard, around 1993.
© Orly Fatal-Warhaftig and Tomari Ruccius.

Myra Warhaftig took up the idea of the hallway-free apartment by architect Alexander Klein. Here, visual and acoustic connections between rooms facilitate communication and childcare. Each apartment is connected to two staircases, allowing large residential units to be divided into smaller ones. This image shows a model of the four-room apartment with a combined living room and kitchen. Model: Joachim Zielke. © Photo: Bernd Seeland.

Myra Warhaftig lived with her family in the IBA project she designed at Dessauer Strasse 39.
© Orly Fatal-Warhaftig and Tomari Ruccius.

View of Myra Warhaftig's combined living room and kitchen, around 1993. She had already developed the concept for the space in her dissertation, *Behinderung der Emanzipation der Frau durch die Wohnung und die Möglichkeit zur Überwindung* (English: Obstruction of Women's Emancipation through the Home and the Possibility of Overcoming It), which she completed in 1982.
© Orly Fatal-Warhaftig and Tomari Ruccius.

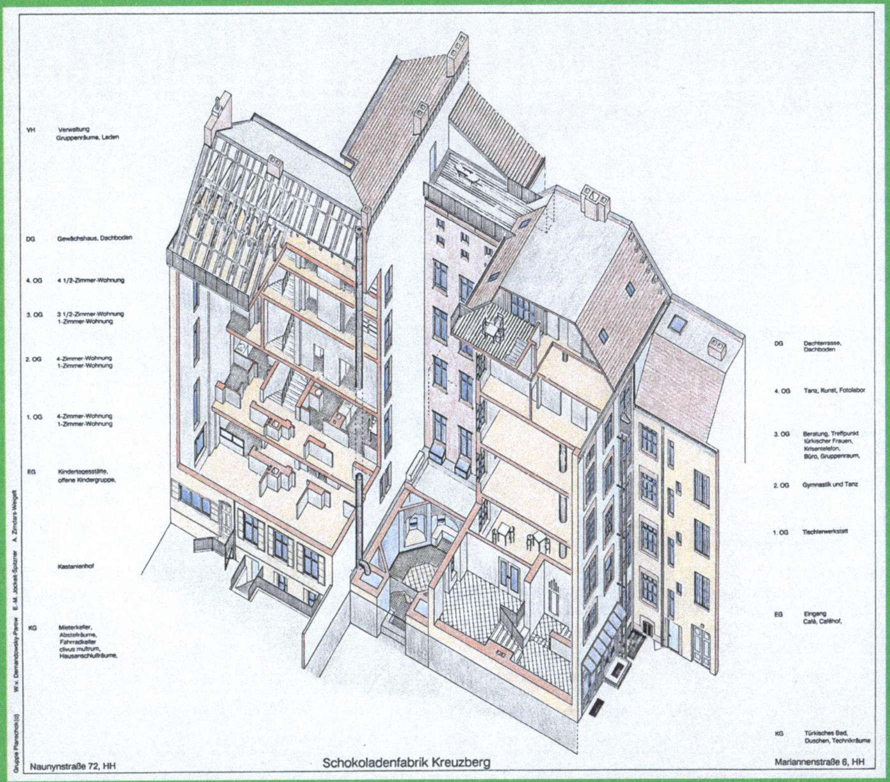

Schokofabrik entrance on Mariannenstrasse 6, around 1981 © Frauenzentrum Schokofabrik e.V.

ISOMETRIC VIEW OF THE DESIGN FOR THE RENOVATION OF THE OLD CHOCOLATE FACTORY IN BERLIN-KREUZBERG.

On May 8, 1981, around 40 women occupied the former Greiser & Dobritz chocolate factory in Berlin-Kreuzberg, responding to threats of it being demolished. Their vision for the building, which had been vacant for eight years, was to transform it into a center for communication and counseling services with apartments and safe spaces for socially disadvantaged women from the neighborhood. Many other activists and students showed solidarity with them, protesting the city's practice of blocking the use of vacant apartments in the city center while demolishing historic buildings and increasing rents. The conversion and development of the Schokofabrik women's center, which was designed within the framework of the IBA and opened in 1986, became an important model project for the strategy of "cautious urban renewal" coined by Hardt-Waltherr Hämer. © Planschok(o)

The Schokofabrik's architectural program includes green courtyards, roofs, and façades; waste recycling; and alternative concepts to save water and energy. The architecture practice Planschok(o), which included Waltraud von Demandowsky-Parow, Margot Gerke, Eva-Maria Jockeit-Spitzner, and Antje Zimdars-Weigelt, worked closely with Schokofabrik members and other women volunteers to create the café, hammam (pictured), a floor for handicrafts and sports, a carpentry workshop, a dance floor, an educational area, and a greenhouse. © Frauenzentrum Schokofabrik e.V.

Schokofabrik volunteers
Photo: Elisabeth Rodé.

racially segregated to this day.[10] Another aspect that fostered urban LGBTQ+ community building in the US and Europe was the political activism sparked by the AIDS crisis in the 1980s, giving rise to queer alliances such as ACT UP and Queer Nation and receiving widespread support from lesbians and feminists.

Newspaper article, *San Francisco Sentinel*, May 29, 1987.

THEORETICAL UPDATES

With the advancement of feminist theory in the 1990s, the focus broadened from women to encompass all dimensions of gender, gender relations, and the critique of a binary gender model. As a result, the category of gender was scrutinized in light of its interaction with other social categories, such as ethnicity, dis/ability, and age. In Germany, this theoretical expansion was reflected in further differentiation among women's projects, for example, dealing with issues of migration and interculturality. Remarks by the social scientist Christina Thürmer-Rohr on the "complicity" of women also provoked discussion in feminist circles, pointing out that many women, particularly white women, participate in patriarchal hegemonic male structures and profit from them or at least approve of them.[11] The critical positions of Black feminism in the US, formulated by the Black lesbian women of the Cohambee River Collective,[12] among others, only gained traction in German discourse in the mid-1990s.[13]

In her 1990 book *Gender Trouble*, Judith Butler introduced a deconstructivist approach to examining gender (social sex) and sex (biological sex) as social constructs.[14] Pointing out that biology and concepts of nature are not indisputable truths but inherently shaped by discourses, she challenged long-held assumptions about the naturally given gender distinctions between "male" and "female." This observation opened up new views on spaces, subjectivities, and identity constructions that transcend the boundaries of the gender binary and heteronormativity in the sense of "undoing gender,"[15] which served as the foundation for the field of queer studies (as an evolution of gay and lesbian studies) and its critique of heteronormativity, homonormativity, and homonationalism. Underpinning this critique is the recognition that, given the intricacies of gender, race, and class that are also evident among LGBTQ+ people, identity politics must address more than issues of sexual orientation in order to strengthen the (self-)empowerment of marginalized groups and tackle structural social inequalities.

The lawyer Kimberlé Crenshaw coined the term "intersectionality" in the late 1980s to describe the interdependencies, entanglement, and simultaneity of categories of inequality such as gender, sexuality, race, social class, disability/ability status, and age. This intersectional perspective is taken up by queer theory to address exclusion, ethnicization, and racialization—also in reaction to violence against LGBTQ+ people in urban spaces—as they are intentionally or unconsciously practiced, even in their own ranks.[16] This criticism still leads to heated discussion within the LGBTQ+ community today, especially against the backdrop of social normalization and compliance with hegemonic norms—a phenomenon that reached a high point in Germany with the 2017 legalization of same-sex marriage, commonly referred to as "marriage for all" (although the definition of "all" in this respect is not yet all-encompassing).

NEOLIBERAL SPATIAL PRODUCTION

In the 21st century, the progressive capitalization of urban (and rural) spaces is showing its effects worldwide. The capitalist production of space is nothing new; what is new, however, is the scope and dynamics that capital unfolds. Today, internationally operating investment firms, banks, as well as real estate, construction, and large planning companies set the tone. At both the macro and micro levels, this leads to an extractivist, infrastructural, and structural arms race in zones of (projected) economic growth—and to processes of precarization, impoverishment, and social disintegration in zones of economic decline. In this regard, we should not forget the Marxist insight that capitalism is a system of crises in which capital is not only invested but also often destroyed at the expense of poorer taxpayers. The mortgage crisis in the United States, a major contributor to the global financial crisis of 2007/8, hit Black and Latinx Americans particularly hard: their assets lost 50 to 60 percent of their value, and many people became homeless.[17] Throughout this and all subsequent crises, the wealth in the hands of the very few has continued to multiply.

This development is a result of the enforcement of neoliberal policies ensuring that as little as possible—and certainly not the state—stands in the way of the investment of capital in what David Harvey refers to as the secondary circuit of capital, i.e., the built environment. While the state does not pull out of the process altogether, the market "itself becomes the organizing and regulating principle of the state."[18] In this context, the selling off of state property, the introduction of New Public Management (NPM), and the formal or material privatization of municipal services are associated with processes of de-democratization, which equally entail a devaluation of spatial and urban planning. State and city, in turn, are concerned with the application of a purported rationalism of economics to as many areas of society as possible, including urban development and housing policy. Here, too, the motto applies: the market will fix it. Private capital—often in combination with state subsidies and deregulation—builds "shining cities"[19] for financially strong target groups with the help of visual, narrative persuasion systems. But what takes place on the other side of the street are demolitions, evictions, rent increases, or the conversion of housing from rental into private property. The consequences of neoliberal policies are well known: privatization of public spaces, gentrification, urban homogenization, loss of affordable housing, and the exacerbation of socio-spatial segregation and social inequality. So far, there seems to have been no significant departure from this policy. The sociologist Pierre Bourdieu saw the targeted implementation of economization policies as part of a "neoliberal utopia" involving the "methodical destruction of collectives."[20] Taking the place of collectives are individualized, flexible, affluent (wherever possible), and self-regulating subjects whose (sexual) identity and diversity represent new target groups, and whose (pink) money creates new markets—with the LGBTQ+ scene(s) relegated to being a tourist attraction and locational factor in city marketing and intercity competition.

DISPLACEMENT AND DISTRIBUTION STRUGGLES

In addition to LGBTQ+ communities, feminist women's projects are not unaffected by these developments. The number of women's projects has decreased significantly in Germany. The remaining projects are in the social sector—befitting of women's socially assigned traditional role. A generational change is also clearly noticeable. Many (young) women do not feel the need for women-only spaces, even though social equality has still not been achieved after decades of feminist struggles for more equality and social participation. The collective struggle by women for autonomy, political self-determination, and alternative lifestyles, housing, and working is no longer addressed mainly by women's projects but through temporary, event-based activism. Although feminist critiques of the city and its spaces have been addressed in a wide variety of publications and practical counter-designs for nearly 40 years, establishing feminist architecture and urban planning theory in German academia has been virtually impossible.[21] Gender mainstreaming as the basis for "gender planning" and "gender budgeting" became legally binding throughout the EU with the Treaty of Lisbon in 2008—and was already laid down as a general equality strategy in the EU Treaty of Amsterdam in 1997–99. In Germany, however, with a few exceptions, it is regarded in architecture and urban planning as an annoyance, if it receives any attention at all.[22] Even modest approaches to gender-responsive urban planning in this country—in contrast to cities such as Vienna, Barcelona, or Stockholm, for example—are, upon closer inspection, light years behind the times. Even when issues of gender-equitable planning are taken into account, the process is not without problems and often leads to exclusion, as sociologist Marguerite van den Berg has pointed out using the example of Rotterdam. The city's urban policy targets young, middle-class families through family-friendly planning, making them agents of gentrification. Van den Berg describes this approach as "genderfication."[23]

For some time, gay and lesbian people were also seen as agents and pioneers of urban gentrification. Yet, many gayborhoods in the US show clear signs of disintegration, a phenomenon supported by the statistics.[24] In the United States, LGBTQ+ people are now moving to different parts of the city or into suburbs, smaller cities, or the countryside. In the English-speaking discourse, gay, lesbian, and queer life in rural areas and small towns is increasingly coming into focus.[25] In this context, critique is aimed at the stereotype of the city as a space of tolerance and freedom and a beacon of the gay, lesbian, trans, and queer community, and how it contributes to the erasure and discrediting of LGBTQ+ people living in rural areas.

In Germany, the LGBTQ+ resident population is not easy to track. One indicator is same-sex domestic partnerships, with evidence of their significant overall increase from 1996 to 2018.[26] An increase can also be seen in same-sex couples by primary residence. These estimates are relatively conservative, as not everyone acknowledges or discloses their sexual identity.[27] Quite a few LGBTQ+ people are necessarily visible or make themselves recognizable as such in everyday (urban) life. Moreover, single people also have same-sex or different-sex partnerships, moving in a network of "alternative kinship arrangements," as Judith Butler has put it.[28]

A comparison of German cities shows a clear correlation between traditional strongholds of LGBTQ+ infrastructures—first and foremost Berlin, followed by Cologne, Frankfurt am Main, Munich, and Hamburg—and a concentration of corresponding resident groups.[29] So far, it superficially appears that Germany has not experienced the same population shifts as the USA. Yet, given the perpetually rising rents, it is becoming obvious that only affluent members of the LGBTQ+ community can continue to afford to live in high-demand cities, a trend set to become even more pronounced in the future. This makes it even harder for more vulnerable LGBTQ+ persons to access housing and urban LGBTQ+ services.

More obvious are the processes of displacement affecting LGBTQ+ social and cultural infrastructures. In his research on gay nightlife in New York City, the cartographer Jeff Ferzoco could locate only 26 gay nightclubs in Manhattan from 1931 to 1960, but 318 for the years from 1961 to 1990. This number dropped to 264 between 1991 and 2010, and to 99 nightclubs in 2015.[30] Significant signs of shrinking infrastructures can also be observed in major German cities, even in well-known trendy neighborhoods such as Berlin-Schöneberg, Cologne's Old Town, or Hamburg's St. Georg "gay village," as it is called in official promotional materials. This loss mainly affects lesbians; in Berlin, for instance, there are no longer any exclusively lesbian bars. Yet, as in the United States, these losses are not solely due to gentrification processes and exploding rents. Processes of recognition and normalization, a diversification of scenes, and different behaviors due to social media use also play a role, so that the average LGBTQ+ citizen no longer seems to be dependent on specific locales and safe places. Community building, collectivity, and solidarity most likely emerge at temporary events like Christopher Street Day or in special-interest clubs.

Nevertheless, the task for the future will not only be to preserve the remaining LGBTQ+ spaces, but to close existing and newly opening gaps. This concerns counseling centers, services for queer refugees, and housing projects targeted mainly at older LGBTQ+ people, to mention just a few examples. Urban policy and planning must finally perceive the needs of LGBTQ+ people of all ethnicities and backgrounds, and meet these needs in cooperation with LGBTQ+

Photo: Yvonne P. Doderer.

organizations. Homo-, bi-, trans-, and intersexphobic violence cannot be answered with police measures alone but require education and active policies promoting gender equality and anti-discrimination that aim to create inclusive, appropriative, diverse, queer- and women-friendly urban spaces—from which *all* city residents can benefit.[31]

Queer feminist (urban) planning

The early feminist demands to change architecture (practice) and urban planning (policy) are still far from being fulfilled, although their reception is, fortunately, experiencing a revival. Even gender mainstreaming, which merely operates in a corrective, compensatory, and regulatory manner, has only been rudimentarily achieved. But the feminist discourse around spatial, urban, and open space planning must also be continued. The discourse on the care economy, which has mainly been conducted in the social sciences, opens up perspectives on reproduction and the gender-specific division of labor. The term care economy applies not only to domestic work but also unpaid and paid care work and all forms of personal services—notably work that continues to be performed mainly by women.

Moreover, discourse about the care economy can and must be directly connected to that of feminist ecology. This entails prioritizing work on and with people and the responsible use of natural resources over notions of added value and growth rate. It represents a fundamental transformation that must include quality spatial development based on genuinely sustainable infrastructures, construction methods, and materials, which aims to meet the needs of daily life and ecological requirements. Going beyond the limitations of traditional gender and family concepts, it must open the window much wider to diverse forms of individual and social coexistence.

Such an approach undoubtedly requires redistribution at all material, social, cultural, and symbolic levels, involving different (spatial) modes of production and redefining the value of work. Urban and rural areas could then be understood as equal, interlocking entities, and spatial disparities and territorial inequalities at all scales could be rectified in the longer term. Advancing these redistributions throughout society cannot be done without an ongoing discussion about post-growth, commons, genuine participation, and the right to the city (Henri Lefebvre), to mention just a few aspects here. However, many of the critical, alternative discourses associated with these terms are not only scarcely intertwined, but also far too often exclude feminist and queer perspectives. Pitting issues of recognition and redistribution against each other cannot be the answer. According to the political philosopher Nancy Fraser, the category of gender and its associated inequities are determined by dimensions related to both economic and social status.[32] Gender justice can only be achieved if both aspects are equally addressed and structurally changed. Not only does the distribution of (reproductive) labor and surplus value need to be balanced, but all those social, cultural, and legal norms and codes must be challenged that situate and devalue women, LGBTQ+ people, and people of color as Other.

Queer perspectives, on the other hand, open up possibilities for action that go beyond the normative, regulatory, and disciplinary delimitations associated with the respective prevailing gender and power systems. From an analytical point of view, in addition to examining sexuality and gender dispositifs, this involves the continuation of critical engagement with Western or Western-influenced centrisms and various dimensions of postcoloniality and decoloniality, intersectionality, and diversity. When seen in a spatial context, and based on an expanded notion of space, the term *queer* can encompass not only heterotopic spaces of deviation, but also non-defined, permeable, fluid spaces and related subjective and collective practices that can contribute to a further opening of society.

Cover of *ARCH+* 60, Winter 1981. © ARCH+

Not least, in view of the climate crisis, we must realize "a different city for a different life" in the 21st century, as the Situationist artist Constant asserted as early as 1959.[33] What is also needed, locally and internationally, is the creation of cross-border, transnational, and equitable solidarity with new forms of collectivity going beyond the dominant spatial, gender, and status systems. This cannot be achieved by planning alone. Yet, the field can and must make a significant contribution to such processes of transformation, which are ultimately unavoidable. The prerequisite to doing so is self-critical scrutiny by the profession and reflection on the social responsibilities of planners (although we have already made much progress in this respect). We must finally stop accommodating capital interests alone, bowing to "master" plans and the idea of sole expertise, stop disregarding findings from other disciplines, and no longer honor purely verbal commitments to participation and sustainability. The current decline in the significance of architecture, spatial planning, and urban planning should be taken as an opportunity to fundamentally transform the industry through conceptual innovation and the political positioning of feminist, queer, and ecological planning.

Photo: Yvonne P. Doderer.

01 Henri Lefebvre, *The Production of Space*, trans. Donald Nicholson-Smith (Oxford: Blackwell, 1991), 416f.
02 See Yvonne P. Doderer, *Urbane Praktiken: Strategien und Raumproduktionen feministischer Frauenöffentlichkeit* (Münster: Monsenstein & Vannerdat, 2003).
03 Dolores Hayden, "What Would a Non-Sexist City Be Like? Speculations on Housing, Urban Design, and Human Work," Signs 5, no. 3 (Spring, 1980), supplement, *Women and the American City*: 170–87.
04 Ulla Terlinden, "Baulich-räumliche HERRschaft – Bedingungen und Veränderungen," in *Frauen, Räume, Architektur, Umwelt: Beiträge zur Feministischen Theorie und Praxis 4*, eds. Petra Berndt et al. (Munich: Verlag Frauenoffensive, 1980), 92–101.
05 See, for example, Ruth Becker, *Frauenwohnprojekte: keine Utopie! Ein Leitfaden zur Entwicklung autonomer Frauen(wohn)räume mit einer Dokumentation realisierter Projekte in Deutschland* (Dortmund: Netzwerk Frauen- und Geschlechterforschung NRW, 2009).
06 Brigitte Karhoff, Rosemarie Ring, Helga Steinmaier, eds., *Frauen verändern ihre Stadt. Selbstorganisierte Projekte der sozialen und ökologischen Stadterneuerung: Vom Frauenstadthaus bis zur Umplanung einer Großsiedlung* (Dortmund: Ebersbach im eFeF-Verlag, 1993), 23.
07 See recent studies, such as Cara Ebert and Janina Steinert, *Gewalt an Frauen und Kindern in Deutschland während COVID-19-bedingten Ausgangsbeschränkungen*, 2020, accessed September 1, 2022, www.hfp.tum.de/globalhealth/forschung/covid-19-and-domestic-violence/.
08 Amin Ghaziani, *There Goes the Gayborhood?* (Princeton, NJ: Princeton University Press, 2014), 16. On the term "great gay migration" see also Kath Weston, "Get Thee to a Big City: Sexual Imaginary and the Great Gay Migration," *GLQ: A Journal of Lesbian and Gay Studies* (June 1995): 253–77.
09 See Susan Stryker, *Transgender History* (Berkeley, CA: Seal Press, 2008).
10 In addition to all-white "gayborhoods," some US cities also have concentrations of Black LGBTQ+ neighborhoods. See Angeliki Kastanis and Gary J. Gates, "*LGBT African-Americans and African-American Same-Sex Couples*," October 2013, accessed September 1, 2022, williamsinstitute.law.ucla.edu/publications/lgbt-afro-am-indv-and-ss-couples.
11 See Christina Thürmer-Rohr, "Mittäterschaft der Frau: Analyse zwischen Mitgefühl und Kälte," in Martina Emme and Christina Thürmer-Rohr, eds., *Mittäterschaft und Entdeckungslust* (Berlin: Orlanda Frauenverlag, 1989).
12 See Combahee River Collective, *The Statement*, 1977, accessed September 1, 2022, combaheerivercollective.weebly.com/the-combahee-river-collective-statement.html.
13 See May Ayim, Katharina Oguntoye, and Dagmar Schultz, eds., *Farbe bekennen: Afro-deutsche Frauen auf den Spuren ihrer Geschichte* [1986] (Berlin: Orlanda, 2020); See also the work of Natasha A. Kelly on the history of Black feminism and organizing in Germany: Natasha A. Kelly ed., *Schwarzer Feminismus: Grundlagentexte* (Münster: Unrast, 2019).
14 Judith Butler, *Gender Trouble: Feminism and the Subversion of Identity* (New York, NY: Routledge, 1990).
15 See Judith Butler, *Undoing Gender* (New York, NY: Routledge, 2004).
16 See Christine M. Klapeer and Karin Schönpflug, "De/constructing Spaces of Queer Fear: rassisierte und klassisierte Stadt- und Raumkonstruktionen am Beispiel Wien," *GENDER* 1 (Spring 2020), 78–94.
17 See Paul Taylor, Rakesh Kochhar, and Richard Fry, "Twenty-to-One: Wealth Gaps Rise to Record Highs Between Whites, Blacks and Hispanics," Pew Research Center, Social & Demographic Trends, July 26, 2021, accessed September 1, 2022, https://www.pewresearch.org/wp-content/uploads/sites/3/2011/07/SDT-Wealth-Report_7-26-11_FINAL.pdf.
18 Thomas Lemke, *Eine Kritik der politischen Vernunft: Foucaults Analyse der modernen Gouvernementalität* (Hamburg: Argument, 1997), 241.
19 See Yvonne P. Doderer, *Glänzende Städte: Geschlechter- und andere Verhältnisse in Stadtentwürfen für das 21. Jahrhundert* (Munich: Metzel, 2016).
20 Pierre Bourdieu, "The Essence of Neoliberalism," *Le Monde diplomatique* (December 1998), accessed September 1, 2022, mondediplo.com/1998/12/08bourdieu.
21 One of the few academic chairs on this topic in Germany, "Frauenforschung und Wohnungswesen in der Raumplanung" (Women and Housing in Spatial Planning) at TU Dortmund University, was abolished in 2009.
22 See also Ute Bauer and Franciska Frölich von Bodelschwingh, "30 Jahre Gender in der Stadt- und Regionalentwicklung: Erfahrungen und Perspektiven," Deutsches Institut für Urbanistik, 2017, accessed September 1, 2022, https://difu.de/publikationen/2017/30-jahre-gender-in-der-stadt-und-regionalentwicklung.
23 Marguerite van den Berg, "City Children and Genderfied Neighborhoods: The New Generation as Urban Regeneration Strategy," *International Journal of Urban and Regional Research* 37, no. 2 (Spring 2013): 523–36.
24 See David Christafore and Susane Leguizamon, "Is 'Gaytrification' a Real Phenomenon?" *Urban Affairs Review* 54, no. 5 (Winter 2016): 994–1016.
25 See Mary L. Gray, Colin R. Johnson, and Brian J. Gilley, eds., *Queering the Countryside: New Frontiers in Rural Queer Studies* (New York, NY: NYU Press, 2016).
26 Statistisches Bundesamt, "Gleichgeschlechtliche Paare (darunter: gleichgeschlechtliche Ehepaare und eingetragene Lebenspartnerschaften) im Zeitvergleich," 2020, accessed July 7, 2021, www.destatis.de/DE/Themen/Gesellschaft-Umwelt/Bevoelkerung/Haushalte-Familien/Tabellen/3-4-gleichgeschlechtliche-lebensgemeinschaften.html.
27 Martin Kroh et al., eds., "Einkommen, soziale Netzwerke, Lebenszufriedenheit: Lesben, Schwule und Bisexuelle in Deutschland," *Deutsches Institut für Wirtschaftsforschung Wochenbericht* 84, no. 35 (August 31, 2017): 687–98, 694.
28 See Judith Butler, "Is Kinship Always Already Heterosexual?," *Differences: A Journal of Feminist Cultural Studies* 13, no. 1 (Spring 2002): 14–44, 17.
29 Kroh 2017 (see 27), 691. In some cities, such as Cologne, a correlation between city districts and living arrangements or civil partnerships can be demonstrated, because the corresponding statistics were collected until the introduction of "marriage for all." See Amt für Stadtentwicklung und Statistik, ed., "Einwohnerinnen und Einwohner nach Familienstand am 31.12.2016," in *Kölner Postleitzahlgebiete: Strukturdaten 2016*, 16.
30 Jeff Ferzoco, "OUTgoing: The Hidden Geography of NYC's Gay Nightlife," accessed September 1, 2022, jferzo.co/outgoing-the-hidden-geography-of-nycs-gay-nightlife.
31 See also Petra L. Doan, ed., *Planning and LGBTQ Communities: The Need for Inclusive Queer Spaces* (New York, NY: Routledge, 2015).
32 See Nancy Fraser and Axel Honneth, *Redistribution or Recognition? A Political-Philosophical Exchange*, trans. Joel Golb, James Ingram, and Christiane Wilke (London: Verso Books, 2003).
33 Constant (Anton Nieuwenhuys), "Eine andere Stadt für ein anderes Leben," *Situationist International* 3, 1959, accessed September 1, 2022, www.si-revue.de/eine-andere-stadt-für-ein-anderes-leben.

Site-Reading Writing Quarterly

Figuring Feminisms in Times of Ecological Crisis and Racial Injustice

TEXT
Jane Rendell

***Site-Reading Writing Quarterly*, no. 2 (March 2020). The image/text collage by Katja Hilevaara and Emily Orley is a response to their reading of *Negotiating Conflict in Lebanon: Bordering Practices in a Divided Beirut* (2019) by Mohamad Hafeda.**

December 21, 2019

Dear Friends,

As we approach the shortest day of the year in the northern hemisphere and the longest in the south, I am sharing the first issue of *Site-Reading Writing Quarterly*, which will go live on December 21, 2019.

Each solstice and equinox, I am inviting two writers to read each other's work, hoping to help generate more interest in the amazing writing in our expanded field, explore ways of "reading writing" that critique the practice of "reviewing" from a situated perspective, and that re-write the genre and texture of the "critical review essay."

My massive thanks to Mona Livholts and Hélène Frichot, who, with everything else they have going on, agreed to inaugurate this reading writing experiment, and it is no surprise to discover that the theme of their dyadic reading writing emerged as "exhaustion"! [...]

And a big thank you to those who have recently sent new projects for site-writing.co.uk and criticalspatialpractice.co.uk; to Maryjane Orley and Martin Purvis for allowing me to use their *Solar Trajectories*; and to Stuart Munro, the designer who makes these websites.

If you have a written work that you've recently completed and/or someone else's work that you'd like to read, please get in touch.

SITE-WRITING

Back in 2002, I introduced the term *critical spatial practice* as one which placed attention on how processes of engaging with sites varied across different modes of artistic and design practices in architecture and in urbanism.[01] I defined these critical spatial practices as ways of questioning and transforming the social conditions of the sites into which they intervened, as well as testing the boundaries and procedures of their own disciplines and their own subjectivities. I stressed three particular qualities of these site-specific projects: the spatial, the critical, and the interdisciplinary, discussing how distinct practices articulate differently relations between the spatial and the social, and the aesthetic and the ethical, depending on position.

In writing "about" critical spatial practice, I began to consider how, since responses to art and architectural works happen *in situ*, we can understand them as taking place *somewhere*, and thus criticism can itself be recognized as a kind of critical spatial practice. The desire to work with variations in voice to reflect and create spatial distances and proximities between works and texts on the one hand, writers and readers on the other, became the motivation for *Site-Writing*, a collection of essays and documentations of text-works produced between 1998 and 2008 which question and perform notions of situatedness and spatiality in critical writing.[02] Here I located site-writing as a feminist form of critical spatial practice, which, because of its interest in situation and situated knowledge, could be connected to the ways in which, over the past 30 years, feminist philosophers and geographers had been articulating new ways of knowing and being through spatial terms, proposing conceptual and critical tools such as "situated knowledge" and "standpoint theory" for examining the relationship between the construction of subjects and the politics of location.[03] I argued, following Donna Haraway, that objectivity is partial and knowledge is situated,[04] and that one constructs one's viewpoint and performs one's critical attitude through writing in relation to one's lived and located experiences. Site-writing draws on the history of feminism, and, like much feminist discourse and critical practice today, it returns to second-wave feminism to rework the politicized yet also personal practices which emerged from that moment, especially Carol Hanisch's notion of "the personal is political."[05]

I defined critical spatial practices as ways of questioning and transforming the social conditions of the sites into which they intervened, as well as testing the boundaries and procedures of their own disciplines and their own subjectivities.

March 21, 2020

I hope you are well in these unsettled and unsettling times.

March 21, 2020, sees the second installment of *Site-Reading Writing Quarterly*, where Katja Hilevaara and Emily Orley read Mohamad Hafeda's *Negotiating Conflict in Lebanon: Bordering Practices in a Divided Beirut* (2019), and Mohamad Hafeda reads *The Creative Critic: Writing As/About Practice* (2018), edited by Katja Hilevaara & Emily Orley.

Already we can see the impact of our current situation—of university strikes in the UK and the impact of COVID-19 globally—on reading and writing activities.

Take care everyone—of (y)ourselves and all (y)our loved and vulnerable ones! [...]

SITUATED PRACTICE

While the notion of situatedness allows us to address the particularities of a site and our relations to it, and may lead us to address the material, political, and emotional qualities of our own subjectivities from both spatial and temporal perspectives, there is still a need to consider in more detail what actually constitutes a change to a condition that can bring us into a situation of critical awareness. This is where feminist concerns with situated knowledge meet the history of politically conscious art.

In her 2014 investigation of the Situationist International (SI) concept of "constructed situations" as a methodology, art historian Frances Stracey describes how SI's theory and practice involved unitary urbanism, psychogeography, and the *dérive*. She writes that "common to all these tactics was the transient, momentary temporality of constructed situations that the SI defined as ephemeral, without a future, mere 'passageways.'"[06] And as critic Ira Ferris has discussed, the SI aimed to allow "moments of life to be experienced in almost laboratory settings where they are highlighted and made obvious and where one can start to critically examine them."[07]

In Sara Ahmed's *Living a Feminist Life*, she refers to Lauren Berlant's elaboration of situation as "something which will perhaps matter."[08] And in "Thinking about Feeling Historical," Berlant herself writes about two men "in the now": "A situation has forced them to think. A situation has changed the ordinary into something they can no longer presume. ... A situation is a state of things in which something that will perhaps matter is unfolding amidst the usual activity of life."[09] The phrase "perhaps matter" led me to wonder about the very process of taking notice and becoming aware and how this is an embodied experience. Iris Marion Young, drawing on Toril Moi's work and existentialist philosophy, uses the term *body-in-situation* to argue that the lived body is a better concept for theorizing subjectivity than gender. Young writes, "The lived body is a unified idea of a physical body acting and experiencing in a specific sociocultural context; it is body-in-situation."[10]

June 21, 2020

Dear Fellow Site-Writers and Critical Spatial Practitioners,

I hope you are well in these turbulent times.

June 21, 2020, sees the launch of the third issue of *Site-Reading Writing Quarterly*, where Marko Jobst, Hélène Frichot, Klaske Havik, and Catharina Gabrielsson read Caroline Rabourdin's *Sense in Translation: Essays on the Bilingual Body* (2020) and Caroline Rabourdin and Matthew Chrislip's *Reading(s) and Writing(s), Unfolding Processes of Transversal Writing*, Issue #3 of *Writingplace Journal for Architecture and Literature*.

Already we have seen how readers' experiences of recent situations—local, such as the university strikes in the UK of 2019–20, and global, like the COVID-19 pandemic—have created writings made out of intimate and located readings. [...]

Ethopoiesis

One way of considering how the interpersonal and epistemological aspects of ethical practice are connected is through practices of "subjectivation,"[11] as advanced by Michel Foucault. These "technologies of the self," as Foucault describes them, place the practices of care for the self over practices of knowing oneself; these are the techniques through which subjects develop themselves, establishing their relation to moral codes and norms with respect to their own lives. Foucault distinguishes between the rule of conduct, the conduct measured by the rule, and "the manner in which one ought to 'conduct oneself'—that is, the manner in which one ought to form oneself as an ethical subject acting in reference to the prescriptive elements that make up the code." These are concerned with what he calls the "*determination of the ethical substance*; that is, the way in which the individual has to constitute this or that part of himself as the prime material of his moral conduct" and "*the mode of subjection* (mode d'assujettissement); that is, with the way in which the individual establishes his relation to the rule and recognizes himself as obliged to put it into practice."[12]

In his essay *Self-Writing* from 1983, Foucault explains how the Stoics understood writing's relation to ethical practice: "As an element of self-training, writing has, to use an expression that one finds in Plutarch, an *ethopoietic* function: it is an agent of the transformation of truth into *ethos*."[13]

He distinguishes between *hupomnemata* and *correspondence* as two modes of writing which differently address the self and the other as reader and writer. While *hupomnemata* are essentially notebooks that constitute a "material record of things read, heard, or thought," *correspondence* is "[t]he work the letter carries out on the recipient, but is also brought to bear on the writer by the very letter he sends, thus involv[ing] an 'introspection'; but the latter is to be understood not so much as a decipherment of the self by the self as an opening one gives the other onto oneself."[14] As Foucault explains, "the first historical developments of the narrative of the self are not to be sought in the direction of the 'personal notebooks,' the *hyomnemata*, whose role is to enable the formation of the self out of the collected discourse of others, they can be found, on the other hand, in the correspondence with others …."[15]

September 21, 2020

I hope you are all as well as can be.

For the fourth issue of *Site-Reading Writing Quarterly*, Marsha Meskimmon and Penny Florence have decided to hold a virtual dialogue about their two new books, *Transnational Feminisms, Transversal Politics and Art: Entanglements and Intersections* (2020) and *Thinking the Sculpture Garden: Art, Plant, Landscape* (2020).

Talking across their two separate-yet-joined Zoom frames, their fascinating conversation stems from their shared interests in art, ecology, and feminist politics. They exchange thoughts about the highly practical events, as well as conceptual concerns, that have informed the realization of their book projects, as well as imagine together the alternative possibilities for economics, knowledge, and life that can be produced out of the challenges posed by COVID-19 and the socioecological crisis of which the virus is a symptom. […]

G E O P O E T I C S

The decision to set up *Site-Reading Writing Quarterly* was driven by a desire to balance the dominance of sole-authored achievements in the academy with opening the possibility of reading and writing together, and to do this by creating a different type of reviewing—not the invisible point-scoring of the academic peer review, nor even the kind of judgement required by the journalistic book review which often does not acknowledge the positionality of the reviewer themselves. Situating the release of each issue at a solstice and equinox in correspondence with the movement of the earth was an attempt to connect a practice of reviewing to planetary patterns, and to forge a link, as Angela Last has done, between geopolitics and geopoetics: "At the same time, the proposal of the 'Anthropocene' has become linked with calls for a new 'geopolitics,' characterized by notions of responsibility and care for the planet and planetary society."[16]

While geographers have been developing new modes of place-writing, and artists and art critics connecting practice and criticism through art-writing, architectural and urban criticism has been slower to experiment with different writing forms. *Site-Writing* has been an attempt to explore the position of the critic, not only in relation to art objects, architectural spaces, and theoretical ideas, but also through the site of writing itself, to investigate the limits of criticism and ask what it is possible for a critic to say about an artist, a work, the site of a work, and the critic herself, and for the writing to still "count" as criticism. Site-writing has aimed to produce criticism as a form of situated practice that sets up different kinds of poetical, political, and ethical relationships with the works it encounters, while it also, as feminism has taught us, takes one's own life experience and responsibilities into account through the situated production of writing and reading. As Judith Butler argues in *Giving an Account of Oneself*, "the 'I' has no story of its own that is not also the story of a relation—or set of relations—to a set of norms."[17]

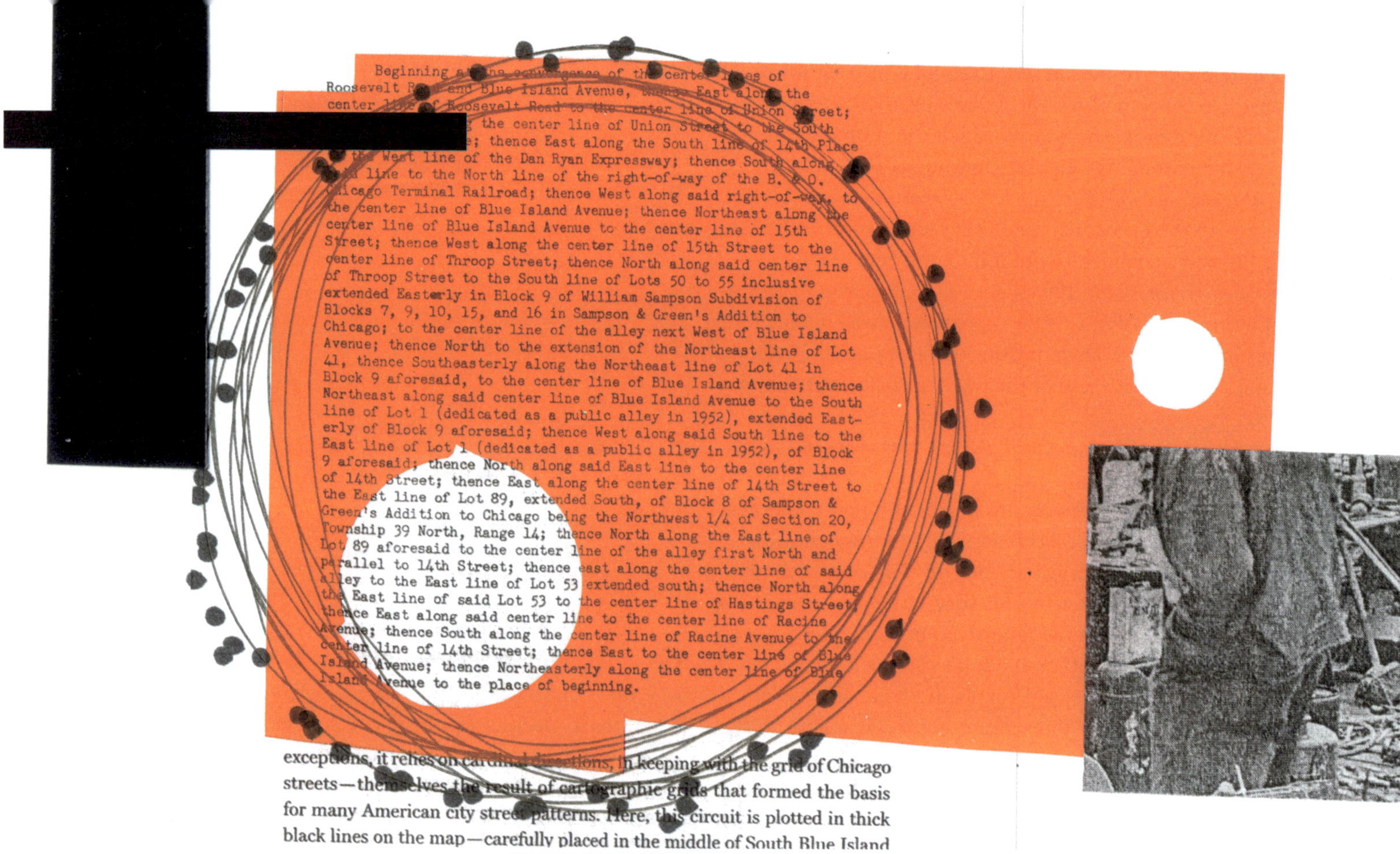

Site-Reading Writing Quarterly, no. 5 (December 2020): Image/text collages *Maxwell St. Pockets* (above), *Maxwell St. Observers* (middle), and *Maxwell St. Roosters* (below) by Kristen Kreider and James O'Leary, in response to their reading of *Maxwell Street: Writing and Thinking Place* (2019) by Tim Cresswell.
© Kreider + O'Leary.

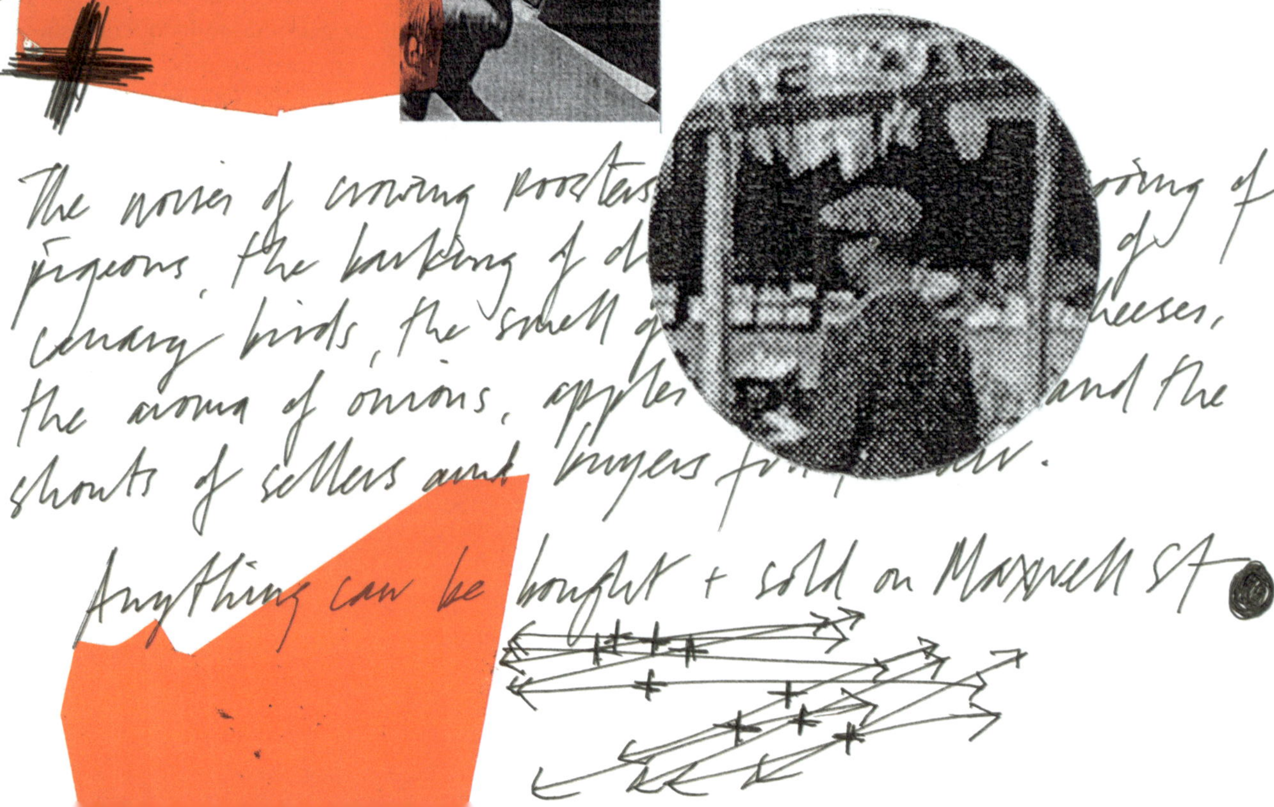

December 21, 2020

For this December 2020 solstice issue of *Site-Reading Writing Quarterly*, I have invited geographer and poet Tim Cresswell and architect and artist-poet duo, Kreider and O'Leary, to respond to each other's books. *Maxwell Street* (2019) is Cresswell's historical and poetic investigation of a specific location in Chicago, while Kreider and O'Leary's *Field Poetics* (2018) explores how text and place intertwine through five of their site-related projects.

2020 has been a year defined by the COVID-19 pandemic. Many have survived so far, but others have not. Lives have been lost. It has been a time of sadness and grief. But we have also shared many moments of kindness, laughter, and joy (perhaps more than usual?). The digital screen has brought people together, not only those who are usually physically close, but communities have been able to extend across the globe. As well as framing working life, we have eaten, cried, and laughed together in the time and space of the digital screen. Many talk of being exhausted by this "screen time." For that reason, it is perhaps no surprise that Tim and Kristen and James decided independently to read each other's books by making images. The visual work they have produced demands no lengthy task of intense reading, line by line. Instead, they have put together parallel series of intriguing combinations of letters and textures. Their compositions allow our eyes to wander around, to explore a bit, creating readings that unwind [...]

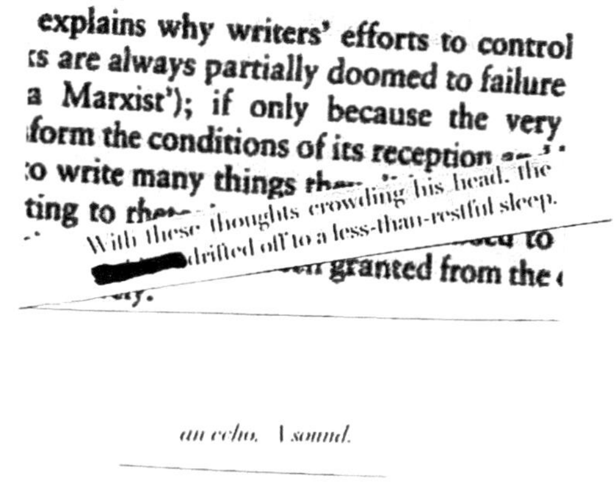

Site-Reading Writing Quarterly, no. 5 (December 2020):
Text collage by Tim Cresswell, in response to his reading of *Field Poetics* (2018) by Kristen Kreider and James O'Leary. © Tim Cresswell.

March 21, 2021

Dear Friends and Colleagues,

As we approach the spring equinox in the north and autumn equinox in the south, night and day rebalance and point to the need to restore equalities in the landscapes of deep social injustice that COVID-19 has brought into stark relief.

For this issue of *Site-Reading Writing Quarterly*, I have invited artist Polly Gould and architectural historian Paulette Singley to respond to each other's books—Gould's *Antarctica, Art, and Archive* (2020) and Singley's *How to Read Architecture* (2019). Through careful acts of positioned observation, these interconnected readings of each other's writings encourage the need for a more ecological approach to criticism and practice—paying attention to how near relates to far. [...]

Sympoeisis

When Donna Haraway reconceptualizes the Anthropocene as the Chthulucene, as a "time of mortal compositions at stake to and with each other,"[18] she notes in *Staying with the Trouble* that this epoch in which the human and nonhuman are inextricably linked is sympoietic not autopoietic. She takes the term sympoeisis from M. Beth Dempster and writes that mortal worlds "do not make themselves,"[19] but rather require a poiesis that thinks-with, makes-with, and becomes-with. This is what she calls SF, defined as "science fiction, speculative fabulation, string figures, speculative feminism, science fact, so far."[20] For Haraway: "SF is practice and process, it is becoming-with each other in surprising relays; it is a figure for ongoingness in the Chthulucene."[21]

SF threads and traces, passes on and receives, makes and unmakes, and, rather than the self-producing generative systems Haraway associates with autopoiesis, is "always partnered all the way down."[22] But SF also, as I understand it, continues the practice, described by Haraway, and Rosi Braidotti, of "feminist figuration."[23]

FEMINIST FIGURATION

In looking into the history of feminist life-writing, I discovered a specific strand of work called "auto-theory," where autobiography itself operates as a mode of theory, described by Lauren Fournier as "the practices of engaging with theory, life, and art from the perspective of one's lived experiences."[24] The early history of such an approach can be located in the writing of women of color second-wave feminists, such as Audre Lorde and Gloria Anzaldúa, as well as Adrienne Rich, as Stacey Young has done.[25] But it is also possible to consider how such feminist life-writing has taken shape through practices of feminist figuration, which Haraway considers to be about "location and historical specificity" and "a kind of assemblage, a kind of connectedness of the

Site-Reading Writing Quarterly*, no. 6 (March 2020): Image collage by Polly Gould, in response to her reading of *How to Read Architecture: An Introduction to Interpreting the Built Environment* by Paulette Singley. It includes illustrations from Singley's book and Gould's own book, *Antarctica, Art, and Archive.
© Polly Gould.

figure and the subject,"[26] and Braidotti describes as "not mere metaphors, but rather markers of more concretely situated historical positions." She writes: "A figuration is the expression of one's specific positioning in space and time. It marks certain territorial or geopolitical coordinates, but it also points out one's sense of genealogy of historical inscription. Figurations deterritorialize and destabilize the certainties of the subject and allow for a proliferation of situated or 'micro' narratives of self and others."[27]

POETHICS

Writing that draws attention to the relation between the poetic and the ethical has been described by poets Seamus Heaney and Joan Retallack as "poethical," and has been developed more recently by Denise Ferreira da Silva through her "black feminist poethics."

In the seventh section of Seamus Heaney's 2001 collection, *Electric Light*, entitled "W. H. Auden, 1907–30," Heaney includes this sentence: "A pause for po-ethics."[28] According to Eugene O'Brian, for Heaney, poetry and ethics are entwined and "Po-ethics allows for a slanted perspective, a swerve, which looks at the ethical demands on life from just such a different perspective." And in her 2003 book, *The Poethical Wager*, Joan Retallack writes of this concept as "a poetics of the swerve" or in terms of "opportunities to usefully rethink habits of thought."[29] For Retallack, poethics is a "distancing form of play" located in the "intermediate zone between self and world," and it is in the distance "engendered by a poethical recognition of reciprocal alterity" that "curiosity and exploration" are stimulated.[30]

For Ferreira da Silva, "black feminist poethics," articulates, as Andrea Phillips has described, "a mode of living and thinking which apprehends and moves beyond the categories of slavery."[31] For Phillips, "this call to the absolute unpicking of the bonds of the capitalist slave narrative of Black history, written through capital accumulation," requires "a total rethink of the temporal-spatial structures of what we serve to display and cherish in the name of poethics."[32] And for da Silva herself, the Black feminist critical worksite is located both in the poet's intention that the Category of Blackness can be emancipated from the scientific and historical ways of knowing that produced it in the first place" and through the ethical as a mandate for "opening up other ways of knowing and doing."[33]

It is this call by Black feminism, for other ways of knowing and doing, that white feminism must now respond to and find ways of figuring, rather than configuring, actions of resistance to racial injustice in this time of ecological crisis, ones that position poethics politically but also relationally.[34]

June 21, 2021

Dear Colleagues and Friends,

For this issue of *Site-Reading Writing Quarterly*, which marks the lightest day in the north and the darkest in the south, I have invited nonbinary researcher and theorist of embodied practice Ben Spatz and writer-artist Emma Cocker to review publications which explore practices associated with the laboratory. As a result of the pandemic, this past year has seen a complete change to our usual operating conditions and required a large degree of experimentation.

Composed of a trilogy of audio recordings of her own readings, Emma Cocker's reading of Ben Spatz's *Making a Laboratory: Dynamic Configurations with Transversal Video* (2020) is a work to be listened to; while Ben Spatz's reading of *Choreo-Graphic Figures: Deviations from the Line* (2017), co-edited by Cocker, with Nikolaus Gansterer and Mariella Greil, takes a more conventional review essay form. Spatz explores the performative methods of artistic research practice presented in the volume, and in drawing attention to *wit(h)ness*—a playful combination of *witness* and *withness*—introduced in *Choreo-Graphic Figures*—calls for whiteness to be taken into account in practice-led artistic research.

That this public act of reading *Choreo-Graphic Figures* has taken place four years after it was published opens up for re-view how the gap between one writing and another reading is always framed by historical difference. Spatz's reading offers a stark reminder that despite an increased awareness of race issues in current academic and artistic practice in the past year—following the murder of George Floyd and the ways in which COVID-19 has laid social inequalities bare—white privilege largely remains invisible. This is a matter to address in future issues of *Site-Reading Writing Quarterly*. [...]

01 See Jane Rendell, "A Place Between Art, Architecture and Critical Theory," Proceedings to *Place and Location* (Tallinn, Estonia, 2003), 221–33; and *Art and Architecture: A Place Between* (London: IB Tauris, 2006). For more recent developments of my work around critical spatial practice, see Jane Rendell, "Critical Spatial Practice as Parrhesia," *MaHKUscript, Journal of Fine Art Research* 1 (December 2016).
02 See Jane Rendell, *Site-Writing: The Architecture of Art Criticism* (London: IB Tauris, 2010).
03 Donna Haraway, "Situated Knowledges: The Science Question in Feminism and the Privilege of Partial Perspective," *Feminist Studies* 14, no. 3 (Autumn 1988): 575–99. See also Jane Flax's "standpoint theory," in *Thinking Fragments: Psychoanalysis, Feminism and Postmodernism in the Contemporary West*, Berkeley (Los Angeles, CA: University of California Press, 1991), 232; Seyla Benhabib's critical articulation of "feminism as situated criticism" in *Situating the Self: Gender, Community and Postmodernism in Contemporary Ethics* (Cambridge: Polity Press, 1992), 225–28; and bell hooks's discussion of the margin as a place of resistance and hope in *Yearnings: Race, Gender, and Cultural Politics* (London: Turnaround Press, 1989).
04 Haraway, "Situated Knowledges" (see note 3).
05 This phrase has been attributed to a paper by Carol Hanisch, originally titled, "Some Thoughts in Response to Dottie's Thoughts on a Women's Liberation Movement" (February 1969), which deals with "therapy vs. politics" and discusses the role of personal experiences in "therapy" or consciousness-raising groups as part of the Women's Liberation Movement. This paper was published in Shulamuth Firestone and Anne Koedt, eds., *Notes from the Second Year: Women's Liberation* (New York, NY: Radical Feminism, 1970); Hanisch states that the title "The Personal is Political" was given to the paper by the editors. See "The Personal is Political," accessed August 15, 2022, www.carolhanisch.org/CHwritings/PIP.html.
06 Frances Stracey, *Constructed Situations: A New History of the Situationist International* (London: Pluto Press, 2014), 9.
07 See Ira Ferris, "Relational Art: An Arty Way to Twitter, with Nothing to Say?," December 21, 2014, accessed August 15, 2022, artiris.wordpress.com/2014/12/21/relational-art-an-arty-way-to-twitter-with-nothing-to-say/.
08 Sara Ahmed, *Living a Feminist Life* (Durham, NC: Duke University Press, 2017), 12–13.
09 Lauren Berlant, "Thinking about Feeling Historical," *Emotion, Space and Society* 1 (October 2008): 4.
10 Young also quotes Moi: "To claim that the body is a situation is to acknowledge that the meaning of a woman's body is bound up with the way she uses her freedom." See Iris Marion Young, *On Female Body Experience: "Throwing like a Girl" and Other Essays* (Oxford: Oxford University Press, 2005), 16. See also Toril Moi, "What is a Woman?" in *What is a Woman?: And Other Essays* (Oxford: Oxford University Press, 2001).
11 It is important to distinguish subjectivation from subjection *(assujetissement)* in Foucault's work. "The history of the subject, from the perspective of the practices of the self and the procedures of subjectivation, is completely separate from the project, formulated in the 1970s, of the history of the production of subjectivities, of the procedures of subjection by the machines of power." See Frédéric Gros, "Le souci de soi chez Michel Foucault, A Review of The Hermeneutics of the Subject: Lectures at the Collège de France, 1981–1982," *Philosophy and Social Criticism* 31, nos. 5–6 (2005): 697–708, 698.
12 Michel Foucault, *The History of Sexuality, Vol. 2, The Use of Pleasure* [1984], trans. Robert Hurley (New York, NY: Vintage Books, 1990), 26.
13 See Michel Foucault, "L'écriture de soi," *Corps écrit* 5 (February 1983): 3–23. See also "Self-Writing," in *The Essential Works of Foucault, 1954–1984, Volume 1: Ethics: Subjectivity, and Truth*, ed. Paul Rabinow, trans. Robert Hurley et al. (New York, NY: The New Press, 2001), 207–22, 209; and "Self Writing," accessed August 15, 2022, foucault.info/documents/foucault.hypomnemata.en/.
14 Ibid.
15 Ibid.
16 Angela Last, "We Are the World? Anthropocene Cultural Production between Geopoetics and Geopolitics," *Theory, Culture & Society* 34, nos. 2–3 (2017): 147–68, 148.
17 Judith Butler, *Giving an Account of Oneself* (New York, NY: Fordham University Press, 2005), 8.
18 "Chthulucene Manifesto from Santa Cruz," revised by "Donna Haraway and Cary Wolfe in Conversation," *Manifestly Haraway* (Minneapolis, MN: University of Minnesota Press, 2016). See "New Narratives of Resilience," accessed August 15, 2022, laboratoryplanet.org/en/manifeste-chthulucene-de-santa-cruz/.
19 Donna Haraway, *Staying with the Trouble: Making Kin in the Chthulucene* (Durham, NC: Duke University Press, 2016), 33.
20 Ibid., 2.
21 Ibid., 3.
22 Ibid., 33.
23 See for example Donna Haraway, "Syntactics: The Grammar of Feminism and Technoscience," *Modest_Witness@Second_Millenium. FemaleMan_Meets_OncoMouse: Feminism and Technoscience* (London: Routledge, 1997), 1–22, 11; See also Rosi Braidotti, *Nomadic Subjects: Embodiment and Sexual Difference in Contemporary Feminist Theory* (New York, NY: Colombia University Press, 1994), 4. For an overview of practices of figuration see Jane Rendell, "Figurations," in *The Architecture of Psychoanalysis* (London: IB Tauris, 2017).
24 Lauren Fournier, "Sick Women, Sad Girls, and Selfie Theory: Autotheory as Contemporary Feminist Practice," *a/b: Auto/Biography Studies* 33, no. 3 (2018): 643.
25 Stacey Young, *Changing the Wor(l)d: Discourse, Politics, and the Feminist Movement* (London: Routledge, 1997). See for example Audre Lorde, "The Master's Tools Will Never Dismantle the Master's House" [1984] in *Sister Outsider: Essays and Speeches* (Berkeley, CA: Crossing Press. 2007); Gloria Anzaldua, *Borderlands: La Frontera—The New Mestiza* [1987] (San Francisco, CA: Aunt Lute Books, 1999); and Cherríe Moraga, *This Bridge Called My Back: Writings by Radical Women of Color* (Watertown, MA: Persephone Press: 1981).
26 Donna Haraway, "Cyborgs, Coyotes and Dogs: A Kinship of Feminist Figurations and There are Always More Things Going on Than You Thought! Methodologies as Thinking Technologies: An interview with Donna Haraway conducted in two parts by Nina Lykke, Randi Markussen, and Finn Olesen" [2000], in *The Haraway Reader* (London: Routledge, 2004), 321–42, 338.
27 Rosi Braidotti, *Transpositions: On Nomadic Ethics* (Cambridge: Polity Press, 2006), 90.
28 Eugene O'Brien, "A Pause for Po-Ethics: Seamus Heaney and the Ethics of Aesthetics," accessed August 15, 2022, www.mdpi.com/2076-0787/8/3/138/htm.
29 Joan Retallack, *The Poethical Wager* (Berkeley, CA: University of California Press, 2003), 1.
30 Ibid., 7.
31 "Annotated by Andrea Phillips," visibleproject.org, accessed September 1, 2022, www.visibleproject.org/blog/book/toward-a-black-feminist-poethics-the-question-of-blackness-toward-the-end-of-the-world-in-the-black-scholar-442/.
32 Ibid.
33 Denise Ferreira da Silva, "Toward a Black Feminist Poethics," *The Black Scholar* 44, no. 2 (2014): 81–97.
34 See for example, Denise Ferreira da Silva and Valentina Desideri's *Sensing Salon* project, accessed August 15, 2022, www.artandeducation.net/announcements/308693/valentina-desideri-and-denise-ferreira-da-silvathe-sensing-salon.

Practice

Dirty Theory
Troubling Architecture

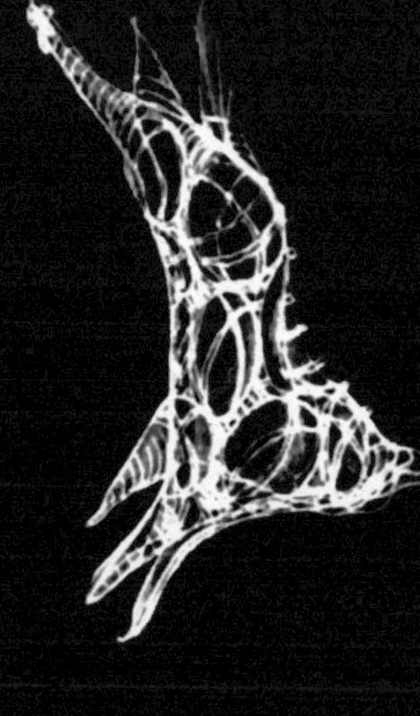

TEXT
Hélène Frichot

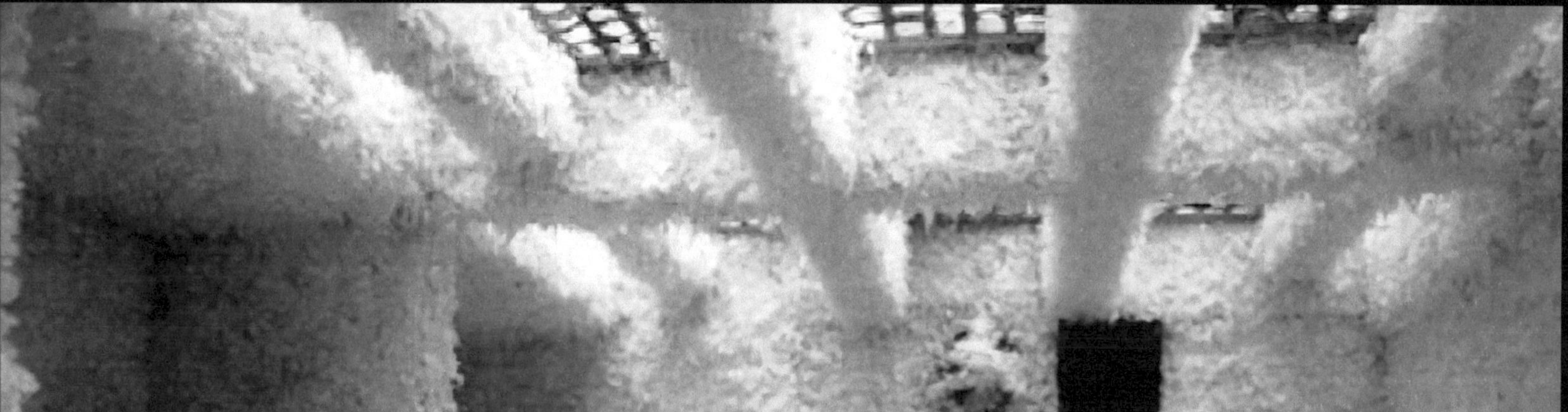

Katherine Shonfield, *Dirt is Matter Out of Place*, installation, 1993. The temporary transformation of a disused Victorian toilet block on Commercial Street in London challenged how architecture defines and keeps out dirt. The interior and toilet were covered with a layer of down that blurred the sharp edges and dissolved transitions between structural elements, throwing their actual function into disarray.
Photo: Frank O'Sullivan. Courtesy Frank O'Sullivan.

There is nothing very respectable about dirty theory. It seeks out approaches and plots trajectories from a position close to the ground. We must move past our disgust to work with the dirt: this is an imperative for coping with our dusty, dirty, defiled world. To think with it, not against it. Dirt never emerges from nowhere, *ex nihilo*, but from beneath your feet, from under your fingernails, from encounters and relations and from the accumulated odds and sods that compose any mode of life. A life, where it is not stultified as *nature morte*, is inevitably dirty, messy, buffeted by contingencies. Theories, ways of actively thinking-with, can be derived from all kinds of sources and situations. The dirty theorist is usually something of an avid collector, accumulating not just the regular set readers—written by the usual theoretical suspects—but pamphlets, brochures, maps and postcards, snatches of conversation and grabs of social media feed, accepting all the while that distinctions between low and high culture are easily undone. (An old lesson we keep forgetting, caught up as we are in a will to purification.) What was once sacred and revered in the next moment may well be expelled as abject, judged to be without sense, useless. The dirty theorist follows the materials, tracks the soiled effluent, observing from where it came and the direction that it appears to be taking. She is unafraid of selecting at will from the sedimented archive of thinking.

Dirty theory messes with mixed disciplines. Showing up in ethnography, in geography, in philosophy, it can just as well find a home in architecture, design, and the creative arts. Dirt and art have an existing long-term relationship, whether rendered as negative sculptures extracted from the earth, or maintenance manifestos or soil revalued as currency. Dirt and architecture—beyond the uptight habits of the archetypal heroic architect's will to purification and hygiene—admits sly allegiances here and there. David Adjaye's Dirty House dabbles in dirt, but better still, Katherine Shonfield's transient installations dig deeper and Jennifer Bloomer's dirty ditties and dirty drawings conspire to imagine architecture otherwise. Dirty theory helps architecture think about the ordinary gestures of care, repair, and maintenance that can form part of its mandate. Most powerfully, following the dirt can be a creative movement, a profound relationship with our local environment-worlds.

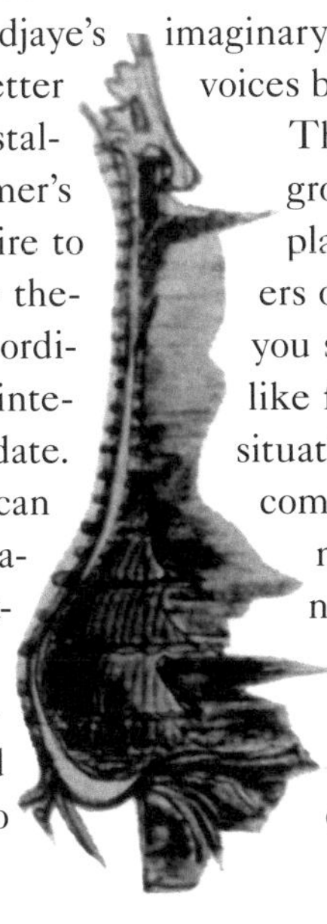

Dirty theory is wary of the strictures of disciplination, preferring instead indisciplination, a wayward approach to problems. It's scattergun, if not scatological. Dirty theory appropriates and critically, knowingly, misappropriates, because ideas do not belong to singular authors, the dirty theorist avers. Dirty theory, the dirty theorist, and the theory slut herself are not very respectable, rational, or reasonable figures. The preferred approach here is one of a "groping experimentation,"[01] to quote that still disreputable pair, Gilles Deleuze and Félix Guattari. Groping the world, prehending it, trying not to grasp it too hard. To be respectable means to have accepted and internalized the status quo, where everything and everyone is agreeable and none are prepared to rock the boat. To rock the boat would be to place oneself at risk of being thrown overboard, only to discover that the mythical island of reason has disappeared into the mists. To be rational assumes that reason has been determined in advance, and that everything can be organized in good measure. To be reasonable, well, it means you are prepared to get along and are certainly not a woman who makes a fuss. The reason that supports the reasonable ("be reasonable now!") assumes that each thing has its proper, measured, and assigned place. Once a title on the lands belonging to reason has been secured, and "a solid foundation to build upon"[02] has been established, why should we not be contented? Why venture further? Beyond the island of truth, as Immanuel Kant has famously expounded, we only risk venturing further into the fogs of illusion. Yet islands, in this age of concatenating global climatic crises, rising sea levels, micro-plastics, and pollutants, turn out to be not so secure after all. Island, land, dirt, all proffering opportunities for the cultivation of reason: there is more than a whiff of the colonial impulse in this territorialization of dirt. Pure reason must be muddied. Dirty theory thus has additional labor in the political project of decolonization, and even in the decolonization of the otherwise too clean imaginary. Dirty theory demands that other voices be heard.

The dirt, the earth, is the required ground in which concepts can be planted and eventually bloom as flowers or weeds (either way). Dirty theory, you see, is neither good nor bad per se; like flowers or weeds it depends on the situation, the relations at hand, on what comes together to form a greater or a meaner composition. The dirt may not be sufficient for anything at all to grow. To territorialize, to deterritorialize, to reterritorialize—all such movements depend on the dirt rendered as the earth, *la terre*, beneath your feet, between your fingers, in your mouth, as you utter a furious expletive. Without these movement sutterances, not much would be achieved, for good or for bad, and you are bound to get dirty either way.

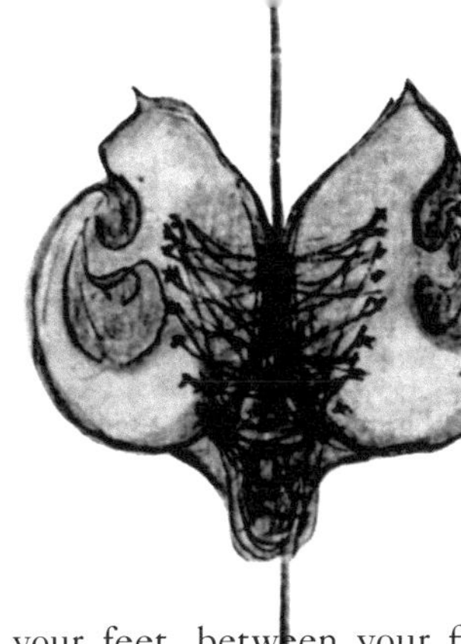

It is the anthropologist Mary Douglas who famously offers the neatest definition of dirt: "Dirt is matter out of place."[03] Matter located where it is judged not to belong. Judged as such by someone, or rather, judged by some societal context organized around societal norms and structures. Douglas explains that this simple formula directs us toward order and then the contravention of ordered relations. Dirt is that which crosses boundaries, challenges decorum, contravenes norms. The low, the reduced, the underfoot, the despised, the rejected, the expelled are at the same moment the accumulated ground upon which the powerful steady themselves in order to reach rarefied heights. Dirt carries material and conceptual weight, it is part of the stuff of all manner of corporeal relation, and it is also symbolic. Dirt registers the conjunction of the material semiotic. It invokes unholy mixtures of concepts and materials, of words and what matters. Jennifer Bloomer puts it plainly: "The world and the language are all tangled around each other."[04] The tangle should be read as a growing vine, a process of entanglement, as of that emerging from the mouth of the young woman in Botticelli's painting *Primavera* [Spring] (1478); either she is choking on, or else she is vomiting up, growing life.

If it is Douglas who represents dirt for the ethnographers, then it is the architectural thinker-doer Jennifer Bloomer who best represents dirt for the architects. She represents it in such a way as to steal it from the grasp of the would-be phenomenologists, and those who would wax lyrical about dirt as an elevated outcome of weathering,[05] or celebrate the aesthetic effects of dust or seek a metaphysics of the imperfect and impure. Much like violence when violence exudes a curious fascination in its beholder, dirt is ever at risk of aestheticization. Despite this risk, cannot a dirty theory enable creative possibilities beyond mere aestheticization—creative possibilities

Dirty Drawing, **section from the installation *Tabbles of Bower.* *Dirty Drawings* are both technically correct and “inappropriately ornamental,” as Bloomer says. The drawings emphasize the material qualities of the installation rather than its geometric dimensions and structural details.**

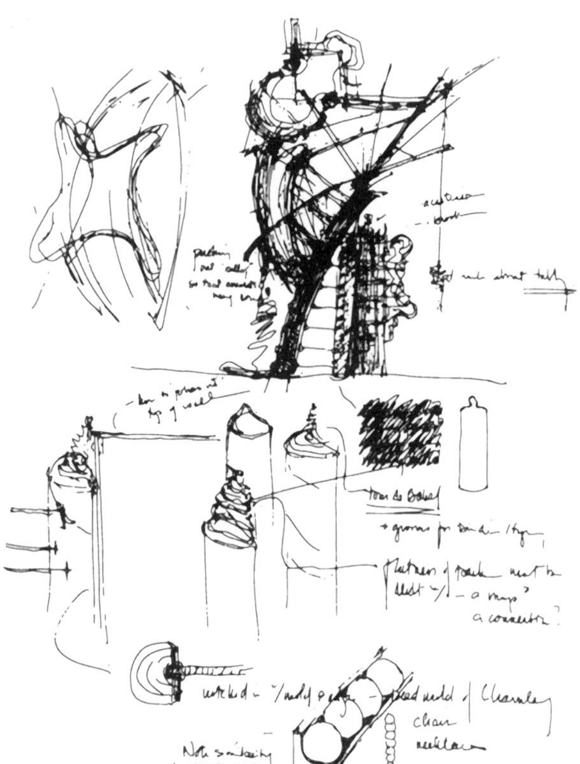

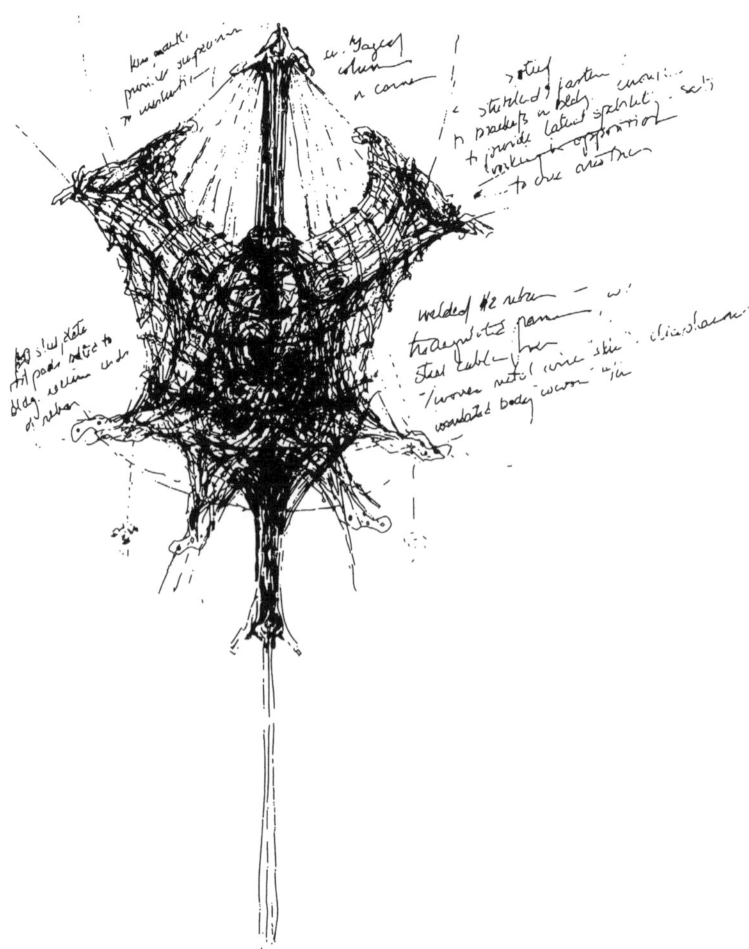

Design studies for *Tabbles of Bower.*

The installation *Tabbles of Bower* consists of 13 allegorical details referencing five main concepts highlighted in the text: colon, fire, cow temple, and dora/doric/d'or.
Photo: King Au.

Unless otherwise indicated, all illustrations are from the work *Abodes of Theory and Flesh: Tabbles of Bower* (1992) by Jennifer Bloomer. With particular thanks to her assistants Adeline "Nina" Hofer and Mikesch Mücke. Courtesy Jennifer Bloomer.

Abodes of Theory and Flesh: Tabbles of Bower (1992) was written by the American architect and architectural theorist Jennifer Bloomer. It is one of the early central works of feminist critical spatial theory and practice.

Starting from a critical examination of Louis Sullivan and Adolf Loos, Jennifer Bloomer reflects on how the conceptual pair ornament/structure was gender-coded early on in Western architectural history and how ornament was attributed with negative connotations of "the feminine," as something decorative, natural, impure, and monstrous.

Through her *Dirty Drawings* and the incorporation of concrete and allegorical symbols of female anatomy, such as uteri, fluids, blood, and udders (the cow as a mythological symbol of fertility and the "good mother"), into architecture and spatial thinking, Bloomer developed a critique of both the sterility of the architectural drawing process and spatial conventions of representation.

Central themes in *Tabbles of Bower* range from intimate accounts of Bloomer's pregnancy to an examination of homelessness as well as the history of the colonization of the Americas and the role that slavery, displacement, and murder of specific ethnic and indigenous communities played in it.

Detail, *Dory Door.*
Tabbles of Bower uses copper and brass wire, buttons, beads, balls, hooks, eyelets, ribbons, fake fingernails, hair, shells, feathers, and bone—materials often used decoratively in domestic environments and body ornamentation.

that can make a critical difference where it matters? Bloomer, I believe, can help show the way.

With architecture, we are ever at risk of rendering dirt bucolic and rustic, of laying it out for our phenomenological enjoyment. Bloomer [...] has darker tales to tell concerning dirt. She mixes water and blood, mixes words and matter, putting things purposively where they do not properly belong. An example: on introducing the beloved architectural motif of the *poché*, the secret that is supposed to properly reveal the deepest phenomenological desires of the architect, she shows instead the hole at the back of the wardrobe through which a young girl escapes from sexual abuse; the *poché* becomes the after-effect of a cigarette burn, the dirt that comes from the violence that is hidden behind the stern façades of what are supposed to be proper family men.[06] Sobering scenes for a dirty theorist. In this sleight of hand Bloomer deploys feminist resistance in response to the accepted definition of *poché*, which instead gives way to matter in the wrong place. Trailing behind Bloomer, suddenly a standard definition breaks into narrative and is off and away. This is no Bachelardian reverie in her discourse, no, it is nothing so saccharine as that. The phenomenological sacred is instead rendered profane and filthy. This is critique, what I would call material semiotic critique, an elegant slippage. The clean sheet turns out to be smudged.

Why get dirty? Why dirty theory now? Dirt is what gives relief to the mark drawn on the dusty ground with a stick to say: inside/outside, included/excluded. To mark, as Michel Serres explains, means to leave a footstep in the soil, and thus to claim, and reclaim, a territory.[07] Dirty theory is a reminder that theories are good for nothing unless they are bound up with the muck of mundane relations on the ground, with the kind of environmental things that are increasingly at stake today, that were at stake yesterday, too, and that certainly will be at stake tomorrow. Make a mud map, find your way through the dirt. The temporalities of dirt take us all the way from property rights to a call for the commons and a return to practices of communing, getting dirty together. These are what Maria Puig de la Bellacasa calls "soil times."[08] Dirt is in the body, the home, the environment[09] and in all that we share and divide. At its best, dirty theory could participate in the imagining of new modes of getting messy together, accepting what Donna Haraway calls our messmates: our more-than-human relations. Dirt demands that we listen to the environment-worlds in the midst of which we lose and find ourselves, becoming and unbecoming. Dirty theory is concerned with discovering new ways of getting along with each other that challenge fixed categories, that track a diagonal and even a zig-zag course across taxonomic charts to invent new kinds of territories. *La terre* is what dirt might aspire to become, as long as the Earth is something that can be adequately, equitably shared.

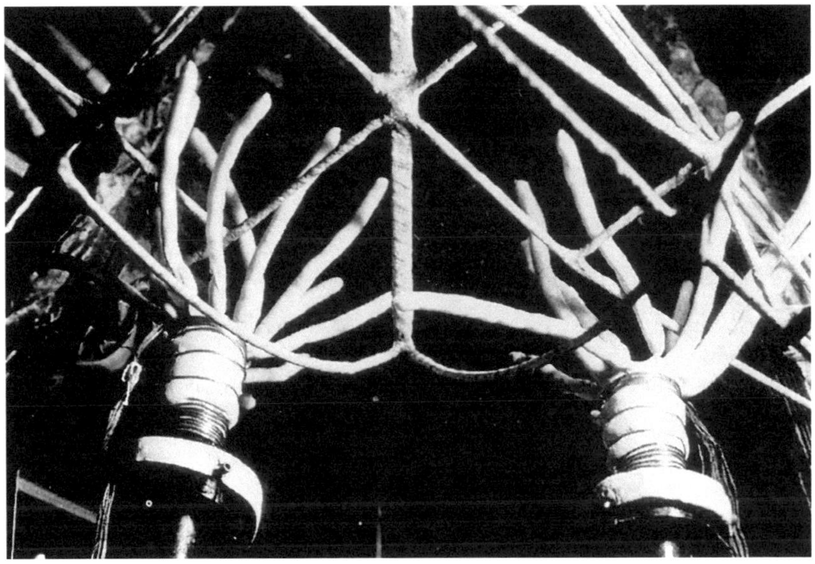

Column capitals in the installation *Tabbles of Bower*. Photo: King Au.

This text is an excerpt from the introduction of Hélène Frichot's book, Dirty Theory: Troubling Architecture, *published by AADR in 2019. Minor changes have been made to orthography and the reference system to conform to* ARCH+ *style (AE). We thank the author and the publisher for their kind permission. Great thanks also to Jennifer Bloomer for permission to reproduce images of artistic work from* Abodes of Theory and Flesh: Tabbles of Bower, *which accompanied her article of the same title in* Assemblage *17 (April 1992).*

01 Gilles Deleuze and Félix Guattari, *What Is Philosophy?* (New York, NY: Columbia University Press, 1994), 41.
02 Immanuel Kant, *Critique of Pure Reason* (New York, NY: Everyman's Library, 1979), 180.
03 Mary Douglas, *Purity and Danger: An Analysis of Concepts of Pollution and Taboo* (London: Routledge, 1966), 36.
04 Jennifer Bloomer, *Architecture and the Text: The (S)crypts of Joyce and Piranesi* (New Haven, CT: Yale University Press, 1993), 87.
05 Mohsen Mostafavi and David Leatherbarrow, *On Weathering: The Life of Buildings in Time* (Cambridge, MA: MIT Press, 1993).
06 Bloomer, *Architecture and the Text* (see note 4), 178–79.
07 Michel Serres, *Malfeasance: Appropriation through Pollution?* (Stanford, CA: Stanford University Press, 2011), 2.
08 Maria Puig de la Bellacasa, *Matters of Care: Speculative Ethics in More than Human Worlds* (Minneapolis, MN: University of Minnesota Press, 2017).
09 Rosie Cox et al., *Dirt: The Filthy Reality of Everyday Life* (London: Profile Books, 2011).

Dealing with Architecture's "Daddy Issues" An Ahmedian Therapy Session

TEXT
Brady Burroughs

Welcome.

I usually don't take on whole disciplines as clients, but since our intersectional-feminist guest editors and *ARCH+* referred you, I'll make an exception. Please take a seat. We threw out the dusty carpet-draped sofas long ago, invited feminist cartoonist (and Freud's most worthy opponent) Liv Strömquist to draw on the modernist white walls, and reupholstered the armchairs in neon green. Critical, *not* clinical! This session takes place around the "kitchen table," where feminist killjoys have (and do) gathered, organized, and supported each other. Choose the place where you feel most uncomfortable. We have a lot to talk about.

You notice the word SNAP written in red marker at the center of a white poster taped to the wall. The poster is hung intentionally askew. Irritating!

From Liv Strömquist, *Kunskapens frukt* (Stockholm: Galago, 2014). © Liv Strömquist & avant-verlag.

First, a little about myself and my methods. I'm trained as an architectural feminist killjoy within the Ahmedian school of thought. That is, my early architectural training, rooted in phenomenological ideas and Bauhausian sensibilities, got a queer-feminist and anti-racist revision. This revision is based on Sara Ahmed's *Living a Feminist Life*, which will also inform our session today.[01] Let me remind you that we're not here to provide you with easy answers, but rather to reflect together over some of your current challenges and difficulties. You still have to be willing to do your "feminist homework."[02]

You look off to the side at a drawing of a menstruating figure skater, leg above her head[03]—a comment on Freud's contribution to the shaming of female sexuality—and feel the heat rise in your cheeks.

I understand your most pressing issue is the unhealthy connection to an inherited architectural authority? Prior to this session, I consulted the well-respected psychoanalytic tool—Google—to find the three most common signs associated with architectural "daddy issues." In this session, we'll briefly go through them one by one, addressing specific examples from architectural research, practice, and education. Don't mind the sleeping cat in the corner, and there's a box of tissues on the table, just in case. Let's begin!

1. YOU'RE ONLY ATTRACTED TO OLDER MEN.

When did you first notice this obsession with older *(white)* men? Was it the homogenous composition of design juries, lecture series, anthologies, panel discussions, book series, architecture awards … should I go on? Yes, I can see that you've made some progress in the last couple of years. Bravo! But let's focus specifically on your bad habit of bromance citations. You know, the "helpful" feedback offered to feminist researchers in seminars or peer reviews, encouraging them to "give [their] love to this or that [*white*/Western] male theorist," to legitimize their work and to make you feel more comfortable?

You look away again only to see a drawing depicting black feminist/activist/scholar Angela Davis receiving the Nobel Prize.[04]

Ahmed describes citations as the "feminist material" we use to build worlds we want to live in. She adopts a "feminist citational policy"—I'm not citing white dudes (i.e., institutions), and I will only cite those who contribute to work that is feminist and anti-racist, in an effort to break the habits of the citational bromance-chain.[05] You ask: what's wrong with a little bromance? Well, it establishes a system of values and expertise that generates a series like Routledge's *Thinkers for Architects*, where the ratio of female/male and racialized/white "contemporary thinkers who have something to say to architects" is 1/17.[06] Good intentions, but balance? Not so much. What would happen if all of your academic practitioners adopted Ahmed's feminist citational policy? Which books would we get then? I'd like you to think about this for our next session, but let's move on.

2. You're clingy, insecure, and need constant validation.

Related to the work we cite is the work we praise. I'd like to explore practice for a moment and the architects (and projects) that you tend to cling to, by offering your sustained validation. As an architectural feminist killjoy, "I am willing to cause unhappiness" and call out the happiness of others that relies on injustice, inequality, even violence.[07] I'll be blunt. What about your undying love and admiration for your architectural ancestors (e.g., Gropius, Johnson, Mies), with their antiquated ideals or even ties to violent ideologies, movements, and regimes? Or the golden boys (and girls) of the present (e.g., Bjarke Ingels, Zaha Hadid/Patrik Schumacher) who continue to accept questionable commissions from shady clients that fund the work you publish in magazines, glorify with awards, and lift up for students in your field to emulate? What are you afraid of? Alienation, loss of status/power, being alone?

You roll your eyes, and the cat jumps up into your lap.

An architectural feminist killjoy's practice celebrates work built on feminist and anti-racist values. It questions neoliberal intentions, rejects (or critically reinterprets) commissions that lead to the gentrification and displacement of vulnerable communities, insists on ethical sources of funding and forms of labor, and is concerned for our planet and its resources. Killjoys also support and inspire each other in this difficult work to transform you. Shout out to AFARAI, WAI Think Tank, Matri-Archi(tecture), Parity Group, Claiming*Spaces, Parlour, among others! When do you, as a discipline, hold the protagonists in your story accountable and reassess who and what represents architectural values worth striving for? Ahmed talks about a collective "feminist snap … to break ties that are damaging as well as to invest in new possibilities."[08] My question is: are YOU "willing to snap any bonds, however precious, when those bonds are damaging to [yourself] or others"[09]?

You jump up to straighten the crooked poster on the wall. The cat darts out of the room, and the door slams shut from a gust of wind through the open window.

Moving on.

3. You have a fear of intimacy.

I see that you're upset. For the remainder of the session, why don't we focus on architectural education and the walls that come up when you feel yourself transforming or opening up "to those who have historically been excluded from [you]."[10] Ahmed talks about the tricky institutional "brick wall" as "a materiality of power" that appears only when something or someone attempts to change things; if nothing challenges the status quo, no wall needed. These fickle, invisible walls only appear to those who seek the intended change, while those that stand to gain (or retain) power "are often invested in not seeing" them.

Your adjustment of the poster reveals the drawing of an anatomically correct clitoris, discovered in 1998 and credited to urologist Helen O'Connell, "after thousands of years of really, really piss-poor research."[11] *You squint and look confused.*

In 2017, Liv Strömquist tried to change the perception of female sexuality through her public artworks depicting menstruating figure skaters in four Stockholm metro stations. The Sweden Democrats (SD), Sweden's third-largest (far-right/anti-immigration) political party, put up a wall: they responded with a proposal to replace her feminist art with 18th-century Swedish landscape paintings, claiming her work was too intimate and provocative.[12] Let's explore some of the places YOUR walls appear and what you're perhaps not seeing (or trying not to see).

I encourage equality and diversity through an institutional policy.

Is this policy actively developed and enforced through paid positions, or just posted on the fridge in the faculty room?

I encourage equality and diversity in my curriculum.

Have you intersectionalized and decolonized the foundations and assumptions of a *white*, male, Eurocentric canon?

I encourage equality and diversity in the recruitment of new teaching staff.

Do you offer anything other than non-tenured, part-time positions?

I encourage equality and diversity within my study culture.

Do you still expect researchers to write and publish on their own time and students to work evenings and weekends?

I encourage equality and diversity through special events and symposia.

Do you provide extra resources, or depend only on personal initiatives and volunteer efforts by dedicated students and faculty?

I encourage equality and diversity within our student body.

How do you promote collaboration over competition, allow for material and cultural differences, and encourage the representation of black, brown, trans, queer bodies and lives?

You begin to sweat, and the squawk from a passing seagull outside startles you.

We should begin to wrap up, but I think we had some real breakthroughs! You still have significant work to do on your feminist citational policy, the feminist snap, and the institutional brick wall, but remember, Ahmed also places humor in her feminist killjoy survival kit.

The cat starts scratching at the door.

I'm sorry, that's all the time we have today. See you same time next week!

01 Sara Ahmed, ***Living a Feminist Life*** **(Durham, NC: Duke University Press, 2017).**
02 **Ibid., 17.**
03 Liv Strömquist, ***Fruit of Knowledge: The Vulva vs. the Patriarchy*** **(*****Kunskapens frukt*****, 2014), trans. Melissa Bowers (London: Virago, 2018).**
04 **Liv Strömquist,** ***Prins Charles Känsla*** **(Stockholm: Galago, 2010), 105.**
05 **Ahmed (see note 1), 29 f.**
06 **See** ***Thinkers for Architects*** **book series website, accessed July 12, 2022, www.routledge.com/Thinkers-for-Architects/book-series/THINKARCH?pd=published,forthcoming&pg=1&pp=12&so=pub&view=list.**
07 **Ahmed (see note 1), 330.**
08 **Ibid., 239.**
09 **Ibid., 341.**
10 **Ibid., 174 f.**
11 **Strömquist,** ***Fruit of Knowledge*** **(see note 3), 79.**
12 **See also Katia Elliott, "Sverigedemokraterna vill byta ut konsten i Slussens tunnelbana" (Sweden Democrats want to replace artwork in Slussen's metro),** ***SvT Nyheter*****, August 23, 2018, accessed July 12, 2022, www.svt.se/nyheter/inrikes/sverigedemokraterna-vill-byta-ut-konsten-i-slussens-tunnelbana.**

Donna Haraway for Architects

TEXT
Elli Mosayebi

Reality

In the practice of our architectural firm, Edelaar Mosayebi Inderbitzin, and in my teaching as a professor at ETH Zurich, the focus is on reality and its relationship to architecture. This confrontation is based on the conviction that architecture is a "medium for experiencing the present" and that architectural practice offers the possibility of "fleshing out the conditions of contemporaneity."[01] This is one of the special features of our discipline: the ability to make visible, tangible, and usable that which may not yet be visible, tangible, or usable, but is undoubtedly *real*. Given the crisis-ridden state of our planet today, we ask ourselves: How can architecture as a discipline critically confront this reality? How can architects assume a critical role in this process?

The work of Donna Haraway gives us a decisive theoretical approach to reality in its everyday abundance. Beginning in the 1980s, the science and technology scholar situated her research at the interdisciplinary nexus of the humanities, natural sciences, and social sciences. Haraway, who speaks about reality with unprecedented conviction, counts herself among those who "tried to stay sane in these disassembled and disassembling times by holding out for a feminist version of objectivity."[02] The power of her argument lies in her desire to "go beyond showing bias in science (that proved too easy anyhow)."[03] According to Haraway, "We unmasked the doctrines of objectivity because they threatened our budding sense of collective historical subjectivity and agency and our 'embodied' accounts of the truth, and we ended up with one more for not learning any post-Newtonian physics."[04] Early on, Haraway recognized the problem that feminism, as a science of deconstruction, risks excluding itself from urgent (secular) debates and, in contrast, argues for an "embodied objectivity"[05] that engages and intervenes in the big questions: "Feminists have to insist on a better account of the world."[06] The feminist concept of a partial and positioned acquisition of knowledge, of a "situated knowledge," describes nothing else than the tipping figure of the "god trick of seeing everything from nowhere,"[07] which exposes it as a male strategy to suggest objectivity and thus (interpretive) sovereignty.

TENTACULAR THINKING

This approach includes various perspectives in considering an object, it does not synthesize them but rather brings them together in structures, condenses them, or hybridizes them. As such, it seems promising with regards to a new kind of architectural practice that is feminist, more equitable, and more ecological. More than any other discipline, architecture is interwoven with philosophical, sociopolitical, and geographical contexts. For Haraway, we must also overcome the problematic dichotomous structure of modernity—a structure, as criticized by Bruno Latour, of "man and nature, subject and object, modes of production, and the environment."[08] For us, as designers, this means that we are always observers and participants at the same time, that our thoughts and actions are equally biologically and culturally (pre)formed, and that our private, individual actions are also political. Or, as Haraway notes, "We are always in the midst of it."[09]

Haraway introduced the notion of "tentacular thinking" in her 2016 book *Staying with the Trouble: Making Kin in the Chthulucene*.[10] It denotes a way of thinking that unfolds in interdisciplinary cross-references. This network creates an image of knowledge supported by various—scientific, historical, mythological, etc.—perspectives. However, "tentacular thinking" is not some kind of network thinking cut off from external references; partial perspectives and one's own positions are decisive. This is because "Nobody lives everywhere; everybody lives somewhere. Nothing is connected to everything; everything is connected to something."[11] Within these conditions of knowledge (and its acquisition), as she describes it, there are only localizable entanglements or entanglements and the possibility to find them, take them up, and pass them on to others.

The concept of the tentacular goes even further. The word comes from the Latin *tentare* and means "to try" and "to irritate." In zoology, tentacles refer to the tentacles in cnidarians or cephalopods. Haraway uses tentacular thinking to counter and critique a visually dominated, anthropomorphic way of thinking. Instead, the world should be perceived by groping, feeling, and trying things out. The metaphor of tentacles represents the *other*, the *non-human*, and implicitly asks how perception that is not two-armed, two-eyed, two-eared, and single-brained but many-armed and many-brained might generate different kinds of knowledge and include other species.[12]

Cyborg cover illustration by Lynn Randolph for Donna J. Haraway, *Simians, Cyborgs and Women: The Reinvention of Nature* (New York: Routledge, 1991). Courtesy Lynn Randolph.

SF

With Haraway, designing becomes speculating about possible futures, what she calls "SF," which stands for both "speculative feminism" and "science fiction"—the combination of natural science and fantasy that invents new worlds.[13] Haraway writes: "The tentacular ones tangle me in SF. Their many appendages make string figures; they entwine me in the poiesis—the making—of speculative fabulation, science fiction, science fact, speculative feminism, *soin de ficelle* [...] I work with string figures as a theoretical trope, a way to think-with a host of companions in sympoietic threading, felting, tangling, tracking, and sorting. I work with and in SF as material-semiotic composting, as theory in the mud, as muddle."[14]

Based on this premise, as well as on the "carrier bag theory of fiction" by the author Ursula K. Le Guin,[15] let us replace the idea of the concept with that of narrative. Only a narrative manages to arrange the contradictory observations, assumptions, and desires, to cement them together into tense and meaningful speculations, and to bring forth new critical realities. This function is also represented by Haraway's neologism of "sympoiesis,"[16] which is rooted in what already exists and can be further spun in interplay with the other and others. In sympoiesis, language is a central design tool that can be implemented throughout the process, from the statement of intent as a catalyst for the design to the review of design decisions.

The narrative thus unfolds *between* situated knowledge and tentacular thinking, between reality and science fiction. The architectural project is nothing more than a fleeting materialization of this dynamic network. What implications does this concept have for design and construction? How can we use it to encounter reality with a critical eye?

In an attempt to answer these questions, I would like to outline three figures that are closely interwoven in terms of content: empathy, mutability, and open form.

As the first figure, empathy is the ability to put oneself in the place of another and relate to others. The ability to observe and critique carefully goes hand in hand with empathy and compassion. The latter are prerequisites for *joint* responsibility. Empathy generates understanding and appreciation, which in our context I relate to the world of things in order to overcome the kind of utilitarian thinking in which things are exploited, consumed and discarded. Empathy creates material cycles in which the new emerges or grows from the old. Empathy makes it possible to live *further* and survive *together*.

The second figure stands for an architecture of changeability, displacement, dissolution, and volatility. Its characteristic is the *non-solid*.[17] If something is changeable, it has the property of being able to change its shape. When, where, and how the transformation will take place is open. What is decisive is why the transformation occurs and what emerges in the end. The transformation process can go through several stages and reach a final state, but the change can also be in constant motion. Shapeshifting can lead to a form that fits the circumstances better than the original form—as in Ovid's *Metamorphoses* or Haraway's hybrid "companion species."[18]

The third figure describes the idea of the open form. Following Umberto Eco's concept of the "open work" in art,[19] our interest lies in the unfinishedness and hybridity of non-traditional or informal forms that are open to interpretation and appropriation. Through our preoccupation with the topos of ruin, we have arrived at the concept of the open form as one "that can be multilayered, multipartite, impure, fuzzy, imprecise, anti-classical, anti-typological, informal, non-causal, fragmented, semantically weakly determined, respectively ambiguous, and sometimes ugly."[20]

Chthulucene

Our reality needs new narratives to meet the challenges of the present. "Chthulucene" is a neologism coined by Haraway, critiquing the use of the notions of Anthropocene and Capitalocene to describe our present times.[21] For Haraway, none of the two can offer a compelling narrative for breaking out of environmentally destructive patterns of thought and action. They only reinforce and consolidate the status quo—namely human supremacy, their individualism, and self-ascribed exceptionalism. For Haraway, the Chthulucene is "a third netbag for collecting up what is crucial for ongoing, for staying with the trouble [...] Specifically, unlike either the Anthropocene or the Capitalocene, the Chthulucene is made up of ongoing multispecies stories and practices of becoming-with [...]."[22]

We live in times of profound upheaval and transformation with an open outcome. The only certainty we have is that we should be prepared for the unknown. Haraway's feminist approach of reflective situatedness, speculation, and sympoiesis gives us the courage necessary to engage—collectively—with difficult and new futures and to dare to embrace the open form.

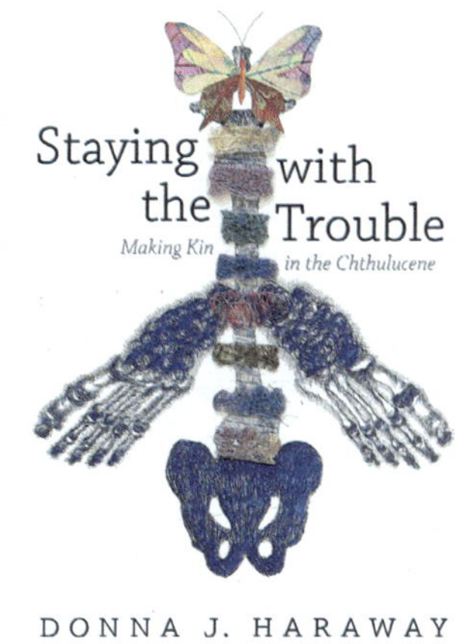

Donna J. Haraway, *Staying with the Trouble: Making Kin in the Chthulucene* (Durham, NC: Duke University Press, 2016). Cover image: Geraldine Javier, *Untitled A (Detail)*, 2012. © STPI/Geraldine Javier.

01 Marcel Meili, "Stand der Dinge – sieben Thesen," IEA Ringvorlesung, accessed September 1, 2022, iea.arch.ethz.ch/wp-content/uploads/2018/05/17HS_Meili_Stand_der_Dinge_Text.pdf, 1.
02 Donna Haraway, "Situated Knowledges: The Science Question in Feminism and the Privilege of Partial Perspective," *Feminist Studies* 14, no. 3 (Autumn 1988): 183–201, 186.
03 Ibid.
04 Ibid.
05 Ibid., 188.
06 Ibid., 187.
07 Ibid., 189.
08 Bruno Latour, *Politics of Nature*, trans. Catherine Porter (Cambridge, MA: Harvard University Press, 2004), 3.
09 Donna Haraway, "Wir sind immer mittendrin. Ein Interview mit Donna Haraway," in Donna Haraway, *Die Neuerfindung der Natur: Primaten, Cyborgs und Frauen* (1991), eds. Carmen Hammer and Immanuel Stiess (Campus: Frankfurt a. M. 1995), 98–122.
10 Donna Haraway, *Staying with the Trouble: Making Kin in the Chthulucene* (Durham, NC: Duke University Press, 2016).
11 Ibid., 31.
12 Hear Julia Grillmayr on Donna Haraway's notion of the tentacular in her podcast: "Tentakulär #1," *Superscience*, podcast audio, June 20, 2019, accessed September 1, 2022, superscience.podigee.io/25-tentacular1.
13 Donna Haraway, *Staying with the Trouble* (see note 10), 2.
14 Ibid., 31.
15 See Ursula K. Le Guin, *The Carrier Bag Theory of Fiction* (1986), intro. Donna Haraway (London: Ignota Books, 2019). For Le Guin, the narrative pattern of a typical heroic story corresponds to a prehistoric hunter-prey myth. Le Guin proposes alternative narrative structures developed from the topos of the collector, who collected found objects of various kinds in so-called carrier bags. According to Le Guin, the structure of such a narrative is polyphonic, non-linear, egalitarian, and inclusive.
16 Haraway, *Staying with the Trouble* (see note 10), 58.
17 See Thesis 11 of our "Twelve Theses on Second Modernist Architecture," accessed September 1, 2022, mosayebi.arch.ethz.ch/zwoelf-thesen/.
18 Haraway, *Staying with the Trouble* (see note 10), 9.
19 See Umberto Eco, *Open Work* (1962), intro. David Robey, trans. Anna Cancogni (Cambridge, MA: Harvard University Press, 1989).
20 Christian Inderbitzin, "Modell und Bild," *trans19* (September 2011): 86–91.
21 Haraway, *Staying with the Trouble* (see note 10), 2.
22 Ibid., 55.

Parity and Diversity in the Context of Higher Education

TEXT
Torsten Lange,
Charlotte Malterre-Barthes,
Daniela Ortiz dos Santos,
Gabrielle Schaad

1 BILDUNG EINES PARITY BOARD BESTEHEND AUS JE EINER VERTRETUNG ALLER INSTITUTE DES D-ARCH, DER PROFESSORENSCHAFT, DES FACHVEREINS DER ASSISTENTINNEN UND ASSISTENTEN DES D-ARCH (AAA), DES FACHVEREINS DER ARCHITEKTURSTUDIERENDEN AN DER ETH ZÜRICH (ARCHITEKTURA), DER PARITY GROUP SOWIE EINER EXTERNEN FACHPERSON. DAS PARITY BOARD IST DAFÜR VERANTWORTLICH, DIE GENANNTEN MASSNAHMEN FÜR EINE GESCHLECHTER-PARITÄT, IHRE GRADUELLE UMSETZUNG SOWIE IHRE ENTSPRECHENDE FINANZIERUNG IN ANGRIFF ZU NEHMEN UND WEITERE ÖFFENTLICHE VERANSTALTUNGEN WIE DIE JÄHRLICHEN PARITY TALKS ZU ORGANISIEREN.

Creation of a Parity Board consisting of representatives from each institute of the D-ARCH, a representative of the professorship, a delegate from the Association of Teaching Assistants at the D-ARCH (AAA), one representative from the architectural students association at the ETH Zurich (architektura), the representatives of the Parity Group and one external expert. The Parity Board would be responsible for instigating the measures by which gender parity is achieved, their gradual implementation, the connected fundraising tasks, and the organisation of future public events such as the annual Parity Talks.

2 JÄHRLICHES INTERNES WIE EXTERNES MONITORING UND VERÖFFENTLICHUNG DER BISHER ERREICHTEN ERGEBNISSE DER GLEICHSTELLUNG.

Annual internal and external monitoring and publication of the achieved parity-related results.

3 GESCHLECHTER-PARITÄT BEI PROFESSUREN, DOZENTUREN, OBERASSISTENZEN, GASTVORTRÄGEN UND GASTKRITIKEN.

Gender parity for professorships, lectureships, senior research and teaching positions, guest lectures, and guest critics.

4 GESCHLECHTER-PARITÄT INNERHALB DER BERUFUNGSKOMMISSIONEN AM D-ARCH SOWIE UNTER DEN EINGELADENEN KANDIDATINNEN UND KANDIDATEN, DIE IN DIESEN KOMMISSIONEN VORSTELLIG WERDEN SOLLEN.

Gender parity within the appointment committees of the department, and of invited candidates that come before such search committees.

5 INTEGRATION UMFASSENDER GENDER-RELEVANTER THEMEN UND VERMITTLUNG GESCHLECHTSSPEZIFISCHER KOMPETENZEN IN DAS CURRICULUM DER AUSBILDUNG AM D-ARCH DURCH WAHLFÄCHER, SEMINARE SOWIE VORTRAGSREIHEN IM BACHELOR-, MASTER- UND IM POSTGRADUALEN STUDIUM SOWIE DURCH EINE BEWUSSTE UNTERRICHTSMETHODIK. EINE MÖGLICHE SOFORTMASSNAHME WÄRE DIE AUFSTELLUNG EINER GESONDERTEN FINANZIERUNG EINES SOLCHEN KURSES AM D-ARCH, DER JEDES SEMESTER VON EINEM ANDEREN LEHRSTUHL VERANSTALTET WERDEN WÜRDE.

Integration of broader gender issues or gender-related skills into the educational curriculum of the D-ARCH through elective courses, seminars, lecture series in graduate and post-graduate studies, and explicit teaching tools. This could be immediately achieved for example through dedicated funding for one such course each semester by different chairs within the D-ARCH.

6 BILDUNG EINES ADVANCED-AWARD-PROGRAMMS, DAS STIPENDIEN AN WISSENSCHAFTLERINNEN VERGIBT, DIE SICH DADURCH GANZ AUF IHRE FORSCHUNG UND LEHRE KONZENTRIEREN KÖNNEN. DIESES STIPENDIUM SOLL IN ERSTER LINIE IN EINER ÜBERGANGSZEIT ZWISCHEN EINZELNEN STUFEN IM AKADEMISCHEN CURRICULUM (DOKTORAT, HABILITATION UND PROFESSUR) VERGEBEN WERDEN, BIS EINE ANGEMESSENE GESCHLECHTER-PARITÄT ERREICHT WIRD.

Creation of an Advanced Award Program, comprising research and teaching grants for female scholars pursuing an academic career. This award is specifically aimed at bridging the gap (the leaky pipeline) in the academic curriculum (doctorate, habilitation, professorship) until reasonable parity is achieved.

7 BILDUNG EINES FONDS ZUR FINANZIERUNG VON GASTVORTRÄGEN EXTERNER REFERENTINNEN UND ZUR BEZUSCHUSSUNG DER REISEKOSTEN VON WISSENSCHAFTLERINNEN DES D-ARCH BEI EXTERNEN VORTRÄGEN, TAGUNGSBESUCHEN ETC. DIESER FONDS SOLL IN ERSTER LINIE IN EINER ÜBERGANGSZEIT DIE WAHRNEHMUNG VON AKADEMIKERINNEN UND ARCHITEKTINNEN ERHÖHEN, BIS EINE ANGEMESSENE GESCHLECHTER-PARITÄT ERREICHT WIRD.

Creation of a travel fund devoted to inviting female scholars for lectures from outside and to support female scholars of D-ARCH to travel for lectures, congresses, etc. This fund is specifically aimed at bridging the gap in academic and professional visibility until reasonable parity is achieved.

8 EINFÜHRUNG EINES STIPENDIUMS FÜR WEIBLICHE UND MÄNNLICHE DOKTORIERENDE, DIE SICH IN IHRER ARBEIT MIT EINER GENDER-THEMATIK IN ARCHITEKTUR ODER STÄDTEBAU BESCHÄFTIGEN.

Creation of a fellowship for female and male doctoral students devoting their thesis to gender-related issues in architecture and town planning.

9 GESCHLECHTER-PARITÄT BEI AUSZEICHNUNGEN AN STUDIERENDE FÜR HERAUSRAGENDE MASTER- UND DOKTORARBEITEN DURCH DIE BEREITSTELLUNG VON JEWEILS ZWEI RESPEKTIVE GERADZAHLIGEN PREISEN. EINE SOLCHE PARITÄTISCHE AUSZEICHNUNG WÜRDE DIE VORBILDLICHE PRAXIS DER AUFNAHME JEWEILS EINER STIPENDIATIN UND EINES STIPENDIATEN PRO JAHR IN DEN LAUFENDEN DOKTORATSPROGRAMMEN AM D-ARCH AUFGREIFEN.

Creation of a fellowship for female and male doctoral students devoting their thesis to gender-related issues in architecture and town planning.

9 POINTS FOR PARITY

The 9-point-program for parity was created in the context of the first Parity Talks in 2016 and articulated measures and demands to implement gender parity in the architecture department of the ETH Zurich. © Parity Group, ETHZ, 2016.

Parity
noun

1. The state or condition of being equal, especially regarding status or pay.

2. Mathematics (of a number), the fact of being even or odd.

Poster for the first Parity Talks symposium "Lets Talk About it" in March of 2016. © Völlm+Walthert, 2016.

Anger and frustration, but also a desire for change, sparked the creation of the Parity Group one December evening in 2014 in the Hönggerberg campus bistro of the Swiss Federal Institute of Technology in Zurich (ETH Zurich). The founding activists had good reason to be disappointed, having just come from an ETH event that had, yet again, an exclusively male panel.[01] Hailing from different countries with various socio-economic backgrounds, gender identities, and sexual orientations, they set their sights on tackling the lack of diversity in architecture.[02] From the start, the Parity Group declared war on the patriarchal order that still prevails in architecture schools. Their preferred term in this fight is "parity," a synonym for equality beyond gender binaries. It came to define a multifaceted battle against patriarchy; against architecture schools too white, male, and cis-gender; against architecture schools' euro-centric, heroic, canonical curricula; against architecture schools' culture of suffering, exhaustion, and competition; against architecture schools at the service of the exploitative offices; against architecture schools' lack of concern about the climate emergency, etc.

Here, Parity work is defined as creating a space for dissent within the discipline and maintaining momentum in the discourse on gender and equality from queer-feminist perspectives. After the #MeToo movement and the negative publicity caused by a sexual harassment allegation in ETH Zurich's architecture department, the school instrumentalized the Parity Group's work as evidence of its supposed engagement with these topics. In response, the Parity Group took advantage of the ETH's reputation and platform to communicate to a broader public about parity, anti-discrimination, and diversity in architecture education. The group has run workshops, events, and public discussions, including the annual Parity Talks, held every International Women's Day since 2016. In doing this work, the group has also helped establish new standards for other universities. Since they began in 2014, several groups within architecture schools have also launched initiatives to push their respective institutions to adopt fairer, more inclusive policies. This has primarily been the work of students and mid-level faculty at institutions such as Vienna University of Technology (Claiming*Spaces, 2019), Munich University of Technology (Parity Board, 2019), and EPFL Lausanne (DRAG lab, 2021). Groups have seen their agenda vindicated and their demands for a diverse teaching body, climate crisis-related curricula, balanced references in studio work, and discussions on working culture taken more seriously. Furthermore, all too common exploitive work practices have been problematized and discussions on the implementation of family-friendly work models have been encouraged. In 2020, the Parity Front, an independent offshoot of the Parity Group, was launched as an umbrella organization offering support and promoting cooperation, global networking, and future knowledge exchange between initiatives in higher education.

Equity, parity, and diversity in higher education cannot, however, be made the sole responsibility of young academics and students. Institutions must face their responsibilities and push structural reforms that go beyond symbolic politics. Shifts in discourse are underway and the awareness for long-ignored problems is increasing. But this is only the start of a long process of decolonizing and depatriarchalizing knowledge and value systems. The looming irrelevance of architecture can only be countered effectively if we, as architects, take a lead in the changes currently impacting all levels of society.

01 These were Katia Frey, Nils Havelka, Friederike Kluge, Kim Förster, Charlotte Malterre-Barthes, Sarah Nichols, Daniela Ortiz dos Santos, Eliana Perrotti, Laila Seewang, Dubravka Sekulic, and Harald Stühlinger.

02 A gender monitoring report from 2014–15, the year the Parity Group was founded, highlighted the "leaky pipeline" at ETH Zurich's architecture department. A leaky pipeline means that men tend to be continuously overrepresented in higher academic positions. While the proportion of women studying at ETH is relatively high, more than 40.5 percent, women hold just 12.2 percent of full professorships. See ETH Zurich, *Gender Monitoring 2014–15*, "Departementsbericht: Architektur," 1, accessed August 16, 2022, ethz.ch/content/dam/ethz/associates/services/Anstellung-Arbeiten/diversity/Strategie_und_Zahlen/monitoring-und-studien/1415/1415_D_ARCH_DE.pdf.

The architecture office WAI Think Tank was invited as a guest speaker to the sixth Parity Talks in 2021 to comment on the 9-point-program for parity and expand it with a global, "planetary" perspective.

1 Assembling of a Planetary network of anti-racist, anti-ableist, anti-capitalist, anti-colonialist, and transfeminist networks of solidarity. This planetary network will dismantle prevalent infrastructures of oppression, and will welcome historically marginalized voices.

2 Seizing mass communication media platforms and redistributing resources. Members of this planetary network will create publications that address new emancipatory, anti-racist, transfeminist, anti-ableist, anti-colonialist, ecologically just imaginaries and foment platforms for the free exchanges of this knowledges, resources and new archives.

3 Questioning through an intersectional lens. In order to make other, better worlds, an intersectional approach that puts anti-racism, transfeminism, anti-ableism, anti-capitalism, anti-imperialism, and ecological justice at the center will transform recruitment and collaborating processes. A critical pedagogy cannot exist without acknowledging the histories of all oppressed people and the imperial and colonial footprint of architecture and its forms of knowledge and power.

4 Creating new radical pedagogies. Radical pedagogies of emancipation are only possible through collaborative processes and networks of solidarity. Teachers and worldmakers will engage in radical and intersectional forms of solidarity and pedagogies of emancipation that challenge traditional hierarchiesand power dynamics.

5 Formulating a Planetary Curriculum. In order to respond to the planetary challenges of our times, a planetary curriculum must move beyond Eurocentric epistemologies and sources of knowledge, and operate at the intersection of anti-racism, anti-ableism, transfeminism, anti-capitalism, anti-colonialism, anti-imperialism.

6 Challenging the Status Quo. Eurocentric, white supremacist, and heteropatriarchal ideologies, customs, and histories must be questioned, challenged, exposed, and replaced with other forms of worldmaking. New strategies that foment, amplify, and empower historically marginalized voices must be implemented. The centers of knowledge must be shifted. New resources that challenge the asymmetrical distribution of power must be disseminated.

7 Relocating resources. Emancipatory pedagogies will relocate resources to support planetary networks of solidarity and provide welcoming platforms for new radical thinking, for the exchange of knowledge, and the proliferation of emancipatory, anti-racist, anti-ableist, transfeminist, anti-capitalist, anti-imperialist, and ecologically just discourses.

8 Reinforcing networks of Solidarity. Intellectual, emotional, financial and material support and mentorship will be provided to people researching and practicing at the intersection of anti-racist, transfeminist, anti-ableist, anti-capitalist, anti-imperialist, and ecologically just imaginaries.

9 Creating alternative models of support for new (and ancestral models) of intersectional, collaborative, narrative, solidary practices of education. Other worlds are possible. Other schools are possible.

SOME POST-NOVIS POINTS FOR A PLANETARY CURRICULUM

Creation of a Parity Board consisting of representatives from each institute of the D-ARCH, a representative of the professorship, a delegate from the Association of Teaching Assistants at the D-ARCH (AAA), one representative from the architectural students association at the ETH Zurich (architektura), the representatives of the Parity Group and one external expert. The Parity Board would be responsible for instigating the measures by which gender parity is achieved, their gradual implementation, the connected fundraising tasks, and the organisation of future public events such as the annual Parity Talks.

Annual internal and external monitoring and publication of the achieved parity-related results.

Gender parity for professorships, lectureships, senior research and teaching positions, guest lectures, and guest critics.

Gender parity within the appointment committees of the department, and of invited candidates that come before such search committees.

Integration of broader gender issues or gender-related skills into the educational curriculum of the D-ARCH through elective courses, seminars, lecture series in graduate and post-graduate studies, and explicit teaching tools. This could be immediately achieved for example through dedicated funding for one such course each semester by different chairs within the D-ARCH.

Creation of an Advanced Award Program, comprising research and teaching grants for female scholars pursuing an academic career. This award *is specifically aimed at bridging the gap (the leaky* pipeline) in the academic curriculum (doctorate, habilitation, professor ship) until reasonable parity is achieved.

Creation of a travel fund devoted to inviting female scholars for lectures from outside and to support female scholars of D-ARCH to travel for lectures, congresses, etc. This *fund is specifically aimed at bridging the gap* in academic and professional visibility until reasonable parity is achieved.

Creation of a fellowship for female and male doctoral students devoting their thesis to gender-related issues in architecture and town planning.

Gender parity in student awards for outstanding master and doctoral theses by offering two or even numbered equal prizes. These awards would follow the positive example set by the doctoral scholarships at the D-ARCH that are currently awarded to one male and one female incoming doctoral student each year.

Parity Front
*2020

© Parity Front.

was founded by Benjamin Groothuijse and Charlotte Malterre-Barthes in 2020 as an independent spin-off organization from the Parity Group (ETH Zurich). It aims to be a kind of umbrella organization, bringing together activist initiatives at higher education institutions around the world, thus creating synergies and building up a pool of collective knowledge. The Parity Group offers strategic consultancy in establishing new bottom-up higher education policy initiatives in the areas of gender equality and diversity. As well as many smaller, informally organized initiatives, the permanent members of the Parity Front include established organizations such as Womxn in Design (Harvard GSD), Womxn in Design and Architecture (Princeton University), Claiming*Spaces (TU Vienna), the Parity Board (TU Munich), and the DRAG lab (EPFL). **VK**
www.instagram.com/parity_front

Womxn in Design (WiD)
*2013
Harvard GSD

© Harvard WiD.

founded in the early 2000s at the Harvard Graduate School of Design (GSD), was relaunched in 2013. The student organization and networking platform advocates for gender equality and better opportunities in personal and professional development for students in design disciplines. Through a variety of projects and formats, WiD works to counter the historical invisibility of women designers and the underrepresentation of women in leadership positions. Since 2018, WiD publishes *WiD Bib: An Annotated Bibliography on Identity Theories*, a feminist reader on intersectional identity-political issues (critical race theories, queer theories, theories of class, cyberfeminism, etc.). **VK**
www.gsdwid.com

Womxn in Design and Architecture (WDA)
*2014
Princeton University SoA

© WDA, Princeton University SoA.

Womxn in Design and Architecture (WDA), founded in 2014, is a student-run organization at Princeton University's School of Architecture (SoA) that campaigns for greater visibility for women in the curriculum and in academic programs and lecture series. WDA also sees itself as an intersectional discourse platform within the academic and professional environment, which can function as a contact point on questions of equal rights and discrimination by class, race, and gender. The international WDA conference, held annually since 2016, addresses the work of important but non-canonical and often under-researched women architects and designers, including Minnette de Silva, Anne Tyng, Norma Merrick Sklarek, and Lina Bo Bardi. **VK**
wda.princeton.edu

Claiming* Spaces
*2019
Technical University Vienna

© Claiming*Spaces, TU Vienna.

is a bottom-up group of students, graduates, teachers, and researchers at Vienna University of Technology (TU Vienna) that promotes intersectional feminist perspectives in architecture and spatial planning. The group's manifesto asks how exclusion mechanisms at universities can be revealed and dismantled, how discriminatory knowledge production and historiography can be exposed and reformulated, and how feminist work practices can bring about much-needed changes in planning and construction. The collective was founded in November 2019 as part of the conference of the same name, which featured lectures, discussion panels, workshops, and performances by international guests and feminist figures in architecture and spatial planning. **VK**
www.claimingspaces.org

DRAG lab
*2021
École Polytechnique Fédérale de Lausanne

© DRAG lab, EPFL.

was founded in 2021 by a group of people studying, teaching, and working at the Swiss Federal Institute of Technology Lausanne (EPFL), who are committed to queering the teaching of architecture. DRAG lab holds public events and workshops on subjects such as "Spaces Challenging Patriarchy," "Architecture as Drag," and "New Habits for Diversity, Equity, and Inclusivity." It also organizes "book clubs," reading circles where texts on queer and feminist topics are discussed, offering a framework for collective reflection and critical conversation about architectural practice and teaching. In the future, this will lead to the development of structural measures to create parity and intersectional justice at the university. **VK**
www.instagram.com/drag.lab/

Parity Board
*2019
Technical University Munich (TUM)

© Parity Board, TUM.

is an open-format organization for students, employees, and professors at the TUM. It was founded in 2019 with the aim of jointly developing strategies for equal working environments at every level of the architecture department. The goals of the Parity Board are to enshrine equality principles in higher education policy and to expand and institutionalize the board. The Parity Jour Fixe has been organized at regular intervals since 2018 by the Parity Board and the university's equal opportunities officers. It addresses inequalities in the distribution of knowledge, funds, and visibility in architecture, raising awareness about equal opportunity and gender equality across higher education. **VK**
www.arc.ed.tum.de/arc/ueber-uns/diversitaet/

OCTOBER 2021

Architecture Lobby Manifesto

Blake Fisher, Sean Higgins, Sben Korsh, Valérie Lechêne, Kaede Polkinghorne, Maya Porath, Priyanka Shah on behalf of The Architecture Lobby

The Architecture Lobby is a democratic, member-driven organization of architectural workers fighting for just labor practices within the architectural field and a more equitable built environment. As the Lobby began to form in 2013, a handful of members penned a ten-point manifesto centered on labor rights for all. Our original manifesto mainly addressed the unjust labor conditions pervasive in the field.

As we campaign for radical change within the discipline, the Lobby continues to grow and attract workers alienated by architectural practice; today we comprise over 16 chapters and 350 dues-paying members across the United States, Canada, the United Kingdom, Australia, and more. In recent years, members have worked to crystallize the intersections between labor rights, heteropatriarchy, and white supremacy. At our 2021 Members Congress, the Lobby ratified a new manifesto that reflects these intersections and our collective revision process.

Our new manifesto is a vision of the world we are fighting for and outlines the changes we seek in the field.

WE ARE PRECARIOUS WORKERS. THESE ARE OUR DEMANDS:

1.

Build worker power and collective agency through unions and cooperatives.

Abusive work environments and irresponsible architectural practices that operate under labor laws favoring employers will endure until we demand change. By building collective worker power towards unionization and enacting cooperative modes of ownership, we can establish more equitable working standards within the discipline of architecture and claim the political agency to advocate for change outside of it.

2.

A living wage, benefits, job security, and wage transparency across the discipline.

Neoliberalism has decimated our social safety nets. In the US, our health insurance, medical leave, pensions and other "benefits" are dependent on employers, leaving pay inequity rooted in white supremacy and heteropatriarchy unchecked. Competitive workplace environments that cultivate shame and secrecy around debt and compensation keep us from naming the problem. We shamelessly demand stability, financial security, and pay equity in our workplaces.

3.

No more free labor; no unpaid internships, unpaid overtime, or unpaid competitions.

Architecture's reliance on unpaid labor fundamentally devalues workers and distorts fee and compensation structures across the discipline. Unpaid internships, unpaid overtime, and unpaid competitions further entrench race, class, and gender inequities while advancing the careers of the privileged. There is no alternative to just compensation. We must collectively demand to be paid for every hour of our labor.

4.

Center the importance of labor in our understanding of architecture. Architecture is work!

The built environment is planned and maintained not only by the professionally educated and credentialed, but also by administrative staff, drafters, BIM managers, marketing staff, and countless other contributors. Architects often prefer to distance themselves from this reality, abstracting both their own labor and the labor of non-architects. We must situate our struggle in the workplace and stand in solidarity with all workers to build collective power.

5.

Stop peddling buildings as products. Demand compensation based on the value and impact our work creates.

Architecture is a practice, not a product. When buildings are seen as innovative objects rather than ever-changing components of the collectively constructed environment, the maintenance labor behind and around them is erased and devalued. We demand compensation not only for the material fact of the buildings we design, but for the material and immaterial value they cultivate in context.

6.

End oppression based on gender within and enabled by the discipline.

The architectural workplace remains a cis-heteronormative environment offering inequitable opportunities, pay, and agency for women, queer people, and other minorities. In the US women enter the architectural work force at equal numbers as men, but they account for only 1/5th of licensed architects and an even lower proportion at the top ranks of the profession. This alarming rate of attrition is due, in large part, to the absence of support for caregiving and reproductive labor, overwhelmingly performed by women. These biases are further compounded along racial and class lines. By decentering capitalist heteronormative values in architectural workplaces, we can open the possibility of a truly creative discipline that empowers a multitude of voices and values.

7.

Confront the complicity of architecture in racism. Confront racism in our workplaces.

Architects rarely acknowledge how their work—both process and product—crystallize long-standing patterns of oppression that have been cultivated through imperialism, settler colonialism and slavery. As a discipline it replicates social biases and perpetuates white supremacy within its own ranks: only 532 Black women hold an architecture license throughout the United States as of October 2021. We demand intentionally anti-racist architectural practice and the continuous confrontation of white supremacy in our workplaces.

8.

Design for the full spectrum of human life. Universal design is not an afterthought.

Architecture reproduces disability by building an environment that is only accessible to bodies deemed normative. Disability rights activists have long recognized this, but architects have historically failed to incorporate their rich critique. We demand a built environment that is fully accessible to all humans.

9.

Challenge the concept of licensure. Expand the right to practice.

The right to practice architecture is predicated on the dual monopoly of elite education and licensure. Riddled with barriers, the path to licensure is guarded by professional institutions and registration boards, maintaining the power of white "professionals" while limiting the legitimacy of other world-making imaginaries. There is no liberatory future within architectural practice without the transformation of these institutions and the end of the "professional."

10.

Celebrate the collective process of producing architecture. Demystify architecture as the work of a solo creative genius.

The starchitect is a white supremacist and heteropatriarchal fever dream: anyone who has worked in architecture knows it is necessarily a collaborative process. We demand that architects turn away from the myth of *one* great white man, and towards the reality of many interdependent collaborators, thinkers, workers and contributors. Obscuring this reality has brought us grossly abusive work practices and made possible the erasure of non-white, queer, and female practitioners' labor across history. In order to build collective power, we must recognize the plurality of architecture.

11.

Climate justice as the basis of all architectural work. There can be no sustainable future without sustainable labor practices.

Architectural work must acknowledge that buildings are not just physical objects but also sites of consumption, extraction, and capitalist property relations. Technocratic "greening" of buildings is not enough to address the deeply embedded inequities that fossil fuel capitalism is built upon. Responding to the climate crisis calls for large-scale systemic interventions that center frontline communities, suppress land speculation, and address climate migration. We must develop means of engaging with the social order threatening the future of the planet and not restrict ourselves to atomized actions on individual buildings, standing in solidarity with the most vulnerable towards a just and carbon-free future.

12.

Fight for democratic alternatives to the capitalist system of development.

Capitalism is based on cultivating profit by devaluing all labor, including architectural labor. The financialization of all forms of real estate further entrenches architectural workers in service of capital rather than society. We demand establishing democratic control over our built environments so that housing, cities, and cultural and governmental institutions be built and planned by social consensus, and not by and in service of private capital.

JOIN US!

architecture-lobby.org

WikiD Women, Wikipedia, Design

Writing Women in(to) the History of Architecture

We Can [edit]!
A parody of the famous "We Can Do It!" poster created for Westinghouse Electric by J. Howard Miller during World War II, intended to boost the morale of women working in the factories.
Collage: Tom Morris, 2012.

Wikipedia currently has 1,827 entries in the category of "Architect (Germany)." Of those pages, just 96—less than 5 percent—are about women architects and urban planners. Wikipedia's global *List of Women Architects* contains the names of 723 women from 79 countries.

These are alarmingly low numbers, but they are in keeping with the centuries of underrepresentation women working in the field have suffered in libraries and archives of knowledge. Few historians took an interest in the archives of the first generation of women architects when they began to die in the second half of the 20th century. This often resulted in the loss or destruction of valuable plans, drawings, and written texts. Even today, our knowledge of countless women architects and their work remains fragmentary. The monograph, early established as a dominant form in architectural history, was primarily reserved for male subjects while also promoting the notion of the architect as a "lone genius." In this way, women architects, who had always worked collaboratively for professional and private reasons, fell victim to collective oblivion.

Although numerous books and articles about women architects have been published in recent years, their names and stories often remain unknown outside of academia. This is where *WikiD – Women, Wikipedia, Design*

01 Despina Stratigakos, "Unforgetting Women Architects: From the Pritzker to Wikipedia," *Places Journal* (April 2016), accessed August 16, 2022, placesjournal.org/article/unforgetting-women-architects-from-the-pritzker-to-wikipedia.

02 *WikiD Guide to Wikipedia Editing* (April 18, 2019), accessed August 16, 2022, www.parlour.org.au/wikid/wikid-guides-to-wikipedia-editing/.

comes in. This international campaign was founded in 2015 by three groups of feminist planners, ArchiteXX, Parlour, and n-ails, located respectively in New York, Melbourne, and Berlin. The project was funded by Wikimedia, the nonprofit foundation and grew into an international network within a very short space of time. The *WikiD* project aims to increase material by and about women from spatial planning disciplines on Wikipedia in order to write them back into the history of architecture. Wikipedia is among the most used online resources and, as such, has a major influence on how architecture and architectural history are perceived, especially by the younger generation. But as well as a shortage of articles on women architects who could serve as role models, the proportion of women among Wikipedia authors is also low. In 2012, just 9 percent of Wikipedia contributors were women. This gap is reflected in the content of the site's articles and how they are later edited and expanded.

The architectural historian Despina Stratigakos, in her essay "Unforgetting Women Architects: From the Pritzker to Wikipedia,"[01] describes the gender bias distortion effect, whereby new posts by women (and about women) are disproportionately flagged for immediate deletion. This often disregards the seven-day critical discussion period customarily granted to new posts. Sometimes sources are questioned, and sometimes the relevance or even the existence of women architects is called into doubt. Relevance is a key criterion for inclusion in the encyclopedia. Wikipedia's "notability guideline" can be problematic: it means that claims to recognition within the profession continue to be determined by the same structures that have traditionally stopped women from being considered architects. For example, having one's own architectural office continues to be a key criterion of professional success in the field.

To familiarize themselves with the various rules and guidelines for developing Wikipedia entries, volunteers meet worldwide in publicly accessible writing workshops, so-called edit-a-thons, where they collaboratively research and write new articles shedding light on women working in architecture and related disciplines in design and spatial planning. Instructions known as "WikiD Guides" have been formulated in various languages. These can help future authors to create new entries independently.[02] By 2019, over 250 authors from all over the world had created or contributed to more than 200 new entries and made some 150,000 changes to 12,000 existing articles. **AM**

ArchiteXX
*2012
in New York

Launched in New York by Lori Brown and Nina Freedman in 2012, ArchiteXX is an international nonprofit organization bringing together theorists and practitioners of architecture. It is dedicated to gender equality, diversity, and supporting women and non-binary people in the world of architecture. ArchiteXX stages lectures, round tables, and exhibitions. It aims to transform the architectural profession through generational change, flexible working time models, and redefining how work is evaluated and remunerated in the architecture industry.
In 2021, it organized screenings of *WOMEN ARCHITECTS ARE EVERYWHERE!*, a selection of short films about women architects, which transposes material from the *WikiD* campaign into video format. **AM**
www.architexx.org

Parlour
*2012
in Melbourne

Parlour is a nonprofit organization working at the intersection of research, activism, and architecture. Through lecture series, public events, workshops, and educational programs, it promotes gender equality in architecture and construction, and works to increase recognition of Australia's indigenous culture. In addition to the *WikiD* campaign, the group maintains *Marion's List*, a growing online public directory of Australian architects, designers, and spatial planners who are women. The list aims to help create more equal representation in lecture series, panels, and juries. Parlour's online lecture series *Light at the End of the Tunnel*, begun in 2020, addresses the world of work and the future of the profession in times of pandemic and climate emergency. **AM**
www.archiparlour.org

n-ails
*2004
in Berlin

n-ails is a network that enables professional, creative, and interdisciplinary exchange between women architects and planners. The group is committed to equal opportunities, women's empowerment within the construction industry, and the adoption of gender-inclusive professional policies by Germany's regional Chambers of Architects. In the summer of 2021, n-ails organized the *Women in Architecture* festival. The festival included exhibitions, film series, guided tours, symposia, lectures, and workshops, addressing historical and contemporary works by women architects as well as subjects related to gender equality in everyday life in offices and construction sites. In recent years, n-ails has played an important role in establishing the nationwide association planerinnen-netzwerk.de and has co-organized specialist conferences for women planners in Georgia, Vienna, and Zurich. **AM**
www.n-ails.de

Essay

Blind Spots

Elisions in Early Accounts of Women in Architectural History

TEXT
Mary Pepchinski

Along with many women of my generation who were born in the postwar years, I expected that a more equitable world was both possible and my undisputed entitlement. Spurred on by Second Wave Feminism, this conviction included a role for women in academic professions as well as architecture. In addition to a desire to transform the present, many of us looked to the past to write historical narratives that explored the experiences of women. As the historian Gerda Lerner notes, these texts would correct the prevailing male-oriented perspective on history and bring about the "development of an alternative vision of the future."[01] In architecture, championing women's history affirmed our intention to become architects by rooting it in historical precedent.

Members of the Women's School of Planning and Architecture lie on a lawn in the form of a Venus symbol at St. Joseph's College in Maine, 1975. The college is considered one of the first in the United States to reorient its curriculum to take a feminist approach.
Photo: Courtesy Women's School of Planning and Architecture Records, Smith College Special Collections.

Starting in the early 1970s, a remarkable collection of texts focusing on the experience of women as architects has been produced. The earliest publications, often exhibition catalogues, surveyed women professionals in national contexts, such as the United States, Germany, and Finland. Monographs about individuals, including Eileen Gray, Lucy Hillebrand, Eleanor Raymond, Lotte Stam-Beese, and Margarete Schütte-Lihotzky appeared, and the collaborators of well-known modernists, including Aino Aalto, Ray Eames, Charlotte Perriand, Marlene Moeschke Poelzig, and Lilly Reich, received attention, too.

Like many women architects and architectural historians of my generation, I avidly consumed these publications and based my own work on this body of knowledge. But in recent years, we increasingly witness enormous disruption and rapid-fire transformation: the feminization of the ranks of architecture students;[02] the extraordinary growth of critical gender-related research in architecture around the globe, particularly in "non-canonical" contexts; the impact of new modes of communication; the repercussions from social and political activism as exemplified by the #MeToo, #AmINext, and #BlackLivesMatter movements; and the upheaval caused by pandemic conditions and rampant climate change, to name a few issues.

When considering the present circumstances, arguably, some of the early histories about women architects no longer seem to reflect the complex reality we inhabit today. Produced by middle-class white women working in mainstream practice or academic settings in "canonical nations," these texts overwhelmingly considered how they could have agency in the male-dominated habitus of architecture.[03] As the writer and activist Audre Lorde observes, differences among women—class, race, sex and sexuality—were suppressed, and their potential as "a springboard for creative change within our lives"[04] was ignored.

What follows are reflections on four intersecting themes—Race and Racism; Religion and Politics; Misogyny, Harassment, Gender Bias; and Private Life—to consider a few seminal publications about women in architecture. It is a reckoning with my (and my generation's) journey, spurred on by this particular moment in time. In conclusion, I argue for the need to write histories of women in architecture that more faithfully reflect their complicated, lived reality to comprehend the manner in which gender inflects architectural practice today.

RACE AND RACISM

The catalogue *Women in American Architecture* accompanied the eponymous exhibition, held at the Brooklyn Museum in New York in 1977. Occupying a capacious gallery, the exhibition featured documentation about women's contributions as architects, artists, critics, and visionaries to shaping the built environment. The presence of middle-class and upper-class WASP (White, Anglo-Saxon, Protestant) women, and their understanding of history, prevailed. Contributions by women of color and the North American First Nations were largely absent, as were the spaces and places devised by the masses of immigrant women, like my maternal and paternal great-grandmothers, who flocked to the United States in the 19th and 20th centuries.

In her study of race and 19th-century feminism, the cultural geographer and sociologist Vron Ware notes that 19th-century British and American feminism "developed as a political movement in a racist society."[05] According to Ware, feminists called for the greater participation of women outside of the home to exert a civilizing influence on public life. At the same time, they understood white womanhood as a category for exclusion, developed in opposition to other socially disadvantaged groups. This included the racist narrative of the hypersexualized black man, perceived as a threat to their morality, and an aversion toward all non-English-speaking immigrants, who were considered foreign to the dominant Anglo-American culture. Intentionally or otherwise, the sentiments about whiteness and womanhood seemed to permeate and distort the depiction of one key exhibit at the 1977 *Women in American Architecture* exhibition: the 1893 Woman's Building. Celebrated as a seminal achievement for both 19th-century feminists and American women in architecture, the monumental neoclassical Woman's Building was a part of the signature "White City" fairgrounds

***Women in American Architecture*, the first survey exhibition of works by American women architects, opened at the Brooklyn Museum in New York in 1977. Photo: Norman McGrath. Courtesy Susana Torre.**

Designed by architect Sophia Hayden, the Woman's Building was a neoclassical exhibition pavilion at the 1893 Chicago World's Fair. Only art and crafts by white women were shown there; works by non-white women were excluded.

(named for the buildings' white stucco façades) at the 1893 Chicago World's Fair (officially called the World's Columbian Exposition). Designed by the architect Sophia Hayden and decorated by middle-class white women, it proclaimed that women were capable of producing seminal public architecture.

Meanwhile, to demonstrate the educational and professional gains they had achieved since the end of slavery in the 1860s, Black American women had vigorously lobbied to be included in the building—but to no avail. To draw attention to their failed efforts, the Black journalist and activist Ida B. Wells produced a brochure titled, *The Reason Why the Colored American is not in the World's Columbian Exposition*, which featured correspondence between Black activists and the white organizers. These exchanges exposed how white women used bureaucratic rules to exclude non-white women from the building. At the 1893 Columbian Exhibition, the brochure was only available at the Haitian Pavilion—representing the Caribbean nation that had been formed after slave uprisings in 1804—and located near the Woman's Building. Nevertheless, the 1977 exhibition and catalogue were devoid of information illuminating the racial and ethnic biases that informed the Woman's Building and the (women's) historiography of that time.

Looking back, there are other details surrounding this exhibition that I now find disturbing as well. In 1977, the Brooklyn Museum was located in a borough of New York City that had a large Black and Brown population. Today, much of downtown Brooklyn and the area around this museum has been gentrified, and the vital inner-city neighborhoods populated by people of color have been transformed. Back in 1977, one wonders, how could a young woman of color from Brooklyn who desired to be an architect find something worth emulating in this show? In recent years, as I visit conferences about gender and architecture throughout Europe, like the 2015 *Matrices* in Lisbon or the 2020 opening of *Frau Architekt* at the Zentrum Architektur Zürich, the 1977 *Women in American Architecture* exhibition continues to be referenced as a feminist milestone. Yet it is time to acknowledge the biases that shaped the 1977 exhibition and find a critical strategy to examine historical events, like the gestation of the 1893 Woman's Building, that played such a pivotal role in them. How can the story of this monument be told in order to have the voices that were silenced, like that of Ida B. Wells, assume a central place in the narrative? How can we, who engage in discourses about gender, architecture, and history, confront racial separation, what Audre Lorde calls the "constant, if unspoken, distortion of vision,"[06] in our work?

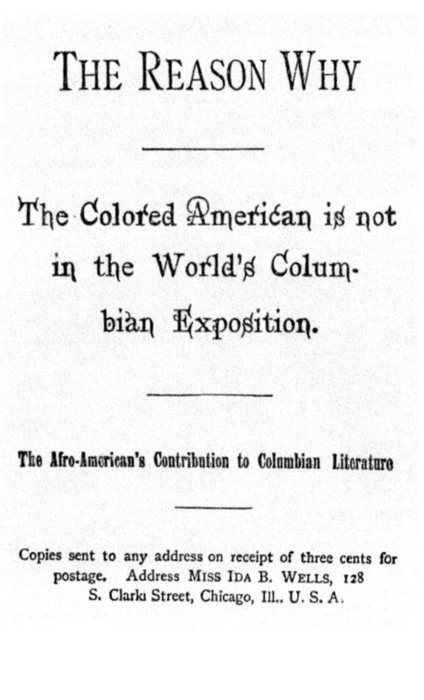

THE REASON WHY

The Colored American is not in the World's Columbian Exposition.

The Afro-American's Contribution to Columbian Literature

Copies sent to any address on receipt of three cents for postage. Address MISS IDA B. WELLS, 128 S. Clark Street, Chicago, Ill., U. S. A.

The pamphlet *The Reason Why the Colored American is not in the World's Columbian Exposition*, published in 1893, documented the correspondence between Black activists and the white organizers of the Woman's Building at the Chicago World's Fair. The latter kept finding new excuses to exclude works by non-white women from the exhibition.
Photo: Hanna Holborn Gray Special Collections Research Center, University of Chicago Library.

RELIGION AND POLITICS

Other elisions are present in *Architektinnenhistorie: Zur Geschichte der Architektinnen und Designerinnen im 20. Jahrhundert. Eine erste Zusammenstellung* from 1984. The catalogue and the eponymous exhibition on 20th-century women architects and designers were produced as part of the 7th International Congress of Women Architects and Town Planners, held in conjunction with the International Building Exhibition (IBA) in Berlin.[07] In this collection, and the accounts that have proceeded from it,[08] Elisabeth von Knobelsdorff-Tippelskirch (1877–1961) is celebrated as the first woman in Germany to break multiple professional barriers: she was the first to receive a Diploma-Engineer degree in architecture from a Technische Hochschule (Technical University); join a professional organization; work as a military architect; register an architectural patent; enter the civil service; and publish an article in the government periodical *Das Zentralblatt der Bauverwaltung*.[09] Her unwomanly passion for architecture was attributed to her illustrious lineage, as the Prussian architect Georg Wenzeslaus von Knobelsdorff, the close friend and chief architect of Frederick the Great, was a paternal relation. Yet her career was short-lived. In 1922 she married the German diplomat Kurt von Tippelskirch and was officially released from the civil service in 1923. From 1927 to 1938, she lived in Boston, Massachusetts, where her husband was posted. We can assume they were a principled couple because the website

Portrait of Elisabeth von Knobelsdorff. Scan from: Union Internationale des Femmes Architectes (UIFA) Sektion Bundesrepublik e.V., eds., *Architektinnenhistorie: Zur Geschichte der Architektinnen und Designerinnen im 20. Jahrhundert* (Berlin: UIFA, 1984), 24.

of the Technical University of Berlin (Elisabeth's alma mater) states: "The diplomat Tippelskirch was recalled to the empire in 1938 because of political differences with the Nazi regime."[10] While undertaking research for *Frau Architekt* in 2017, I came upon other aspects of her life. Correspondence in public archives reveals her to be a dedicated architect who attempted to remain professionally active long after her marriage to Kurt von Tippelskirch.[11] Although devoted to her husband, she bitterly bemoaned her enforced idleness as the wife of a German diplomat in a provincial American city.

But there is more to the story. Whereas her father was a Prussian general, Elisabeth von Knobelsdorff-Tippelskirch's mother came from a wealthy Jewish family in Breslau, which converted to Christianity in the 19th century. Her maternal aunt, Gertrud Dyhrenfurth, was a bourgeois activist committed to improving the situation of women farm workers. It can be assumed that she had to "closet" her Jewishness while active in the mainstream women's movement—as she went on to be an avid supporter of the National Socialists.[12] With this in mind, for the aspiring woman architect who broke so many barriers, playing down her Judaism was as necessary for her professional acceptance as the need to stress her aristocratic Christian heritage.

Research by the historian Stephen Norwood shows Elisabeth von Knobelsdorff-Tippelskirch (identified in published archival photographs as "Baroness von Tippelskirch") and Kurt von Tippelskirch welcoming the commander and crew of the ship *Karlsruhe* when it docked in Boston in 1934 on its controversial propaganda tour of the USA.[13] As the diplomat and his wife, they were required to represent the government of their nation, so their actions should be understood in this context. However, according to the current state of research, there is no evidence to suggest they were opposed to official German policies at this time.

The question for architectural historians is: How is it possible to retell Elisabeth von Knobelsdorff-Tippelskirch's story using an intersectional framework, acknowledging her desire to become an architect, longing for integration shared by many Jewish citizens, aristocratic identification with Prussia, and fears of anti-Semitism? For Elisabeth von Knobelsdorff-Tippelskirch, the passion for working in architecture was inflected by complex issues about personal identity, not merely the wish to transcend rigid gender roles.

Officers and diplomats from Nazi Germany visit Kurt von Tippelskirch in Newton, Massachusetts, 1934. In the front right of the photo is his wife, Elisabeth von Tippelskirch, née von Knobelsdorff. Photo: Boston Herald-Traveler Photo Morgue, Boston Public Library.

Misogyny, harassment, gender bias

Many of the early texts about women in architecture demonstrated women's pathbreaking achievements. Two other literary forms, the biography and the autobiography, attempted to portray the *gendered* experience of studying and working in architecture.

Margarete Schütte-Lihotzky (1897–2000) is acknowledged as a feminist icon for her social engagement and decades-long work in architecture. Starting in the 1970s, she was also a witness to history, who recounted her contributions to the social welfare architecture of the 1920s and 1930s along with her political activities. Her *Erinnerungen aus dem Widerstand* (Memories from the Resistance) *1938–1945* was first published in East Berlin and Hamburg in 1985 and reissued in Vienna in 1994,[14] and her 1984 memoir about her education and early professional years, *Warum ich Architektin wurde* (Why I Became an Architect), appeared posthumously in 2004. She remains one of the most prolific female architect-authors and was well aware of the power of the written word to shape her image and keep herself firmly anchored in the public eye.[15]

We expect biographical and especially autobiographical writing to go beyond a simple accounting of facts to illuminate the subject's agency and reveal her feelings, motivations, and reactions. We want to know *why* Margarete Schütte-Lihotzky, for example, has made her choices and, perhaps most importantly, how she *felt* during crucial moments in her life and career. For example, resistance towards female professionalism, especially in architecture, was pronounced when Margarete Schütte-Lihotzky made her bold decision to study this subject. In reading *Warum ich Architektin wurde*, I am astonished to learn how little she reflects upon such sentiments in her narrative. At best, the gender-based resistance she encounters is brief; in one short sentence, she mentions her family's initial opposition ("No one would ever let a woman build a house," they asserted) while her favorite teacher, Oskar Strnad, warns her of the inherent difficulties this profession presented to men, let alone a young woman. Only the slightest personal reaction is revealed when she recalls Josef Hoffmann, who refused to admit women to his architecture class at the Kunstgewerbeschule (School of Applied Arts) in Vienna. After recalling that she did not feel like a "suffragette" at the time, she nonetheless found his position "unjust" and "reactionary."[16]

Nevertheless, in a few instances, she does recall how gender played a role in her professional endeavors. In 1920, in the context of a competition for a garden colony and a housing estate, her presence among the prizewinners caused disruption. When it was revealed that a woman was among this group, she notes that the jury suspected it was the design that featured "romantically decorated buildings, kitschy painted perspectives, and the theme 'back to nature.'"[17] Her project was quite different because it displayed a competent, technical-constructive solution. Later in the text, she describes her work for Ernst May on the *Neues Frankfurt* urban development plan and the "Frankfurt Kitchen" in the late 1920s. Although she did not know how to cook or run a household, for propaganda reasons Ernst May insisted it was no coincidence that "the Frankfurt Kitchen was created by a woman for women, because a female architect knows best what is important for cooking."[18] Her authorship, she recalls, was necessary to convince housewives of the usefulness of this innovation.

Margarete Schütte-Lihotzky rarely discloses how she *felt* when on the receiving end of gender biases or the lingering scars such as derision (concerning the competition) and stereotyping (regarding the Frankfurt Kitchen) can leave on one's psyche. Yet all women experience some form of prejudice during their lifetime. The literary scholar Jacqueline Rose notes that acts of prejudice or harassment are not violence per se, but they are related because both are an expression of unequal power relations, carried out by those who wield privilege and influence.[19] In the context of architecture, such behavior is often perpetrated by those who control access to employment, education, commissions, or the means to disseminate one's work. The consequences of eliminating such experiences from writing history are clear: according to the cultural theorist Sara Ahmed, not calling out injurious behavior, reflecting on its origin and consequences, is a means to perpetuate it.[20]

Considering the barriers that women have had to confront in the past century, it is remarkable how biographies and autobiographies rarely engage with the subject's experience of misogyny, or what the sociologist Paul Bourdieu identifies as "symbolic violence": the production and reproduction of structures of domination, which are

Margarete Schütte-Lihotzky with her colleagues from the Frankfurt building department, c. 1928. © Universität für angewandte Kunst Wien, Kunstsammlung und Archiv.

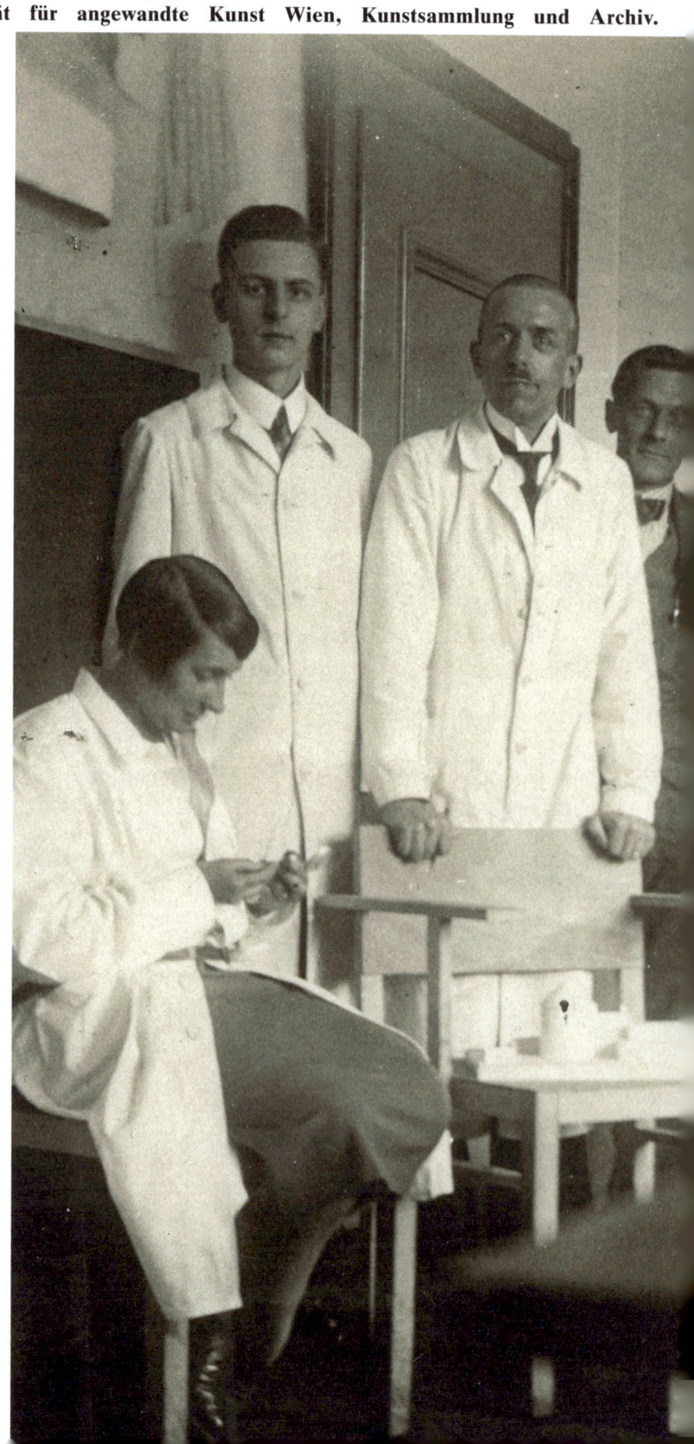

historically rooted and are carried out by institutions that govern our lives.[21] It is well known that the architect Patty Hopkins was photoshopped out of the 2014 group portrait of British high-tech pioneers for the BBC television series *The Brits Who Built the Modern World* (she was originally standing next to Norman Foster and Richard Rogers), and that the 1991 Pritzker Prize was denied to Denise Scott Brown and given only to her partner, Robert Venturi. Another example is Marlene Moeschke-Poelzig. Her studio and home in Berlin-Westend, designed in 1930 and demolished in November 2021 despite international protests, is considered an "outstanding example of modernist architecture and the emancipation of women in the early 20th century."[22] And yet, the memorial plaque in front of the building only pays tribute to her well-known husband: "Prof. Hans Poelzig: the great architect and teacher lived in this house from 1930 to 1936."[23]

Although Margarete Schütte-Lihotzky was wholly unfamiliar with housework, Ernst May tasked her with the design of a prototype for the Frankfurt Kitchen. He would later claim that it was conceived "by a woman for women" in a bid to convince homemakers of the innovation's usefulness. Photo from the magazine *Das neue Frankfurt* 5, 1926–27.

But there are innumerable, less spectacular acts, like those alluded to by Margarete Schütte-Lihotzky, I would argue, that fall into this category, too. And though I do not doubt her sincere commitment to the design of social welfare architecture, particularly for children, I wonder how she felt about her career becoming so closely focused on this one theme, especially in her later years. Certainly, Schütte-Lihotzky's unwavering devotion to communism in the context of postwar Western Europe, and not simply her gender, contributed to this situation.[24] Yet if her correspondence dating from the 1950s and 1960s with colleagues like Walter Gropius[25] and especially Ernst May[26] is any indication, she clearly desired new challenges and the opportunity to take part in another large, collective effort.

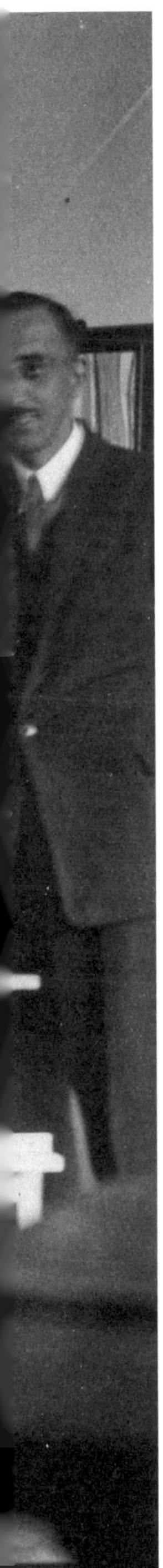

Private life

Like Margarete Schütte-Lihotzky, the majority of the women and men who entered architecture in the past century hailed from the middle class, and the ideals and practices of this caste were integral to their identity. Starting in the 19th century, one key attribute was the need for a private life that was separate from one's public life.[27] Private life was centered on the nuclear family, where women and children were subject to the authority of the father. According to the historian Ingeborg Weber-Kellermann, the increasing democratization of public life in the 20th century has engendered a more egalitarian conception of the private sphere, including the weakening of the *pater familias*, a greater sense of equality among the members and the recognition of their desire for self-determination.[28] Non-traditional families, such as singles, queer partnerships, patchwork families, etc., have arisen, pointing to greater tolerance of social diversity and the changing nature of personal affairs.

For many women architects, this has meant the need to think about what kind of private life—remaining single, living in a collective household, or collaborating with a partner to share parenting and professional work, for example—is best suited to support their career.[29] But private life does not merely consist of how one chooses to live and with whom. In my role as an architectural historian and researcher, on more than one occasion, I have been taken aside by someone with knowledge of a particular woman architect. They feel it necessary to convey to me facts about her life that are absent from the official record, including: domestic abuse of her or her offspring, her perceived deviant sexuality or decision to remain celibate, alcoholism, mental illness, or inherited trauma. Why is this important? Should it even be made known? Certainly, when telling someone's story for public consumption, the wishes of someone concerning how her life should be publicized should be respected.

Nevertheless, one can ask the question: Why would knowing about such intimate facts shed light on someone's life in architecture? The recent research about Mies van der Rohe by Franz Schulze and Alice Friedman[30] along with the personal recollections of Anne Griswold Tyng and Nathaniel Kahn[31] on Louis I. Kahn offers some clues. Taking the form of memoirs, biographical accounts, and a film, these projects expose their subjects' messy personal relationships and, in the case of Mies, his physical infirmities. The resulting information is not a mound of gossip, I would argue, but rather an accumulation of facts that lead one to question why society feels the need to tolerate the complicated behavior of perceived male geniuses at all costs.[32] My suspicion is that when more information about women architects and their personal lives comes to light, it will be possible to glean insights about them, their buildings, and other facets of the gendered nature of architectural practice in our time, too.

Essay

The German sculptor and architect Marlene Moeschke and her later husband, the architect Hans Poelzig, founded the architecture firm Bauatelier Poelzig in 1920. They worked together on many projects, such as the Haus des Rundfunks (House of Broadcasting) and the Messe Berlin exhibition grounds. The Poelzig House, their studio and home in Tannenburgallee in Berlin-Westend—whose topping out ceremony was documented by this photo in 1930—was designed by Marlene Moeschke-Poelzig alone. It was symbolic of the emancipation of female architects in the early 20th century and an important monument of modernist architecture.
Photo: Archiv Bauwelt.

Lieber Herr Conrads,

gelegentlich gerne bemüht, die leeren Seiten Ihres Blattes zu füllen – manchmal würde ich allerdings auch die allzu vollen gerne etwas lichten –, ist mir auf Ihre ¾-Jahrhundert-Frage eingefallen:
Hans Poelzigs Frau Marlene war Architektin und hat das eigene Poelzigsche Wohnhaus in der Tannenbergallee in Berlin-Neuwestend allein entworfen.
Der Meister hat sie machen lassen, das ist Liebe.
Zugegeben: Diese Erinnerung ist nur ein Vorwand, um Ihnen ein Foto zu zeigen, das Fritz Jaenecke aus Schweden mitbrachte, als wir 1974 unter Peter Poelzigs Vorsitz im Preisgericht für die Neubauten im Rudolf-Virchow-Krankenhaus gemeinsam, aber vergeblich den Entwurf von Ludwig Leo durchsetzen wollten (übrigens auch im Sinne Ihrer Fragestellung eine der betrüblichen Fehlentwicklungen, daß dies nicht gelungen ist).
Das Bild zeigt beim Richtfest für das Haus in der Tannenbergallee vorne rechts Hans Poelzig, dahinter seinen noch schwarzhaarigen Sohn Peter, links vorne die linke Hand der Architektin (ob Fritz Jaenecke den Körper abgeschnitten hat?), dahinter die rechte Hand Poelzigs, den Bürochef Zimmermann, auch mit Zigarre, neben ihm Martin Wagner und im Hintergrund Jaenecke – noch ganz Otto Normalverbraucher –, der die Bauleitung der Marlene-Villa machte, darüber aber scheiterte.
Er hat uns das ausführlich geschildert.
Nochmal zugegeben: Auch dies ist immer noch ein Vorwand. Was ich wirklich – von Jaenecke authentisch verbürgt und berichtet – weitergeben möchte: Hans Poelzig, von Frau und Bauleiter nach besonderen Wünschen befragt, hatte diese Antwort: Mir ist ganz egal, was Ihr baut, Hauptsache Ihr legt das Lokusfenster so, daß ich beim Scheißen in den Grunewald sehen kann!
Ganz in diesem Sinne
Ihr Cornelius Hertling, Berlin

1984

An article in *Bauwelt* in 1984 featured a photo of the topping-out ceremony, but Marlene Moeschke-Poelzig was cropped out of the picture. © Bauwelt 1984.

The Poelzig House, where the architect couple lived with their three children, was tailored to the needs of the family: the kitchen, living room, and dining room, which formed the spatial and social center of the house, acted as an acoustic buffer zone between the studio spaces in the west wing and the children's play area in the eastern part of the building, while allowing views via the terrace, so that professional practice, artistic activity, and childcare were compatible.
Photo: Alfred Krügelstein, *Bauwelt*, 1930.

Photo: Alfred Krügelstein, *Bauwelt*, 1930.

Renovations on the house in the 1950s included drastic changes to its architecture, leading to the rejection of the application for historical preservation in 1990. In 2020, the Initiative Haus Marlene Poelzig launched a campaign to preserve the building, which had been left to decay, and to recognize Marlene Moeschke-Poelzig's work as an architect. In early November 2021, most of the Poelzig House was demolished. The events were accompanied by protests, as pictured here, on November 2, 2021, the first day of demolition. Photo: Initiative Marlene Poelzig.

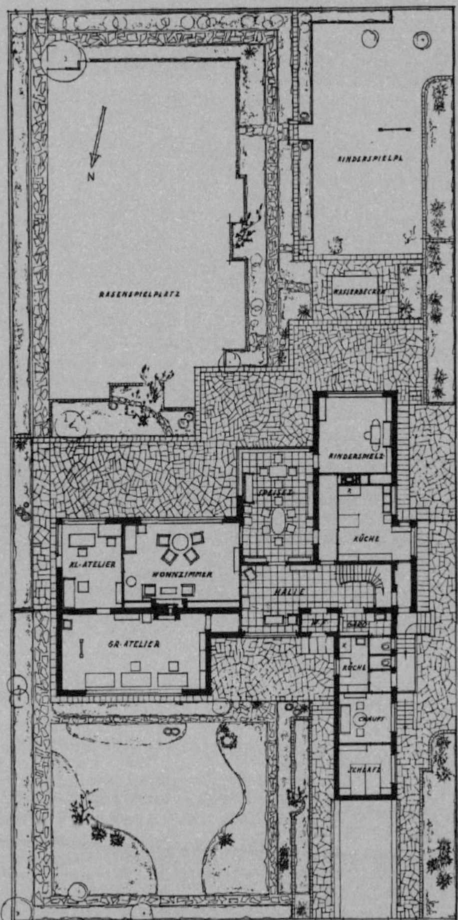

Floor plan with the garden designed by landscape architect Herta Hammerbacher, scan from: *Wasmuths Monatshefte für Baukunst und Städtebau* 14, 1930.

View onto the terrace from a bedroom on the upper floor.
Photo: Alfred Krügelstein, *Bauwelt*, 1930.

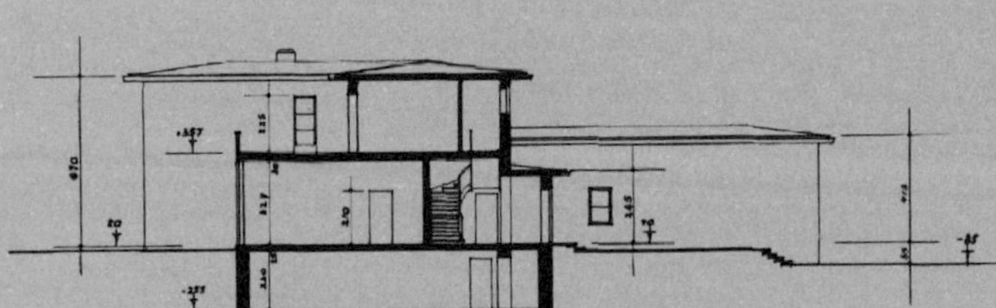

SECTION.
Scan from: *Wasmuths Monatshefte für Baukunst und Städtebau* 14, 1930.

Terrace on the upper floor.
Scan from: *Wasmuths Monatshefte für Baukunst und Städtebau* 14, 1930.

WHY NOW?

Looking back at these first attempts at writing architectural history with a focus on women, I do not approach this body of writing as a dry academic subject but rather as a part of my own biography. In 1977, while studying in New York, I visited the *Women in American Architecture* exhibition, and, upon coming to West Berlin in the late 1980s, I sought out *Architektinnenhistorie: Zur Geschichte der Architektinnen und Designerinnen im 20. Jahrhundert.* Over the years, many colleagues who are exploring the phenomena of women architects have shared anecdotes, insights, and stories with me. At the same time, I feel the time has come to acknowledge that feminist architectural history has a past.

Referencing Michel Foucault's concept of *parrhesia*, the architectural theorist Jane Rendell argued in her 2016 essay "Giving an Account of Oneself Architecturally" for the unity of *bios* (life) and *logos* (rational knowledge), like having a steadfast and well-grounded moral compass, to orient the activities we undertake in an academic context.[33] Certainly, every researcher should consider how this imperative should play out in their life and professional endeavors. For myself, it means that the assumptions which informed the recent histories of women and architecture have to be examined, without sentiment or nostalgia, to pave the way for a truly transformative and inclusive "alternative vision of the future" to unfold. For writing biographies of women architects, this means not portraying them as impossibly ideal heroines, but rather as real human beings struggling in the world they inhabit to make architecture.

01 Gerda Lerner, ***The Creation of a Feminist Consciousness*** **(Oxford: Oxford University Press, 1993), 274.**
02 **See Hermann Kaufmann, Susanne Ihsen, and Paula-Irene Villa Braslavsky,** ***Frauen in der Architektur*****, Technische Universität München, Fakultät für Architektur, Munich, 2018, 13, accessed September 1, 2022, mediatum.ub.tum.de/doc/1519783/1519783.pdf.**
03 **One notable exception: Doris Cole,** ***From Tipi to Skyscraper: A History of Women in Architecture*** **(New York, NY: ipress/George Braziller, 1973). Cole discusses women of the North American First Nations (referred to as "Indians") and the Black women activists who created educational institutions in the post-Civil War era.**
04 **Audre Lorde, "Age, Race, Class and Sex," in** ***Audre Lorde: Your Silence Will Not Protect You*** **(London: Silver Press, 2017), 96.**
05 **Vron Ware,** ***Beyond the Pale: White Women, Racism and History*** **(1992) (London: Verso, 2015), XIX; 202; and 167–224.**
06 **Audre Lorde, "The Transformation of Silence," in** ***Audre Lorde: Your Silence Will Not Protect You*** **(see note 4), 3.**
07 **Union Internationale des Femmes Architectes (UIFA) Sektion Bundesrepublik, eds.,** ***Architektinnenhistorie: Zur Geschichte der Architektinnen und Designerinnen im 20. Jahrhundert. Eine erste Zusammenstellung*****, catalogue for the eponymous exhibition during the 7th International Congress of Women Architects and Town Planners, October 11 to 30, 1984 (Berlin: UIFA, 1984).**
08 **See Verena Dietrich,** ***Architektinnen: Ideen, Projekte, Bauten*** **(Stuttgart: Kohlhammer, 1986); Despina Stratigakos,** ***Skirts and Scaffolding: Women Architects, Gender and Design in Wilhelmine Germany*****, PhD Dissertation (Bryn Mawr College, Philadelphia, 1999); Kerstin Dörhofer,** ***Pionierinnen der Architektur*** **(Tübingen: Wasmuth 2004); Ute Maasberg, Regina Prinz,** ***Die Neuen kommen: Weibliche Avantgarde in der Architektur der zwanziger Jahre*** **(Hamburg: Junius, 2005); Mary Pepchinski et al., eds.,** ***Frau Architekt*** **(Tübingen: Wasmuth, 2017).**
09 **Technische Universität Berlin,** ***Persönlichkeiten: Elisabeth von Knobelsdorff*****, accessed September 1, 2022, www.tu.berlin/ueber-die-tu-berlin/geschichte/persoenlichkeiten/elisabeth-von-knobelsdorff.**
10 **Ibid.**
11 **Mary Pepchinski, "Wollen und Wirklichkeit," in** ***Frau Architekt*** **(Tübingen: Wasmuth, 2017), 25–36, footnotes 11, 17, and images 3, 6.**
12 **See Marion Kaplan, "Sisterhood under Siege: Feminism and Anti-Semitism in Germany 1904–1938," in** ***When Biology became Destiny*****, eds. Renate Bridenthal, Atina Grossmann, and Marion Kaplan (New York, NY: Monthly Review Press, 1984), 186–87.**
13 **Stephen Norwood,** ***The Third Reich in the Ivory Tower*** **(Cambridge: Cambridge University Press, 2009), 27–56; photos on 46, 47.**
14 **Margarete Schütte-Lihotzky,** ***Erinnerungen aus dem Widerstand*** **(Vienna: ProMedia, 1994).**
15 **Margarete Schütte-Lihotzky,** ***Warum ich Architektin wurde*** **(Salzburg: Residenz Verlag, 2004), 16–17.**
16 **Ibid., 21, 28.**
17 **Ibid., 39–40.**
18 **Ibid., 149–50.**
19 **See Jacqueline Rose,** ***On Violence and On Violence against Women*** **(London: Faber, 2021), 39, 46–47.**
20 **Ibid., 68–69, on Jacqueline Rose's references to Sara Ahmed regarding sexual harassment. See also Sara Ahmed,** ***feministkilljoys*****, accessed September 1, 2022, feministkilljoys.com/2016/06/02/speaking-out/.**
21 **See Pierre Bourdieu,** ***Masculine Domination*** **(1998), trans. Richard Nice (Stanford, CA: Stanford University Press, 2001), 34.**
22 **"Haus Marlene Poelzig," accessed September 1, 2022, http://hausmarlenepoelzig.de/wp-content/uploads/2021/11/20211105_HMP_Presseeinladung_Laternenumzug_11.11.pdf.**
23 **See photo, accessed September 1, 2022, de.m.wikipedia.org/wiki/Datei:Gedenktafel_Tannenbergallee_28_(Weste)_Hans_Poelzig.jpg.**
24 **Irene Nierhaus, "Nicht zuschütten: A personal remembrance of Margarete Schütte-Lihotzky," in** ***Women Architects and Politics: Intersections between Gender, Power Structures and Architecture in the Long 20th Century*****, ed. Mary Pepchinski and Christina Budde (Bielefeld: transcript, 2022), 21–26.**
25 **Margarete Schütte-Lihotzky–Walter Gropius correspondence, Bauhaus Archiv Berlin and the Houghton Library, Harvard University.**
26 **Margarete Schütte-Lihotzky–Ernst May correspondence, DAM/Deutsches Architekturmuseum Archiv.**
27 **See Antoine Prost,** ***A History of Private Life*****, intro, vol. V, eds. Antoine Prost and Gerhard Vincent (1987), trans. Arthur Goldhammer (Cambridge: The Belknap Press, 1991), 3–8.**
28 **Ingeborg Weber-Kellermann, "The German Family between Private Life and Politics," in** ***A History of Private Life*****, eds. Antoine Prost and Gerhard Vincent (1987), trans. M. J. Maynes and M. Mouton (Cambridge: The Belknap Press, 1991), 503–38.**
29 **Mary Pepchinski, "Emancipated Women, Liberated Living: Three Pioneering Women Architects in Germany and Their Domesticity," in** ***Modern Woman Architect: Projection and Reality in Central Europe since 1900*****, ed. Helena Huber-Doudová (Prague: UMPRUM, 2021), 66–73.**
30 **Franz Schulze,** ***Mies van der Rohe: A Critical Biography*** **(Chicago, IL: University of Chicago Press, 2014); Alice. T. Friedman,** ***Women and the Making of the Modern House*** **(New York, NY: Harry N. Abrams, 1998), 126–59.**
31 **Anne Griswold Tyng, ed.,** ***Louis Kahn to Anne Tyng: The Rome Letters 1953–1954*** **(New York, NY: Rizzoli, 1997); Nathanial Kahn, director,** ***My Architect: A Son's Journey*****, 116 minutes (2003).**
32 **Another example: Richard Meier's recent fall from grace due to the sexual harassment of his female employees. See Robin Pogrebin, "Five Women Accuse the Architect Richard Meier of Sexual Harassment,"** ***New York Times*****, March 13, 2018, accessed September 1, 2022, www.nytimes.com/2018/03/13/arts/design/richard-meier-sexual-harassment-allegations.html.**
33 **Jane Rendell, "Giving an Account of Oneself: Architecturally,"** ***Journal of Visual Culture*****, October 4, 2016, accessed September 1, 2022, https://doi.org/10.1177/1470412916665143.**

A meeting at Grüntuch Ernst architects in Clausewitzstrasse in Berlin, ca. 1996. The practice was founded in 1991 by Almut Grüntuch-Ernst and Armand Grüntuch. Since 2008, the practice and the home of the couple and their five children has been located in a self-designed multifamily home in Berlin-Mitte. Short distances, a loose separation of private life and work, and a reliable private environment facilitate the organization of work life and family life.
Photo: Edgar Rodtmann (Neumann und Rodtmann).

Practice

Coupling Portraits
Inés Toscano

Ray Eames & Charles Eames – Why Not?
Collage by Ovid Mahfuz Houry, 2021.
© Inés Toscano, DIA, Anhalt University of Applied Sciences.

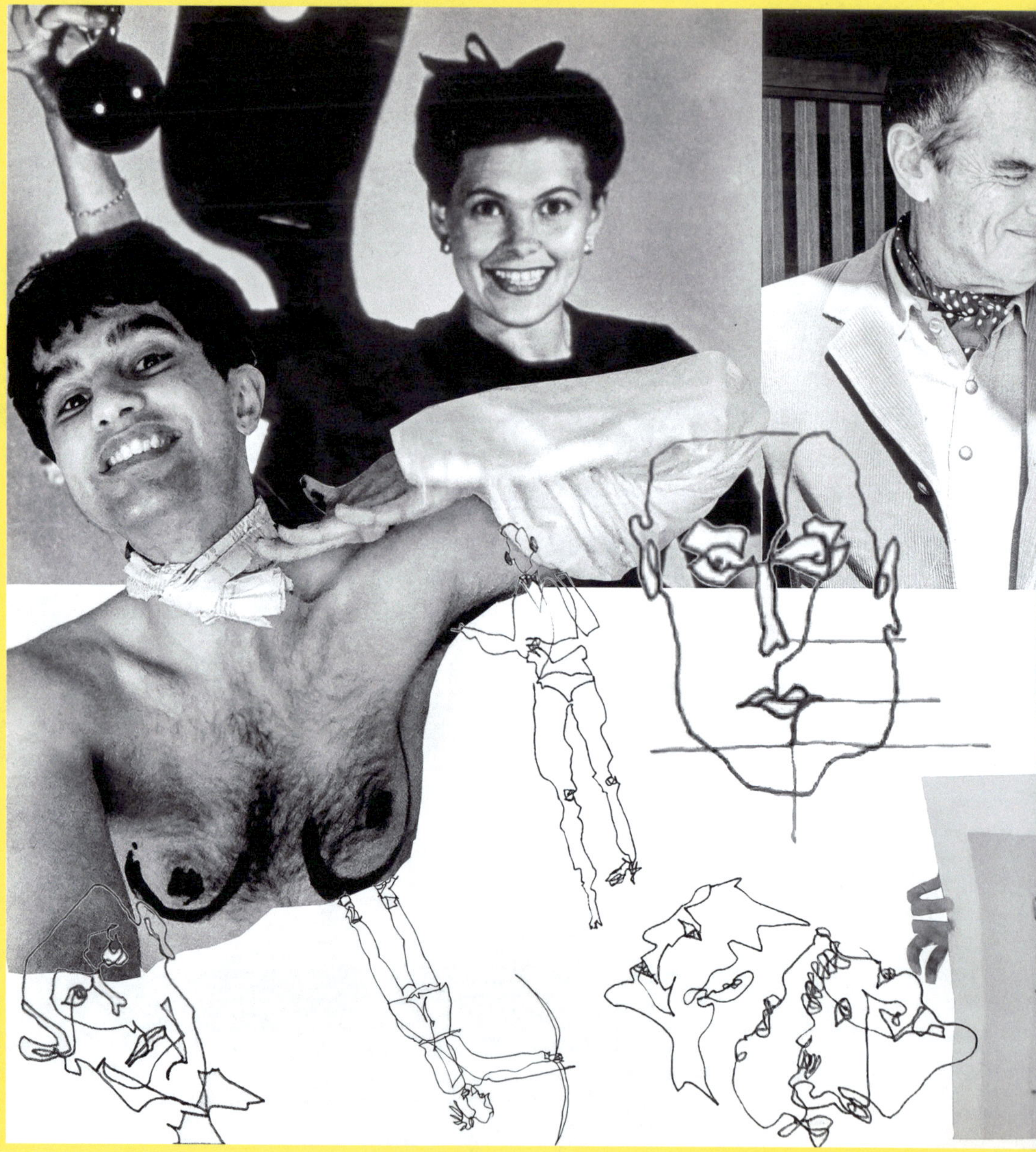

www.couplingstactic.com/coupling-portrait

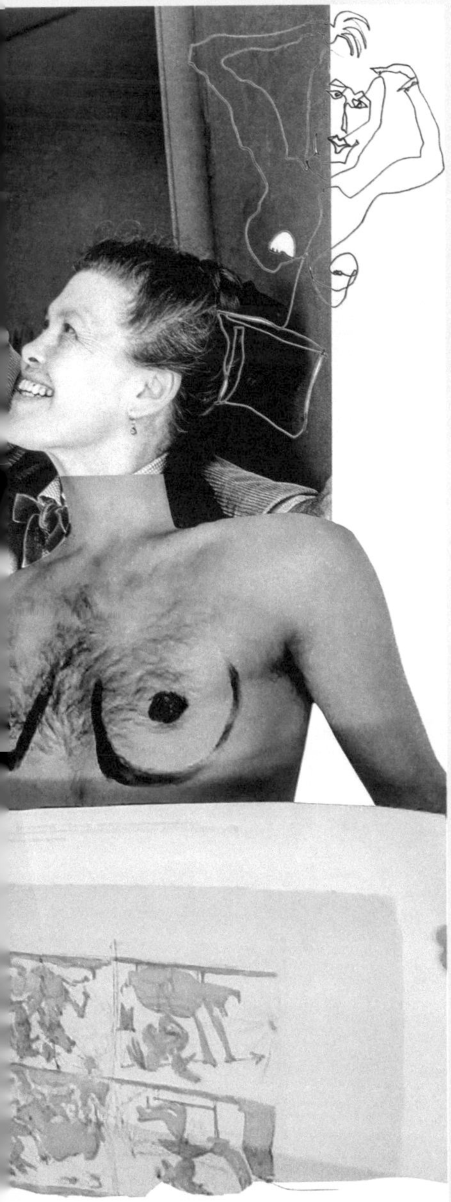

Margaret MacDonald & Charles Rennie Mackintosh: Togetherness and Equality.
Collage by Jayati Doda and Mary Dwomoh, 2021.
© Inés Toscano, DIA, Anhalt University of Applied Sciences.

It is no coincidence that our subconscious associates the surnames *Poelzig* or *Aalto* mainly with Hans and Alvar. The architectural canon, curriculum, and discourse largely ignore the fact that *Marlene* and *Aino* worked alongside them. So does the accompanying iconography, which romanticizes the creative genius, who takes a contemplative pose alongside his creation. Inés Toscano's critical reappraisal of these representations takes up the complex, gender-specific dynamics that emerge among couples who work and live together. The architectural theorist Beatriz Colomina coined the term “couplings” in 1999 to describe this working strategy.

In the intersectional feminist seminars that she teaches at Anhalt University of Applied Sciences and Bauhaus University Weimar—with titles such as *Coupling Portraits* and *Gender Masquerade*—Toscano takes the struggle for equality into architectural teaching. She uses roleplay as an interactive method to address and stimulate thinking about discrimination based on gender, racial attributions, class, and disability. The topics she explores include: How can feminist activism empower and inspire future architects to think critically about architectural discourse? How can it help them define their professional and social roles so they can learn and work together as *equals*? For that is the ultimate goal. **FG**

ARCH+ features

106

KATE MACINTOSH

in conversation with Kristina Herresthal and Ariane Wiegner

“INSTEAD OF *HE* ... WE PUT IN *THEY* OR *THEM*.”

KATE MACINTOSH in conversation with Kristina Herresthal and Ariane Wiegner

Kate Macintosh was only 28 years old when her design for Dawson’s Heights social housing estate won the internal competition held by the London Borough of Southwark planning department. Beginning in the mid-1960s, she led the planning and implementation process for the iconic development of nearly 300 residential units in the southern part of the city. The oeuvre of the Scottish architect, born in 1937, includes not only social housing but also numerous public facilities, such as the fire stations and their distinctive drill towers in Rushmoor, Maresfield, and Hastings; projects for assisted living such as the housing estate on Leigham Court Road in London; several schools, such as Solent Infants School in Portsmouth, the primary school in Battle Langton, and a playground and building for the Weston Adventure Playground in Southhampton. Macintosh has always been politically active and was chair of the RIBA Architects for Peace Group and the RIBA Women Architecture Group. In 2021, she was awarded the prestigious Jane Drew Prize for her life’s work. Kristina Herresthal and Ariane Wiegner spoke with Kate Macintosh.

Kristina Herresthal: In 2021, you received the Jane Drew prize, which honors women in architecture for their design excellence and contribution to the built environment. What does this prize mean to you?

Kate Macintosh: It is wonderful to have this recognition so late in my career. While I was a student, there were so few women architects around, only about 4 percent of the profession. Jane Drew was one of the few names in the UK that I knew of. In the 1930s, she became a member of the Modern Architectural Research Group (MARS), a group of British architects who advanced the British modernist movement after the CIAM congresses. As one of the pioneers of tropical modernism, Drew realized several well-known buildings around the world in the 1950s, including in the newly independent states of India and Iran. She proposed to the Indian government that Le Corbusier should be the mastermind behind the construction of Chandigarh. In 1964 she was the first woman to be elected as a RIBA councilor. That was where we met. Jane and I always had similar interests in important architectural themes. We both spent much of our expertise and work throughout life on the development of low-cost social housing and public projects.

KH: You’ve just indicated how overwhelmingly male-dominated the architecture profession was back then. What drew you to architecture in the first place?

KM: Both my parents were socialists. And I was the eldest of a family of four children: two girls and two boys. My father always worked in the public sector as a matter of principle, despite the fact that his father had a private architectural practice, which was moderately successful. My father eventually became the head of the Direct Labour Organization (DLO), which provided social housing across the length and breadth of Scotland. After I finished school, I wanted to do something that would combine art and science, and I wanted to do something that was socially useful. My father suggested that architecture might be a suitable profession; he saw no reason why women shouldn’t become architects, which was unusual for a man of his generation. That greatly supported my decision to apply to the Edinburgh School of Art to study architecture.

Ariane Wiegner: What were the requirements for pursuing a degree in architecture at that time?

KM: The exam qualifications they were calling for were quite modest, so you could say it was a course which was endeavoring to open the field to people from not-privileged backgrounds. One of the entrance tests was to do a drawing and a rendering of an architectural scheme, and they seemed to place great emphasis on the skills of craftsmanship. In my year, there were only two women of about 30, and by the time I got into my second year, I was the only woman. Most of the chaps on the course had come through male-only schools, and some had also done military service. They had never had to relate to a woman on an equal basis, and they were absolutely puzzled about how they should behave. I remember a construction tutor who, after a lecture, bent my ear and said, “You know, it’s a waste of time teaching women because they are only going to marry and fail to get their final qualification, and even if they qualify, they will probably not practice.” That sort of assumption was hanging around.

AW: After graduating from art school in Edinburgh, you decided to go to Poland for a year to study at Warsaw Polytechnic on a British Council scholarship. Why did you choose Poland of all countries?

KM: On graduating, I applied for a number of post-graduate courses and was offered two. One from the Warsaw Polytechnic and the other from Columbia University in New York. Many of my contemporaries would find Warsaw Polytechnic a strange choice. But as a person of the left, I was very influenced by the chilling effect of the McCarthy era, with its anti-communist propaganda and persecutions of intellectuals and the Un-American Activities trials, which lasted from 1947 to 1959.

On the other hand, a cultural thaw had occurred in Poland following Joseph Stalin's death. In 1956, protests by workers in Poznań resulted in the rise in power of the reformers' faction, led by Władysław Gomułka. After brief but tense negotiations, the Soviets permitted Gomułka to stay in control and made several other concessions, resulting in greater autonomy for the Polish government. For Poland, that meant a temporary liberalization, which was also expressed in the country's lively art scene and met with great interest beyond the country's borders. I remember seeing the two films: *Ashes and Diamonds* and *Canal* by director Andrzej Wajda at the Edinburgh Film Festival at that time. The films of the Łódź Film School were every bit as gripping as Sergei Eisenstein's *Battleship Potemkin* or Ingmar Bergman's *Wild Strawberries*.

AW: So you used your year abroad to explore the creative scene in Warsaw, but it was probably more focused on the liberal arts than architecture?

KM: Yes, one could say so. Regarding the architectural course—I wasn't so much attached to the Warsaw Polytechnic, but a place called the Experimental Office for the Development of Precast Structures (*Biuro Studiów i Projektów Typowych Budownictwa Przemysłowego*). It was full of brilliant engineers, such as Jan Szymczyk and Wacław Zalewski, who later became a professor of structural design at MIT. So, it was mainly engineers that I was associated with, who had all these ideas, but they couldn't get them executed because the construction industry in Poland was in a much more primitive state than in the West.

Work from architecture school, sectional view, 1960.
© Kate Macintosh.

AW: After your stay in Poland, you decided not to return to the UK but instead went to Finland, Sweden, and Denmark, where you took your first jobs as an architect. How did this decision come about?

KM: While in Warsaw, I joined a course on improving my Polish, and in the same class, there was a Finnish journalist who generously said that if any of us wanted to turn up in Helsinki, she could offer them a bed. So I carefully noted her contact details, and in July of 1962, I caught a ferry from Gdansk to Helsinki. I spent about three weeks touring around not just Helsinki but further afield, mostly looking at Alvar Aalto's buildings but also Heikki Sirén's. I was perfectly sure that this was where the most interesting architecture was going on at that time. In October of that year, I set out for Stockholm, where I worked initially on a competition in Leonie Geisendorf's office and later for Lennart Bergström. I found my jobs going to each office personally with my heavy roll of drawings. After that, I went on to Copenhagen, where I managed to get a job for three months with Claus Bremer. His wife, Gunhild Westergaard, was also an architect-planner and had her own office, which was not uncommon in Scandinavia. Still, it was morally boosting to see that a woman could succeed this way, independently of her spouse. I went from Copenhagen to Helsinki to seek work there, which I found with the practice of Toivo Korhonen. My spell in that office was entirely taken up with competition entries. Almost every practice in Finland established itself through a competition win. As there are so many the wastage is not so great and it is extremely stimulating.

AW: Did the greater independence of women in Scandinavian countries play a role in your decision to gather your first professional experiences there?

KM: Yes, in Finland, for instance, the women there had won the right to vote in 1906, and the first Finnish women had qualified and entered the institute in Helsinki well ahead of anything of that sort in the UK. So that was an incentive.

I was also fascinated by Scandinavian architecture and building culture, which in many respects was more developed and also more committed to social justice. In Britain, there is a strict stratification in terms of the budget allocated to different kinds of work: there is prestigious work, and then there is non-prestigious work. Whereas in Scandinavia, everything, even the humblest thing, is a design opportunity. You try to make it as good and delightful as possible within your budget.

So the appreciation of the profession is much higher there. For instance, in Helsinki, there is a museum of architecture in a very central location. Whenever an architectural competition is held, the shortlisted schemes are all on public view. The general public takes an interest in what's going on, and of course, that's the case not just in architecture but in all design.

AW: That's something we also struggle with a lot here: the acknowledgment of the work of architects and often the lack of education in those fields. Did the architectural scene in London share your view of architectural production in Scandinavia?

KM: During my student days, there was a struggle for allegiance between the more Miesian approach, where structural expression was what you took the aesthetics from, and the more humanistic approach, which was the one that was dominant in Scandinavia. I would say that Aalto was probably the leader in this, but Arne Jacobsen was, of course, also very influential. I count myself as belonging to the more alternative tradition, as advocated by Colin St. John Wilson, who did the British Library and wrote a book in 1995 called *The Other Tradition of Modern Architecture*. His approach focuses on taking your key from the environment, including the architectural context, the landscape context, and even the historical context, which immediately influences your thinking.

The ziggurat-like structures of Dawson's Heights on the horizon of London's Forest Hill neighborhood.

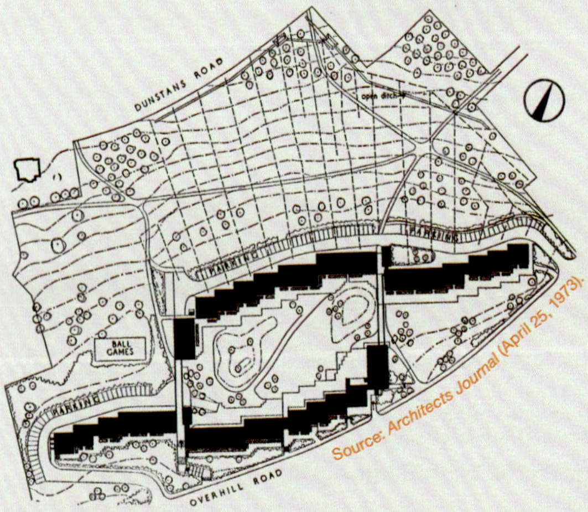

SITE PLAN.

A dramatic, building-deep offset breaks up the long facade and creates connecting spaces in between. A sense of dynamic is created by the various nested maisonette apartments, each with its own balcony.

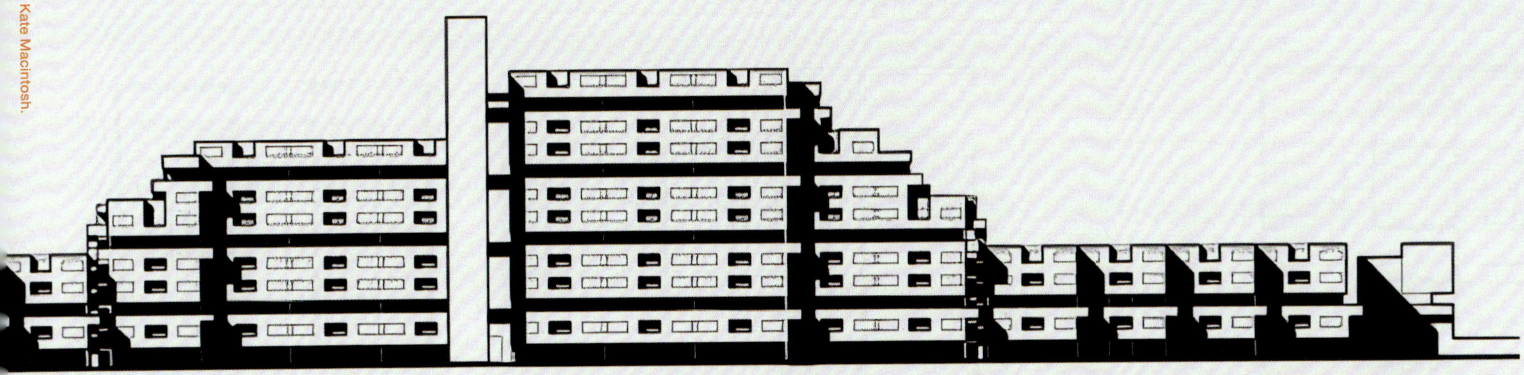

VIEW FROM THE NORTH.

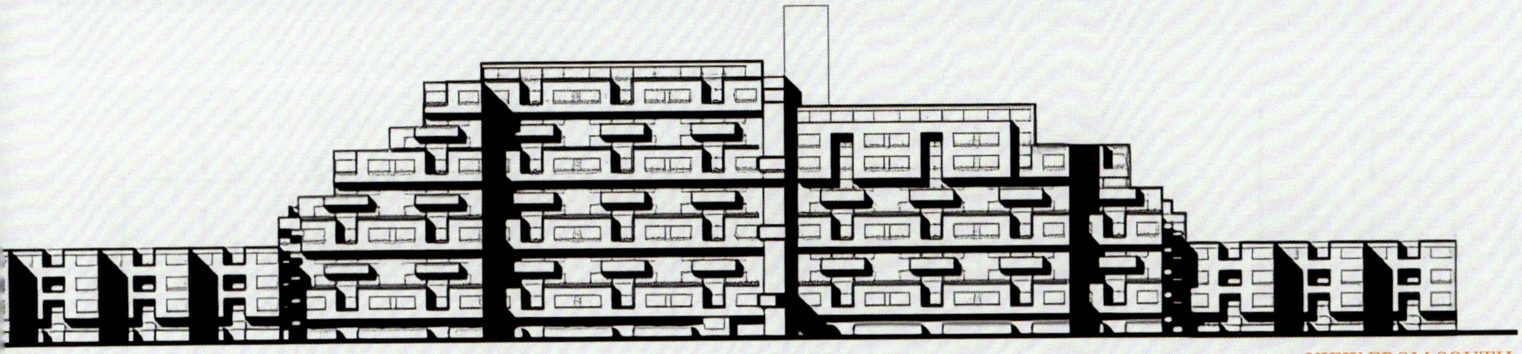

VIEW FROM SOUTH.

Dawson's Heights, 1964–1972
For the London Borough of Southwark

In the front, one of the two now-defunct pedestrian bridges along the courtyard that connected Dawson's Heights buildings.

FLOOR PLANS,
5-room maisonette.

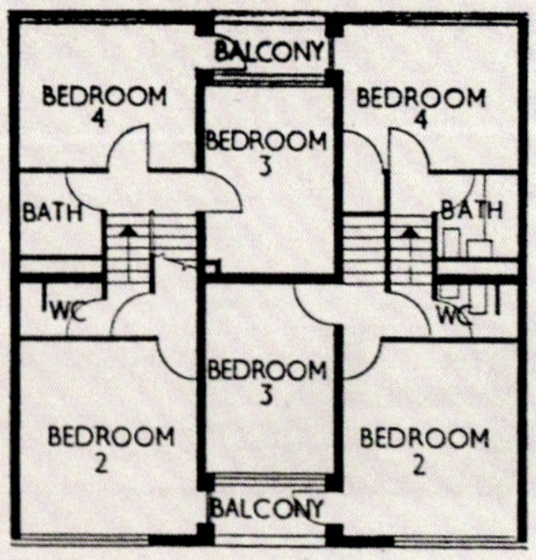

UPPER FLOOR.

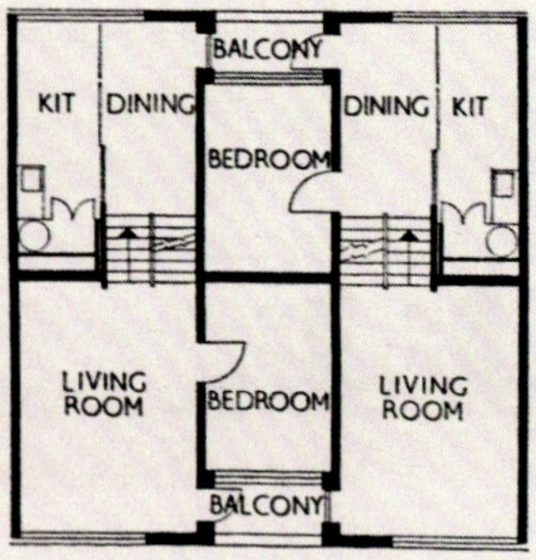

LOWER FLOOR.

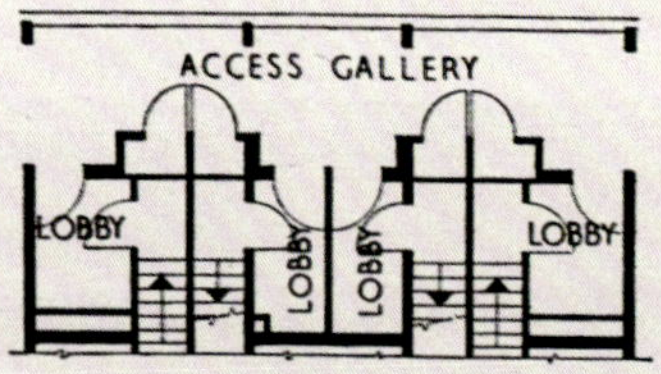

ACCESS FLOOR.

FLOOR PLANS of the 3-room (right) and 4-room maisonette (left).

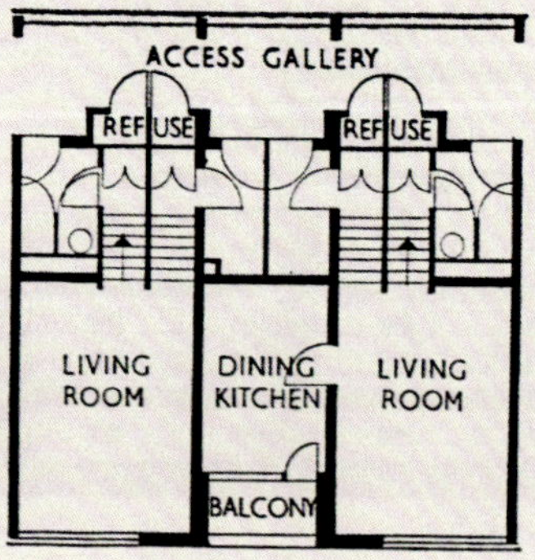

UPPER ACCESS FLOOR.

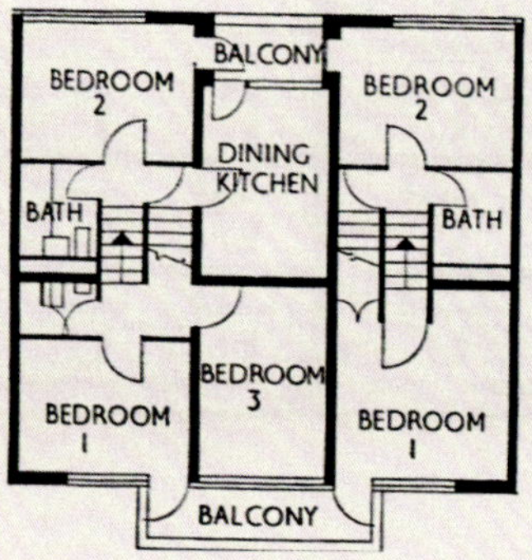

LOWER FLOOR.

FLOOR PLANS,
2-room maisonette.

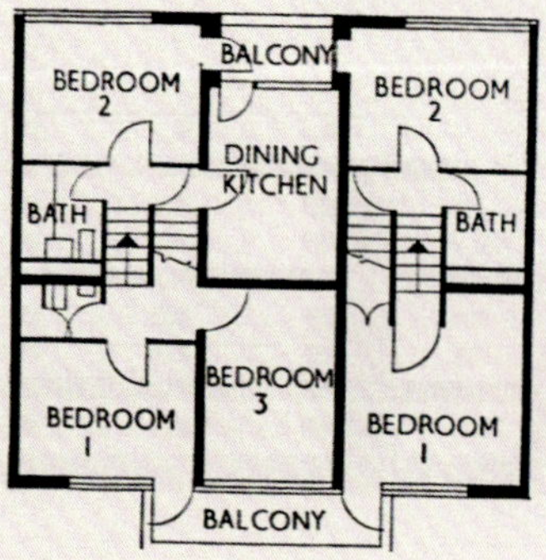

UPPER FLOOR.

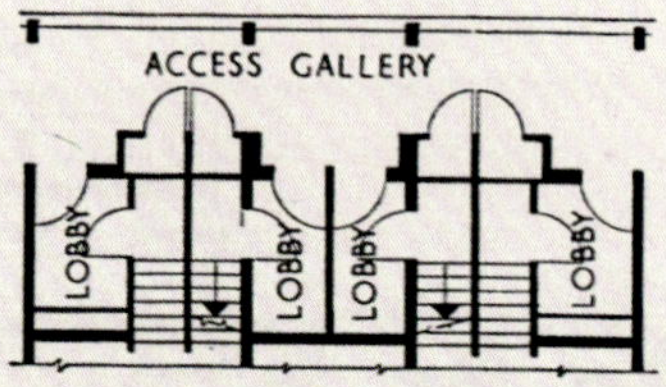

ACCESS FLOOR.

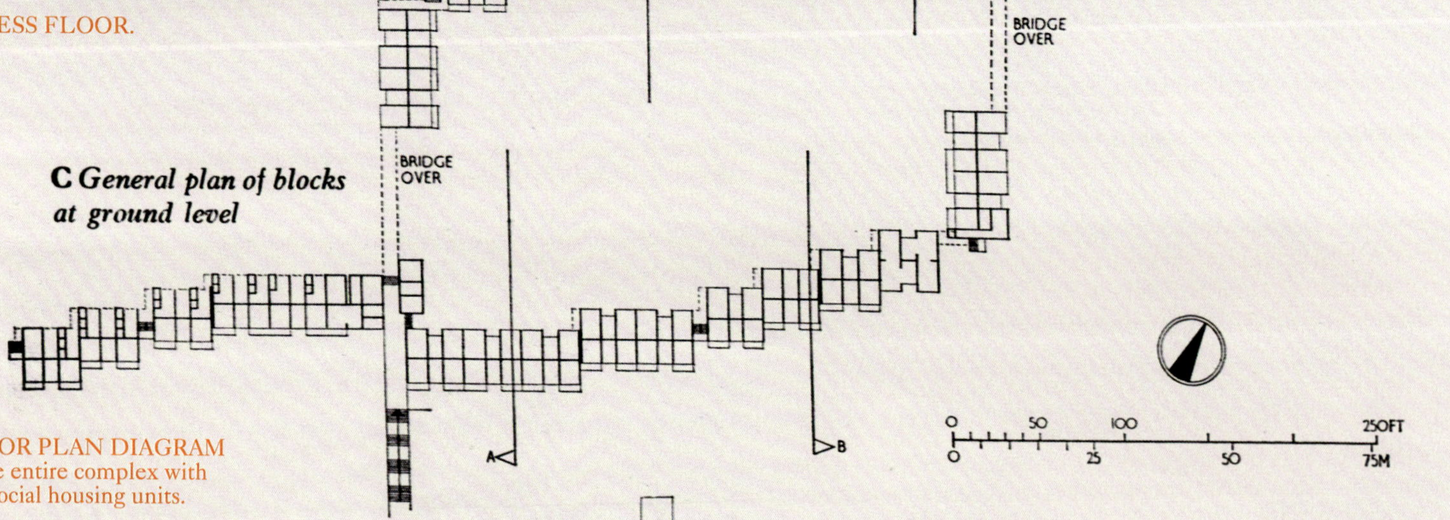

FLOOR PLAN DIAGRAM
of the entire complex with 298 social housing units.

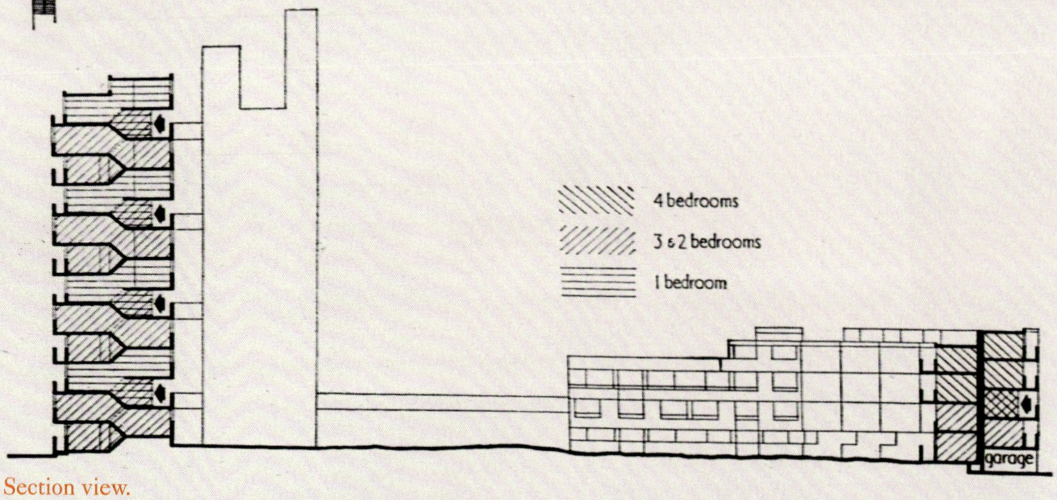

Section view.

The apartments are accessed along exterior walkways on every third floor.

Source: *Architects Journal* (April 25, 1973).

KH: How did your career develop after you returned to the UK and started working in London?

KM: First, I worked for a year in Denys Lasdun's office on early designs for the National Theatre in London. But I was the most junior member of the design team and did not play a significant role because I had little or no practical experience. So, in 1965 I decided to start working for the Borough of Southwark's building department, where I was soon placed in charge of developing the big social housing project, Dawson's Heights.

KH: How did you approach this big task?

KM: There were two housing designs that were just being completed at the time, which became important models for me in the development of the project. The first one was Park Hill in Sheffield, one of the earliest big deck access schemes, produced by the local authority. The other one was Lillington Gardens by Darbourne and Dark, located on Vauxhall Bridge Road and built in dark brick. What I resolved as a desirable characteristic from both these schemes was the emphasis on the expression of the individual dwelling within the totality. A lot of the large local authority housing from that time has a rather institutional look; it has been subdued to the production process and is very repetitive. I wanted to avoid that uniform look for Dawson's Heights, a large complex with nearly 300 residential units.

KH: A large amount of council housing was being produced at the time, with a peak of above 400,000 homes per year in the late 1960s. What were the design specifications? Was there a catalogue of standards you had to follow, and how were you able to incorporate the idea you mentioned of highlighting the individual apartment in the overall complex?

KM: In 1961, the Parker Morris report, *Homes for Today and Tomorrow*, outlined the overall space standards for dwellings of different sizes. Its adoption meant a big liberation for architects working in the public sector. The space standards were supposed to be minimum standards intended to improve dwelling conditions, even as people's demands grew. It was a very optimistic time, and we thought everything would improve for everybody. All the London Boroughs voluntarily adopted these space standards in 1964 before they became mandatory for public housing in 1969. This legislation was swept aside by Margaret Thatcher's government following complaints by speculative house builders that they could not meet those standards and achieve the profits they expected. This resulted in housing in the UK built post 1979 having the lowest space standards in Europe.

KH: To what extent did the Parker Morris report play a role in shaping Dawson's Heights?

KM: The Parker Morris report defined standards for natural lighting, among other things. In Dawson's Heights, the two interlocking ziggurats are staggered to minimize the blocking of sun and view; each dwelling gets at least one distant view, and roughly two-thirds get a fine view to the north and south. They are all dual-aspect split-level dwellings, which means they can all get cross-ventilation on hot summer days. The reduction in height at the extremities reflects the scale of surrounding housing. The Parker-Morris report also required a certain allocation of communal outdoor space. But in Dawson's Heights, we have an excess of that.

I was determined that my dwellings were going to have balconies. So I designed the scheme so that every balcony acted as a means of escape in case of fire. So you would have two doors onto the balcony: one was the door that belonged to the dwelling that looked onto the balcony, but at the other end of the balcony, there was a door with a special lock with a break glass to enter and a key inside, so you could escape to the adjoining dwelling if yours was full of smoke. In that way, the balconies couldn't be cut out.

KH: Can you tell us a little bit about working on Dawson's Heights? How many people worked with you on the project? As the project architect, how did you manage the team? How long did it take to complete Dawson's Heights?

KM: The design stage went fairly rapidly—up to the planning stage. During that time, I worked as the sole architect in an interdisciplinary context with other building professionals. After that stage, I built up a small team, including one experienced architect and two or three students, but the team was never sufficiently large. I was desperately inexperienced, but I ran the site meetings on my own. I learned a lot on the job. I kept sending memos, though, saying I needed more staff, but no one ever took any notice.

The consequence was that the contractor started writing letters claiming delays in information, and I got the blame for this and was taken off the job. Later I met one of the project's structural engineers, who was very critical of how I had been treated. He said they had had more engineering staff working on that project, purely on the structural side, than I had on the architectural side. But anyway—it's still there, so I have to be grateful.

KH: In terms of teamwork in the office or the borough, did people see themselves as a team working together for better architecture?

KM: In the main, they were. There were some—inevitably, you get this in local governments—what you call time-servers who just wanted to do the minimum. But people were generally very motivated, and there was a good *esprit de corps*, you might say. The Lambeth architecture department, where I started working right after I left Southwark in 1969, was much better organized. Not only did we have good structural consultants but also our own quantity surveyors, our own landscape architects, our own graphic designers—we had the whole range of skills in-house. When engineer Ted Hollamby took over as director of architecture, planning, and development in Lambeth in 1969, he brought over the organizational structure from the London

View into the living room of a multistory 4-room apartment.

Dawson's designer?
From Kate Macintosh, RIBA
Sir:
I was very interested to read Richard Padovan's fair and well-researched appraisal of the scheme I designed while at Southwark—Dawson's Heights. I was also interested to see Felix Trenton's 'seminal' sketch, which I had not seen before.
Kate Macintosh
London SE5

After the design of Dawson's Heights was attributed to the head of the building department, this correction by Macintosh appeared in the September issue of *Architects' Journal.*

Source: *Architects' Journal* 157 (September 1973), 1093.

County Council (LCC), where he had previously worked. Each group operated as a semi-autonomous atelier, so you knew your colleagues and who might be able to help you with a design.

KH: What role did the clients and residents of the housing projects play in your designs?

KM: In Lambeth, we worked with a housing manager who was very forward-thinking, open-minded, and had excellent relations with the architects. The sheltered housing scheme in Lambeth was on a suburban site where there wasn't much going on in the locality. So we put in a shop on the road frontage that could be both a meeting place for the residents and a convenience store serving the general public. He agreed to that immediately. That was rather unusual for the time, as paternalistic guidelines by managers and client-departments usually left little room for participatory models in housing.

KH: Earlier, you mentioned working in an atelier structure, which was remarkable because you could work for the public sector while becoming a renowned architect in your own right. How could you stand out as an individual while working collectively in the public sector?

KM: When I first went into the public sector in the UK, that was not the case at all. Everything that was built went out under the name of the chief architect. As an architect working on the project, you went in on the understanding that you would be anonymous. That was also the case when Dawson's Heights was first written about. *Architectural Review* did a special issue on housing, and they listed Dawson's Heights under the chief architect's name. That didn't go down greatly with me, but it was an experience shared by many women in architecture whose endeavors were subsumed into the work of their male colleagues.

But this led me to get involved in a rebellion against certain things that the RIBA (Royal Institute of British Architects) was doing, and I ended up being a lead player. We organized a referendum on a new membership structure that the RIBA wanted to bring in, which would have led to a dramatic under-representation of architects working in the public sector; at that time, about 50 percent of all British architects worked in the public sector. To our great satisfaction, our campaign was successful. The president called on the RIBA council to resign and have an extraordinary election. About a third of the council refused to resign. But with that election, a whole slate of people working in the public sector was elected, myself included. Because of this network, the next time Dawson's Heights was featured, in *Architectural Design* in January 1968, it was attributed to me.

KH: In 1970, you decided to leave London and move to East Sussex to work for the county architecture department. You once mentioned that your three-year-old son was one of the reasons for your move. You and your partner George Finch both pursued careers in architecture. How did you manage it all with a small child?

KM: With great difficulty! By the time Sean was born, the local government had introduced maternity leave (which I took) at a much lower level than it is now in the UK. Luckily for me, I had a doctor who signed me off sick until Sean was three months old.

It was 1968, and all sorts of thinking was going on about the nature of the nuclear family and how people could live more communally. George and I had set up a large household in a very large early-Georgian Victorian house in Camberwell in South London, which consisted of four adults and six children, Sean being the youngest of these. And we let out the basement, a self-contained flat, at no rent in return for child-minding services. That was as good as it gets, I think, because I could stipulate the way I wanted him cared for, I didn't have to drive him somewhere, re-drive to work, etc. But by the time Sean was three years old, the domestic situation had become a bit fraught, and life in London was getting extremely difficult. The miners had gone on strike, and there were power cuts, and the Edward Heath government announced the three-day week to save power, so they didn't have to give in to the miners. By that time I was working for the architectural practice Ahrends, Burton & Koralek and was trying to travel from South London to Camden Town. It was all getting very stressful. I was conversing with a friend of mine about how I didn't think London was any longer the place to bring up a young child. And he said, "Well, why don't you apply to Sussex (where he had gotten a senior post); we've got lots of interesting work, and we're recruiting staff." Eventually, I got the job and had to sort out the issue of moving and working out child-minding facilities, which was tricky. My mother had to step in and help with that for a while.

KH: How long did you work for the county architects?

KM: I was nearly 13 years in East Sussex. I had quite a throughput of buildings. If you average it out, I completed a building every 18 months. I did three buildings for the fire brigade, a primary school, a children's home, and an old person's home combined with sheltered housing—it was a great time. But the planning constraints became greater and greater there toward the end.

A proposal came up that the architects should not produce their own technical details but that the quantity surveyors would select a range of standard technical details and that we would have to use them. Well, I thought, this is the beginning of the end. So I decided not to work there anymore. From there, I went to Hampshire, where the Architects' Department was the most prestigious in the country at that time.

KH: After so many years in the public building sector, you founded your private practice in 1995 with your partner George Finch. What prompted you to make this decision?

KM: There were political reasons. Prime Minister Thatcher sought to reduce the power of the local governments by fragmenting their power at the local level and allowing larger cities, known as Unitary Authorities, to return to their original smaller-scale structure. Hampshire subsequently lost the port cities of Portsmouth and Southampton, where the bulk of the need for public building investment was located. The rumor circulated

View of the fire department drill tower.

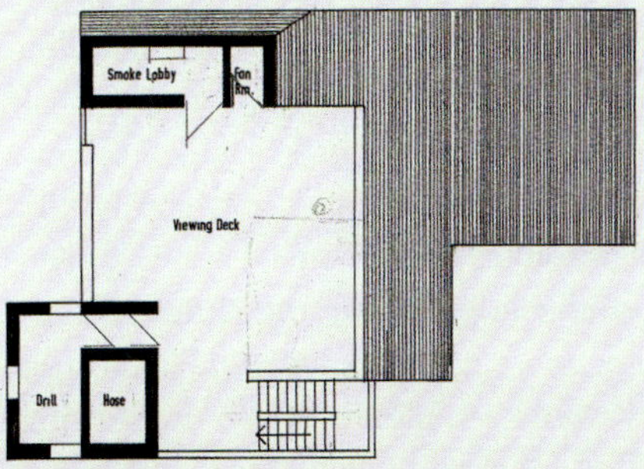

SECOND FLOOR
of the drill tower.

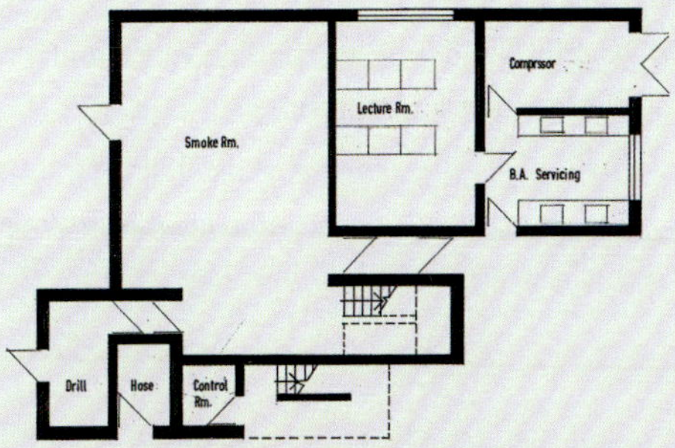

GROUND FLOOR
of the drill tower.

View from the northwest.

SITE PLAN with drill tower
and main building.

Source: *Architects' Journal* (November 1979).

Maresfield Fire Brigade Training HQ, 1979
For the East Sussex County Council

that as we would lose one-third of our workload we would all have to reapply for our own jobs. I chose to avoid any such upheaval and negotiated an early retirement package.

That was the start of my period of self-employment as an architect. I built a studio at the end of our garden, large enough for two architects to practice but also so that we had a separation between work and domestic life.

AW: Looking back on your life's work, it is interesting that much of your oeuvre is referred to today as Brutalism. How do you feel about this label?

KM: I have no reason to object, I suppose, because in a way, it has benefitted me; there has certainly been a revival of Brutalism in recent years. But I think it has to be very confusing for the general public because of the very different ideas of what Brutalism is. When the term "New Brutalism" first arose in the 1950s, it was intrinsically associated with the *beton brut* of Le Corbusier's late work. But on the other hand, it distinguished itself from these buildings and generally stood for the authenticity of materials and construction and the ethical claim of architecture with a social purpose. Today, on the other hand, any building that is heavily modeled and has a bit of concrete—what building does not?—gets labeled Brutalist. That ignores the ethical dimension of Brutalism and how so much of the so-called Brutalist oeuvre was built during an era of social commitment by architects. And that is what the Tory Party and the neoliberal economists want to erase. They want to eliminate the memory that those things were possible.

AW: It is impressive how you have continuously worked to create such socially engaged architecture. As one of the first chairs of the RIBA Women Architects Group, you were also an early advocate for greater equality and participation for women in architecture. What did this group do to improve women architects' situation at the time?

KM: Well, the first thing we did was to go through the recruiting material that the RIBA was producing and eliminate all the male pronouns. Instead of "he"—it was always a "he"—we put in "they" or "them." We used the plural to make it neutral. We also introduced illustrations showing women in hard hats and so on. We also ran returner courses for women who had had a career break, and they were always over-subscribed. In 1984, the RIBA had an architecture festival to celebrate the 150th anniversary of the RIBA's founding, for which we co-curated an exhibition—the first ever—of designs by women in the RIBA. The Women Architects Group has since morphed into the Diversity Group, which is trying to eliminate all forms of discrimination—sexual, racial, class-based, religious, or whatever.

AW: These various forms of discrimination and exploitation are often interrelated. Most of all, it requires structural changes to eliminate them.

KM: Yes. A key problem is the persistent gender pay gap. One of the things that I think got even worse for architects since my time is the long hours culture. Against the backdrop of the increasing neoliberalization of our society and the dismantling of welfare state policies over the past decades, everything has become so commercially oriented—which makes it increasingly difficult to maintain a balance between work and family life. And that is extremely regrettable. In Scandinavia, where they have affordable and very reliable childcare, the gender difference within the profession doesn't exist anymore. The cost of good childcare in the UK would completely eat up the starting salary of a woman who is just launching herself in her first job. So you often have to choose between a career in architecture and having children. That's just not fair!

AW: There is still a lot to do—which leads me to the last question: Do you see yourself as a role model for future generations?

KM: Well, I think that is for others to judge and for history to judge, but I hope that I am.

A curved staircase connects the "quiet" administrative rooms on the upper floor with the "noisy" operational rooms on the ground floor.

"They want to eliminate the [built] memory that those things were possible."
– KATE MACINTOSH

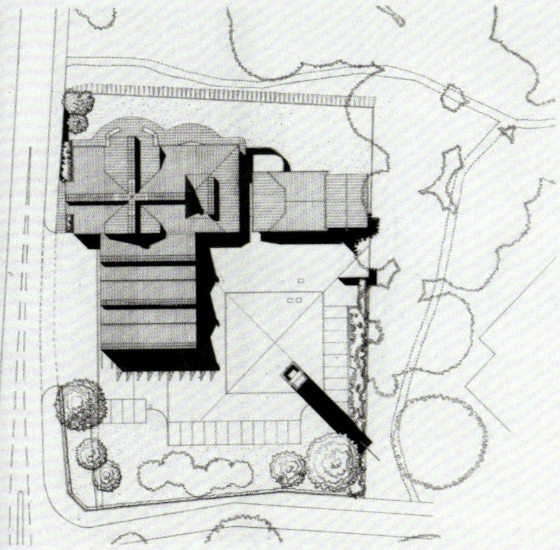

SITE PLAN.

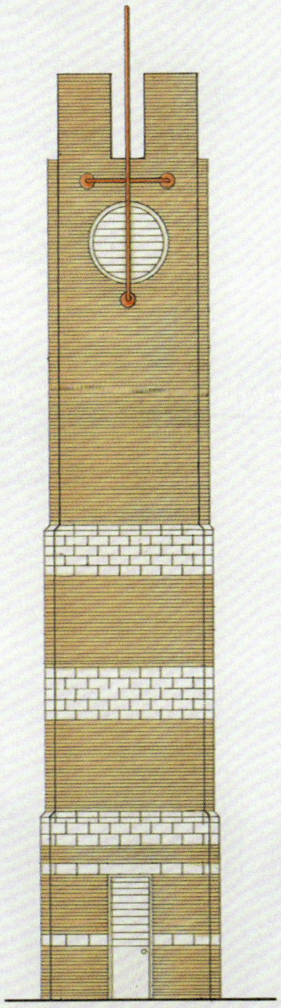

View of the drill tower from the southwest.

The sliding pole is in the middle of the cross-shaped fire station. The side facing the stairs is enclosed by a cylinder of white perforated metal sheet and dramatically staged by the glazed gable and double-column steel structure in fire-engine red that characterizes the building.

VIEW FROM THE NORTH.

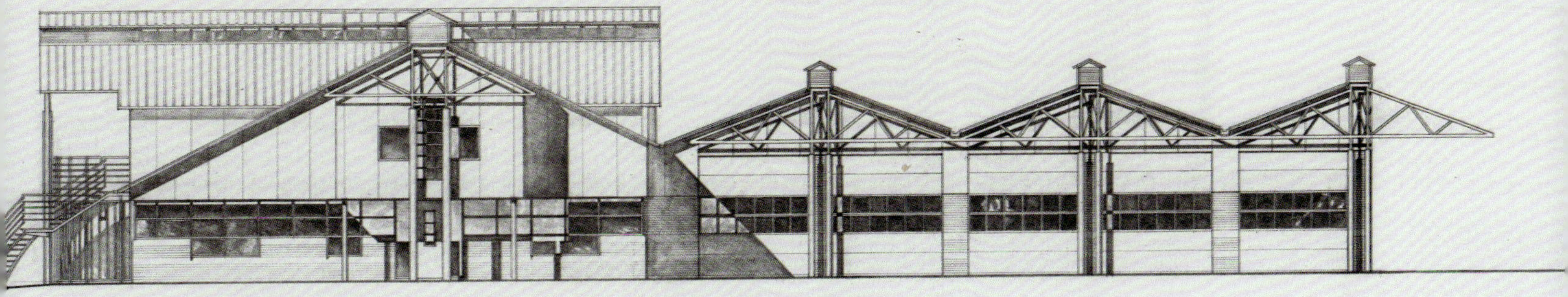

North Elevation
RUSHMOOR FIRE STATION

Rushmoor Fire Station, 1984–1990
For the Hampshire County Architects

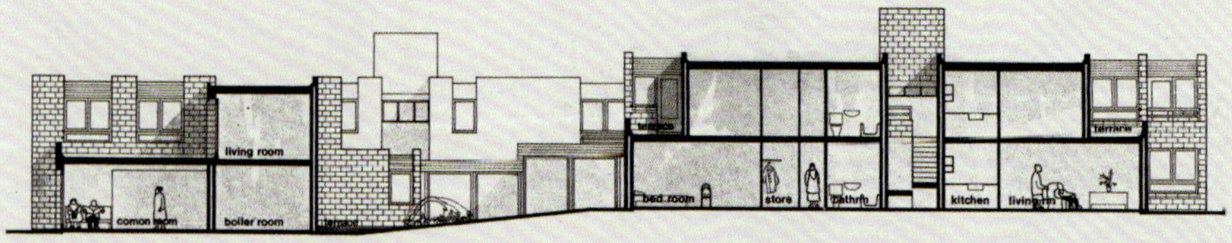

SECTION.

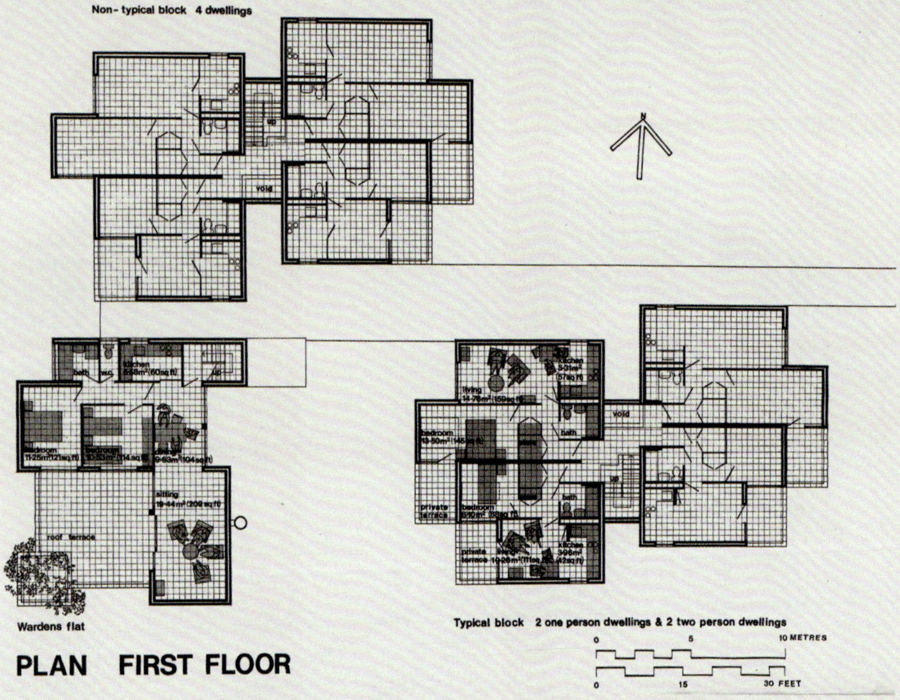

FLOOR PLAN,
FIRST UPPER FLOOR.

AXONOMETRIC SITE PLAN.
A central covered walkway connects the building volumes into a large structure and provides a space to meet outdoors.

269 Leigham Court Road, 1969–1973
Housing for senior citizens
For the London Borough of Lambeth

View of the settlement surrounded by trees, 269 Leigham Court Road, London, 1969–1973.

Classrooms are fitted with porthole windows and share a terrace along the southern slope.

Solent Infants School, Portsmouth 1994
For the Hampshire County Architects

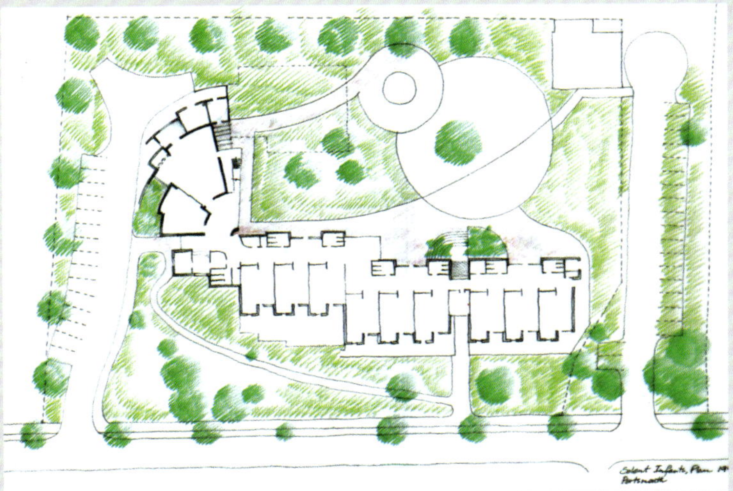

GROUND FLOOR PLAN.
Situated on a hill, the building has two entrances. The entrance to the west next to the auditorium is for teachers and parents, while children use the entrance to the south. The latter cuts into the terrain, leading under the building to a staircase in the schoolyard.

The wide hallway provides space for group activities and accommodates the school library. Natural light enters the interior via a staggered monopitch roof design, which continues above the classrooms.

GLOSSARY Kate Macintosh: References, Role Models & Current Affairs

THREE-DAY WEEK

From January 1 to March 7, 1974, the Conservative government under Prime Minister Edward Heath imposed a three-day workweek in Great Britain in response to a dispute with the coal miners' union and related strikes. Commercial establishments were allowed to use electricity only three consecutive days a week; hospitals, grocery stores, and newspaper printers were excepted.

COLIN ST JOHN WILSON, *THE OTHER TRADITION OF MODERN ARCHITECTURE*, 1995

Opening with the question "What Went Wrong?" St John Wilson argues in *The Other Tradition* that modernism is not a historical movement of the past but part of an ongoing tradition, an "uncompleted project." He points out how the strict formal specifications of CIAM were challenged by a group of architects, most notably Alvar Aalto, Hans Scharoun, and Hugo Häring, who offered an alternative reading of modernism focusing on the residents and the context.

Photo: Stephen Richards.

CENTRAL HILL, LONDON ROSEMARY STJERNSTEDT & ROGER WESTMAN, 1966–1974

The social housing complex with more than 450 dwellings was built for the London borough of Lambeth and included a dormitory, a senior citizens daycare facility, and a doctor's office. The development was designed to be low-rise with a high overall density. Parker Morris' spatial standards were implemented in the design: each residential unit has a private front garden and a large rear terrace with a view of the city.

DAME JANE DREW (1911–1996)

The British architect and urban planner founded her practice during the Second World War and initially employed only women. Because of her buildings in West Africa, she and her husband Maxwell Fry were commissioned to plan the city of Chandigarh, for which they enlisted the support of Le Corbusier and Pierre Jeanneret. Since 1998, the annual Jane Drew Prize has been awarded to women architects whose work exemplifies "innovation, diversity, and inclusion." Kate Macintosh was the recipient in 2021.

Photo: Julián Varas.

PARK HILL, SHEFFIELD** JACK LYNN & IVOR SMITH, 1957–1961

With more than 900 apartments, this building complex is exemplary for the mass housing construction of the 1950s in Great Britain. Despite its large size, a sense of community was fostered by re-homing neighbors next door to each other and naming the pathways after old street names from the area. Kate Macintosh fought for many years to preserve the building, which was listed in 1998.

LCC

Established in 1889, the London County Council (LCC) was the city's central planning and administrative body. After the Second World War, much of the housing was designed in the LCC architectural department. This allowed for the immediate implementation of policy objectives and the realization of high-quality projects. Functioning at times as the world's largest architecture firm, the LCC was a stepping stone in the career of many architects in the UK; Kate Macintosh also worked there during her studies. With the Borough Reform of 1965, the LCC was restructured into the Greater London Council (GLC). The GLC shared the responsibility for all new housing with the London boroughs, which were given the authority for all planning decisions.

NATIONAL THEATRE, LONDON DENYS LASDUN, 1967–1976

With its exposed concrete facade, the National Theatre is one of Britain's most iconic Brutalist buildings. Its design was based on Lasdun's concept of architecture as an "urban landscape." The building holds three auditoriums, the largest of which seats over 1,160, as well as restaurants, bars, workshops, and technical facilities.

LÉONIE (LOLA) GEISENDORF (1914–2016)

The architect was born in Warsaw when the city was still part of the Tsarist Russian Empire. Geisendorf studied at the ETH Zurich and went on to work for Le Corbusier. In 1938 she moved to Sweden and from 1950 led an architectural practice with her husband, Charles-Edouard Geisendorf. She became known, among other things, for the Riksrådsvägen townhouse development in Stockholm. Kate Macintosh found her first job in Sweden at Geisendorf's practice.

Photo: Ewan Munro.

LILLINGTON GARDENS, LONDON** ROGER WESTMAN AND DARBOURNE & DARKE, 1961–1971

The project in central London was one of the last major public housing projects before the reform of British housing policy. The cubature of the brick ensemble emphasizes the individuality of the apartments, each of which has its own private outdoor spaces.

1940 1950 1960 1970

1792 *A Vindication of the Rights of Women*, by Mary Wollstonecraft

1898 Ethel Charles becomes the first female member of the RIBA

1906 Women gain the right to vote in Finland

1928 Women gain the right to vote in Great Britain

1937 Kate Macintosh is born in Edinburgh

1947–1956 McCarthy era; first phase of the Cold War

LCC is a pioneer in equal pay for women and men

1961 Graduation from Edinburgh School of Art

1962 Scholarship in Warsaw

1963 Working stay in Finland, Sweden, and Denmark

1964 Return to England

LATE 1960s Introduction of paid maternity leave in the British civil service

Equal Pay Act
London County Council implements equal pay earlier

1972 Dawson's Heights, London

1973 Leigham Court Road, London

1978 Halton Fire Station, Hastings

Margaret Thatcher becomes British prime minister
Maresfield Fire Brigade Training HQ

PARKER MORRIS, *HOMES FOR TODAY AND TOMORROW*

The 1961 study by Sir Parker Morris for the Ministry of Housing and Local Government presented recommendations for new housing standards based on a user survey. Instead of calling for minimum room sizes, it defined functional necessities. The minimum dwelling size was made dependent on the size of the household. Furniture, but also technical requirements, played an important role, for example, providing heating for individual rooms so that a household member could withdraw from the central living space.

Photo: Kallerna.

ENSO-GUTZEIT HEADQUARTERS, HELSINKI* ALVAR AALTO, 1959–1962

The timeless office building is the administrative headquarter of one of Finland's largest paper and pulp companies. Clad in Carrara marble, the façade was designed to blend into the maritime skyline. Kate Macintosh studied the Aalto building during her travels.

Photo: Holger Ellgaard.

VILLA ERSKINE, DROTTNINGHOLM, SWEDEN* RALPH ERSKINE, 1956–1963

The exterior walls of the architect's private residence are made of lightweight concrete elements. The facade corners and the roof are arched. Macintosh visited Erskine at the villa shortly after its completion.

Photo: Jørgen Jespersen.

KINGO HOUSES, HELSINGØR, DENMARK* JØRN UTZON, 1956–1960

The housing development with 60 L-shaped courtyard houses provided a high standard of living at low prices thanks to their modular design, which enabled their mass production. All units have a private exterior space.

WEEGEE HOUSE, TAPIOLA, FINLAND* AARNO RUUSUVUORI, 1964–1967 (PHASES 1–2)

The print shop building became famous for its imposing concrete structure. Four 27 × 27-meter units structure the building, each with a three-meter-diameter column in the center. In 2006, the WeeGee House was converted into a museum.

Turku

Helsinki

Stockholm

Copenhagen

Warsaw

SUPERSAM SUPERMARKET, WARSAW JERZY HRYNIEWIECKI, MACIEJ KRASIŃSKI, AND EWA KRASIŃSKA, 1962 (DEMOLISHED IN 2006)

With its 1,000-square-meter column-free salesroom, the building was a landmark of Polish modernism. Wacław Zalewski was responsible for the statics and was part of the circle Macintosh moved in during her time in Warsaw. Zalewski developed further ideas for long-span structures made of precast concrete elements.

THE RONAN POINT DISASTER

In 1968, only two weeks after its opening, the entire corner of the 22-floor slab apartment building collapsed due to structural flaws and poor execution. Ronan Point was part of the post-World War II reconstruction effort and was built by a private housing company to provide low-cost housing. The collapse shattered public confidence in high-rise residential buildings and prefabrication.

ROSEMARY STJERNSTEDT (1912–1998)

After studying in Birmingham and at the AA in London, the British architect and urban planner moved to Sweden, where she had previously visited on a tour of new urban development projects as a student. She returned to London at the end of the Second World War and became the first woman to work in a senior position at the LCC, including on the design of the Alton East Estate.

* Reference projects for Dawson's Heights.
** Excursion destinations during Kate Macintosh's working stay in Scandinavia.

1980 — RIBA Women Architects Group is formed

1981 — Polegate Old Persons Home (demolished); Chair of the newly founded nonprofit organization Architects for Peace

1982 — Thornwood Old Persons Home & Sheltered Housing

1984 — 252–253 Preston Road, family center, Brighton

1985 — Lewes Fire Brigade Communications Centre

1987 — Battle and Langton Primary School, Battle

1990 — Rushmoor Fire Station

1993 — Priory Secondary School Sports Hall & Music Suite, Portsmouth

1994 — Solent Infants School, Portsmouth

1995 — Finch Macintosh Architects founded with George Finch

1995 — Studio, Winchester

1995 — Audley's Close Centre for Handicapped Adults

2000

2004 — Weston Adventure Playground, Southampton

2005 — Winner of the RIBA Award

2016 — 269 Leigham Court Road in London renamed as Macintosh Court

2021 — Winner of the Jane Drew Prize

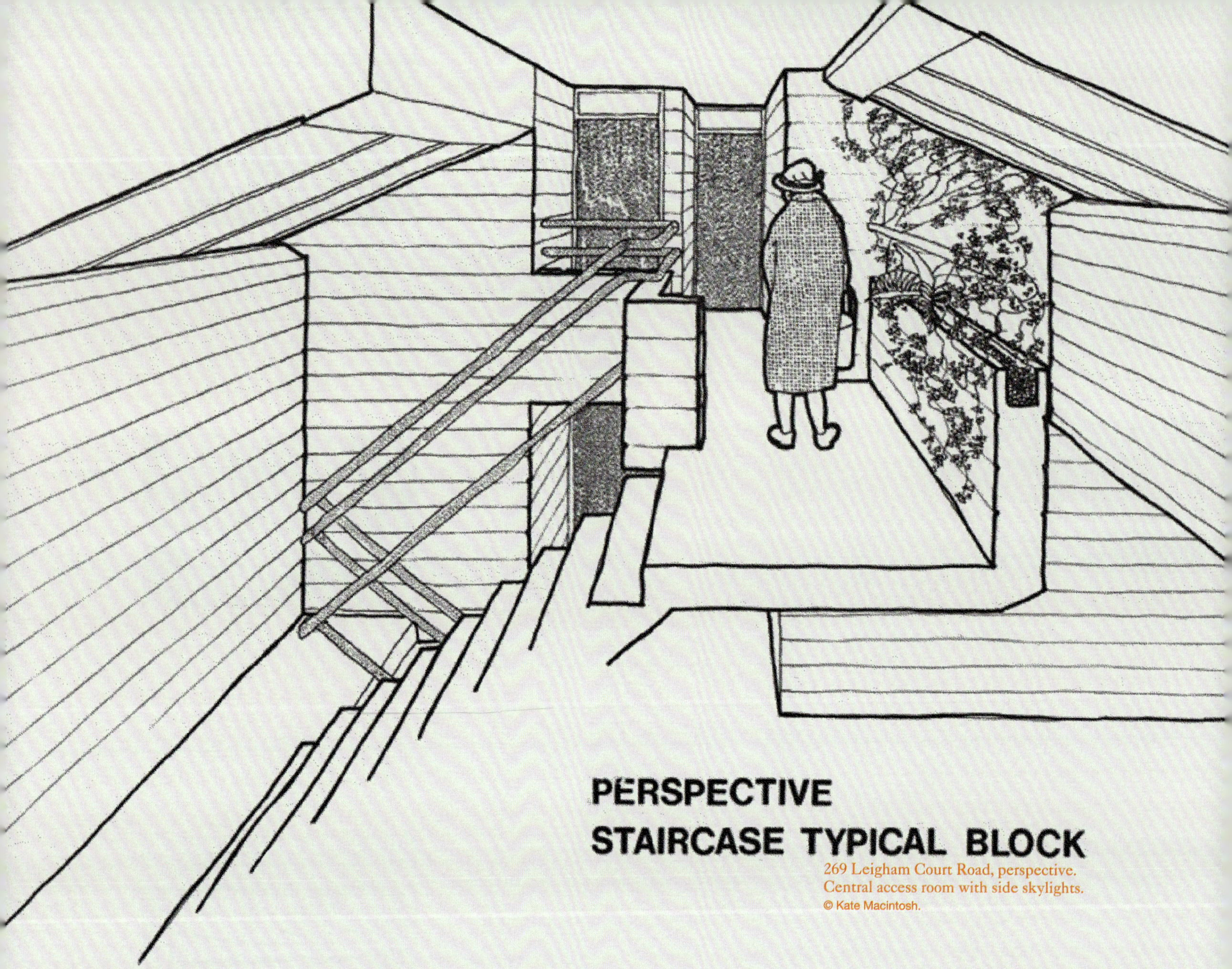

269 Leigham Court Road, perspective. Central access room with side skylights. © Kate Macintosh.

ARCH+ features

A platform for discourse by ARCH+ and Siedle

SSS SIEDLE

PUBLISHERS: ARCH+, Berlin/Spector Books, Leipzig
EDITORS: Anh-Linh Ngo, Melissa Makele, Markus Krieger
CREATIVE DIRECTION: Max Kaldenhoff
MANAGING EDITOR: Nora Dünser
ART DIRECTION: Mike Meiré
DESIGN: Charlotte Cassel, Meiré und Meiré
TYPESETTING: Stan Hema, Daniel Vandré
COPY EDITOR: Alisa Kotmair
PROOFREADING: James Copeland
PRINTING: Medialis Offsetdruck GmbH, Berlin
PREPRESS: max-color, Berlin
COVER: © Michael Franke.

With the ARCH+ features series, ARCH+ regularly presents select positions on the contemporary conditions of architectural production. ARCH+ features is curated by Anh-Linh Ngo. The series is made possible by Siedle as the initiative partner.

The interview with Kate Macintosh was conducted by Kristina Herresthal and Ariane Wiegner in writing and by video conference in February 2021.

The timeline on pages 14–15 was developed by Ariane Wiegner and Kristina Herresthal with Prof. Dr. Hermann Schlimme, the Chair of History of Architecture and Urbanism at the Technical University of Berlin in the seminar "Inhabiting the Survival Lounge." Participants: Sarah Rivière, Prof. Hermann Schlimme, Luise Albrecht, and the students Tamar Gürciyan, Eléonore Sophia Hayar, Katjuschka Ama Owusu, Paul André Walter, and Anis Ziaei. Special thanks to Paul André Walter for additional contributions and the timeline's visual concept.

"We Need Forms of Reproduction That Do Not Separate Us from Each Other"

Silvia Federici in conversation with Lilian Chee on domestic work and the role of architecture in processes of emancipation.

Since the 1970s, Silvia Federici has been at the front line of the international feminist movement, first in Italy and then in the United States. In 1975, she founded the American branch of the activist group Wages for Housework. Since then, Federici has been living and teaching in New York. Her writings have become a fundamental reference for feminist groups demanding the recognition of full labor rights for domestic workers worldwide. Lilian Chee is an Associate Professor at the National University of Singapore Department of Architecture. Her research investigates topics such as public housing, domesticity, and how gendered divisions of labor affect the production of space.

LILIAN CHEE (LC): In my research, I have looked at different understandings of domesticity and, more specifically, at how, in architecture, we adopt clear semantic differences between "home" and "housing," while domesticity—understood as a set of practices that defines the occupation and production of the household—is largely left out from architectural discourse because it entails a certain amount of labor that lies outside the realm of capital. Domesticity is maintenance work, and maintenance work is often not accounted for in architecture. In collaboration with Singaporean filmmaker Lei Yuan Bin, I developed the movie *03-Flats*, in which we followed three single women who helm their domesticities at different stages in their lives. They live in three of the much-celebrated and much-politicized public housing blocks developed by Singapore's Housing and Development Board (HDB). Public housing in Singapore is a concession. The flats are leased to citizens by the state. While the provision of public housing in Singapore successfully fulfills a fundamental social need, HDB flats are specifically designed for the nuclear family. Marriage is still a precondition of eligibility to apply for new flats at a subsidized price. Therefore, behind this socially progressive housing scheme lies a very specific idea of what constitutes a family. Singles are only allowed to purchase public housing flats upon reaching 35 years of age, which is coincidentally the time when women are considered to have passed the age of procreation. As a result, we see young people who either marry to gain access to public housing or make some other kind of creative living arrangements. For example, they are in homosexual relationships but marry people of the opposite sex and live separately. This is in a country where housing is considered a fundamental right, so, for a Singaporean citizen, if you can't access public housing, you are giving up a significant aspect of your citizenship.

Furthermore, some people don't qualify for housing at all because they are not Singaporean citizens. Among these are tens of thousands of foreign domestic workers, mostly women from other Southeast Asian countries, who come to Singapore with a special working visa granted as part of a public scheme initiated in the 1970s. They leave their own families behind to care for the families of others in a country with higher pay so they can send remittances back to their families at home. I have a foreign domestic helper who has been with me for eight years. In Southeast Asia, domestic workers don't have the same rights and freedoms as the rest of us. This is a situation that touches me very personally and that, as a feminist, I find very difficult to deal with because, to a certain extent, I am a part of the problem: my helper is taking care of my children so that she can afford to give her two teenage daughters a better education. While there is a sense of professional and personal empathy between us, the class divide and power relationships are such that my attempts to build a truly amicable relationship often result in an awkwardness that vacillates between solidarity and patronizing.

SILVIA FEDERICI (SF): I see three main topics here. The first is the question of care work; the second is the question of how space and architecture have the power to shape social relationships; the third is the question of the rights of domestic workers in the global economy. All three are profoundly interrelated and are extremely important topics.

First, the concept of care work: I would start by acknowledging that there is a growing critique of the idea of care work. There is a powerful article by Premilla Nadasen on this topic titled *Rethinking Care Work: (Dis) Affection and the Politics of Caring.*[01] Nadasen argues that the concept of care work is problematic because the stress on "care" ties the rights of domestic workers to their emotional involvement with the people they are working for. It is like saying that these women have rights not because they are workers, not because of their labor, but only insofar as they make their employers happy, only if they care for people who have more resources than them. Nadasen suggests that feminists need to avoid using the concept of care work. We never used the words "care work" in the 1970s; we spoke of housework and later reproductive work because we realized that the work that goes into the reproduction of daily life goes beyond the house, for example, when a woman takes a child to school or goes to talk with the teacher, or when her work contributes to the regeneration of the social environment. Nevertheless, it is important to stress that the house remains central because procreation, sexuality, and housework are the nerve center for the reproduction of daily life and the workforce.

Second is the question of space and architecture. On this front, there are major transformations underway, but first, I would like to mention a book that, although it was published exactly 40 years ago, is still fundamental to understanding how space and architecture regulate relationships of power between the genders. It is *The Grand Domestic Revolution* by Dolores Hayden.[02] Hayden traces the history of women's struggles from the 1870s to the 1920s in the United States and how they led to new types of homes and neighborhoods. Some of those women were revolutionaries, anarchists, and utopian socialists; others were reformers. They came from different social and political backgrounds, but they all had one thing in common: they struggled against the organization of the home as a place where women would work in isolation from each other and imagined a different, more socialized form of reproductive work. As the Italian feminist thinker Leopoldina Fortunati taught us, the development of capitalism united workers in the factory but separated them in the home. In *The Grand Domestic Revolution*, Dolores Hayden shows how this fundamental separation between production and reproduction drove the American feminist movement to the forefront of the struggle for collectivizing and socializing domestic work. Some of these women, even if they weren't architects, laid out floor plans for revolutionary buildings that featured collective kitchens on the ground floor replacing individual kitchens inside the units. Hayden argues that the development of the neighborhood restaurant in the USA was shaped by these women's efforts to socialize the kitchen. In her book *Redesigning the American Dream*,[03] Hayden shows how during the Second World War, in order to recruit women in the war industry while men were deployed in the army, authorities provided a whole system of collective reproduction. Women, for instance, could go in the morning and drop off their children and dirty clothes and came back at night to pick them up. But this came to an end after the war when the great migration towards suburbia started, and the nuclear family became the primary subject of the American consumerist economy, inaugurating a new phase of isolation for many women. Hayden also shows in her book how thoroughly the architecture of the suburban home was shaped as a means to institute a sexual division of labor, tie the housewife to domestic work, and keep men workers away from each other to prevent them from organizing unions. This is how deeply the politics of space relate to questions of labor, particularly regarding the organization of reproductive work. We now have two realities in the United States. On the one hand, we have the dissolution of the traditional family. On the other, we have a growing number of people living alone or forming new types of families that are not connected by blood or marriage but only by economic necessity or cultural or political affinities. This leads to a new communalization of reproductive life and a radical rethinking of the home, both aiming at socializing reproduction. You have to consider that, for most women, the problem is not domestic work itself but the miserable conditions in which it is performed. The fact that the work is their responsibility, that it is devalued, that it is unpaid, and that it makes you economically dependent on a man are all fundamental problems. Still, what mainly concerns the great majority of women is how reproduction is organized, how it separates us from other women, and how it keeps us alone all day with a small child or with an older person who is ill and whom we have to take care of all alone. If we collectivize the work, one person can take care now, and someone else will do so later. Tasks are shared, and so is responsibility. Much of my work throughout my career has been a struggle against the devaluation of reproductive work and a call for re-channeling our social wealth to support its collectivization.

We have seen incredible changes in recent years, particularly in places like Chile or Argentina, countries that have gone through big economic crises and where people have found themselves with close to nothing, and the only way out was to communalize reproductive work. Women pushed in the direction of developing things like urban farming, collective kitchens, and local support groups to guarantee that every child gets at least a glass of milk or a *merienda* afternoon snack. We, too, must fight for cities and houses to include spaces where we can come together and collectivize

FILM STILLS FROM *03-FLATS*, 2014.
Conceived by Lilian Chee and directed by Lei Yuan Bin, the film *03-FLATS* looks at the promises and realities of Singapore's public housing system. In Singapore, nearly 80 percent of the population lives in Housing and Development Board (HDB) apartments, and about one-third are singles. However, single people under 35 are ineligible for government-subsidized housing. The heteronormative nuclear family is favored by both housing policy and housing design, which considerably limits women's autonomy.
The film portrays three single women in Singapore striving for their independence at different stages of their lives. *03-FLATS* is based on an academic research project by Lilian Chee on the architectural representation of domesticity.

All photos: Courtesy Lei Yuan Bin and Lilian Chee.

"Much of my work throughout my career has been a struggle against the devaluation of reproductive work and a call for re-channeling our social wealth to support its collectivization." – SILVIA FEDERICI reproductive work. This is particularly important in places like the United States, where there are traditionally few places for collective gatherings. Most towns in the United States don't even have a square. This is inconceivable in Europe, where cities are built around squares dating back to the Middle Ages when there was a strong economic need for collective spaces. Today, both in Europe and in the United States, new struggles have emerged over public space and communal housing. There is a push to break down the isolation of the suburban house and develop new forms of reproduction that do not separate us from each other.

Finally, there is the issue of the relationship between the feminist movement and the struggles of domestic workers. In the last 20 years, I have seen an enormous growth of domestic worker movements globally, such as Domestic Workers United in the United States and Territorio Doméstico in Spain. These movements are the alternative to the micro-struggle that we experience daily. They change the power relationships between women. The relationship between the madam and the maid is an old dilemma. It does not matter how good and sincere the intentions are; there will always be an unequal power relationship between the employer and the employee, but that's precisely why looking at things through the lens of feminism is so powerful. Domestic worker activists are saying: "We are not fighting against the women who employ us; we are asking them to join us in the movement. We ask them to join forces and fight with us for the institutional change that has to occur for domestic workers to have the same rights as every other worker, to have the same set of guarantees, because all of the small abuses that domestic workers have been subjected to have been made possible by the grand abuse that comes from governments and institutions, which ultimately is the grand abuse that comes from the national regimes." Take Canada, for example: you have to live in Canada for two years in your employer's house before you can apply for a permanent working visa. Just try to imagine all that can happen during these two years. In these two years, women are bound to accept anything. If you are abused, you have no power to protest because, if you do, you can compromise your opportunity to get the visa.

LC: That's very interesting. I have never seen it that way. Political movements are often seen in terms of "us versus them." It's binary. But if you build an argument of cross-solidarity between women and say, "I need your labor in my home because I have to go out and offer my own labor to another kind of economy, and as a woman, I too will demand that your labor comes with full institutional rights," then we are both fighting together. We are fighting for the same thing.

SF: Yes! And there is even a more profound issue at stake: the devaluation of domestic work affects all women, not just domestic workers, because the devaluation of their work is the devaluation of the reproductive work that every woman is subjected to simply for being a woman. The struggle of domestic workers is the struggle of every woman.

LC: Yes, for example, here in Singapore, there are many older women who are not officially domestic workers but who offer childcare informally. Most have already retired and have time to care for young children after school. They do the work that grandparents traditionally are expected to do. In Southeast Asia, leaving kids with their grandparents after school is common, but not everyone has this opportunity, especially if the grandparents live in another city. So, parents leave their kids with informal caregivers, usually trusted older women in the neighborhood. But if care work is devalued, their informal work is devalued too, and so is that of the grandparents.

SF: And this is mostly the work of the grandmother, usually the mother's mother.

LC: Yes, it's always the maternal grandmother we rely on because, as a mother, you don't always feel comfortable asking the father's family for help. It feels like you are taking a debt, and then you end up doing all kinds of things to overcompensate. I am quite surprised you mentioned this, Silvia, because I thought it was an Asian thing.

SF: No, not at all. It's happening everywhere. I know it from Italy, and the same happens here in the United States. It's usually the mother's mother who cares for the children. One thing that happens a lot here in the US is that women who don't have the money for childcare will care for their children at home but also take in the children of other women in the community for a small fee. Childcare has become very expensive here. Public, institutional childcare has been defunded. As a mother, you depend mainly on the private sector, and that's very expensive. Most women cannot afford it, so they organize childcare informally. There are also official women's cooperatives that have organized themselves to provide childcare or eldercare locally. Cooperatives can give great power to domestic workers and women in general. When organized cooperatively, caregiving becomes less of a one-to-one relationship, which is always tricky because it generates emotional involvement that is not always easy to manage. Ultimately the solution lies at the institutional level. We need more money, we need more resources, we need public buildings, we need space, and we need welfare in order to be able to provide a reproduction that is worth this name. We must reproduce a life that is worth living. And this is why we need the struggle over the revalorization and socialization of reproductive work and why feminist struggles must have a material base.

Currently, there is a debate in the United States about the government issuing some kind of subsidy for childcare. This is a major feminist struggle that concerns all women and is closely linked to the struggle of domestic workers. As in many other situations, however, women are made to fight against each other over resources, work, and time. I call it the redistribution of poverty. The feminist movement has relied too much on the struggle for better-paid jobs, but that is not enough. It's not enough because you may have better pay, and you might be able to afford some extra help at home, but if you have to pay more and more for a privatized and individualized daycare service, at the end of the day, you are left with nothing. In the United States, women are going into

"We need more money, we need more resources, we need public buildings, we need space, and we need welfare in order to be able to provide a reproduction that is worth this name. We must reproduce a life that is worth living. And this is why we need the struggle over the revalorization and socialization of reproductive work and why feminist struggles must have a material base." – SILVIA FEDERICI

debt because what they earn is not enough; they use their wages as collateral to take out a loan. Today a wage is the road to a loan. You have to work more so you can get more debt, but the root of it all is the devaluation of reproductive work.

GUEST EDITORS (DOS): I would like to jump into the conversation and introduce my point of view as a female architect because I believe that Lilian's personal struggle also has to do with the architecture profession, as well as with the condition of domestic workers. Architecture is a very elitist profession; nevertheless, the work of architects is completely devaluated. It is almost impossible to make a living as a young architect, especially if you come from a poor background. We all like to think of our profession as charged with great social responsibility, but we also have this latent awareness that this is an elitist profession that, for the most part, works at the service of a system that reproduces the same social injustices that we wish to resolve. Our work ethics clash completely with the day-to-day reality of the profession. For example, I come from Brazil. In Brazil, the majority of undergraduate students in architecture are women. But by the time they have finished their degrees, they realize that life gets tough, especially if you want children. The level of commitment and precariousness in the architecture sector does not support motherhood. And then, there is this moment of epiphany when you think, "I work late every day, and I still can't afford to have a domestic worker to take care of my children while I design and build apartments that, by law, must include a domestic worker's room with a separated toilet." This is the law in Brazil; you don't get planning permission if you design apartments above three rooms without including a separate toilet for the domestic worker. And so, that's when you realize that there is quite a sophisticated model in place in which architecture is systematically reproducing preexisting divisions of gender and class rather than eliminating them.

SF: I have been talking with domestic workers in Brazil and the national organization of domestic workers there. One of the main struggles in Brazil is to refuse to live-in because once you live in your employer's house, life becomes very difficult. It becomes difficult to be able to go out at the end of the day, to have a life of your own, and to develop mentally, emotionally, and politically. When you become part of the family, it is hard to say no, set boundaries, deal with the emotional ties, and ask to get paid for overtime. Many domestic workers cannot even close their door, or their room doesn't have a key. They can be woken up at any time.

DOS: Lilian, what is the situation in Singapore in terms of the living arrangements? Where does your domestic worker live?

LC: She lives with us. In Singapore, foreign domestic workers cannot live outside the home where they work unless they come into the country with some other kind of work permit. If you come from abroad as a domestic worker, you must move in with the family who sponsors your visa. In the beginning, I had a hard time sharing my home. It is still hard sometimes. My helper comes from the Philippines. I encourage her to go back twice a year and to go out of the house on the weekends. She has friends from her hometown and even other members of her family who work in different parts of Singapore. But she must live with me; there is no other option. It's even worse than in Canada because she can't get an independent working visa after two years. As long as you are a domestic worker, you must live with your employer. Some families only use the program to sublet an extra room to foreign domestic workers who then work for a different family, but that's technically illegal.

The visa policy creates a problem that architecture actively supports by producing specific kinds of spaces that accommodate it. If you are recruited to come to Singapore as a domestic worker, you must do a short professional training before you start. One of the things they teach you is that you should not close your door. Can you imagine? Not only do you have to live in your employer's home, but you are taught that you should not even close the door of your room. I found myself in an awkward situation when I asked the helper to close her door, and she replied, "No, it's fine." Then I had to insist and say, "No, really, your door doesn't need to be open all the time." But hierarchies are so ingrained here, and until we change the policy and give domestic workers more autonomy, this will not change because they simply don't have the same rights.

SF: Yes, negotiating spatial relationships at home is difficult. It's difficult with your partner, with your children, with your friends, and it is especially difficult with a person with whom there is an objective hierarchy. This makes it immensely complicated to negotiate the relationship because many different factors come into play: guilt, things that are said or not said, things that are repressed. Some things cannot be negotiated in a one-to-one relationship.

LC: And when we look outside the home, the way the architecture profession is organized is still very patriarchal. The structures of employment, the working hours, and the ethics of the building industry. This is not only a sector that lacks the consciousness of care but one that benefits from the exploitation of labor at every possible level. The profit-making of the building industry is well-documented. In the past year, due to the pandemic, the state's response to Covid-19 has created situations at the limits of human rights, where foreign construction workers are literally incarcerated inside workers' housing. Lockdowns have only exacerbated preexisting labor hierarchies in the construction industry and, more generally, all the structural weaknesses in society. We want to build faster and cheaper, but where do you find the labor? Where do you find the materials? How do you pay the workers? The scale at which new buildings are erected is astounding. But do we really need so many buildings? Obviously, many people's livelihoods depend on this industry. A lot of these buildings are just a way to generate money, create jobs, and support livelihoods, but is this an effective way of doing it? It's a vicious cycle. Can we think more creatively and ethically about the decisions we make? About what gets built and what doesn't? All these questions are feminist questions.

SF: Architecture and urban planning are critical to the feminist struggle. For example,

DARLING

one trend that has to change is that of making residential buildings taller and taller, disconnecting entirely from the street. Streets should join homes, not separate them. Every little aspect of architecture that goes in the direction of moving away from the street and isolating the family from public life goes against a century of feminist struggles. Every tendency to individualize de facto weakens the infrastructures of support that women have worked hard to build in order to emancipate themselves. Architects who wish to support women's struggles should fight against the individualization of reproduction. In New York, apartments that accommodated many people 30 years ago have now been sliced up. Every slice has one small washing machine, one small television, and one small seat for the computer. You enter the room and bump right into the bed. You cannot have friends over. You cannot invite other people. There is no social life in the house. If you want a social life, you have to go to a cafe. You have to pay money to meet people. This is the home the new entrepreneurial young men and women presumably want. Impossible! We need to create spaces that do not individualize, that do not separate, places that do not fragment reproduction. We need buildings that include communal spaces.

TEAM
Guest editors: Daniela Ortiz dos Santos (DOS) and Charlotte Malterre-Barthes;
ARCH+: Mirko Gatti, Melissa Makele.

"We want to build faster and cheaper, but where do you find the labor? Where do you find the materials? How do you pay the workers? The scale at which new buildings are erected is astounding. But do we really need so many buildings?" – LILIAN CHEE

01 Premilla Nadasen, "Rethinking Care Work: (Dis) Affection and the Politics of Caring," *Feminist Formations* 33, no. 1 (Spring 2021): 165–88.
02 Dolores Hayden, *The Grand Domestic Revolution: A History of Feminist Designs for American Homes, Neighborhoods, and Cities* (Cambridge, MA: The MIT Press, 1981).
03 Dolores Hayden, *Redesigning the American Dream: The Future of Housing, Work, and Family Life* (New York, NY: W. W. Norton & Co., 2002).

Kitchenless Cities

Anna Puigjaner

At the Hotel Belleclaire apartment building in New York, completed in 1903, residents had access to a rich offer of communal facilities, including laundries, cleaning services, and childcare centers. Meals were taken in the communal dining hall, which, starting at the turn of the century, was often located on the roofs of the apartment buildings. Not only the invention of the electric elevator but, above all, Central Park and the underlying notion of having a "view over the city" spurred the development of rooftop gardens in the new public spaces of the metropolis. Postcard, Hotel Belleclaire. © Collection Kyle Jolliffe.

Since time immemorial, the home has been not only a personal shelter but also a reflection of society's economic and social structures. As a vehicle for capitalist division into productive and reproductive labor since the 19th century, the kitchen has played a central role in the production of gendered power relations in the domestic environment. It has sparked discussions about the role of women, the construct of the nuclear family, and the valuation of housework, which to this day is essentially based on the principle of unpaid care. Despite rationalization and technological progress ranging from the mechanization to the digitalization of household technologies (like the "smart home"), not much less time is spent on housework in industrialized countries today than 100 years ago, with more food consumed and more waste produced than ever before.

In her dissertation *Kitchenless City* (2014), Anna Puigjaner explored the economic benefits of communal kitchens, the professionalization of domestic labor, and the impact of corresponding changes on urban space. Her research focused on apartment buildings without private kitchens, which were built throughout New York City as a new housing typology in the wake of the sharp population increase resulting from industrialization in the second half of the 19th century. These individual "kitchenless" apartments were served by collective facilities, such as dining halls, laundromats, cleaning services, and childcare centers. The outsourcing of reproductive activities from the realm of housing and recreation was not only consistent with concepts about comfort at the time but also with the principle of rationalization, reducing the individual costs of household management. In addition, eliminating kitchens made space for more rental units; the additional rental income helped keep household services affordable for low-income earners. It also enabled women to work without having to additionally manage their household. The new kitchenless housing typology was an open system of rooms, often arranged along long corridors. Individually accessible, the rooms could be connected or separated as needed, allowing for a variety of flexible apartment configurations. They attracted a social mix of single people, families, and residential communities of different sizes and ages. The outsourcing of domestic

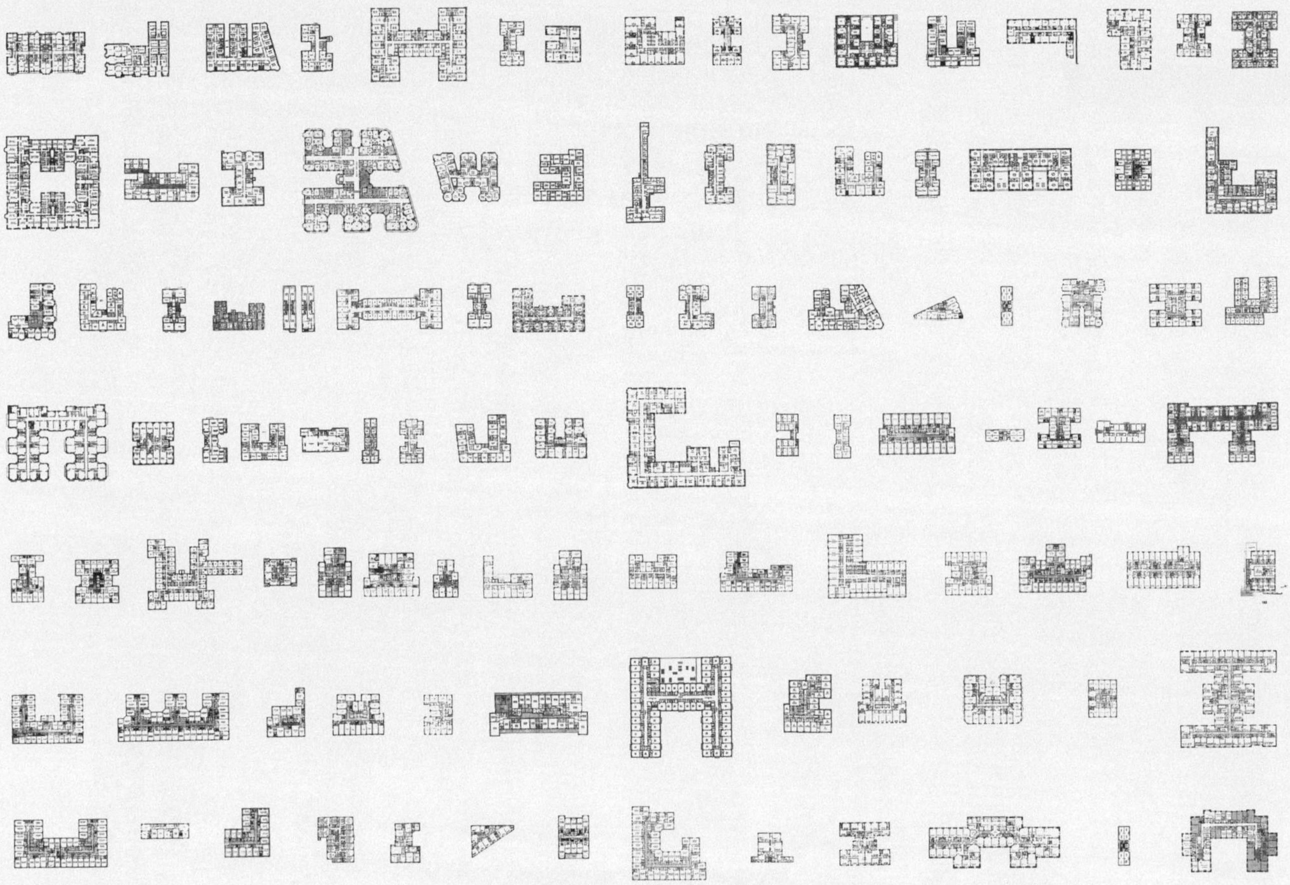

Kitchenless Housing Typologies.
Kitchenless housing typologies: The first small, kitchenless apartment buildings were established in the 1870s. By 1900, they were rapidly spreading as a new housing typology throughout the urban areas west and east of Central Park. The number and size of buildings increased sharply, partly due to a revision of the laws governing the construction of new apartment buildings, which redefined the minimum size of buildable lots. Following the stock market crash of 1929 and the new focus on the home as a place of female productivity and individual domestic consumption, kitchenless apartment buildings waned in popularity.
© Anna Puigjaner.

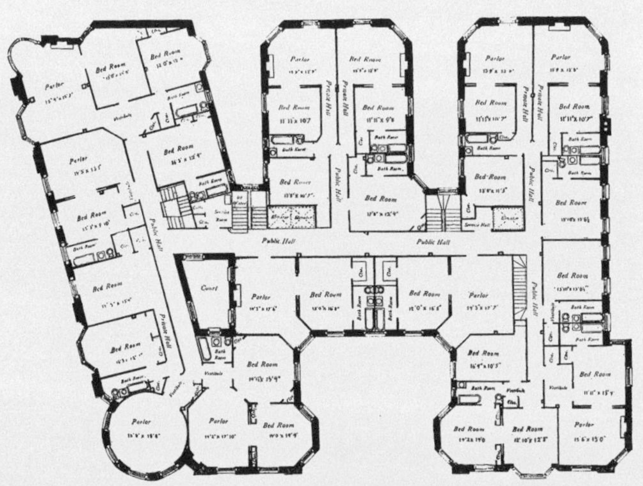

FLOOR PLAN, HOTEL BELLECLAIRE.
A system of open-use spaces and access corridors allowed flexible apartment sizes for various user groups in the kitchenless apartment buildings.
Courtesy Avery Columbia University.

Drawing of Hotel Belleclaire from 1903.
Courtesy Avery Columbia University.

Comedor Comunitario Las Margaritas, located in a converted sports center in Mexico City, serves around 400 people daily. In addition to a public dining room, there are several medical offices, classrooms, and shops. © Anna Puigjaner.

From 2009 onwards, hundreds of government-subsidized community kitchens, known as *comedores comunitarios*, were set up in Mexico City to relieve the financial burden on the population hit by the global economic crisis and to provide warm low-cost meals. Homeowners with a room larger than 30 square meters could apply to the social program to host a kitchen and were provided by the city with industrial kitchen appliances, utensils, and supplies. The boundaries between private and public space often blur in such places—as seen in this living room, where rice and beans are stored for use in the communal kitchen. The influence of *comedores comunitarios* went far beyond individual homes; entire neighborhoods developed into urban networks of collective care. © Anna Puigjaner.

Both photos: © Anna Puigjaner.

activities to communal and sometimes even publicly accessible areas promoted the emergence of new forms of urban collectivity that went beyond the individual building community; the dining halls and recreational facilities, for example, were often located on the roofs of the high-rise buildings and were usually open to the public.

Today, the nuclear family is increasingly losing its normative binding force. Accompanying this phenomenon are louder calls for alternative forms of communal living combined with pressing questions about the socioecological restructuring of society and approaches to household activities, living, working, and care. The design of the home in general—and the kitchen in particular—plays a central role in the transformation of society, particularly in the reorganization of domestic and care work.

In many government housing complexes in Singapore, the ground floor is not rented out to residents but is left as a "void deck" for community activities. For their project *GoodLife! Makan* in 2016, DP Architects designed a neighborhood kitchen for elderly citizens on the ground floor of a building at the Marine Parade residential complex. The aim was to foster social exchange through communal cooking and eating experiences to prevent loneliness and isolation.

Practice

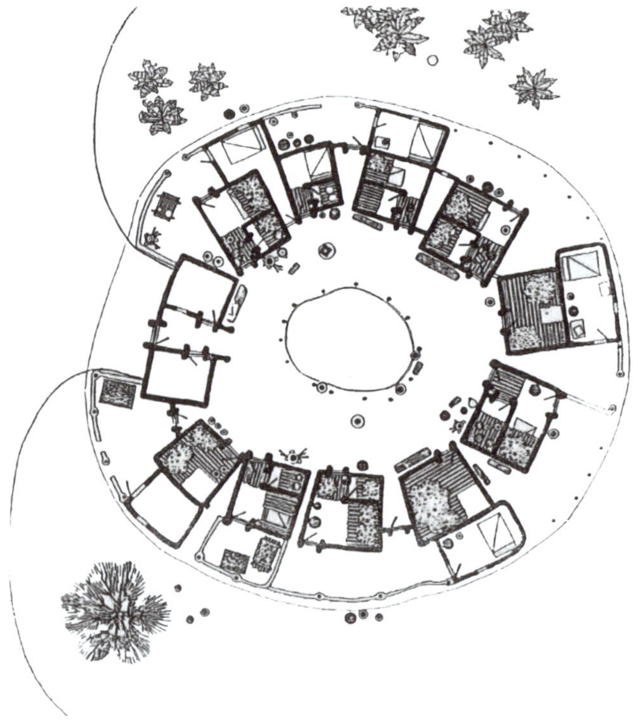

© Patrick Dujarric.

The *maison impluvium*, pictured here in the village of Niambalang, is widespread in rural Senegal. It houses several families who share a common space for cooking. Surrounding the round common room are private rooms, which are divided among the families according to the residents' needs. Photo: Anna Puigjaner.

Building on her dissertation with the project *Kitchen Stories* (2016–18), Anna Puigjaner documented contemporary case studies of collective kitchens around the world, including in Peru, Mexico, Canada, Senegal, Singapore, Thailand, China, and Japan. The reasons for their establishment differ in terms of economic, social, and cultural factors. What they all have in common, however, is their effect on the community and culture of coexistence, redrawing the boundaries between production and reproduction, public and private, and the urban and the domestic.

Anna Puigjaner focuses on examples where the kitchen, as a central spatial organizational element, defines a specific architectural typology that can inspire ideas for the contemporary redefinition of the domestic sphere. She looks to the *maison impluvium* for inspiration, a housing typology common in rural Senegal, in which a series of open-use private rooms surround a communal space with firepits in the center. Building on this principle, Puigjaner formulates her vision of a "diffuse city" with generic living spaces and strategically located collective "activity centers." A kind of "fragmented domesticity" results from private and public spaces scattered throughout the city, which are used flexibly by the residents. **AM**

In Lima, half a million people receive warm daily meals in so-called *comedores populares*—neighborhood community kitchens that are often housed in private dwellings. Pictured here: Comedor Popular Jesús de Nazaret Vizona. These collective kitchens emerged in the 1970s during a phase of social mobilization and politicization against the military regime. During a national teachers' association strike, women from the neighborhood began cooking for the community. Even today, *comedores populares* offer women in particular the opportunity to work independently of their home and family and earn their own income.

Both photos: © Anna Puigjaner.

Comedor Popular La Balanza is one of the few planner-designed community kitchens at a large community center in Lima.

Intervention

110 Rooms

Anna Puigjaner / MAIO

USE (SIZE): Multistory apartment building for collective living (2,795 m²)
CLIENT: private
LOCATION: Barcelona
DESIGN TEAM: Anna Puigjaner, Maria Charneco, Guillermo López, Alfredo Lérida
YEAR: 2013–2016

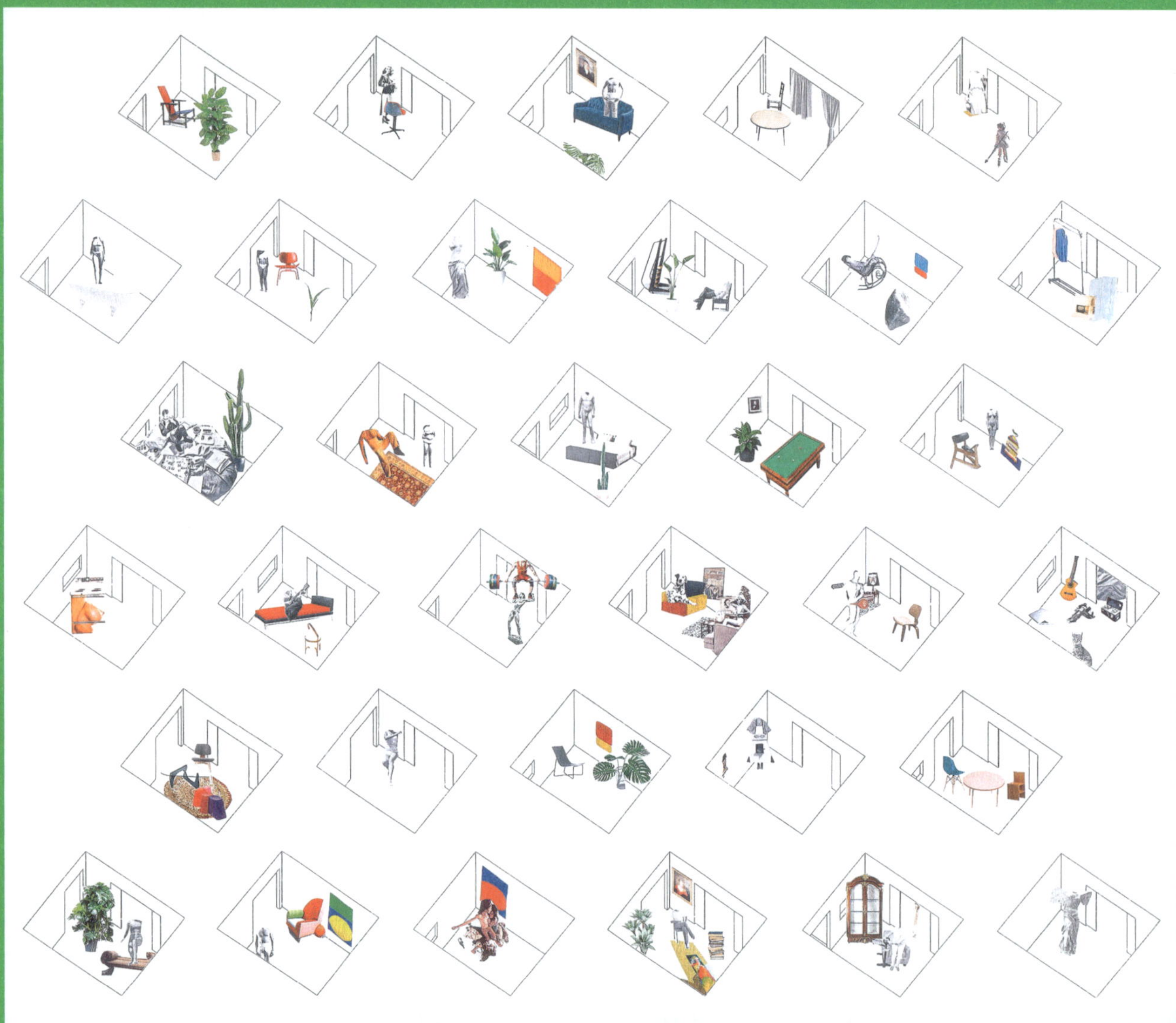

Completed by MAIO in 2016, the multistory apartment building in Barcelona consists of 110 rooms, which can be used flexibly as bedrooms, living rooms, children's rooms, or study rooms.

In 2013, Anna Puigjaner and her partners from the architecture firm MAIO designed 110 Rooms, a residential project in Barcelona. It builds on the findings of her research on the "Kitchenless City" and the idea of open use of generically designed living spaces. The multistory building is a system of 110 rooms without predefined use, whose function is defined by the residents. With their design, the architects intentionally resist hierarchical apartment typologies that cater to the image of an ideal nuclear family with a fixed living room, parents' bedroom, and children's bedrooms. They also reference the historic buildings of the Eixample neighborhood, built in the 19th century according to the plans of Ildefons Cerdà. Thanks to their generic room sizes, they have accommodated various uses over time without significant structural intervention. A central sculptural staircase divides the structure into two building sections comprising 20 residential units with five rooms each. The units can be enlarged or reduced according to the residents' needs by adding individual rooms from the neighboring apartment or combining multiple residential units. Even within an apartment, users can decide for themselves where they live, sleep, and work. This flexibility is provided by the uniform room size of about ten square meters, connecting doors, and clear zoning. Multipurpose rooms are located along the facades, which open outward to the street and inward toward the atrium. Between that are the sanitary facilities, installation shafts, and kitchens, which, due to their central position, serve as both the central access room and the social center of the dwellings.

MAIO based the ground floor design on the surrounding 19th-century townhouses and the architecture of their magnificent entrance halls. Freestanding geometrically

Street facade.

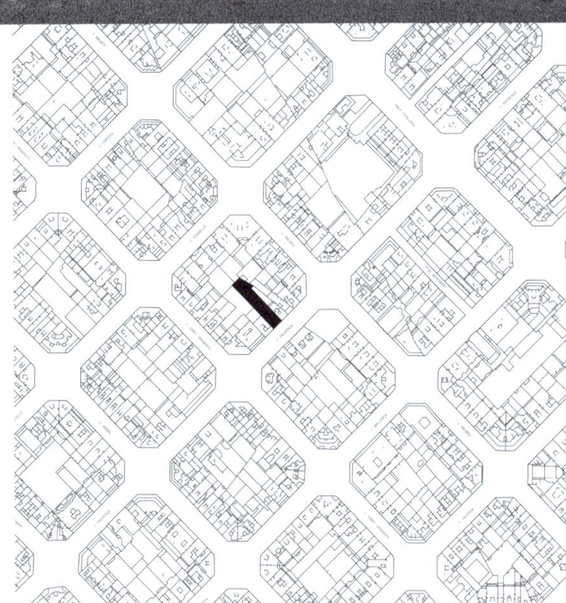

Site plan.

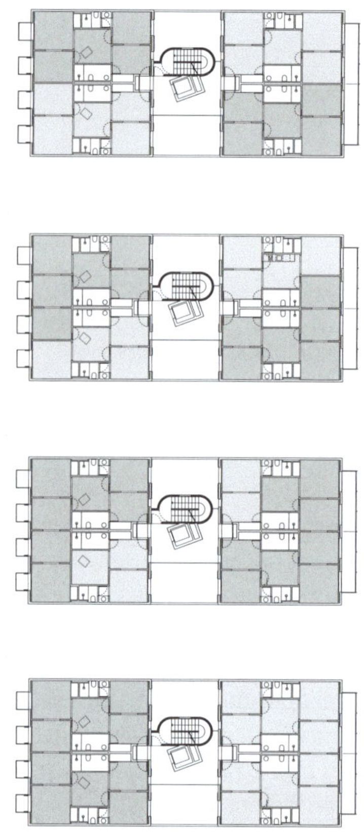

Examples of different room use and dwelling configurations.

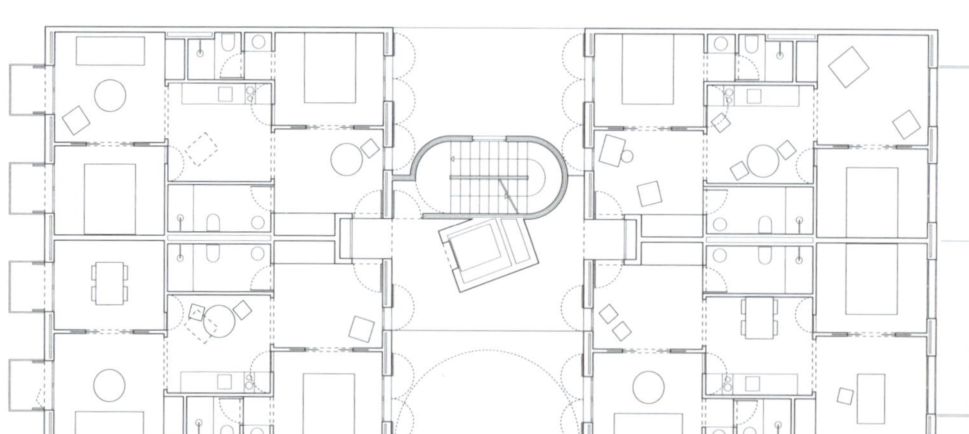

The neutral-use rooms on the upper floors can be divided among the residential units according to the residents' current needs. Between them, in the middle of the apartment, the kitchen acts as a central access room (there are no storage rooms or corridors). The kitchen also serves as the social heart of the dwelling.

The function of the rooms is determined by their respective occupants. Neutral colors and materials such as plaster and wood contribute to maximum functional flexibility.

Abstracted textured floor plan of the entrance hall on the ground floor.

Longitudinal section of the building.

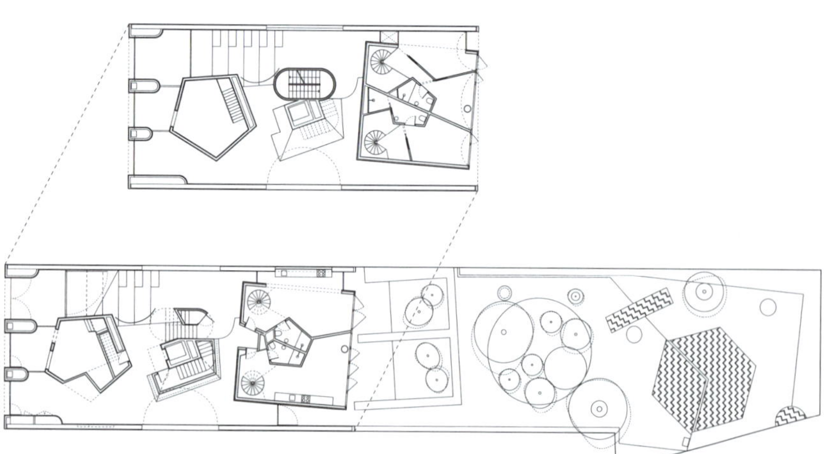

Ground floor plan showing the volume above it.

shaped volumes clad in differently colored marble characterize the space of "collective representation," as the architects call it, which opens onto the street. The spacious entrance hall on the ground floor contrasts with the minimalist, pragmatic living spaces on the upper floors, which were realized in neutral colors and inexpensive materials such as plaster and wood. This juxtaposition of simplicity or economy with architectural generosity, as well as the linking of the generic with the specific, is also reflected in the facade to the street. With its small balconies, wooden shutters and stucco ornaments, it responds to the characteristic elements of the historic building facades. On the other hand, the uniform window openings and the homogeneous mint-green paint testify to the generic structure of the rooms behind them. **AM**

The "collective representation" space that opens to the street on the ground floor contrasts in its generosity and eye-catching design with the reduced and pragmatic living spaces on the upper floors.

Intervention

San Riemo

Non-load-bearing facades are built in timber frame construction, visually combined by a curtain of corrugated-iron panels. In the south, facing the forecourt, the architects planned a partially closed "display facade" based on the idea of a public town house.
© Petter Krag.

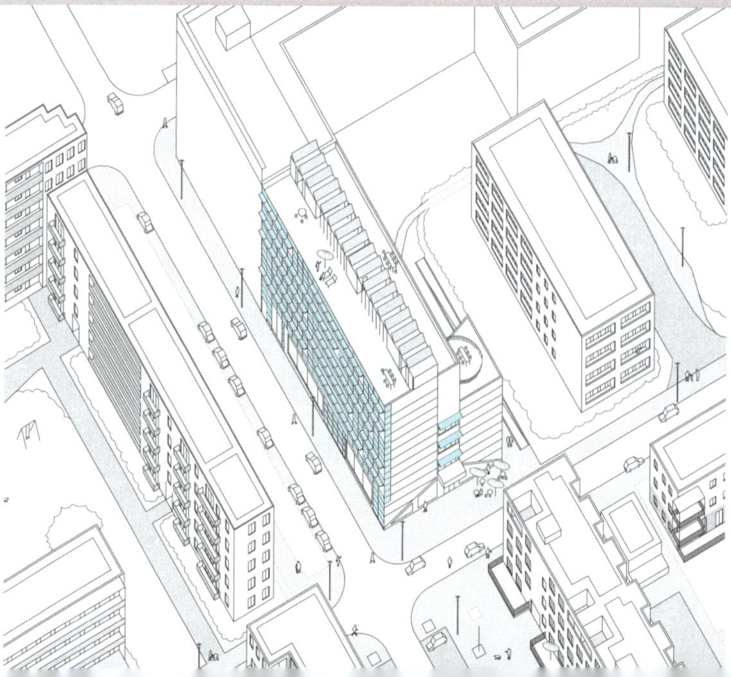

Axonometric of the building during the competition phase.

USE (AREA): Cooperative residential building with 27 residential units (4,250 m²)
DESIGN TEAM: Anne Femmer, Juliane Greb, Petter Krag, Florian Summa
CLIENT: Kooperative Großstadt eG
PLACE: Munich (Riem)
YEAR: 2017–2021

ALL DRAWINGS: © ARGE Summacumfemmer and Büro Juliane Greb.

In 2017, the Kooperative Grossstadt building cooperative launched an open design competition for their first residential building in Munich-Riem. From across Europe, 62 architecture practices submitted designs for a residential building with communal and commercial areas. Founded in 2015, the cooperative aims to create housing with high architectural standards at moderate rents. It takes a solidarity-based approach to project financing, which enables people with very different income levels to become part of the building community. Although a design by Tim Schäfer, Pablo Donet Garcia, and Tanja Reimer from Zurich was awarded first prize, questions of economic viability meant the second-place entry—Project San Riemo, by the German-Belgian working group Summacumfemmer and Büro Juliane Greb—was ultimately chosen as the design to be implemented.

In addition to conventional apartment types, the final project offers space for more experimental forms of shared living. The 27 residential units can house a total of around 100 residents and include small apartments, family apartments, large shared apartments, and a therapeutic shared flat for women with mental illnesses. In keeping with the principle of the "breathing house," individual residential units can be enlarged or reduced as necessary by adding rooms, dividing up spaces, or giving rooms to neighbors. This calls for a large number of doors, allowing

ARGE Summacumfemmer and Büro Juliane Greb

East facade with continuous ribbon windows. © Florian Summa.

The west facade features a "winter garden" layer of full-length balconies behind translucent corrugated panels. Pale turquoise curtains serve to protect from the sun and provide privacy. The four-meter-high ground floor spaces, with large openings onto Heinrich-Böll-Strasse, are currently rented by the Lichtblick Foundation for its child and youth welfare facility.
© Petter Krag.

Residents have planted flowers and vegetables on the roof terrace. Outdoor communal cooking is possible in the summer kitchen. © Petter Krag.

rooms to be linked together without making structural alterations, but also requires an open load-bearing system of reinforced concrete beams and columns. This enables the creation of new openings and the installation of non-load-bearing walls made of plasterboard. The floor plan is based on a basic unit of 14 square meters (roughly 3.5 × 4 meters), allowing for great flexibility for current and future projects.

The concept of non-hierarchical, "breathing" architecture seeks to transcend the prevailing model of the heteronormative nuclear family. The social and functional impact of the nuclear family model underlies the traditional floor plan divided into a living room, a parents' bedroom, and children's bedrooms. Rather than follow this model, the architects introduced new housing typologies such as "nucleus" apartments, where individual rooms can be connected to different living units depending on specific needs, and "filial" apartments, where several rooms are combined into a shared open area by the residents of a single floor. Different forms and intensities of collective living and mutual care can be tried out, depending on the position and permeability of shared spaces on any given floor.

To maximize the spatial efficiency and flexible use of the apartments, the building is strategically zoned along a long, single axis. Functionally neutral spaces are positioned along the facades. The middle zone contains the access areas, bathrooms, and multifunctional gathering areas holding the entrance, central connecting space, and kitchen, which can be rearranged according to each resident's needs. An outer "winter garden" layer of enclosed balcony spaces serves as a buffer zone to the street, expanding the apartments with an unheated outdoor space. Further communal areas include a cobbled inner courtyard, which also offers access to

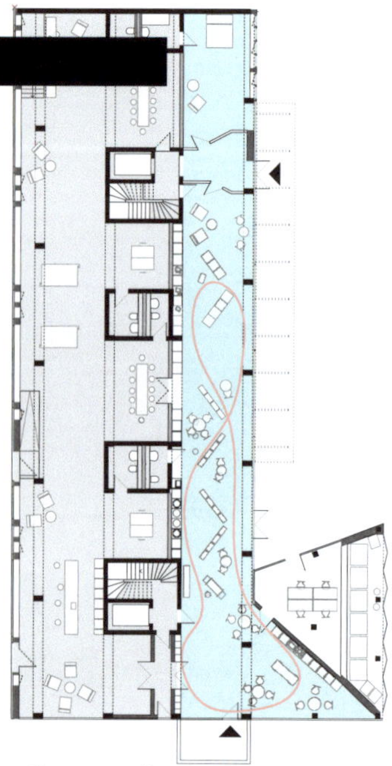

Promenade.

Shared living.

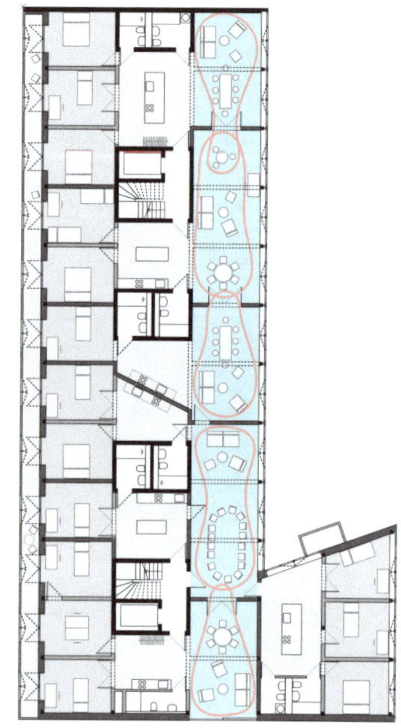

Family living.

The apartments have no corridors or storage rooms and are accessed through a central zone, which also houses the kitchen. The uniform size of the rooms on the facade side make them suitable as bedrooms, play areas, living rooms, or offices. Larger spaces can be created by combining several rooms into a single unit.
© Florian Summa.

the apartments, and a roof terrace with a collective garden and summer kitchen.

While the interior spaces are characterized by plurality and multiple definitions, the building's facade is uniform, featuring a corrugated iron curtain, in keeping with the sober, functional design of the surrounding area. The overall design embraces the interplay between universality and individuality, private space and open public areas, exploring the possibilities of sustainable and more diverse living arrangements and providing space for many different needs and lifestyles. It allows for change over time while increasing autonomy for the individual residents. Users of the building were involved in the design of the apartments, as well as in earlier planning processes, including the distribution of residential units and coordinating with future neighbors about the number of rooms available. Residents used sheets with cut-out figures

Loft living.

Nucleus living.

Filial living.

The project's diverse living arrangements include classic shared apartments, family apartments, lofts with full-length living and dining spaces, and flexible concepts like "nucleus" apartments, where rooms can be added to or subtracted from different units as needed, and "filial" apartments, where rooms are combined into a shared open area by the residents of a floor.

The ground floor includes a guest apartment and a "flexi room" that can be used as a workshop or for crafts, as well as a four-meter-high "inner street" with a laundry area, a communal kitchen, and other shared spaces.
© Petter Krag.

Both photos: © Florian Summa.

to decide how individual rooms in their apartment would be used, including the placement of walls, doors, and electrical sockets. Residents also participate in organizing the building's use and maintenance. Chat channels are used to distribute mail and packages, plan clean-up actions, and develop neighborhood care concepts. The open common area on the ground floor—a four-meter-high "interior street"—provides access, storage for baby carriages, a shared laundry area, a library, a kitchen for events, and an in-house cinema.

The deliberate approach to the building's design is reflected in the labor structures of the architectural offices involved. During the planning process, both Summacumfemmer and Juliane Greb's office placed great importance on non-hierarchical and collective (negotiation) processes. At first glance, it may seem inefficient to have both partners of both design offices involved in every design and decision-making process. In fact, it just meant adopting a high-quality approach to communications. With shared knowledge and joint responsibility, the planning community was given more leeway in (re)distributing tasks flexibly. This proved a real advantage, given the everyday pressures on participants—a relatively new office, teaching responsibilities, parenthood—and the many unpredictable aspects. **AM**

A "winter garden" system of enclosed, non-heated balconies is mounted along the west side of the building. This space can be used for growing vegetables, storing groceries, or drying laundry. Apartment partitions were done away with in favor of shared use, with the winter garden serving as a communication zone for neighborly encounters.

Intervention

La Comunal

Lacol

Taking up half a block, the complex stands out from the structure of the surrounding urban area. The original set of buildings was complemented by distinct extensions made of timber and steel. © Lacol.

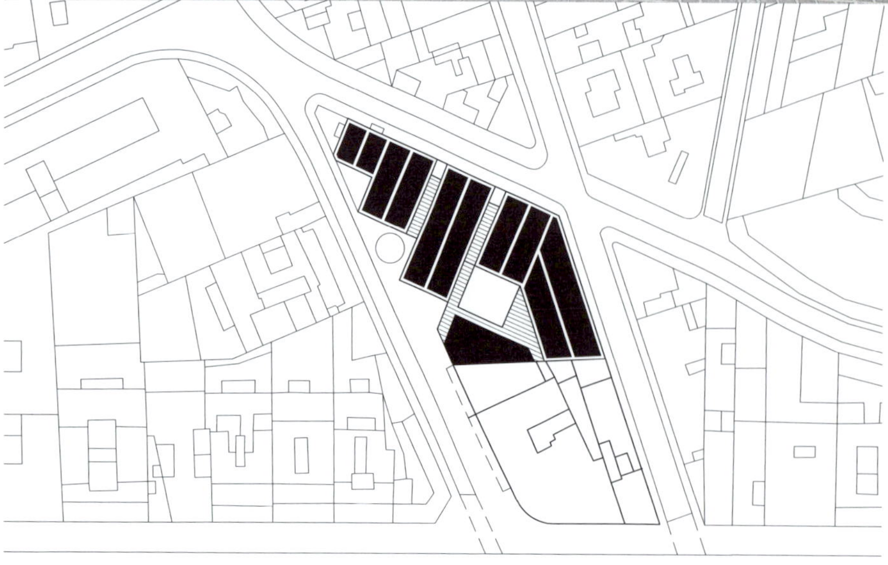

Cooperativa d'arquitectes Lacol was founded in 2009 by a group of students from Universitat Politècnica de Catalunya and Escola Tècnica Superior d'Architectura de Barcelona as a cooperatively organized office. They took this step in response to the financial crisis, which had greatly impaired the professional prospects of future architects. The collective of 14 members is committed to flat hierarchies, active participation, and transdisciplinary work in their practice. It is also politically active and, in the spirit of the global social movements of the 2010s, advocates for a right to the city and housing and the radical expansion of political participation at a municipal level.

The construction of a new, southeastern part of the building created an inner courtyard. The new build and the divided multi-purpose space merge into one another, forming the spatial center of the community. © Lacol.

USE (AREA): Cooperative community space, building for service and cultural cooperatives (1,400 m²)
DESIGN TEAM: Cooperativa d'arquitectes Lacol
CLIENT: La Comunal
LOCATION: Barcelona
YEAR: 2018–2019

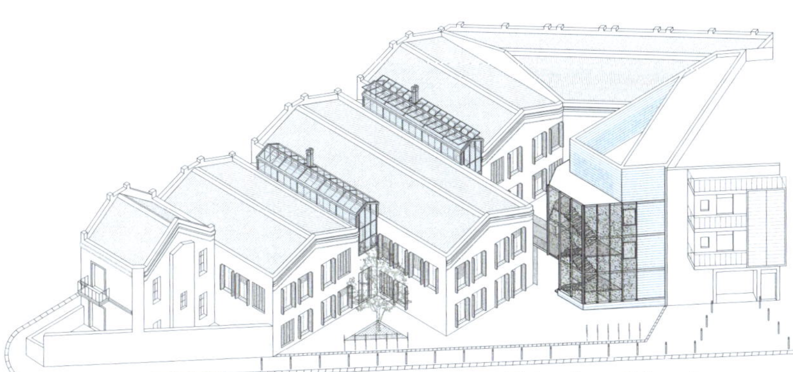

All drawings: © Lacol.

What kind of architectural practice can emerge from a milieu that works consciously in the tradition of activist social movements? In Sants, a former working-class district of Barcelona, those developing new forms of self-government are in dialogue with the area's historic anarchist traditions. The Barcelona housing crisis around 2016 also had a substantial impact on cultural and nonprofit organizations. Against this backdrop, Lacol founded a cooperative scheme to work with other cooperatives. The so-called Cooperative of Cooperatives aimed to create spaces and new development opportunities for all its members and developed a programmatic concept for the adaptive reuse of a complex of industrial buildings originally built for the 1929 Barcelona World's Fair but which had lain empty since 2003.

In addition to Lacol, the cooperative consists of nonprofit organizations and includes a bookstore, a nonprofit language school, a human rights organization, a cooperative newspaper, an IT cooperative, and a restaurant with a music bar. Not only do the cooperatives share the building but also social and economic aspects of their work. The complex was designed with this in mind and architecturally encourages interactions and collaborations between the various organizations. The common areas and shared meeting rooms are organized around an inner courtyard, occupied on the ground floor by a restaurant, which is open to the public but also serves as the canteen for cooperative members.

Conversion work undertaken included restoring the building's original geometry. The structure was originally a warehouse facility for large textile production, including sails and tarpaulins. The stucco facade from 1926 was uncovered and restored in its original style. The ground floor, which had been entirely closed off, was transformed into a permeable zone with open corridors and entrances leading directly onto the courtyard. This inner courtyard has now been completed by a new building built at the end of the site. Constructed with steel, timber, and concrete blocks, it stands out from the existing buildings in its form, materiality, and function. Moreover, the new structure can be entirely dismantled for future demolition. New glass passages linking the preexisting parallel volumes lend structure to the overall form. To ensure flexible options for use, versatile modular components were created using minimally invasive interventions to the existing building. The architects describe La Comunal as a working space that reflects the many changes to the working world. Once an industrial complex, today the structure is a hybrid site of service and communication, and has now become an important cultural hub for the district. **VK**

Wide raised walkways flank the formerly built-up courtyard, which is now an open space. The galleries are transparent spaces with wire mesh covering. This, along with the large windows, creates good interior lighting conditions.
© Álvaro Valdecantos.

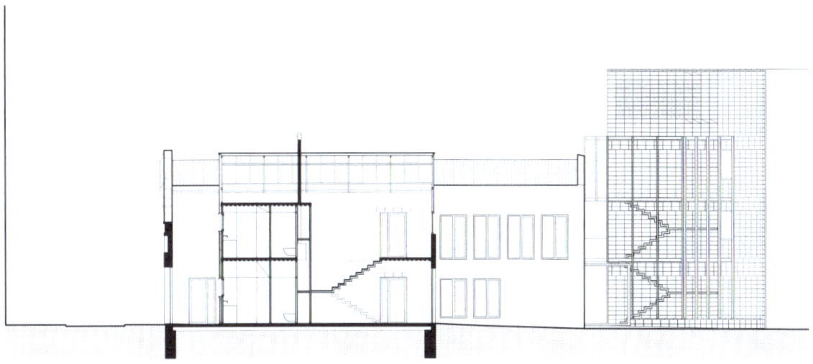

Inner courtyard, cross-section.

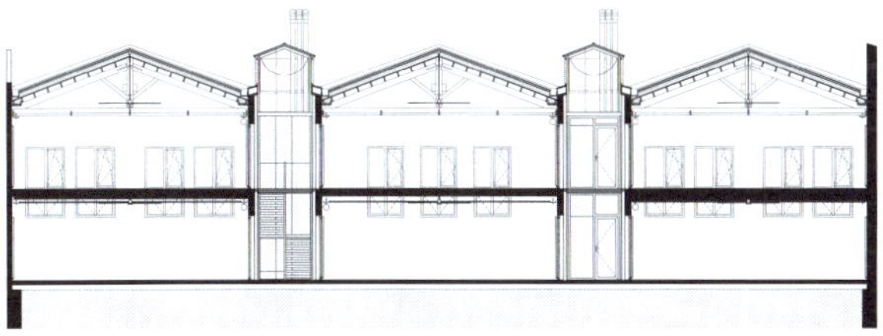

Longitudinal section.

The gaps between the preexisting row-like buildings were roofed over with glass. This lends visual structure to the overall form while creating a thermal buffer thanks to the greenhouse effect. © Álvaro Valdecantos.

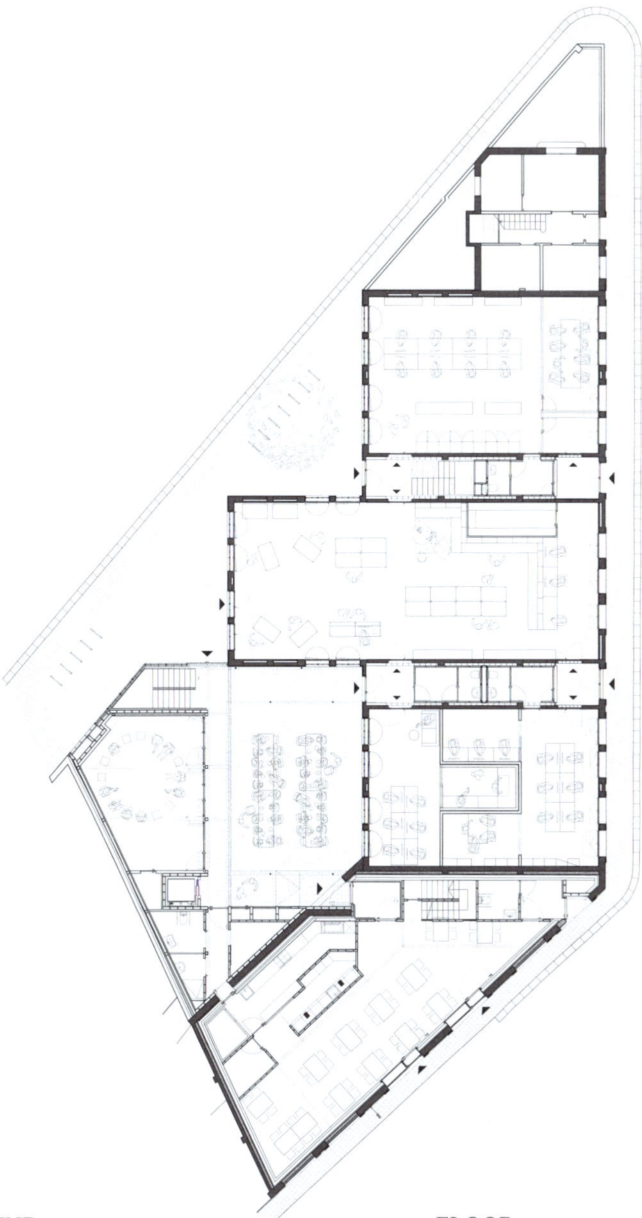

GROUND FLOOR
Except for the restaurant and concert hall, the building's interiors are almost unchanged; versatile, modular components were added, allowing the space to be occupied in flexible ways.

In 2011, local initiatives in the working-class district of La Bordeta, just outside of Sants, occupied the empty Can Batlló textile factory, which dates to the 19th century. Residents cited a 1976 plan announcing the end of industrial use for the site, which led to the demolition of some newer factory buildings and the creation of green spaces in one of Barcelona's most densely populated neighborhoods. The snail's pace of the redevelopment process and plans to build private luxury apartments on the site sparked citizens to present the city administration with an ultimatum, threatening to take matters into their own hands and undertake conversion work themselves. Two days before the deadline they had set, the local authority handed over one of the buildings to the initiatives.

Lacol supported residents' demands for communal facilities and affordable housing and worked with them to expand a wing of the large factory complex. The decision to preserve this part of the building also sparked a debate about what should be conserved from the historic fabric of the site—Barcelona's last surviving urban industrial complex of this size. Eventually, the municipality decided to renovate and convert the vast majority of the existing buildings. In addition, it was decided to boost the historic location by siting a new city archive in what was previously its large warehouse. For this, the local authority announced a two-phase competition.

Another streetside section of the former Can Batlló site was leased to La Borda housing cooperative on a 75-year leasehold. Speculation is prevented by building cooperative housing on public land. In cooperation with Coop 57, an ethical financial service provider, La Borda was able to set the average basic rent at about 450 euros a month for the 28 cooperative apartments, a level that covers the current overall loan interest. Once the debt has been paid off, rents will be reduced further from their current levels (around half the market rate), and collective reserves will be built up.

USE (AREA): Cooperative housing (3,000 m^2)
DESIGN TEAM: Cooperativa d'arquitectes Lacol
CLIENT: La Borda (Cooperativa d'habitatge en cessió d'ús)
LOCATION: Barcelona
YEAR: 2014–2018

La Borda
Lacol

Street view of La Borda with polycarbonate curtain wall facade. Above the small grocery store on the ground floor are living spaces and a large, communal roof terrace. © Lacol.

Continuous balconies are the main feature of the courtyard's southern interior facade. © Lacol.

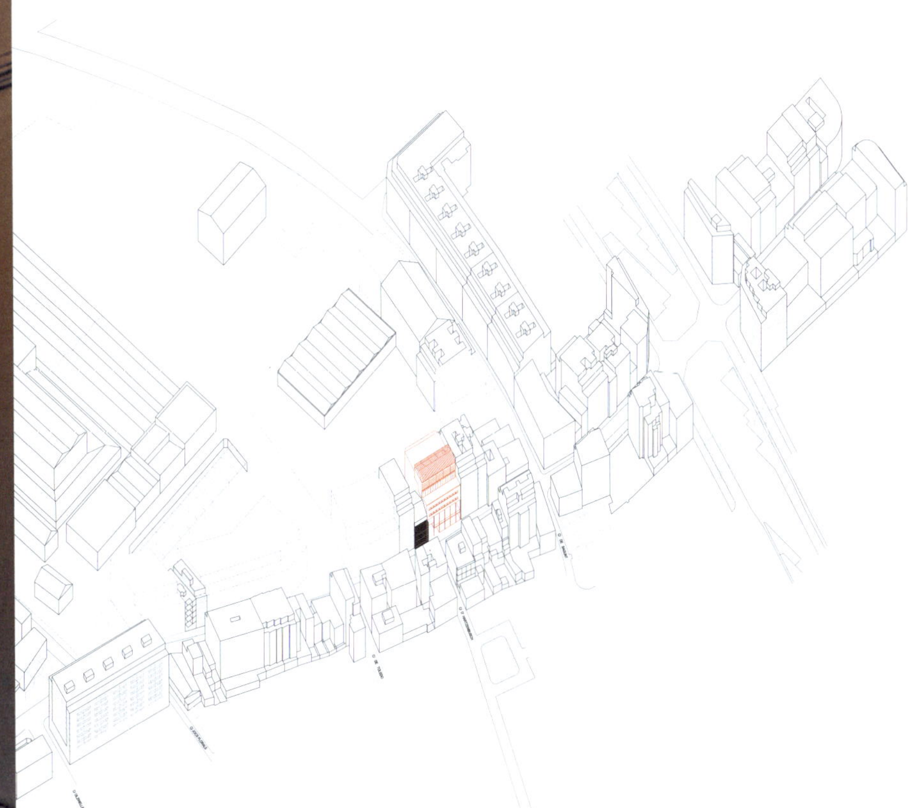

All drawings: © Lacol.

La Borda seeks to make collective forms of living possible and promotes mutual support in areas like housework and care work.
© Institut Municipal de l'Habitatge i Rehabilitació de Barcelona.

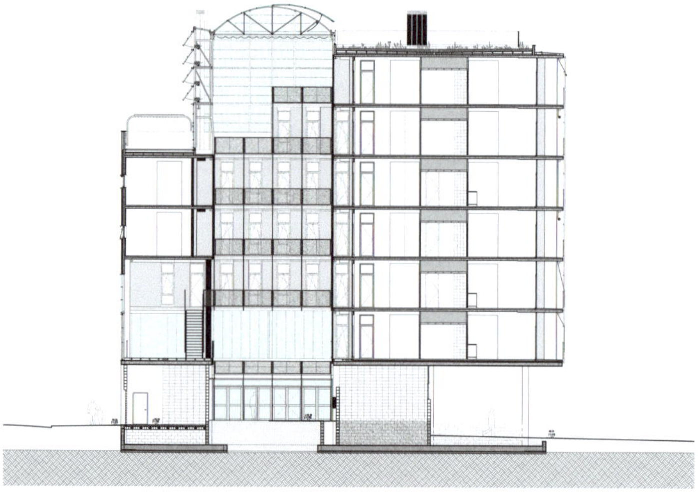

Cross-section.

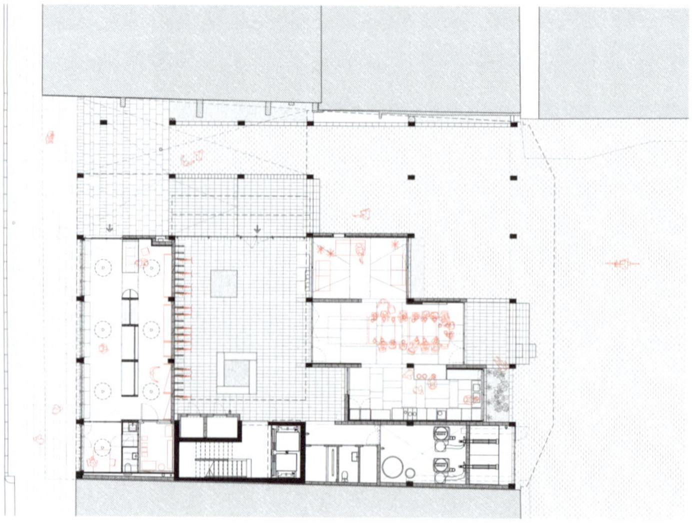

Ground floor.

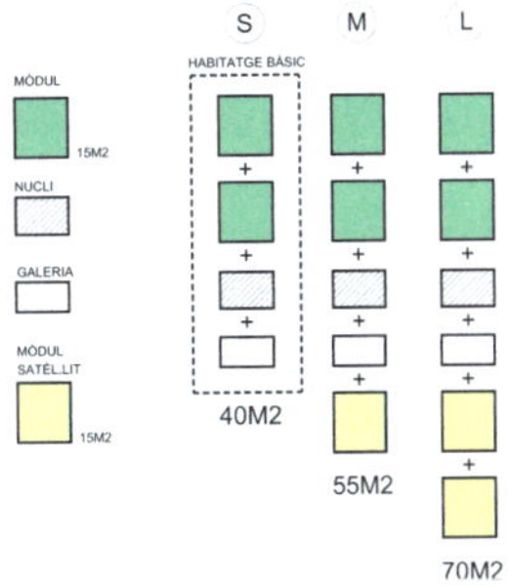

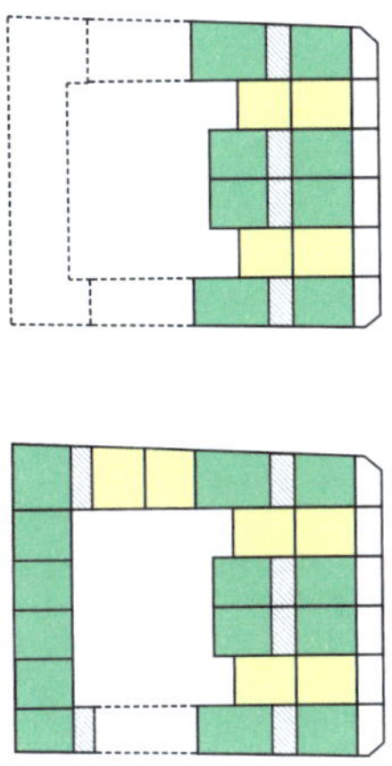

If necessary, optional spaces can be added to the layout of a typical apartment, allowing it to be expanded by up to two rooms. These "elastic apartments" adapt to their residents' changing requirements.

The balconies around the courtyard function as access zones but are above all meant as spaces for interaction, where plants can be cultivated, and conversations held.
© Lluc Miralles.

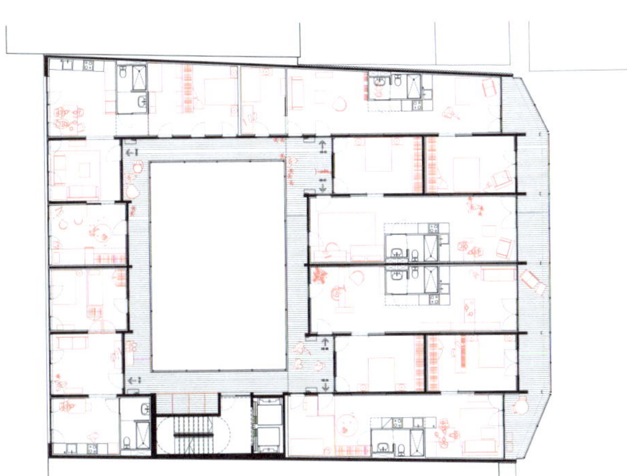

Standard floor plan.

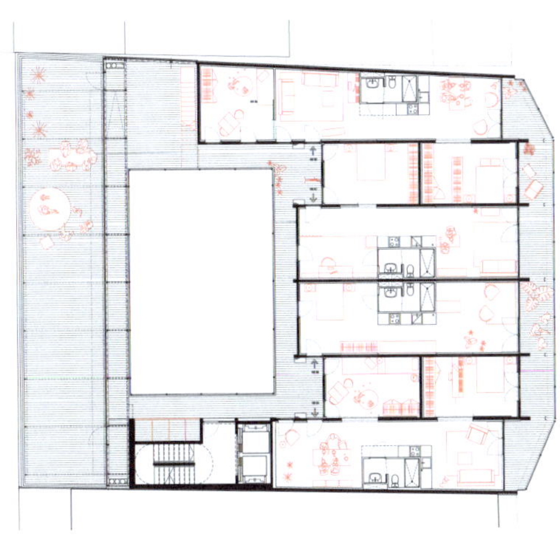

Rooftop.

Intervention

Lacol was the architectural bureau tasked with planning and executing the project. It developed the building in constant communication with future residents, who included some of its own employees. During the design and construction phases, an internal participatory structure was put in place with various working groups and monthly general meetings. The plan was designed to strengthen neighborly relationships while allowing cooperative structures to operate in areas such as budget, maintenance, and care work. The architectural concept for supporting the community is supplemented by structural support, such as a general emergency fund and spaces dedicated to emotional support and conflict prevention. In addition to 40-, 60- and 75-square meter private residential units built in modular timber construction, residents have an additional 300 square meters of covered communal space at their disposal. This communal space corresponds to about one-quarter of the site's gross total area. The common spaces include a large collective kitchen with a dining room, laundry room, guest rooms, several indoor lounge areas, and a large outdoor terrace. These spaces are sited on the gallery level, arranged around a central glass-roofed atrium, which serves as a transition zone to the private apartments. This spatial typology—an inner courtyard with multilevel arcades—is widespread in southern Spain. At La Borda, it also acts as natural air conditioning for the apartments, which have windows on two sides. In winter, the glazed atrium doubles as a thermal buffer; in summer, the chimney effect promotes air circulation. Using local laminated timber for the construction and the flexible spatial concept that accommodates changing needs of different generations of residents makes the building highly efficient and both economically and ecologically stable. **VK**

The courtyard forms a communicative center, widening at street level into an open space along the street facade to create a threshold area opening onto the streetscape. © Lluc Miralles.

Shared roof terrace, north side of the building. © Lluc Miralles.

Edit Collective

Honey, I'm Home (2018–)

"As early as 1969, Carol Hanisch used the slogan *The Personal Is Political*, which was then popularized by publication of the 1970 book *Notes from the Second Year: Women's Liberation*, edited by Shulamith Firestone and Anne Koedt. In contrast to the first wave of feminism and its efforts to achieve political participation and equality (including the right to vote), second-wave feminism distinguished itself in particular by opening up a new, immediate field of struggle within *first-person politics* situated in the arena of the domestic sphere. This is where we come in with our intersectional feminist collective Edit, founded in London in 2018. Our research and design strategies lie at the crossroads of architecture, design, and art and aim at a fundamental critique of power in private domestic space. In addition, we want to make visible the gendered hierarchies and power structures that shape our built environment. Our methods and modes of mediation (fictional narratives, photomontages, gifs, etc.) often depart from conventional architectural modes of representation to create works that are accessible to a broader audience. In doing so, we avoid large-scale, technocratic narratives. Instead, the smallest possible intervention that can be implemented from within the existing building is often the starting point for our thinking."
– Edit

Installation view, *Gross Domestic Product* at the Oslo Architecture Triennale with the three-person vacuum cleaner in the middle.

In their ongoing study *Honey, I'm Home*, Edit examines performative aspects of housing as well as the rituals, hierarchies, and power relations in the gendered appropriation of space codified in and through the floor plan. They attribute the typical domestic floor plan of spatially segregated functions—an "architecture of wall boundaries, corridors, and enclosed spaces" (Edit) that continues to dominate the Anglo-American landscape today—to two developments from the first half of the 19th century: the typical Victorian row house and the emergence of the bourgeois nuclear family, whose rigid roles became a social norm. The ground floor of a typical Victorian home was characterized by a clear separation of public and private spaces. The kitchen—a place of work for women or domestic servants—was situated far from the dining room and salon, prestigious spaces where guests were received and entertained. The division into public and private spheres, into production and reproduction, into paid gainful employment and invisible and unpaid (or poorly paid) domestic labor and care work continues to shape society and the organization of our everyday lives. At the heart of this phenomenon is the traditional nuclear family as the incontestable basic unit of our socioeconomic system, in which the pursuit of home ownership as the "safe haven" of the nuclear family consolidates the capitalist model of society based on private property.[01] As part of their research project *Honey, I'm Home*, Edit develops spatial interventions that stimulate a (re)ordering of the domestic sphere. They awaken the desire to explore ways of living together beyond the institution of the nuclear family. They renegotiate the labor of care and relationships beyond the bourgeois divisions of private and public. **FG**

TEAM: Alberte Lauridsen, Alice Meyer, Hannah Rozenberg, Marianna Janowicz, Saijel Taank, Sophie Williams
LOCATION: London
FOUNDED: 2018

Members of the Edit Collective demonstrate the use of the three-person vacuum cleaner.

Gross Domestic Product (2019)

With their project *Gross Domestic Product* (GDP), Edit continues their research for *Honey, I'm Home* on an experimental, speculative level. This is a design for a vacuum cleaner that can only be operated when used by three people at the same time. *Gross Domestic Product* was presented as part of the Oslo Architecture Triennale under the title *Enough: The Architecture of Degrowth.* It represents an antithesis to the capitalist growth economy and its underlying idea of efficiency and performance based on individualism and autonomy. The market launch of the commercial vacuum cleaner in 1919 is emblematic of the development in the 1920s when electric household appliances became mass-produced goods, and the expansion of the domestic infrastructure with water, gas, and electricity promoted a culture of private housework. Within this temporal framework, Edit situates the fictional story of the three-person vacuum cleaner. The collective introduces it as the forgotten invention of Jenny Spangler, the daughter of the actual inventor of the modern vacuum cleaner. The design for *Gross Domestic Product* contradicts the promise of the time; the vacuum cleaner was advertised as a household appliance optimally geared toward individual use, which would relieve isolated care workers thanks to its high efficiency. In contrast, the three-person vacuum cleaner makes collective use mandatory in order to distribute the housework among several members of a (household) community. *GDP* is less a concrete proposal for a solution than a speculative object that invites us—starting from the small scale of the design of everyday objects—to question our common notions of housework and explore its potential as a collective, sociable, and political act. **FG**

01 See Dolores Hayden, *Redesigning the American Dream: Gender, Housing, and Family Life* (New York, NY: W. W. Norton & Company, 1984), 87 f.; see also Friedrich Engels' interpretation of historical materialism in his text *The Origin of the Family, Private Property and the State* (1884) with an introduction by Jennifer Doyle (London: Verso Books, 2021).

Home Revolution (2020)

Home Revolution collage.

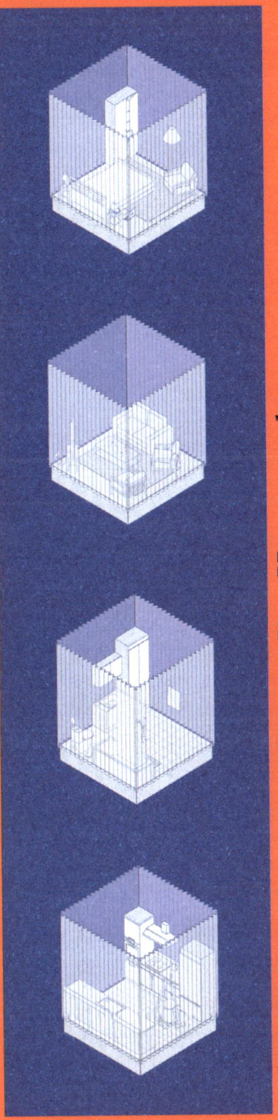

Representation of the *Honey, I'm Home* study as a moving image to remove the functional and physical separation of individual spatial units.

Home Revolution **suggests stripping rooms of their dedicated functions, rearranging furniture, and creating connections to explore the home as a new learning environment.**

The Covid-19 pandemic led to an enormous shift in social power relations. It showed the extent to which care and reproductive work are constitutive (as "essential workers") for the survival of us all. While doctors and nurses in hospitals and workers in the service sector reached their physical and psychological limits, consumption, work, and leisure shifted to the digital—and the domestic. With the closure of care facilities such as all-day schools and daycare centers for children and senior citizens, a considerable part of the welfare apparatus disappeared. This left an indelible mark on domestic behavior and the reappropriation of living space for activities such as homeschooling. In response to the opportunities and challenges presented by this reorganization of the domestic sphere, Edit launched the *Home Revolution* learning materials in May 2020, geared toward parents and children isolated at home. The project was part of the *Architecture at Home* series, established by the organizations Open City and Celebrating Architecture as a learning platform to advance the proactive transformation of neighborhoods by residents of different ages, social backgrounds, and expertise during the pandemic. For *Home Revolution*, Edit used comics as a communication tool to help children engage with their new learning environment through drawings, collages, models, and 1:1 prototypes. They were encouraged to think about how the spaces and things that surround them affect the way they live. **FG**

Practice

Mona Mahall, Aslı Serbest

LOCATION: Berlin
FOUNDED: 2010

TEXT
Mona Mahall, Aslı Serbest

When we study spaces from an aesthetic, historical, speculative, performative, or academic perspective, are we doing theory and not practice? Reproduction (overthinking, invisible), and not production (making, visible)? Can we afford the hesitation that this scrutiny implies, or don't we—like the rest of the world—need to act (build) even faster and more rationally?

In fact, our work, which combines space, image, video and text, represents a sense of hesitation about the architecture of a reasonable (good) common world. We hesitate at both the sensible and the common aspects of this world, which we think of as a kind of "Delirious New York," only bigger and more Western.

Our reason and "our" world are determined by the dualism of our thinking, which also marks the unreasonable outside, with facts provided by our technical equipment and evaluations associated with our practices. Our world, an extremely expansive West with even more expansive war zones, insists (like our architecture) on a horizon, a perspectival vanishing point that generates, here and there, inclusion and exclusion: an inside and outside that is resisted not only by practice (by which we mean living, not building) but also by (feminist and decolonial) theory. Both subvert this world and its boundaries through bodies that do not form an impermeable, closed form and with politics that do not simply demand community but coexistence. For us, architecture does not have to decide where bodies end or begin; it can enable intimacy between strangers in concrete situations and for specific moments (see Köçek Pisti) between theory and practice.

INTIMACY

Doesn't the connection between theory and practice refer to intimacy between strangers? An intimacy that means being drawn to beings, things and forms of knowledge that, thought of in binary terms, lie outside, not inside, from which the word "intimate" derives. For us, intimacy with so-called strangers creates liminal spaces beyond the binary of inside and outside (theory and practice), where multifaceted social and architectural configurations can emerge. Where border regimes are challenged. In the (re)production of an in-between space, a collectivity with strangers, lies for us a politics of form.

Like any form of intimacy, the intimacy between theory and practice testifies to the impossibility of a distanced, disembodied rationality and its apparent objectivity. It consists of lived experiences that transcend practical, theoretical, and social contexts. Together and overlapping, intimacy subverts the grand narratives of "techno-patriarchal capitalism" (Paul B. Preciado), in which rationality distances itself from sensitivity to assert objectivity. Such intimacy implies expanded practices, new languages, and thinking and acting out of methodological weakness rather than instrumental mastery, which can make connections between contexts, knowledge, and affects.

Intimacy with strangers can be seen as the realization of a desire that defies given boundaries, norms, and disciplines. In this regard, contemporary changes in intimacy, sexuality, and reproduction are not merely questions of subjectivity or identity but transformative vectors for multiplying differences and for a kind of corporeal or transdisciplinary rationality.

Rational architecture

A rational architecture, seen from this perspective, would not be merely the (causal) response to the immediate social world for which it builds in order to improve it. In this, we side with the autonomous form. For us, however, this has less to do with self-reference and identifying with a (Western classical) typology understood as the essence of architecture. On the contrary, the autonomy of the form opens up possibilities for variation, or more precisely, for creolization, as intimacy with strangers can also be called. For us, rational architecture consists in the recognition that forms reach a design from different (even foreign) places, and that the design is determined by forms before it determines forms. So, for us, the focus is less on the design of the form than on the forms of the design: the concepts, principles, hierarchies, conventions, unexpected convergences, and intimacies that shape it. These forms structure not only the design but our experiences everywhere; they order and exclude, compete and collide, and can redirect each other.

It is clear to us that aesthetic (architectural) and political forms are intertwined and that each of them is capable of disrupting the regulatory power of the others. Therein lies the radical potential: in acts of rearrangement, in which the sensual form is broken open to question the way order is arranged inside it.

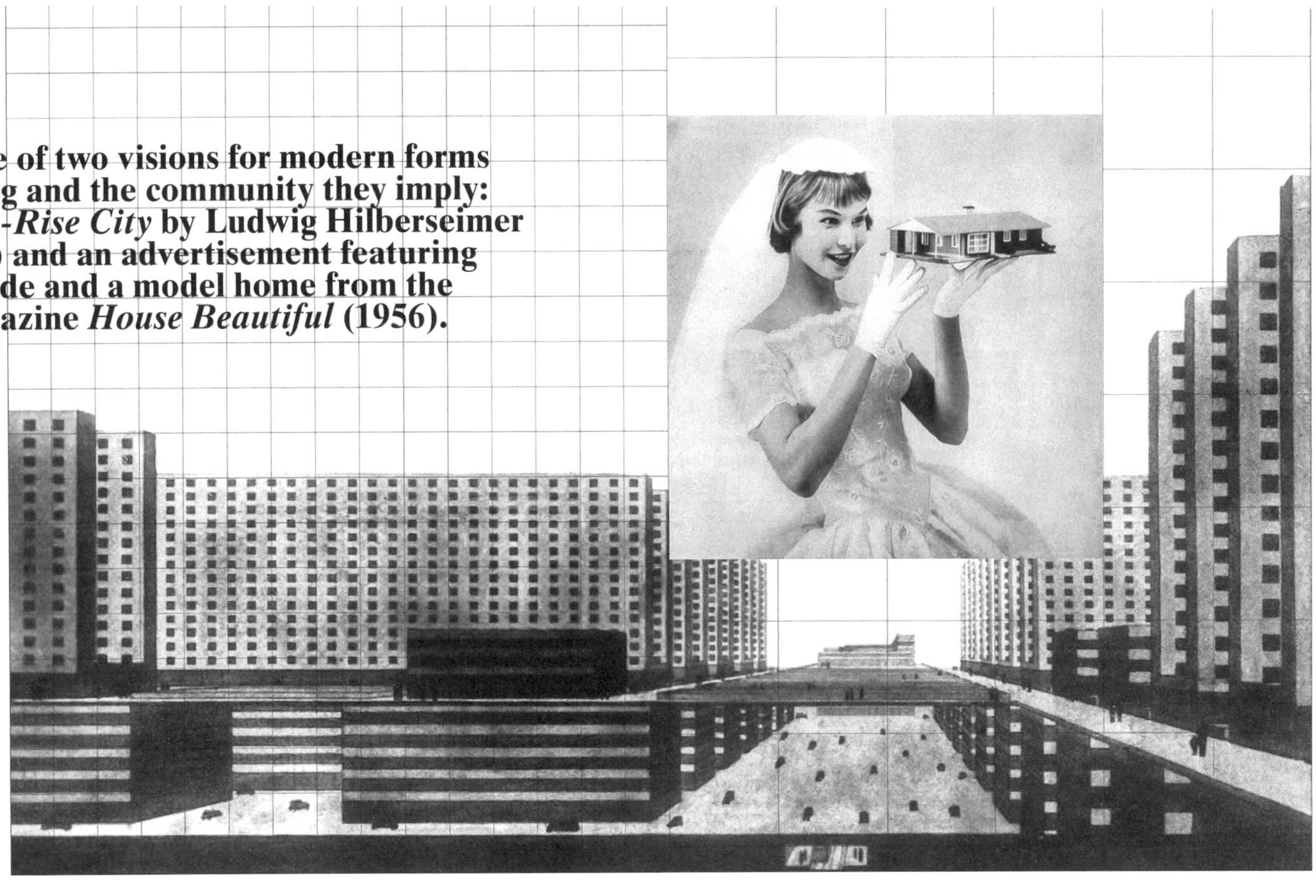

Collage of two visions for modern forms of living and the community they imply: *The High-Rise City* by Ludwig Hilberseimer (1924) and an advertisement featuring a bride and a model home from the magazine *House Beautiful* (1956).

The House Alice Built (2018)

With the installation *The House Alice Built*, which comprises fragments of a speculative excavation site, we refer to a socialist and architectural utopia of early modernism. In 1915, the American architect Alice Constance Austin submitted a development plan with kitchenless houses for a commune in California. The individual kitchens were to be replaced by a community kitchen run by paid professionals. It was not just about freeing women from unpaid and invisible domestic work. Subtracting the kitchen from the body of the building left room for an open patio. These permeable houses foresaw a shift in the social relationships between family members and community members and their surroundings. We understand the subtraction of the kitchen as a strategy of the minor form.

The House Alice Built at *Riverrun: Bunker Exhibitions,* Istanbul. Installation, detailed view: Fragments on tea glasses.

This installation forms a (dance) space within a (museum) space, with video screens relating the history of the so-called *köçek*. These "queer boys" were dancers, at the same time slaves and coveted stars of courtly culture in pre-modern Islamic societies with multiple gender differences. *Köçek* mostly performed for male audiences and used design elements such as long, tiered skirts, tinsel, colorful silks, jewelry, and makeup. Colonial travelers identified the *köçek* as an unmanly, morally objectionable (but desirable) figure of the deviant Orient. With the modernization processes introduced during the Tanzimat period of reform (1839–1876), Ottoman civil and religious authorities adopted the Western heteronormative position and enforced strict censorship of the *köçek*, which persists today through homophobic policies. The installation *Köçek Pisti* was accompanied by weekly DJ sets and invited all visitors and staff to participate in a queer environment: to dance, that is, to mobilize our politically passive bodies.

Köçek Pisti (2016) at Istanbul Design Biennial, *Are We Human?*, installation view of the (dance) space in the (museum) space with a video about the queer dancers. For the weekly DJ sets at the museum, the curtain was opened, and with it, the dance floor.

Köçek Pisti (2016)

Minor form/fragment

We see the potential for greater separations or disruptions, especially in minor forms. With a minor form, everything is political. Political in the sense that everyday, family, or domestic lives and concerns are always linked to larger social issues; that a minor architecture does not take place elsewhere or separate from the larger one but operates out of it—from within—as an intimate stranger. If a minor shape is political, it is because it can open up to the outside more easily. This is why Gilles Deleuze and Félix Guattari perceived Gregor Samsa's "becoming-animal" (shrinking to become an insect) as a political form: it draws a line of flight from marriage, the nuclear family, and the patriarchal order. The character in Franz Kafka's well-known story becomes a pest that hides under the canopy of the family apartment to escape his father (the family). Minor forms, that is, rearranged fragments of larger forms, can subvert dominant categories. They find gaps and dark corners in the dominant scientific, technological, and commercial spaces. They can invent new spaces that enable us to imagine other social organizations of ways of living (see *The House Alice Built*). Minor architecture is based on the forms of different, usually marginalized geographical, cultural, and historical places. We consider both feminist and postcolonial practices and theories to be minor in this sense. They emerge where systems of order already seem established or territories already apparently vacated in order to question and disrupt the associated boundaries. A minor architecture is always collective; it has no great authors. It is collective in that it perceives labor production as already collaborative. It considers labor as an affective body and does not attach subjectivity to the individual (male, rational, white) and his seemingly delimited body. Paradoxically, we can thus understand minor forms as a kind of extension into ways of life that are differently connected, be they individual or social (or even non-human). For us, this is the utopian function of minor architecture: to imagine intimacy transversally, in the co-relation of bodies.

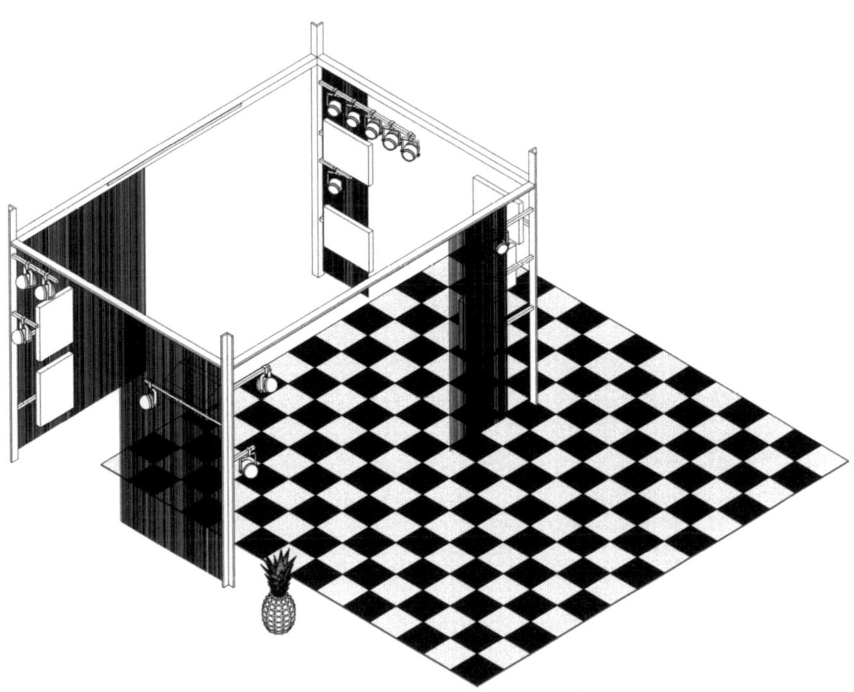

UTOPIA

For us, utopia consists of a plurality of processes, a kind of (theoretical and practical) practice: spatially smaller, not in the future but continued in time. It is politically troubling and negates the idea of a seemingly ideal, universal society that neutralizes bodies, points of view, interests, perspectives, and differences. Utopias are utopias for us when they multiply by making neutralizations visible as such. They are invitations to take up the work of social and aesthetic coexistence and to reject attempts to present our present as approximately normal.

The utopias we are interested in are not about a goal or an ideal place where process or time becomes negligible but, conversely, about a contextual process that deconstructs that goal. Because the goal arises from a dominant present and history, which is only one among many possible stories. For us, utopias lie in practices of architecture that have either been discarded or ignored or never invented or explored: in the foreign, its recognition, or re-adoption. Contrary to any modern attitude, we do not see a gap between the past and the present. The gap is closed by perceiving and actualizing positions that have not yet been perceived by anyone (see the *Feminist Utopian Spaces Lexicon*).

The utopian process can supersede the modern idea of the new as being better and bearing the future, and can render architecture unrecognizable in terms of the forms it is expected to take. With it, we can loosen the disciplinary grip and allow for a non-hierarchical connection of design with political and institutional languages that yield different formations in each project. Perhaps we can also generate diversity, complexity, and contradiction, as described by Denise Scott Brown and Robert Venturi, in the sense of an inclusive process over time, an architectural practice that is at once social, exploratory, and emancipatory.

Practice

Lexicon for Feminist Utopian Spaces (2018–)

The *Lexicon for Feminist Utopian Spaces* is an open-ended, transversal collection of articles that introduce alternative conceptions of space informed by feminist ideas and practices. It serves as a tool to rethink (Bauhaus) modernism, its history and future, its authors, inhabitants, and its discourses from feminist perspectives.

Including the still influential experimental counter-architecture projects around 1968, such as Archigram, Superstudio, and Haus-Rucker-Co, the architectural utopia has not yet been able to free itself from its masculine-paternalist, technopositive, and colonialist views. Women and non-binary persons are entirely absent, as if they would not think in utopian terms. Our lexicon focuses on feminist approaches to reclaiming and redefining utopia.

Structurally, the lexicon represents a mutable archive that can move from a sentence to a text, from a drawing to a floor plan, and from an image to a model. References, parentheses, and speculations play an important role. We are expanding our work to include, in particular, non-Western contributions through collective workshops in Istanbul, Yekaterinburg, São Paulo, Ouagadougou, and other locations.

La Cité des Dames, 1405
Christine de Pizan

Urban utopia of a space occupied and inhabited by women, without a final state or fixed rules and characterized by processuality. Written about 100 years before Thomas More's *Utopia*, the book addresses the *querelle des femmes* (women's question), which, unlike the *querelle des anciens et des modernes* (quarrel of the ancients and the moderns, Charles Perrault), continues worldwide to this day.

Master of the City of Ladies: Detail from *Livre de la cité des dames* (Book of the City of Ladies).

Dauerwelle, since 2018
Aslı Serbest, Mona Mahall

Passenger ship from the 1960s converted into a nomadic art space. This is less an art container that can be visited than an act of visiting itself. The name *Dauerwelle* (permanent wave) refers to its feminist agenda (and the hairstyle) and its confrontation with static institutional thinking, fixed spatial conditions, and organizational structures.

Collage and axonometry of the reconstruction. © Serbest/Mahall.

Alpha 7, 1968
Film by Roger Vadim

Alpha 7 is the spaceship in which Barbarella travels through the universe in the year 4000 AD. The "feminine" place in space exposes gender stereotypes, masculinized space travel, and techno-utopian narratives. In response to Adolf Loos's bedroom, the cockpit is furnished with (faux) fur, and the pilot operates her flight instruments from a bed embedded in the floor.

Collage: Serbest/Mahall; photo of the Loos bedroom. © MAK, *Barbarella* film still. © IMAGO/Allstar.

Cookbook, 1954
Alice B. Toklas

Recipe collection and report on the events of World War II and their consequences for the public space of the metropolis. The book contains a recipe for "space cakes," intended to expand space and consciousness, and more effective than the *Mind Expander* by Haus-Rucker-Co 15 years later.

Space Cake Sketch. © Serbest/Mahall.

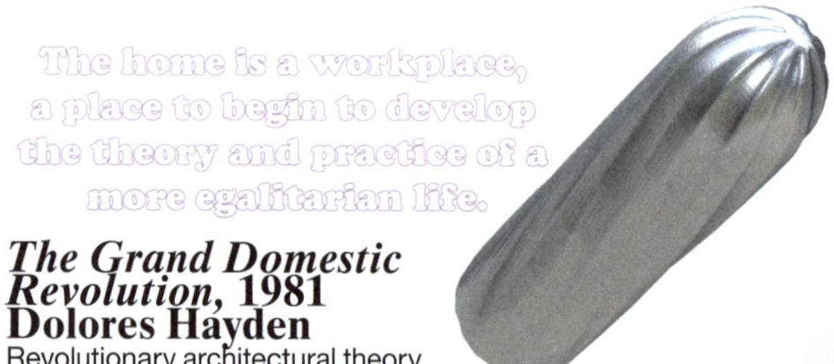

The Grand Domestic Revolution, 1981
Dolores Hayden

Revolutionary architectural theory (after 2,000 years of writing about architecture) on the domestic environment and life and its reorganization by feminist thinkers, designers, and activists around 1900.

Collage. © Serbest/Mahall.

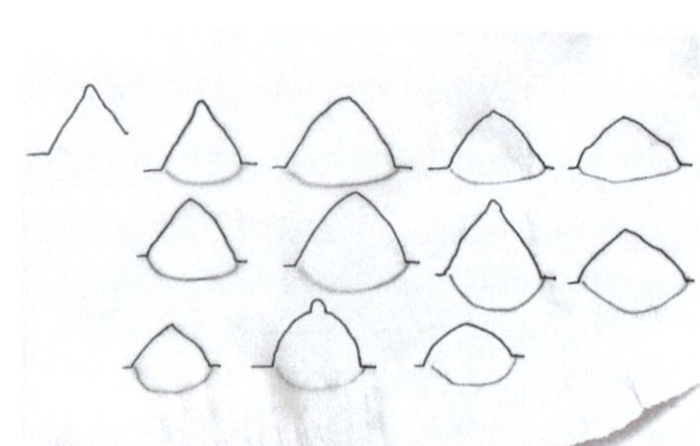

Airless Spaces, 1970/1998
Shulamith Firestone

Climate capsules, similar to dome-like cooling rooms below the deck of a (sinking) ocean liner, but which warm rather than cool. They replace the airless space of the female uterus to enable reproduction outside the biological female body.

Dome sketches. © Serbest/Mahall.

Dover Sun House, 1948
Maria Telkes, Eleanor Raymond

First solar-heated passive house with a pent roof, built in Boston, which has received little attention. Nearby and around the same time, Walter Gropius in Cambridge elevated the Bauhaus to the International Style without addressing environmental or energy issues.

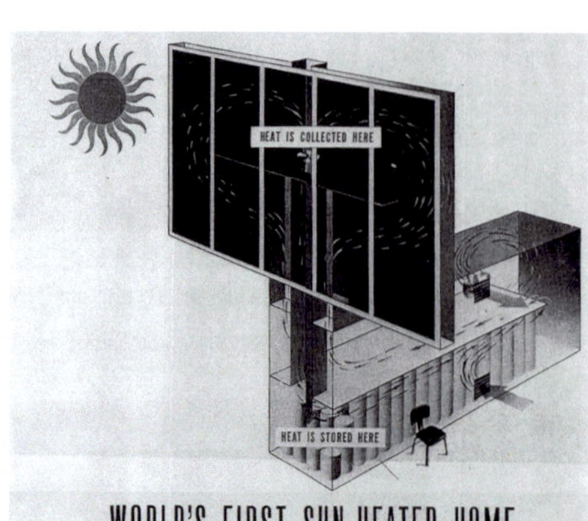

Unisex Uniform, 1923
Varvara Stepanova

Designs for white shirts and dark striped pants with a "central core" (Judy Chicago, 1977) depicting a vaginal shape. As a second skin (architecture is the third), the androgynous uniform minimizes natural differences between bodies and imagines the classless and genderless body.

Collage: Varvara Stepanova /Janelle Monáe. © Serbest/Mahall.

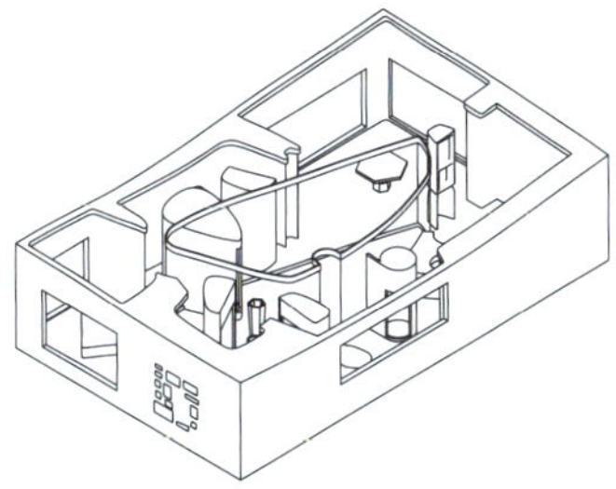

House of the Future, 1956
Alison Smithson

Design of an ideal home, a prototype housing unit made of plastic composite material, anticipating the way of life of the future. Residents are surrounded by technical installations that allow them to perform housework "at the push of a button."

Model and drawing. © Serbest/Mahall.

Jinwar, since 2017
Free Women's Village (Kurdish women's movement)

An independent community settlement that follows jineology (the science of women) and free living. The ecological village is located in the center of Rojava (Western Kurdistan or Northern Syria) and is currently under construction.

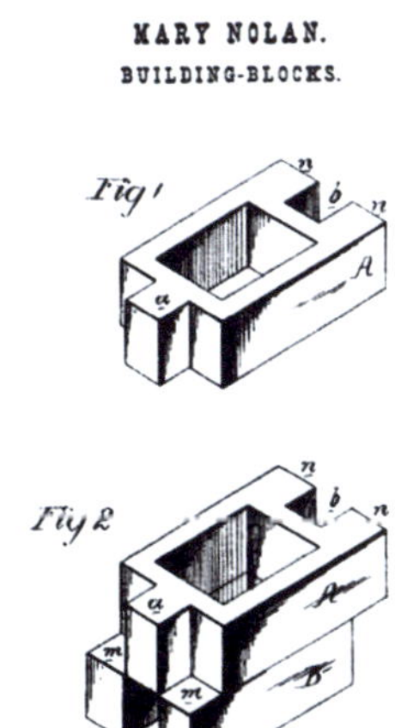

Nolanum, 1876
Mary Nolan

Award-winning, refractory hollow brick made from a blend of Missouri clay, which can be interlocked and joined to form walls. Their connection is virtually seamless, so plastering is unnecessary.

Lesbian Garden, from 1905
Jeanne Ghyka

Part of Villa Gamberaia, near Florence. The redesigned garden offers the homosexual community a protected space for their meetings. With it, the classical association of nature and female eroticism is reclaimed and re-established in aesthetic practice.

© Minneapolis Institute of Arts.

Self-Cleaning House, 1984
Frances Gabe

Patented invention made from 68 parts that the house can use to clean and dry itself. It represents a truly liberating counterpart to the Frankfurt kitchen.

Model with bellows. © Serbest/Mahall.

Цирkеннале [Circus: Circus+Biennial], 2021
Alice Hualic, Lolja Nordic, Xenia Peshekhonova, Natalia Tikhonova, Aslı Serbest, Mona Mahall

Campaign for animal rights and utopian institutional critique in Russia on the occasion of the use of the Yekaterinburg State Circus as a venue for the 6th Ural Biennial. There is a demand to end the exploitative and deadly circus business worldwide, and to turn circus spaces into retirement homes for circus animals and people.

Collage with the Yekaterinburg Circus. © Serbest/Mahall.

Kitchenless House, 1885
Marie Howland and Alice Constance Austin, 1915

Plans for kitchenless house typologies in cooperative communities near Topolobampo, Mexico, and Palmdale, California. Both communities have a socialist administration that opposes privatization and land speculation and works for equality and the economy of labor, raw materials, and space.

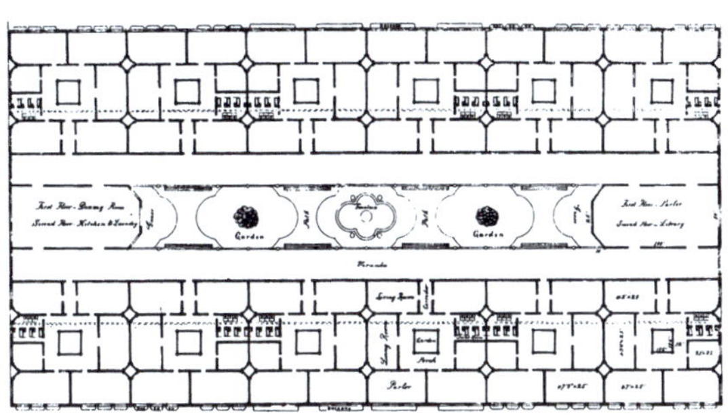

Eileen Gray, *Untitled*, c. 1930.
Courtesy Eileen Gray Estate.

Queering Architecture Histories

For decades, the architecture historian Beatriz Colomina has restlessly challenged dominant narratives about modern architecture by meticulously deconstructing the public and private lives of the heroes of the modern movement. Since the 1990s, her irreverent academic contribution has introduced topics of sexuality, privacy, perversion, and illness into the mainstream architectural discourse. For this ARCH+ issue, she engaged in conversation with the architect and theorist Katarina Bonnevier, whose explorations of the spatial dimension of queerness transcend a narrow definition of architecture to encompass the fields of design, theater, art, and critical theory.

Beatriz Colomina in conversation with Katarina Bonnevier about the queering of architecture history, the use of labels, and the challenges faced by feminist architecture practice today.

KATARINA BONNEVIER: Beatriz, your work has been a huge source of inspiration throughout my career. As a student, all the queerness that I could lay my hands on in architecture theory was very masculine. Take, for example, Aaron Betsky's seminal work *Queer Space: Architecture and Same-Sex Desire*; he only spends two lines talking about lesbian spaces.[01] This was a very important book for me, and yet, at the time, it was hurtful to see that women didn't seem to take part in that discourse. And then, one day, Catharina Gabrielsson, a dear colleague of mine, pointed me towards a passage from your book *Privacy and Publicity,* in which you talk about Adolf Loos's *Ornament and Crime*:

> "And what of modern woman? The figure of modernity for Loos, as for most writers of modernity, is emphatically male. Women and children are 'primitive,' 'ignoble savages,' as distinct from the heroic figure of modern man as primitive 'noble savage.' [...] The ornament, which for 'the child, the Papuan and the woman' is a 'natural phenomenon,' for modern man is a 'symptom of degeneration.' [...] And when this 'degeneration' becomes clearly identified as homosexuality, Loos's raid against ornament is not only gender-loaded but openly homophobic."[02]

Reading this as a young queer woman who was trying to find her place in a largely male-dominated architecture system was very important. I would like to start our conversation from this quote and ask you how topics like gender and femininity first came to intersect queerness in your research as an architecture historian.

BEATRIZ COLOMINA: *Privacy and Publicity* was first published in 1994. Not many people know this, but it was my PhD dissertation. *Sexuality and Space* was published even before that.[03] When I arrived at Princeton, in 1988, at my first faculty meeting, I looked around and immediately realized that sitting at the table with me were only men. When I remarked that I was the only woman in the room, they said, "True, but it's the same everywhere, isn't it?" "No," I said, "I was at Columbia University before, and it's not the same there." That was in November. Robert Maxwell, who was dean at the time, had a pot of money which we either had to use by the following March or lose it. He said, "Beatriz, why don't you organize a conference?" That's the story of how *Sexuality and Space* came about. It was a kind of "dare to" situation. I was still very young and had three months to organize my first conference. That was also when I started realizing that there was a widespread internalized homophobia in architecture culture that nobody was addressing. And when I say nobody, I mean really nobody. Aaron Betsky's book *Queer Space* only came out in 1997. The *Sexuality and Space* conference was in 1990. The exhibition, with the same title, *Queer Space*, which I co-organized at Storefront for Art and Architecture in New York, was in 1994. Storefront had asked me to do an exhibition based on *Sexuality and Space*, but I said, "No, not again; more than two years have passed—we have to move forward." So I proposed the topic of queer space. That was the first time I named it. The other organizers included Eve Kosofsky Sedgwick, whom I invited to be part of the team. She had written the book *Epistemology of the Closet*,[04] and I had already invited her to Princeton to give a lecture. But even before that, I had a critical sense that my quest was not only a matter of gender but of sexuality at large. This is why—partly inspired by Jacqueline Rose—I chose the name *Sexuality and Space* and not, for example, "architecture and gender" or "women and architecture." When I arrived at Princeton, a first restructuring of the curriculum was already partially underway. In the English faculty, you had people like Diana Fuss, who was putting together transformative lesbian and gay studies, but architecture was relatively slow to catch up. Initially, I thought it would pick up very fast, but it didn't. It took a long time before these topics reached a big audience.

The quote about *Ornament and Crime* you mentioned must be placed in this context. You have to remember that I was still writing my PhD when I wrote it. I was not even an assistant professor yet. The quote should be understood as a spontaneous first encounter with a topic that was relatively new to me. Since then, my research has become charged with many more questions. For example: was Loos's homophobia real or staged? Why does a man so obsessed with his own outfits have such strong opinions about the outfits of other men, like Joseph Hoffman, which he describes as too feminine? Why, while very publicly expressing appreciation for glamorous and successful women like Josephine Baker, does he get married three times to girls who are little more than adolescents? In 2015, *Der Fall Loos*[05] brought to the surface new information that was largely ignored before: that Adolf Loos was convicted for pederasty. Apparently, he used to seduce little kids in the Prater and take them back to his apartment. Seen in this light, Loos's misogynist and homophobic statements seem to reveal new deep and complex layers of his personality that until then were completely hidden behind the theatrical and heroic public figure.

KB: I personally get somehow irritated when people try to bring back Loos as this fundamental canon against which to measure someone's work. Many times, I asked myself: Why? Why should we still spend so much time talking about this man? Why is *Ornament and Crime* still a topic in architecture history if we know that the text is so explicitly misogynist and homophobic? Instead, what I try to do with my students is to go further back in history and put other works in the spotlight, like those of Eileen Gray, for example, whose designs were a source of inspiration for Loos himself, as well as for Le Corbusier, Frank Lloyd Wright, and other so-called "masters" of the modern movement. This way, I wish to trick the canon and deconstruct the male-dominated narrative we have become so accustomed to in architecture history.

BC: There are multiple ways of undoing the patriarchal structures behind dominant architectural discourse. One way, like you say, is to shift the focus to lesser-known female and queer protagonists like Eileen Gray. Another way is to hit right at the core by exposing what lurks behind the myth of the masters. This is what I was suggesting before with my reassessment of *Ornament and Crime*: that there is a complexity and a vulnerability hidden behind the public figure of Adolf Loos which is largely overlooked—or explicitly denied—by architectural discourse. In my view, the simplistic reading that has been made of *Ornament and Crime* is based on a refusal to acknowledge the complexity of Loos' own identity. Of course, here we are talking about a white man, but the same refusal could be directed toward a person of color or someone who identifies as a woman or as queer. I want to talk about Loos to my students because I want to present his case

> “Every work of architecture is a deeply collaborative enterprise, but we work so hard to deny it.”
> **– Beatriz Colomina**

as a symptom of what architectural discourse generally does to the complexities of identity: it denies them. I find this more productive than not talking about Loos because if you don't talk about him, the discourse will continue, with or without you, and the complexities will remain forever buried under the surface. But if you hit right at the core, you might find that a deep vulnerability lies behind the myth of the heroic masters or that the masters are themselves queer in some way or another, even if they are straight men.

Another strategy would be to talk more about collaborations, which is to say: Look, there are plenty of women out there. There have always been, but all too often, they stay in the background because the dominant narrative favors the idea of the individual martyr genius. So many women who played key roles have been systematically thrown out with the bathwater. Every work of architecture is a deeply collaborative enterprise, but we work so hard to deny it. Designing a building is much closer to making a movie than producing a work of art in the traditional sense. There are so many people involved at all stages of the creative process, and this is something we can expose with our work as historians.

KB: Absolutely. I myself am working in a collaborative practice called MYCKET. We don't necessarily commit to architecture with the big A but combine architectural design with theater, film, and art. One of our core values is that whatever we produce, we always put our own bodies into the product, which I believe conceptually is a very queer, feminist way of doing things because we start from the principle that one's own body is the key to how you experience the world. For example, when we designed a public beach, in order to understand specific local needs, we went swimming there with the people we were designing the space for. How could we find out unless we went swimming together? Of course, while doing this, we also found out many more things that didn't have anything to do with swimming, but that helped us understand what needed to be done to make the place more inclusive.

BC: That's a very bodily way of being collaborative. I was thinking of less material understandings of collaboration, such as intellectual or creative collaborations. Architecture is always a product of multiple overlapping and interacting forms of collaboration. This is why I am interested in the characters behind the heroic narration of modernity, you know, people like lovers, gay partners, clients, employees, consultants, critics, publishers … These people contributed with their material labor but also their intellectual, creative, and technological input. And the collaborating agents in any scene are not only human bodies and brains but also systems, technologies, software, protocols, etc. The very concept and even the sensual reality of the body are changed in all this. The body changes ideas, and ideas change the body, and I am interested in that confusion, that plasticity.

KB: True; nevertheless, I would like to stay in the material dimension and continue to talk about bodies. In particular, I would like to talk about the body of the architect. In 2012, I wrote an article analyzing the design of Mårbacka—the iconic 20th-century Swedish manor house that Nobel Prize–winner Selma Lagerlöf staged for her queer lifestyle—in terms of drag. I used the term “cross-cladding,” a combination

In 1909, the Swedish writer Selma Lagerlöf was the first woman to receive the Nobel Prize in Literature. She repurchased her childhood home in Mårbacka (painting by Christoffer Wallroth) in 1907–10 and transformed it into a stately manor house with a portico and mansard roof (photo below).

of cross-dressing and cladding, as a way to describe architectural design as a complex, layered, and manifold performance of gender and sexuality.[06] Similarly, in your works, you have talked about the image of themselves that architects project when, for example, they do physical exercise or design a mansion supposedly modeled around a neutral genderless figure, which in fact is a young, athletic male body.

BC: Yes, the body of the architect is a work of architecture itself. Architects perform a kind of "bodybuilding," real or metaphorical, as an act of identity construction. It's a kind of artificial body. This is something I am especially interested in right now because I am working on a project about architecture and epidemics and, more generally, about the relationship between architecture and sick bodies. During my research, I discovered that many famous architects have been affected by illnesses they don't talk about. Loos's health was extremely fragile. He had syphilis at a very young age and suffered from progressive hearing loss. That's why he went around with a big trumpet. Later in life, his stomach, appendix, and part of his intestine were removed due to cancer. Right at the beginning of his career, Le Corbusier lost sight completely in one eye. Can you imagine? A man with one eye and another who is almost completely deaf; these are the heroes of modern architecture! The list continues: Richard Neutra had tuberculosis and suffered multiple nervous breakdowns. That's why he was interested in preventing tuberculosis with his architecture—the architect as a doctor. Once streptomycin was discovered as a treatment for tuberculosis, he shifted to the idea of the architect as a kind of psychoanalyst and the house as a form of therapy. Alvar Aalto was very sick just before he designed the Paimio sanatorium. He claimed that being in bed for such a long time was very important for his understanding of the problem. There is a beautiful sketch in which he shows how architecture is always conceived for the vertical person, but when you have to design a space for someone who is constantly lying horizontal, the whole architecture has to change.[07] The top half of the drawing shows a vertical figure standing in a regular room with a light on the ceiling, and the bottom half shows a figure lying in bed. The sketch shows how the room was designed for the vertical person. But from the irritation of having a direct light shining in your eyes from the ceiling if you have to lay in bed all day, to the air circulation and heating system, and the view of the landscape outside the window, everything should be rethought from the perspective of this horizontal body. Aalto even argued that architects should always design for the person in the weakest position, which is, if you think about it, an extraordinary statement and so at odds with the athletic white body male endlessly redrawn, from Renaissance treatises to modern architecture manifestos, from Leonardo to Le Corbusier.

So, you see, these architects have always been described as heroes, but look closer and you discover that the heroic bodies they worked so hard to construct during their careers were actually very fragile, sick bodies. One might even think that all these efforts they put into producing an image of a healthy, exercised body were, in fact, some kind of cover-up to hide the fact that their bodies were not healthy at all.

GUEST EDITORS (CMB): Beatriz, I would like to know more about your idea of what a queer or feminist spatial practice should look like today, also in light of a broader call for an intersectional approach in all cultural fields.

BC: I think that the question of intersectionality is not new. This is something that was already very present in the 1990s—how to integrate questions of gender and sexuality with questions of race and colonialism and understand the unique, often unacknowledged, specificity of each intersection. I do not have an example of a best practice or a definition of a queer or feminist way of practicing architecture. There are many ways

In her research paper "Dress-Code: Gender Performance and Misbehavior in the Manor" (2012), Katarina Bonnevier describes the strictly representative architecture of the manor house serving as a patriarchal facade and masquerade, a "cross-cladding" behind which Lagerlöf lived a life of companionship with her lovers, friends, and employees, far removed from heteronormative standards. © Mårbacka.

of undoing patriarchal structures, and they are all very valuable. There are many deeply transgressive feminist practices, theories and histories that never used the word "feminism" at all. I myself have avoided using the term all my career precisely because if you do, you are dismissed immediately. Nowadays, it is a little bit less so, but generally speaking, if you start by saying, "I am a feminist architecture historian," people immediately put you in a box. Once again, the complexity of your identity or identities is immediately dismissed. That is why I was never interested in that label or any label. There are many incredibly transgressive practices that are feminist and queer; nevertheless, they don't label themselves as such. They are just who and what they are. When you go back historically, they didn't even have the terms, but we do. We can use these labels to describe past works that were not necessarily recognized as queer or feminist in the context in which they were created. The queering of architecture history has yet to happen.

KB: Of course, queerness and feminism are not something you can put solely at the margins; they are also in the midst of the mainstream and the understanding of a specific work as queer depends on the definitions of norms and normativity relative to the context in which the work was created. In this sense, I don't think that the queering of architecture history has yet to happen. I think it has happened and is still happening, but it depends on the perspective from which you look. It depends on where you are situated in the world. Take, for example, Jean Badovici's editorial work at *L'Architecture Vivante* or the contributions by Eileen Gray in the same magazine, which was already queer in the 1920s.

BC: Yes, but only if you read it so retroactively. When I started writing about Eileen Gray, no one even knew she was lesbian. People largely ignored the complexity of her relationship with Jean Badovici. In the 1920s, Gray's work was widely recognized because it was published in all the magazines of the time, especially in France and the Netherlands, but after the Second World War, it fell into oblivion. It would be interesting to analyze what role Le Corbusier—who was a close friend of both Gray and Badovici—played in all of this. It was only in 1972 that Gray's work reemerged, after one of her lacquer screens reached a stellar price at an auction in Paris of a furniture collection. Before that, the only academic text ever published about Gray was an article by Joseph Rykwert in *Domus* in 1966, followed in 1971 by his article in *Perspecta*: "Eileen Gray: Two Houses and an Interior."[08] There was nothing else. She was completely ignored by all major histories of modern architecture and is even absent in the more recent ones, like Kenneth Frampton's or Alan Colquhoun's. I agree with you that the queering of architecture history is an ongoing process, but I would not say that it has been happening for a long time. I see it as a relatively recent process that has started to unfold in the last 30 years and is opening countless new perspectives on the history of modern architecture.

GUEST EDITORS (GS): You said that if you used the label "feminist," they would immediately put you in a box, but nowadays, it is less and less so. If you were to set up a new edition of *Sexuality and Space* today, what would it look like? Would questions of intersectionality and feminism be more explicitly in the foreground?

BC: I wouldn't do a new conference on the topic today. It was a great experience that had an enormous impact. Every time *Sexuality and Space* was reprinted, I couldn't believe my eyes. The way it went all over the world was really a surprise. It also generated a tremendous response from other authors and scholars, and now it stands on its own. But in the meantime, the questions have changed. That was a moment when I felt that sexuality was something that had to be discussed in architecture, so I reached out to people who were already developing a similar discourse in other fields, like Laura Mulvey, Meaghan Morris, and Liz Gross, who took part in the original project. Ever since, people have asked me, "Why don't you organize *Sexuality and Space 2*?" They all want a sequel, like in the movies, but no, there is no sequel. I am happy with the momentum that *Sexuality and Space* generated in the 1990s, and I have enormous confidence that the next generation will write their own chapter with new questions, new topics, etc. That's also why I like teaching so much. Every year new students come in with different questions and different viewpoints. My role as an educator is to take all this potential and facilitate the work of the next generation that is yet to emerge.

KB: Personally, when I think of the profound systemic changes we are experiencing today, the ways in which the pandemic has affected democracies worldwide, for example, or the challenges posed by climate change, I would suggest that a new conference about sexuality and space should also include non-human actors. In a future threatened by the absence of other species, questions of sexuality should be more than just human.

BC: Yes, definitely. This was, of course, the very point of our extended *Are We Human?* project and is going further with our new work on trans-species collaboration that rethinks figures like the brilliant Lina Bo Bardi.[09] There are countless queer and feminist practices today, with or without the label, that challenge existing systems of power and raise new interesting questions about sexuality, but one very important thing for me is that, however these practices operate, we must not forget that being a feminist is not a moral imperative, a singular self-assured direction, but a multitude of questions. Whatever shape queer and feminist architecture practices will take in the future, it cannot be singular. It should be collaborative, including and producing multiple histories and strategies. We don't know yet what the big systemic changes will bring us, but not knowing sometimes is good because it leaves room for optimism. Personally, I am looking forward to the surprising, shocking, and beautiful new set of discoveries that will transform all of us. I am an incurable optimist by nature.

TEAM
Guest editors: Charlotte Malterre-Barthes (CMB) and Gabrielle Schaad (GS);
ARCH+: Mirko Gatti, Franziska Gödicke, Melissa Makele.

01 **Aaron Betsky, *Queer Space: Architecture and Same-Sex Desire* (New York, NY: William Morrow, 1997).**
02 **Beatriz Colomina, *Privacy and Publicity: Modern Architecture as Mass Media* (Cambridge, MA: MIT Press, 1994), 37–38.**
03 **Beatriz Colomina, ed., *Sexuality and Space* (Hudson, NY: Princeton Architectural Press, 1992).**
04 **Eve Kosofsky Sedgwick, *Epistemology of the Closet* (Oakland, CA: University of California Press, 1990).**
05 **Christopher Long, *Der Fall Loos* (Vienna: Amalthea Signum, 2015).**
06 **Katarina Bonnevier, "Dress-code: Gender Performance and Misbehavior in the Manor," *Gender, Place & Culture: A Journal of Feminist Geography* 19, no. 6 (2012): 1–23.**
07 **Drawing by Alvar Aalto illustrating his article "The Humanizing of Architecture," *The Technology Review*, November 1940.**
08 **Joseph Rykwert, "Eileen Gray: Two Houses and an Interior, 1926–1933," *Perspecta* 13/14 (1971): 66–73.**
09 **Beatriz Colomina and Mark Wigley, *Are We Human? Notes on an Archeology of Design* (Zurich: Lars Muller, 2016).**

The ideal of the (healthy) body and its place in modern architecture, pictured here in Richard Döcker's single-family home in the Weissenhof estate (Weißenhofsiedlung) in Stuttgart, ca. 1926. Scan from Richard Döcker's book *Terrassentyp: Krankenhaus, Erholungsheim, Hotel, Bürohaus, Einfamilienhaus, Siedlungshaus, Miethaus und die Stadt* (Stuttgart: F. Wedekind, 1929).

11

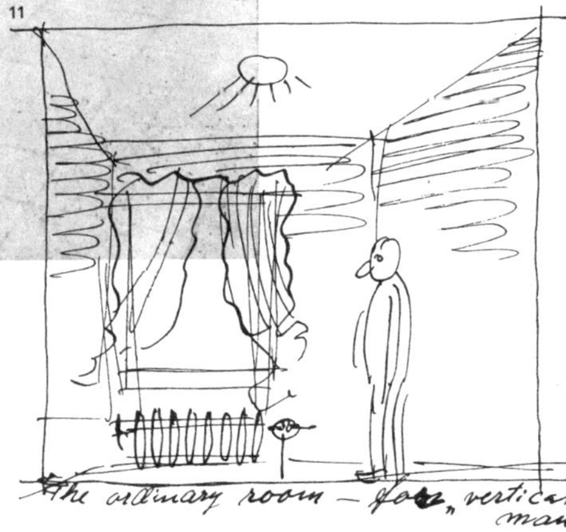

"The body of the architect": Le Corbusier and his cousin, Pierre Jeanneret, boxing on the beach, 1933.

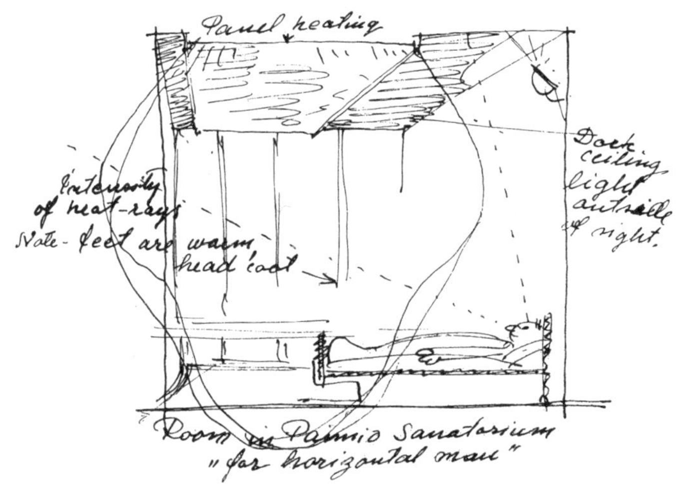

Sketch by Alvar Aalto for an "ordinary room" for a "vertical person" (top) and a room at the Paimio Sanatorium for a non-healthy "horizontal human being" (bottom). From Alvar Aalto, "The Humanizing of Architecture," *The Technology Review*, November 1940. Courtesy Alvar Aalto Foundation.

Eileen Gray, *Intérieurs français*, 1922. Boudoir de Monte Carlo presented at the 14th Salon des Artistes Décorateurs, 1923. Eileen Gray designed the interior of E.1027 herself. She had already made studies in the early 1920s for some of the (built-in) furniture and the room divider. Courtesy Gilles Peyroulet & Cie, Paris.

Eileen Gray's design for a room divider in black lacquered wood.
Courtesy Misia Arte Bari.

"[Q]ueerness and feminism are not something you can put solely at the margins; they are also in the midst of the mainstream and the understanding of a specific work as queer depends on the definitions of norms and normativity relative to the context in which the work was created."
– Katarina Bonnevier

In 1926–29 the Irish architect and designer Eileen Gray designed E.1027, a villa for herself and her then companion Jean Badovici in Roquebrune-Cap-Martin, Côte d'Azur. The building's design was long falsely attributed to Le Corbusier; Gray was only recognized as its official architect and designer in 2000. © National Museum of Ireland.

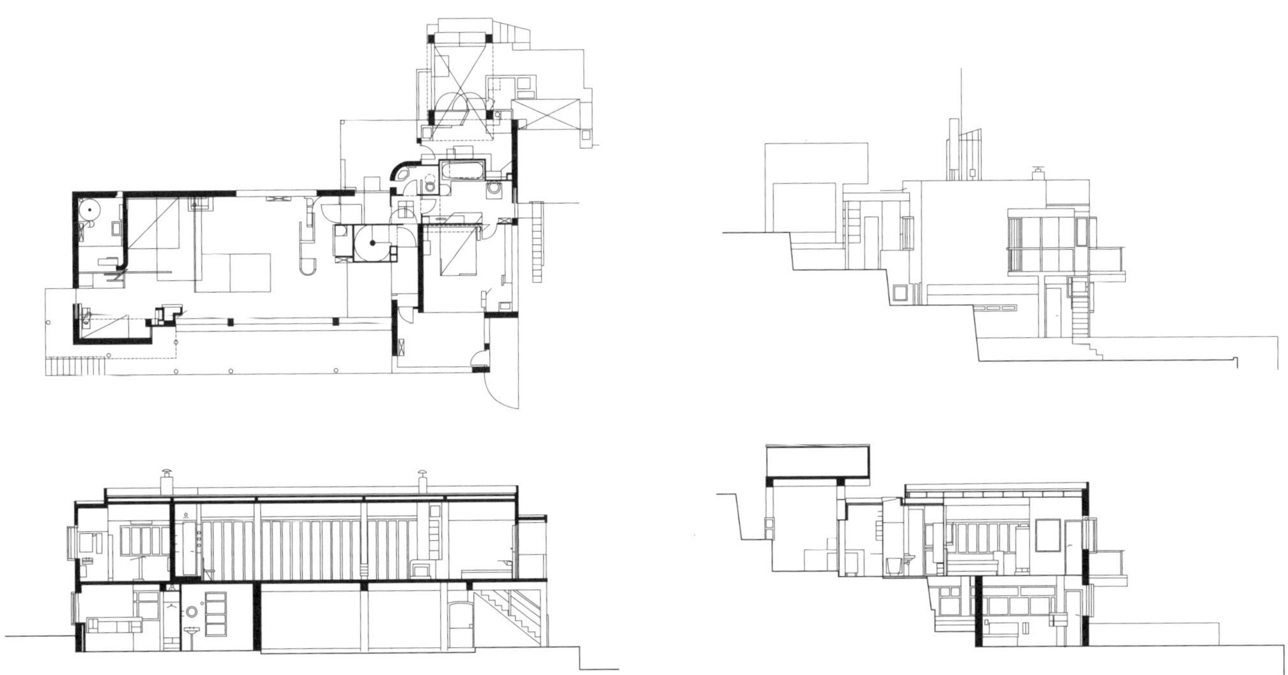

Eileen Gray, E.1027, 1926–29, floor plan, sections, elevation. The long, narrow building has a front terrace with a view of the sea and an open floor plan. The only fixed walls are between the common areas and the private rooms. Courtesy Claire Ludewigs, Mark Cooper, and Emmeily Zhang, University of Waterloo, 2012.

Practice

MYCKET Collaboration

TEAM: Mariana Alves Silva, Katarina Bonnevier, Thérèse Kristiansson
LOCATION: Stockholm
FOUNDED: 2012

Courtesy *Girls Like Us.*

Cover of the Belgian queer feminist magazine *Girls Like Us*, for which MYCKET was guest editor in 2021. In the special issue, the collective presents its research on the history of queer nightclub architecture. Courtesy *Girls Like Us.*

TEXT
MYCKET

As the art and architecture collective MYCKET, we have been working with spaces of repair, sharing, and learning in different ways since 2012. We engage in dialogue and practice of intersecting perspectives, positionings, and experiences—queer, feminist, class-, anti-racist, more-than-human.[01] In addition to (re-)designing permanent public spaces, our interdisciplinary projects include theater and performance, exhibitions, animations, text and theory production, and educational activities, to name just a few.

In our work, we develop and apply methods that are both critical and constructive. Building on a wealth of references, we never try to make a copy or a direct reenactment but rather a critical fiction. We consider normative narratives of history inadequate. Instead, we favor thought experiments and imaginary worlds. As Gloria Anzaldúa noted in 1987, "Nothing happens in the 'real' world unless it first happens in the images in our heads."[02]

We are firmly rooted in the study of gender and space, which makes itself felt in the topics we work on and how we work. There is a didactic element in our careful handling of public design issues and our efforts to take responsibility for the spatial situations we create. This, in turn, opens up space for constructive and reparative criticism. We practice non-violent communication striving for respect and connectedness. We practice "staying with the trouble," as Donna Haraway puts it.[03] We support development processes based on attempts, mistakes, and detours.

What this didactic attitude means for our artistic practice is perhaps best explained by a method we call DIG. Instead of DIY (do it yourself), our approach is "doing in group"—a collaborative practice where everyone's contribution remains visible in the details and as part of the whole. In the beginning, no one knows how it will turn out.

Struggleoke is a pop-up karaoke bar that MYCKET installed in front of the Royal Palace in Stockholm in 2019 as part of the *Choreographies of the Social* festival. © Ricard Estay.

By featuring only protest songs in the karaoke sessions, the collective drew attention to historical and contemporary civil rights struggles. © Ricard Estay.

From 2016 to 2020, MYCKET developed the project *The Ball Cap* at the invitation of the Swedish Public Art Agency, which was created in the Jönköping district of Råslätt in collaboration with various local groups.
All photos: © Ricard Estay.

The project features an oversized baseball cap that serves as the roof of a fully equipped public dance studio. The aim was to provide a space for the mostly female members of the local Mix Dancer's Academy and other interested parties to complement the many outdoor sports opportunities used mainly by local boys and men.

“We practice ‘staying with the trouble,’ as Donna Haraway puts it.”

It is a shared process of finding out through materialization. We first developed this method in 2016 in our project *Dream Castles: When We Build the City We Want to Live In*, in which sewing circles created large inflatable pavilions from recycled umbrellas, plastic bags, and sails. We continued this approach in Sweden with *The Grotto of the Naiads* (2018), a pedestrian tunnel for the municipality of Haninge, and with *The Ball Cap* (2020), a new public space in Råslätt, a district of Jönköping, in the course of which we collectively renovated the open village stage and created a new dance pavilion in collaboration with the local Mix Dancer's Academy.

In early 2021, we concluded our research project, *The Club Scene*, on the history of queer nightclub architecture, conducted over nearly nine years. We summarized our work as guest editors of a special issue of the cultural journal *Girls Like Us*, titled “When Walls Speak.” In our latest artistic research project, *Troll Perceptions in the Heartlands: Artistic Research to Widen our Imagination Capacity*, we turn to folktales and legends and the perception of trolls, fairies, and other creatures to investigate our relationship to nature and explore new ways of designing and living for the future.

01 See also María Puig de la Bellacasa, *Matters of Care: Speculative Ethics in More Than Human Worlds* (Minneapolis, MN: University of Minnesota Press, 2017).
02 Gloria Anzaldúa, *Borderlands / La Frontera: The New Mestiza* (San Francisco, CA: Aunt Lute, 1987), 87.
03 Donna Haraway, *Staying with the Trouble: Making Kin in the Chthulucene* (Durham, NC: Duke University Press, 2016).

Together with the children and youth of Råslätt, MYCKET renovated the district's open stage.

Intervention

The Restroom Pavilion

Your Restroom Is a Battleground

Matilde Cassani,
Ignacio G. Galán,
Iván L. Munuera with
Leonardo Gatti,
Pablo Saiz del Rio,
Joel Sanders,
Paula Vilaplana de Miguel

Urban sites of structural interdependency related to sanitary infrastructure are marked with corresponding flags. In this way, the city itself becomes an exhibition space.

Drawing by Pablo Saiz del Rio.

Toilets are not neutral spaces. The question of who can use which toilet is the result of political discourses and social norms, whether through racist segregation in historical apartheid systems or the kind of gender-specific separation still in force today. This also applies to the portable toilets at the Venice Architecture Biennale, which testify to the barriers inherent to binary gender separation in a cis-heteronormative social system.

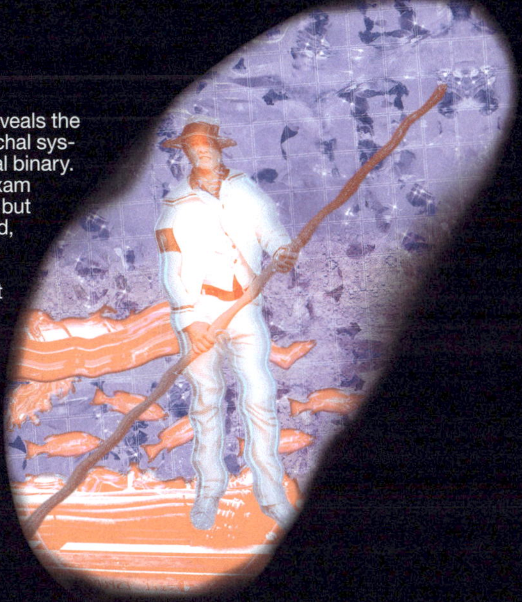

The case of Alex Hai reveals the extent to which patriarchal systems enforce the sexual binary. In 2007, Hai took the exam to become a gondolier but was repeatedly rejected, apparently because of his transgender. He is contesting a policy that dates back to the year 1094, in which the professional guild of gondoliers only allows cis-male candidates.

Differences in the construction of women's and men's toilets are by no means functionally necessary. Instead, the distinction between cubicles and urinals involves idealizations: femininity goes along with discretion maintained by opaque partitions, with users acting as singular individuals. On the other hand, public urination while standing describes the preferred constitution of heterosexual masculinity. For this reason, men's restrooms are spaces where men can connect in sexual complicity.[01] Precisely because toilets are such stages for performative sexuality, they can also be a venue for fears of people outside the norm, where those people might experience exclusion. These include non-binary, homosexual, and trans people and people with disabilities, as well as people with different cultural and religious understandings of hygiene, who are rarely taken into account in the design of those spaces. Moreover, the norm in this context has received little critical reflection. This is exactly where the intervention of the group around Matilde Cassani, Ignacio G. Galán, and Iván L. Munuera at the Architecture Biennale comes in.

With their *Restroom Pavilion*, the group redefined the toilet building at the Giardini, doing away with all gender assignments. Distinguishing signs were removed; instead, the entrance to the pavilion was marked with variously shaped yellow flags, which reappeared within the urban space of Venice. The *Restroom Pavilion* at the Giardini was woven into a dense narrative that ranged

Every day, the lagoon's tides wash contaminated water from Venice and into the Adriatic basin. The MOSE project, intended to protect the city against flooding, will significantly reduce these flows and may lead to local accumulation of pollutants and sediments in the lagoon.

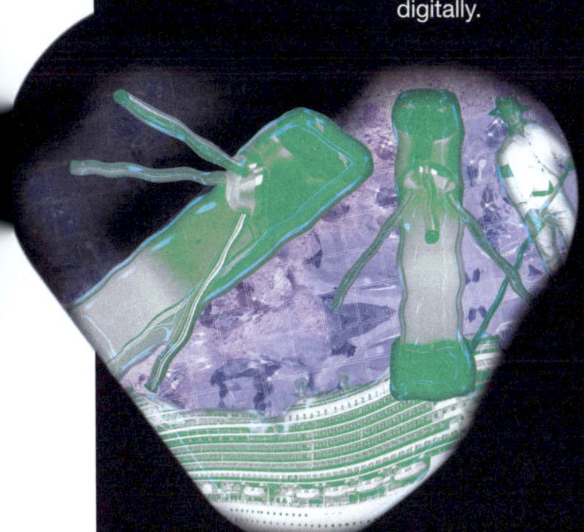

The few existing public toilets mostly have turnstiles, which exclude some people with disabilities. Users without a smartphone also suffer discrimination since the use fee is charged digitally.

All drawings on this page by Paula Vilaplana. © Matilde Cassani, Ignacio G. Galan, and Ivan L. Munuera, *The Restroom Pavilion* (2021).

01 See Paul B. Preciado, "Trashgender: Urinate/Defecate, Masculine/Feminine," *The Funambulist* 13 (October 2017): 15–17.

View of the *Restroom Pavilion.* Photograph by Imagen Subliminal. © Matilde Cassani, Ignacio G. Galan, and Ivan L. Munuera, *The Restroom Pavilion* (2021).

from a trans man being rejected from gondolier training to Japanese invasive species and suffocating fish, to a Venetian fog heavily laced with disinfectants. In this way, human beings are understood to be part of a larger whole, making clear the dramatic consequences of their behavior on non-human existences. The short stories displayed inside the pavilion on the walls, together with colored lighting, removed the clinical, antiseptic aspects associated with public toilet facilities, integrating the toilet building into the context of a comprehensive ecosystem.

Your Restroom Is a Battleground, on display at the Arsenale, demonstrated the degree to which toilet architecture remains a site for the cultural definition and material articulation of issues of gender, religion, race, disability, hygiene, health, and environment. Displays in showcases exemplified the struggle for inclusive public sanitary facilities for people outside the norm. Thus a young man in a wheelchair, along with his mother,

In the mid-1990s, cruise ships brought the seaweed *Undaria pinnatifida* to the lagoon Originally from Japan, the plant is now displacing native species, threatening to clog the wastewater system of local toilets. Drawings by Paula Vilaplana. © The authors, *The Restroom Pavilion* (2021).

Both drawings by Paula Vilaplana. © Matilde Cassani, Ignacio G. Galan, and Ivan L. Munuera, *The Restroom Pavilion* (2021).

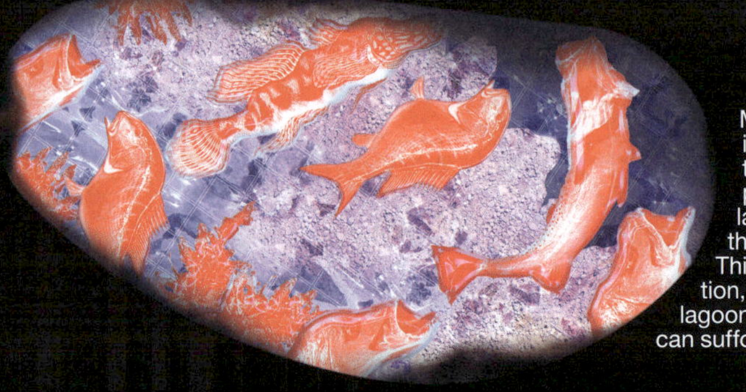

Mass tourism and an increase in domestic technology have prompted an accumulation of sediment at the bottom of canals. This causes eutrophication, a change in the lagoon's ecosystem that can suffocate fish.

The use of detergents like Lysoform in sanitation facilities pollutes the lagoon's waters, endangering food chains and animal populations within the Venice ecosystem. In its evaporated form, Lysoform forms part of the famous Venice smog.

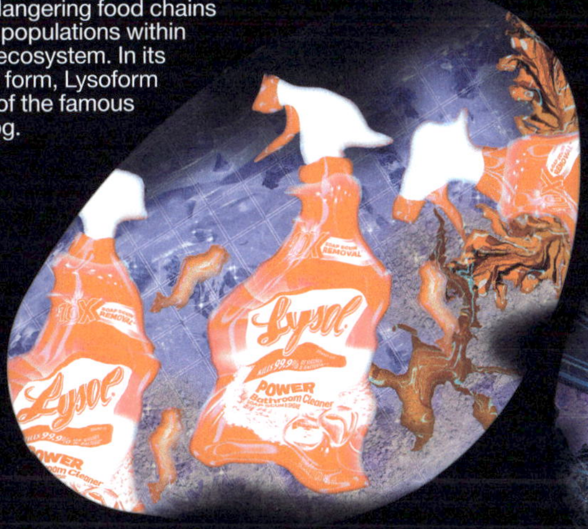

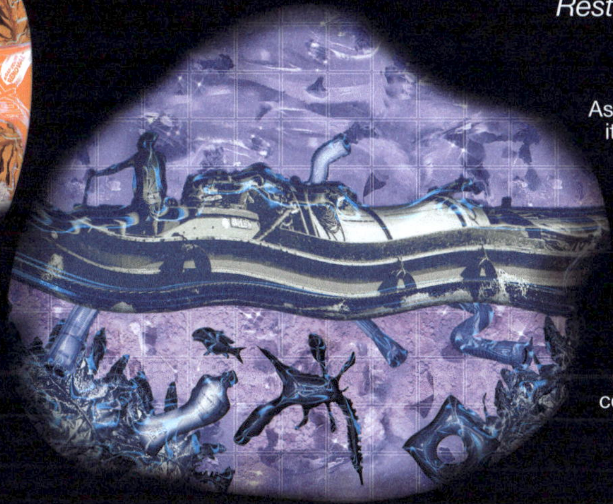

Both drawings by Paula Vilaplana. © Matilde Cassani, Ignacio G. Galan, and Ivan L. Munuera, *The Restroom Pavilion* (2021).

As tourism in Venice increased, its historic sewage system—a network of 16th-century underground brick tunnels known as the *gatoli*—became increasingly overburdened. In the 1990s, the city began to install wastewater tanks as standard. However, these only offer temporary sewage storage and must be emptied regularly into mobile containers, which then transport their contents out of the city.

The critical appropriation of the flag format challenges the rhetoric of nation-states and their forms of representation at the Biennale. This is why the entrance to the *Restroom Pavilion* is marked with all flags rather than a single one.

Drawing by Pablo Saiz del Rio. © Matilde Cassani, Ignacio G. Galan, and Ivan L. Munuera, *The Restroom Pavilion* (2021).

The exhibition *Your Restroom Is a Battleground* at the Arsenale uses a series of display cases to tell the story of contemporary struggles for barrier-free and inclusive access to sanitary infrastructure.
Photograph by Imagen Subliminal. © Matilde Cassani, Ignacio G. Galan, and Ivan L. Munuera, *The Restroom Pavilion* (2021).

Canterbury Prison is the first British prison used solely to house foreign prisoners. As part of major renovations, footbaths and squat latrines were installed for use by approximately 100 Muslim inmates. Various groups protested against using government funds to support inmates' religious and cultural practices.

Matilde Cassani, Ignacio G. Galan, Ivan L. Munuera, Joel Sanders; model: Pablo Saiz del Rio; photo: Natalia Guardia, Pablo Saiz del Rio. © The authors, *The Restroom Pavilion* (2021).

fights for better access within social housing. For several decades, day-to-day politics in their home country of Colombia was marked by unrest and armed conflicts. Many people were wounded, some very seriously, resulting in a high proportion of people with disabilities. However, their needs, and associated technical and spatial requirements, have hardly been taken into consideration by Colombia's sanitation infrastructure, making it almost impossible for them to participate in public life.

Toilets cannot be regarded as an isolated design issue but rather as symptoms of larger controversies, which can be conveyed in architectural terms. Toilets are a form of political architecture and a field of social conflict. At the same time, they are spaces of mutual dependency, with the potential to become the site of radical and queer ecologies. **FG**

After the wrongful arrest of two people of color at a Starbucks in Philadelphia, Black Lives Matter activists called for a boycott of the coffee chain. According to reports, white people were given access to restrooms even without having placed an order, while Black people were denied this. Starbucks responded to the allegations by removing the obligation to buy beverages or food in order to use their toilets. But some of its toilet rooms were equipped with blue lights to make the use of intravenous drugs more difficult, exposing their underlying prejudices.

As part of the Occupy Men's Room movement, 20 women occupied men's public toilets in Guangzhou and Beijing in 2012. They demanded that building standards be changed to reduce waiting times at women's toilets. This would mean that three new women's toilets would be built for every two new men's toilets.

All images on this page: Matilde Cassani, Ignacio G. Galan, Ivan L. Munuera, Joel Sanders; model: Pablo Saiz del Rio; photo: Natalia Guardia, Pablo Saiz del Rio. © The authors, *The Restroom Pavilion* (2021).

In 2010, the island nation of Haiti was shaken by an earthquake. Shortly afterward, a cholera epidemic struck the population, killing thousands of people. The epidemic was thought to have been caused by the contamination of the Artibonite River, caused in turn by poor wastewater management on the part of UN peacekeeping troops in the country for reconstruction, as well as the poor condition of Haiti's water and health systems.

Office for Political Innovation

The age of digital dating apps, social media, and the globalization of lifestyles has seen the formation of new economies, territorial dependencies, and infrastructures of desire. Accompanying this is the increasing dissolution of rigid categories such as inside–outside, domestic–public, female–male, and heteronormativity in general. The Office for Political Innovation, founded by Andrés Jaque in 2003, explores the dimensions, dynamics, and potentials of these developments in its queer spatial practice of design, performance, activism, and research—most recently with projects such as *Pornified Homes* (2016), *Transurban Love: The Architecturalization of Romance* (2017), and *Sex and the So-Called City* (2018), among others.

TEAM: Andrés Jaque;
Roberto González,
Paola Pardo-Castillo, Alberto Heras
LOCATIONS: New York / Madrid
FOUNDED: 2003

Poster for the installation *Transurban Love: The Architecturalizacion of Romance*, Seoul Biennale of Architecture and Urbanism, 2017.
In this project, the Office for Political Innovation explores four historical sociocultural turning points from the perspective of spatial politics to show how love or romance could become one of the driving forces for neoliberal ideology, technological developments, and the domination of the real estate market.
© Andrés Jaque / Office for Political Innovation.

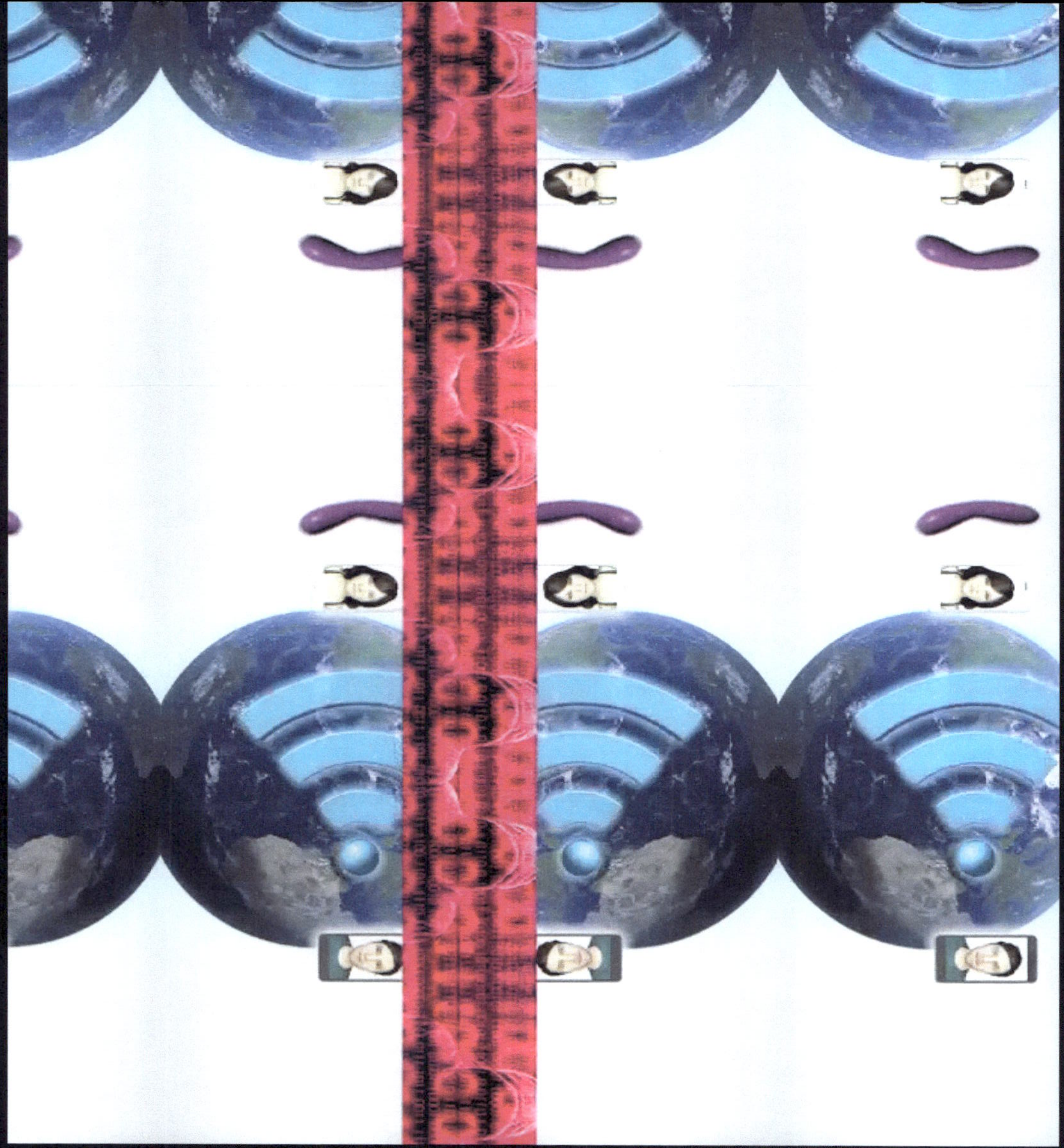

Video stills from the installation *Transurban Love*, 2017. In 2016, the Canadian erotic products manufacturer Standard Innovation Corporation was sued for collecting and transmitting to servers highly sensitive data, such as the temperature and vibration strength of smartphone-controlled dildos. Security gaps in the app also allowed hackers to access this sensitive data. © Andrés Jaque / Office for Political Innovation + Miguel Mesa.

Intimate Strangers
The Politics of Grindr Archiurbanism (2016)

In a two-year-long research project on the dating app Grindr, the Office for Political Innovation investigated how the tool's development has contributed to the emergence of new forms of urbanism—the way we inhabit cities. The results of this study were incorporated into the 2016 multimedia installation *Intimate Strangers* (2016) and the text "Grindr Archiurbanism," published in 2017 in the journal *Log*.[01] In the late 20th century, predictions about life in the future assumed that digital technologies and the increasing shift of amorous relationships into digital and virtual space would make the physical location of people increasingly unimportant. But as the Office for Political Innovation points out, precisely the opposite is the case today. That is because the market penetration of smartphones with global positioning (GPS), starting in 2008, spurred the rapid technological development of geosocial networking applications, such as location-based dating apps, Facebook's "Nearby Friends," and other so-called hook-up software that make it easier than ever for people to date. In just a few years, technology has fundamentally changed how we seek friendship, love, and sex.

Grindr was founded in 2009 by Joel Simkhai and the company Nearby Buddy Finder LLC. It was the first geosocial mobile dating app targeted at gay, bisexual, transgender, and queer men. More than ten years later, with over 72 million users in 192 countries and a growth rate of 10,000 daily downloads, Grindr produces a stream of hundreds of millions of messages per day—not just in the darkness of the bedroom, but in offices and bars, on the street, and in trains, factories, gyms, and institutes of higher education. The available user profiles are not determined by fixed distances but by constantly changing spatial density ratios. In rural areas, hundreds of kilometers separate potential lovers; in cities and airport hotels,

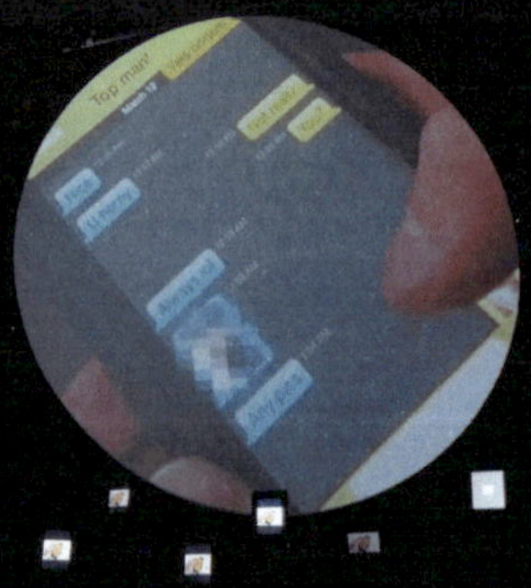

Intimate Strangers, exhibition views.
Most dating apps work through GPS-based tracking systems. However, various auxiliary apps can be used to disguise the user's actual location. With Grindr version 3.0.9 from 2016, the recognizable orange frame disappeared from the user interface so that users would not give themselves away when using the app in public.

"In many Western cities, Grindr is, in part, both a cause and a consequence of the displacement of queer urban space."

For some time now, cruising areas and darkrooms have increasingly shifted into the digital space, where flirtations and initiations of (sex) dates occur. The interface of the dating app Grindr includes a finely tuned rating system based on age, body measurements, ethnicity, sexual preferences, identities, and relationship status. Categories such as "poz" for HIV-positive people or "trans" for trans people enable contact with specific groups.

it may be just a few feet. The Office for Political Innovation describes the specific manifestation of "Grindr Archiurbanism" as follows:

"Not just accommodated by the urban, Grindr has become a kind of urbanism in its own right. It is both super-immaterial and super-material. It is a network of constantly moving parts linked by desire. The setting is permanently active, constantly being produced by updating profiles, dragging one profile to the next, and disappearing from one person's screen to become available on another's. If Buckminster Fuller dreamed of a world of omnidirectional connectivity in the air, Grindr is the fulfillment of his vision."[02]

In many Western cities, Grindr is, in part, Grindr creates a networking platform for individual, one-to-one encounters that are often highly preselected by detailed filter categories. At the same time, this form of anonymous outreach provides a global group of isolated LGBTQ+ individuals with an alternative space for interaction and dialogue.

The Office for Political Innovation also turns its attention to states where LGBTQ+ people and their activities are criminalized and prosecuted, highlighting cases where queer dating apps were weaponized by local authorities to track, harass, and arrest users. In 2014, for example, Egyptian police used Grindr to locate and arrest queer people in

Practice

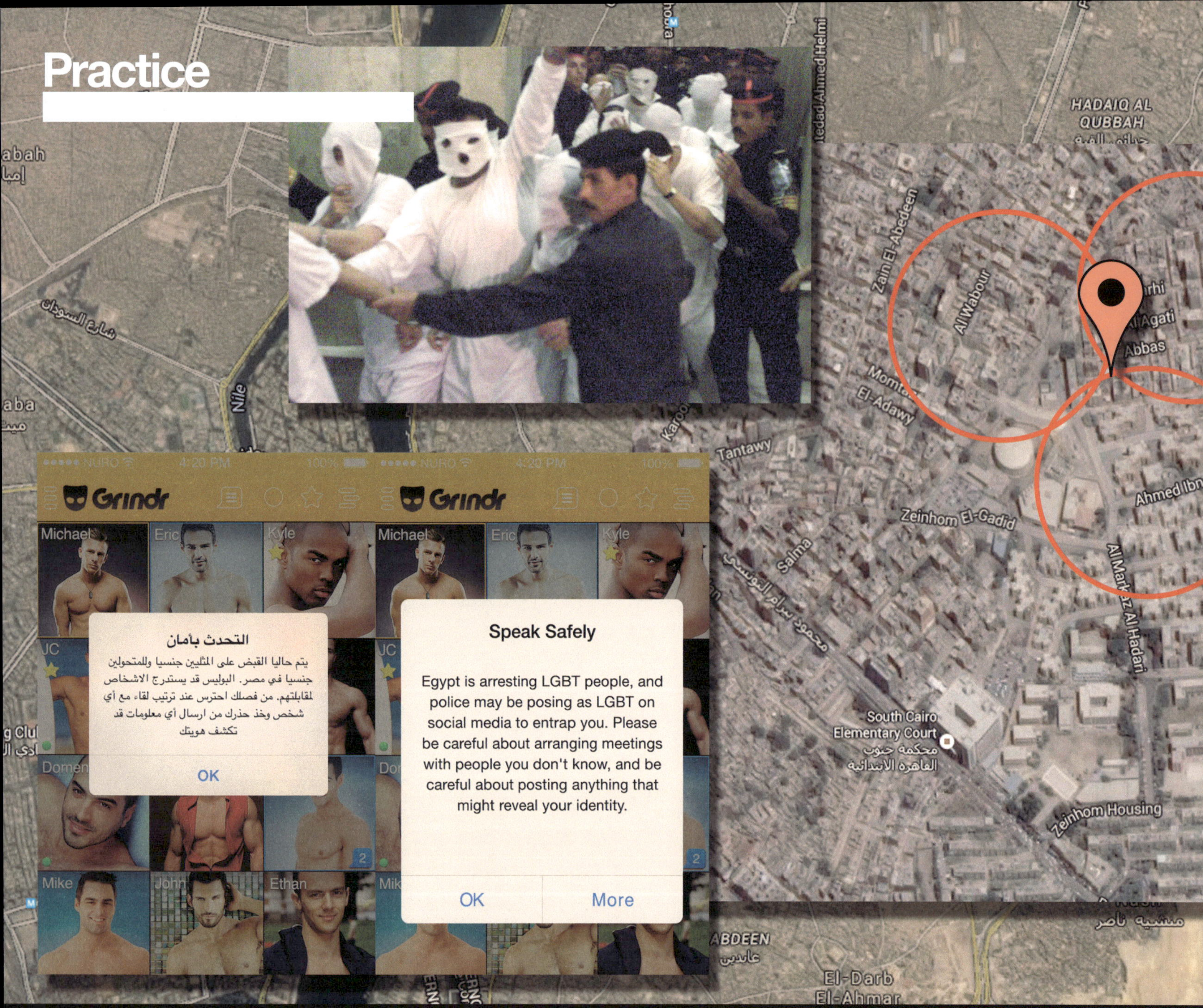

Same-sex sexuality is still prosecuted in 69 countries worldwide, making geosocial networks like Grindr a place where LGBTQ+ realities are both constructed and threatened. In 2001, four gay men were arrested at a party in Cairo. They attracted media attention when they appeared in court dressed entirely in white with white cloth masks to hide their faces. They did so to prevent the government from using their images for its own purposes. Grindr's logo, which shows a mask, refers to this event.

Although the victims used fake GPS or VPNs to disguise their location, it also made dating more difficult for them. By making minor changes to their location (for example, in border areas), queer people who are on the run can also make contact with people in neighboring countries who are willing to support them. For example, in October 2015, a man fled Kabul and was navigated by 15 Grindr users. While most fugitives rely on information from fellow fugitives or distant friends, the Afghan could find nearby strangers on Grindr who helped him with up-to-date local information. Some LGBTQ+ activists specifically use the network to provide refugees with accommodations and information for LGBTQ+ persons among them.

The Office for Political Innovation shows the transurban or transnational character of Grindr in this context: the platform is a hybrid interface between digital and physical space where privileged citizens and disenfranchised people can interact, network, show solidarity, and collaborate. **FG/MAK**

In 2016, Grindr sold 60 percent of its shares to Beijing Kunlun Technology, a Chinese gaming company, and subsequently entered into more collaborations with partners in the entertainment, fashion, and design industries to transform the app into a broader gay lifestyle platform.

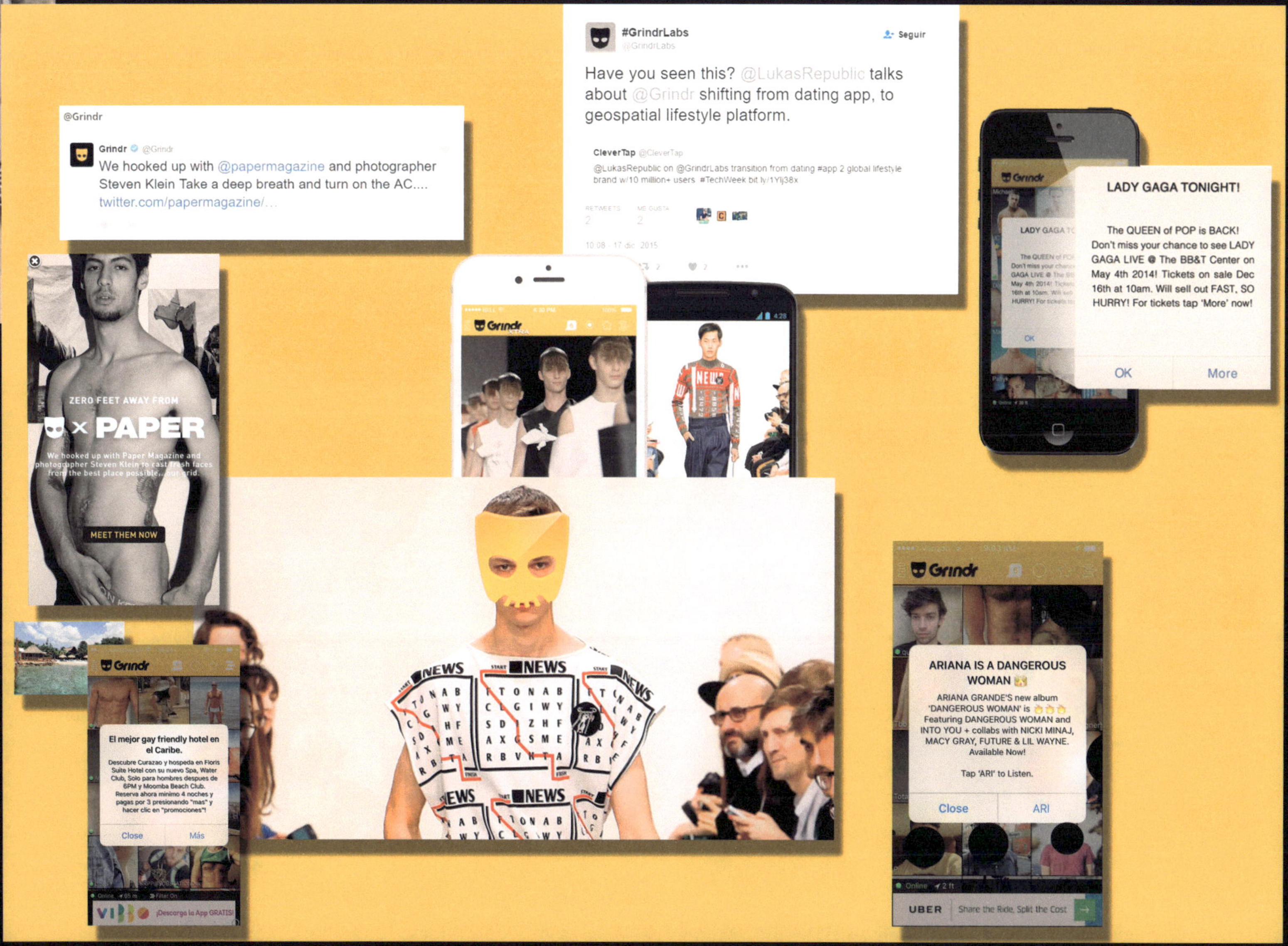

Xcessive Aesthetics

TEAM: Teresa Boulting, Rhiarna Dhaliwal, Ibiye Camp, Darcy Chittmittrapap, Jade Blanchard-McKinley, Emmy Bacharach
LOCATION: London
FOUNDED: 2019

A collage by Xcessive Aesthetics appeared in the first issue of *Terraforma Journal*. In addition to *XAMA: Augmented Salon*, the project *Data Deli* can also be seen here. The project proposed a speculative pavilion to make data collection in public space and invisible digital infrastructures both physically and spatially tangible.

Xcessive Aesthetics (XA) is an all-female intersectional feminist collective founded in London in 2019. The collective consists of six architects who met while completing their master's degree from the Royal College of Art. As part of unit ADS8, they all focused their final thesis on Digital Infrastructures, Data Networks, and Posthuman Futures. The practice examines the implications of new technologies and data politics for physical and digital spaces in order to explore augmented realities and possible counter-worlds. With a techno-ambivalent philosophy, their interactive, virtual-physical installations play with low-threshold spaces that are often read as clearly "female," subverting them into locations for critique and experimentation. Neither for nor against technology, they believe in the importance of criticism from a design perspective through working at the interface of architecture, art, digital media, and science. Their practice aims to examine alternative forms of producing space, as well as different ways of research and teaching with the goal of questioning traditional forms of architectural communication and overcoming prejudices within the profession. "We want to critically explore the limits and possibilities of architecture as well as its future direction and development." **–XA**

XAMA_Augmented Salon

In its biggest event during its inaugural year, XA hosted *Augmented Salon*, a live nail salon and augmented reality workshop, engaging audiences in discussions about digital rights, internet freedom, and social platforms. The setting was designed to resemble a typical Brazilian beauty salon.

In her project *XAMA* (2019), XA cofounder Teresa Boulting explored these salons as traditionally female centers for social interaction and informal knowledge sharing. Reference was also made to the historical idea of the French *salon* as a space for political and cultural discussion, led mainly by women. Here, the salon was expanded into an "augmented salon," using augmented reality, screens, and other digital tools. Various objects within the nail salon—including magazine covers, nail stickers, and graphics—could be scanned with a smartphone using a code, augmenting the physical space of the nail salon into the digital space. Workshop participants at *Augmented Salon* learned how to access and address the content within augmented reality.

In this context, Teresa Boulting gave a lecture titled *XAMA: Internet at Your Fingertips!*, in which she presented her research into digital inequality in Brazil. Access to the internet in that country still depends heavily on users' socioeconomic status and the quality of the connectivity infrastructure available to them; most people in rural areas still only have internet access through their mobile phones. Teresa Boulting presented an analysis of the internet as both a material-technical infrastructure and an immaterial-political one, and proposed further exploration of beauty salons as the physical manifestation of existing social networks. Appropriately equipped salon hubs could help to create a network-like structure of internet access, undermining the practice of large platforms offering their own services and applications free of charge through the so-called zero-rating practice, which threatens net neutrality. *XAMA* thus revealed the potential for an alternative bottom-up communication network to advance women's digital empowerment in rural communities in Brazil.

The *Augmented Salon* project also connected to other contemporary feminist questions. These include the ambivalent relationship between feminism, beauty (industry), and consumption; body positivity and body diversity; the reproduction/rejection of patriarchal ideals of beauty; and establishing one's own ideas of beauty as a moment of self-empowerment. *Augmented Salon* is a visible location in the public space that counters gender clichés, seeking to reclaim women's own beauty standards and their agency over their own appearance. **VK**

Augmented Salon, interior view.

Various objects in the salon, including nail stickers and magazine covers, can be scanned with a smartphone, expanding the salon into the digital sphere.

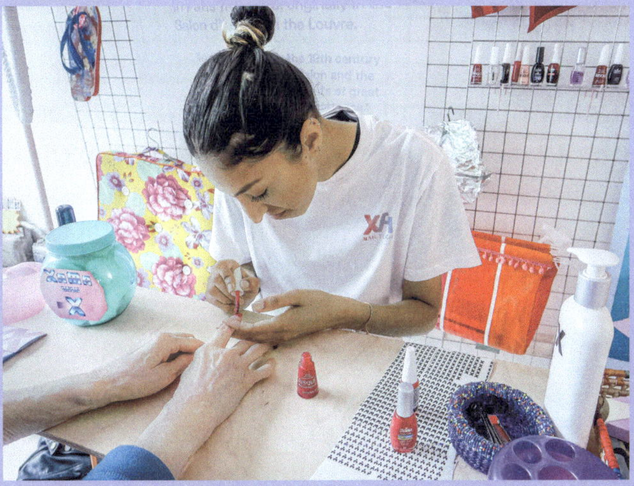

The AR content and information could be accessed in the salon with mobile phones.

GOSSIP, shop window installation at Kottbusser Tor, Berlin.

fem_arc

"Against the backdrop of ever louder debates about social inequality, which is also centrally expressed in spatial issues, we see it as our duty as young architects to make a contribution. We are a group of six women; none of us identifies as an architect in the sense of the classical guidelines of the Chamber of Architects, nor are we proven specialists in the field of feminist theory. We are, however, interested in spatial body politics. We are at a point where we are fundamentally questioning the structural boundaries of the discipline that have historically been set by the white male elite and which continue to shape the scholarly canon and the methods and concepts taught in architecture schools today. Given the problematic state of contemporary architectural practice in terms of inequitable gender relations and other forms of structural disadvantage, homogenous office structures, and unquestioned professional paradigms (from norms to overtime culture), we want to use the gender discourse to build alliances and initiate an ongoing dialogue on the future of feminist practices in art and architecture. For us, critical spatial practice can also consist of refusing to build physical structures. We seek new points of departure and entry, as well as transversal thinking and design, to radically expand the conventional boundaries of our discipline."

– fem_arc

TEAM: fem_arc: Océane Vé-Réveillac, Amelie Schindler, Insa Streit, Lara Stöhlmacher, Lucía Gauchat Schulte, Aslı Varol, Ana Rodriguez Bisbicus
LOCATION: Berlin
FOUNDED: 2018

All photos: © Duygu Atceken.

MAP KEY:

OUR CONVERSATION

„Interview quote"

"Literature quote"

"Edebiyat alıntı"

„Literaturzitat"

fem_arc

ETYMOLOGY:

COMMERE = co-parent — F. rapports familiers — F. indiscrète et bavarde — **F. COMMERE** — racontars; **M. COMPERE** — compagnon

GOSSIP = (old eng.) godsibb (god + sib) — **F. close friend, someone you trust** — Idle talk; a relative — godfather + godmother

KLATSCH = lautmalerisch

Silvia FEDERICI, *Caliban and the witch*

"Tracing the history of the words frequently used to define and degrade women is a necessary step if we are to understand how gender oppression functions and reproduces itself. The history of 'gossip' is emblematic in this context. Through it we can follow two centuries of attacks on women at the dawn of modern England, when a term commonly indicating a close female friend turned into one signifying idle, backbiting talk, that is, talk potentially sowing discord, the opposite of the solidarity that female friendship implies and generates. Attaching a denigrating meaning to the term indicating friendship among women served to destroy the female sociality that had prevailed in the Middle Ages, when most of the activities women performed were of a collective nature and, in the lower classes at least, women formed a tight-knit community that was the source of a strength unmatched in the modern era."

"Cinsiyet baskılarının tekrar tekrar nasıl oluştuğunu anlamak istiyorsak, kadınları tanımlamak ve aşağılamak için sıklıkla kullanılan kelimelerin geçmişinin izini sürmek gerekli bir adımdır. Dedikodu'nun tarihi semboliktir. Dedikodu kavramının tarihi ile, kadınlara karşı yapılmış iki yüzyıllık saldırıları takip edebiliriz. Modern Ingiltere nin kurulmasından hemen önce aslında yaygın olarak 'yakın bir bayan arkadaş' anlamına gelen dedikodu kelimesi, zamanla baskalarına zarar veren, anlaşmazlıklara sebep olan, boş, gıybet konuşma anlamına gelmeye baslamıştır. Bu anlam, aslında kadın arkadaşlığının ima ettiği dayanışma ve destek olma duruma tamamen zıttır. Kadınlar arasındaki dostluğu belirten bir kelimeye aşağılayıcı bir anlam yüklemek, zamanla kadınların sosyal toplumdaki yerlerini yok etmeye yardımcı oldumuştur. Orta Çağ'da kadınların gerçekleştirdiği çoğu aktivite kolektif bir yapıya sahipti – en azından toplumun ekonomik anlamda alt sınıflarında. Kadınların birbirine inanan ve birbirine bagli toplulukları, onların Modern Çağ'da eşine rastlanmayan gücünün kaynağıydı."

„Sich mit der Geschichte der Wörter auseinanderzusetzen, die verwendet wurden, um Frauen zu definieren, zu degradieren und zu verfolgen, ist eine notwendige Voraussetzung dafür, um zu verstehen, wie die Unterdrückung des Geschlechts funktioniert und reproduziert wird. Die Geschichte des Klatsches ist sinnbildlich in diesem Zusammenhang. Dadurch können wir zwei Jahrhunderte der Angriffe auf Frauen zu Beginn des modernen Englands nachvollziehen, als aus einem Begriff, der ursprünglich eine enge Freundin bezeichnete, ein Begriff wurde, der Müßiggang bedeutet, verleumderisches Gerede. Das heißt Reden, das potentiell Zwietracht säen könnte, das Gegenteil von Solidarität, die auf weiblicher Freundschaft aufbaut und ihr innewohnt. Dem Begriff der Freundschaft zwischen Frauen eine abwertende Bedeutung zuzuweisen, diente dazu, weiblichen Zusammenhalt zu zerstören, der sich im Mittelalter verstärkt durch kollektive Aktivitäten unter Frauen herausbildete und zumindest in den unteren Schichten ein enges Gemeinschaftsgefühl auszubilden vermochte, das in der Neuzeit seinesgleichen sucht."

KLATSCHTHEMEN
TOPICS OF GOSSIP
BIR NESNE OLARAK DEDIKODU

"Klatsch is more like exchanging the news, Tratsch is more sharing knowledge that is actually not real, but making it real. And often it's to put people down, or to tell a story through your own point of view even though it's not the reality. Maybe creating stories, sort of Kiez Politics."

"Klatsch daha çok haber alışverişi gibidir, Tratsch daha çok aslında gerçek olmayan bilgiyi paylaşmaktır, onu gerçeğe dönüştürmektir. Ve çoğu zaman insanları kötülemek ya da gerçek olmasa bile kendi bakış açınızdan bir hikaye anlatmaktır. Belki hikayeler yaratmak, bir nevi Mahalle Politikaları."

"I feel like it fills up the space that I'm not here, it for me fills up the image of this place"

NAMING IT?
NASIL DENİR?
WIE WIRD ES GENANNT?

GAYRIRESMİ SÖZEL AKTARIM
INFORMAL ORAL TRANSMISSION
INFORMELLE MÜNDLICHE ÜBERMITTLUNG

BIR ILETIŞIM SÜRECI OLARAK DEDIKODU
GOSSIP AS A PROCESS OF COMMUNICATION
GOSSIP ALS KOMMUNIKATIONSPROZESS

Estelle DANSEREAU, *Lieu de plaisir, lieu de pouvoir*

«Aussitôt que produit, l'énoncé disparaît, se fond dans l'énonciation d'une nouvelle parole [...] cette voix qui déborde le sujet. Quand Lamy définit le bavardage comme ›une énonciation sans énoncé‹, elle souligne par là le fait que le sens des mots est secondaire par rapport à l'acte de parler. C'est donc cet acte qui devient porteur de sens.»

"Ifade, üretildiği anda ortadan kalkar ve yeni bir sözcüğün telaffuzunda erir. Sesin kendisi, ifade esilen konuyu asar. Gevezelik 'ifadesiz bir beyandir' Yani kelimelerin anlamını konuşma ediminden sonra ikincildir. Konusma eyleminin kendisi, gevezelik, aslinda anlami tasiyan seyin kendisidir."

„Sobald sie hervorgebracht wird, verschwindet die Äußerung, verschmilzt mit der Aussprache eines neuen Wortes [...] diese Stimme, die das Subjekt überflutet. Wenn Lamy Geschwätz als ‚eine Äußerung ohne Aussage' definiert, unterstreicht sie damit, dass die Bedeutung der Worte dem Akt des Sprechens untergeordnet ist. So wird dieser Akt selbst zum Bedeutungsträger."

fem_arc WEBSEITE

We see listening as a critical practice, an active practice capable of developing and elevating consciousness. Listening is the starting point for relational processes, a starting point for conversations with oneself and others.

F_WALKS audio walk, embodied practice

How can we collectively experience feminist spatial practices despite physical distance? How can listening to stories about the feminist appropriation of (urban) spaces facilitate the reassessment of our own bodies in space?

Audre LORDE, *The Master's Tools Will Never Dismantle the Master's House*

"In our world, divide and conquer must become define and empower."

„In unserer Welt muss aus Teilen und Herrschen Bestimmen und Ermächtigen werden."

VERGNÜGEN
ENTERTAINMENT

SELBSTAUSDRUCK
SELF-EXPRESSION

RESISTANCE
DIRENMEK
WIDERSTAND

WISSEN TEILEN
SHARE INFORMATION
BILGI PAYLAŞMAK

Ne tür bir bilgi? What kind of information? Welche Art von Wissen?
What is the intention? Amaç nedir? Mit welcher Absicht?
How much trust is there? Gibt es ein Vertrauensverhältnis?

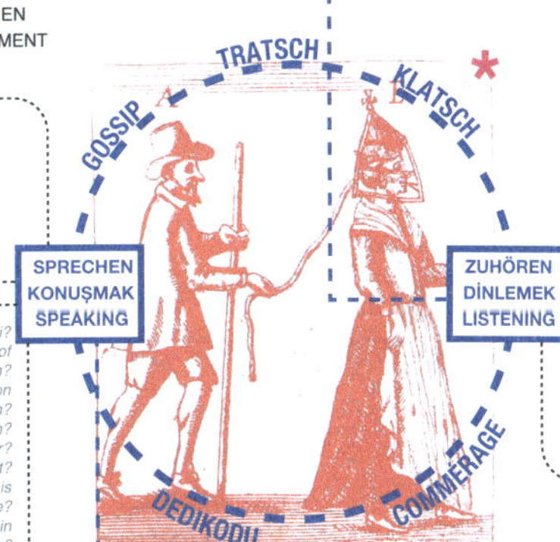

*

BİLGİ TOPLAMAK
WISSEN AUFNEHMEN
COLLECT INFORMATION

Ursula K. LE GUIN, *The Carrier Bag Theory of Fiction*

"All of us, maybe have like a piece of information by our own experience of this person, then if you share it, you construct like a whole personality of that person. And then you can experience yourself if it's according to your perception or not. I find it really nice actually. Like you are creating new characters from little pieces around."

YANINDA OLMAK
SOLIDARISIEREN
BOND

START A DIALOGUE
IN DEN DIALOG TRETEN
MUHABBET BAŞLATMAK

HEGEMONIC KNOWLEDGE PRODUCTION
HEGEMONIALE WISSENSPRODUKTION

Gayatri Chakravorty SPIVAK, *Can the Subaltern Speak?*

"Epistemic violence"

„Epistemische Gewalt"

Donna HARAWAY, *Staying with the Trouble*

"It matters what thoughts think thoughts. It matters what knowledges know knowledges. It matters what relations relate relations. It matters what worlds world worlds. It matters what stories tell stories."

"Hangi düşüncelerin düşünceleri düşündüğü önemlidir. Hangi bilginin ne bildiği önemlidir. Hangi ilişkilerin ilişkileri ilişkilendirdiği önemlidir. Hangi dünyaların dünyalar dünyaladığı önemlidir. Hangi hikayelerin hikaye anlattığı önemlidir."

GÖRMEZDEN gelme, küçümseme, itibarsızlaştırma, küçümseme
IGNORIEREN abwerten, diskreditieren, herabsetzen
IGNORE devaluing, discrediting, diminishing

GOSSIPS.CITY WEBSEITE

We want to create spaces to express ourselves, spaces to be on the record, spaces to define ouselves, spaces to collecivly engage our varied experiences in and with the city.

Pamela J. WALKER on Melanie Tebbutt, *Women's Talk? A Social History of Gossip in Working Class Neighbourhoods*

"Erkekler, kadınların konuşmasını küçümsedi, söylediklerinin önemini azalttı ve kadınları ev içinde tutmaya çalıştı"

"Men disdained women's talk, disminished its importance, and attempted to contain women within the household"

„Männer verachteten das Reden von Frauen, würdigten seine Bedeutung herab und versuchten, die Frauen im Haushalt zu halten"

BEZIEHUNGEN HERSTELLEN
BUILD RELATIONS
İLİŞKİ KURMAK

GOSSIPING

EXTERNAL GOSSIP

"Bildiğimizi biliyoruz"

"WE [WOMEN] KNOW THAT WE KNOW"

„Wir [Frauen] wissen, dass wir wissen"

Luce IRIGARAY, *Ca sexe qui n'en est pas un*

«La femme ne parle jamais pareil. Ce qu'elle émet est fluent, fluctuant. Flouant. Et on ne l'écoute pas, sauf à y perdre le sens (du) propre. D'où les résistances à cette voix qui déborde le ›sujet‹. Qu'il figera donc, glacera, dans ses catégories jusqu'à la paralyser dans son flux. ›Et voilà, Messieurs, pourquoi vos filles sont muettes.‹ Même si elles jacassent, prolifèrent pithiatiquement en mots qui ne signifient que leur aphasie, ou le revers mimétique de votre désir.»

Silvia FEDERICI, *On the Meaning of Gossip*

"In many parts of the world, women have historically been seen as the weavers of memory. Those who keep alive the voices of the past and the histories of the communities, who transmit them to the future generations and, in so doing, create a collective identity and a profound sense of cohesion."

"Diğer bir çok kültürel geleneğe bakıldığında, bu 'boş kadın konuşması' aslında oldukça farklı görünecektir. Dünyanın pek çok yerinde, kadınlar tarihsel olarak hafızanın dokumacıları olarak görülmüştür. Kadınlar, geçmişin seslerini, toplulukların tarihini ve hikayelerini gelecek nesillere aktaranlardır. Böylece kolektif bir kimlik ve toplumsal bağlılık duygusu oluştururlar."

„In vielen anderen kulturellen Traditionen außerhalb Europas wird Frauen die Weitergabe von Geschichte(n) zugeschrieben. Sie halten die Stimmen der Vergangenheit lebendig und auch die Geschichten ihrer Gemeinschaften. Sie tragen diese weiter an zukünftige Generationen. So bauen sie eine gemeinsame kulturelle Identität auf und ein tiefes Zusammengehörigkeitsgefühl."

EINGRENZEN
CONTAIN

BEHERRSCHEN
CONTROL
KONTROL ETMEK

KOLLEKTIVE MACHT
COLLECTIVE POWER
KOLEKTİV GÜÇ

"Information Is Power"

"I think gossip brings me a feeling of belonging also"

"Dedıkodu yapmak, bana bir aitlik duygusu veriyor"

Estelle DANSEREAU, *Lieu de plaisir, lieu de pouvoir*

"Chatter can function as a counter-discourse, as an instrument of transgression; it is then transformed into a 'place of pleasure' and of speaking, or, on the ideological level, a place of power. [It is a] chat based on connivance, complicity that creates a space where speech does not have to be forced or coerced."

"Gevezelik etmek bir karşı-söylem işlevi görebilir. Gevezelik; konuşmanın zorlanmadığı veya zorlamadığı bir alan yaratan, göz yummaya, suç ortaklığına dayalı bir sohbettir."

„Laut Lamy und Anderen „kann Geschwätz als Gegendiskurs, als Instrument der Überschreitung fungieren; es verwandelt sich dann in einen ‚Ort der Freude' und des Sprechens – oder auf ideologischer Ebene – in einen Ort der Macht."

"It's about also sharing how I feel, those maybe not so significant feelings but those tiny feelings I have in that moment. Maybe not towards one particular person but in general a feeling, that I share maybe."

"Dedikodu aynı zamanda nasıl hissettiğimi paylaşmakla da ilgili, belki o kadar önemli hisler değil ama o an sahip olduğum o küçücük hisler gibi. Belki bir kişiye karşı değil ama genel olarak paylaştığım bir duygu belki."

KADIN AĞLARI
WOMEN NETWORKS
FRAUENNETZWERKE

"Also sometimes it's about seeking support, I think. I can imagine, if one customer is super rude and behaving in a very unpleasant way, and I took it personal, and if I talk with other people about this experience and this specific person. And if the other person tells me, No, it's the same for everyone ... Because for me, I sometimes can imagine that it is because I'm not german, I'm not european, I'm not white, so they treat me differently ... If I tell other people what happened to me, and if other people experienced the same, and then I would not take it personally – then this is a big help for me."

SEEKING FOR PEOPLE TO RELATE
AUF DER SUCHE SEIN NACH MENSCHEN, DIE DAS GLEICHE ERLEBEN

confirmation, validation of one's feeling through gossip

* "Dizgin", sivri dilli kadınları cezalandırmak için kullanılan demir bir aletti. Benzer bir cihaz Avrupalı köle tüccarları tarafından Afrika'da esirlerini köle gemilerine yüklerken dizginlemek için kullanıldı.

[T]he "bridle" [was] an iron contraption used to punish women with a sharp tongue. Significantly, a similar device was used by European slavetraders in Africa to subdue their captives and carry them to their ships. (Silvia Federici, *Caliban and the Witch*, New York, 2004, p. 101.)

Map of conversations across levels of informal talk and their historical and contextual meanings.
© fem_arc.

City of Gossips

Listening As an Urban Strategy of Resistance

TEXT
fem_arc

What if the most important achievement is not building but collecting and sharing the stories that cities comprise? Shop-window installations, such as this one at Kottbusser Tor in Berlin, intend to provide visible access points in the urban space for an examination of the various overlapping narratives of a place. Some of the elements are readable from a distance, while others can only be deciphered up close.

The term gossip is currently used in a somewhat derogatory way to describe a type of informal speech perceived as unproductive, opaque, or even disingenuous. The principle is repeated in other languages: *commérage* (French), *dedikodu* (Turkish), or *Klatsch* (German) all have negative connotations, despite their sociability. Gossip derives from the Old English *godsibb* and originally meant something like "close friend."[01] *Godsibbs* were connected through a relationship of trust in which they could confide intimate thoughts and feelings unfettered by the restrictive expectations of patriarchal societies. This parallel world of women's networks enabled mutual support and backing in the most vulnerable situations, such as childbirth. It served the beneficial exchange of information and goods and offered a protective space for personal conversations during work or leisure time. It was precisely this unsupervised conviviality (of oppressed women) that outside observers often dismissed as "idleness" or "useless chatter." *Godsibbs* were accused of neglecting their duties as wives, mothers, or plantation and factory workers. Yet, gossip also played a significant role in the resistance movements of the 20th century. Here it was a resource for the oppressed, a means of mobilization, and a central form of solidarity. At the same time, gossip has the power to penetrate the political realm of everyday life. It reports on urban and domestic life, violence and oppression, sexuality and friendship—stories that impact the public sphere but remain mostly hidden from the public. Where these stories intersect and intertwine—through urban, social, digital, or media spaces—they unfold their own urban spatial impact.

This is where our ongoing project *GOSSIP* ties in, which we have been developing based on the urban context in Berlin since spring 2021. Berlin is a site and object of entrepreneurial activity that has led to rapid urban changes and the displacement of local communities in recent years. In our process-oriented project, we reflect from a feminist perspective on the urban dimension of (informal) conversations and explore their value as a bottom-up strategy in local communities for building, transforming, and resisting. In doing so, we understand everyday face-to-face conversations as an act of care and a participatory practice for mutual empowerment that focuses on listening. The act of listening is at the beginning of every relationship and is a prerequisite for every conversation—with yourself and others. What can listening to other people's stories do to us? How can we bring together listening with a spatial moment? Can listening become a collective spatial practice?

Going beyond exclusively feminist readings to trace the themes and methods of contemporary urban gossip, we work closely with diverse protagonists, initiatives, and communities in the districts of Neukölln and Kreuzberg. In interviews and workshops, we collect subjective narratives in which the intersections of individual experiences and their interaction with urban space become legible. These experiences have been shaped by aspects such as social gender and non-heteronormative identities (gender and queerness), racial attributions or religious affiliation (race and religion), and economic status or discrimination based on disability (class and dis/ability). We bring these narratives back to the site, presenting them in window installations, so they reverberate back into the urban space and spark further conversations.

01 See also the comments by Silvia Federici in "On the Meaning of Gossip" in Silvia Federici, *Witches, Witch-Hunting, and Women* (Oakland, CA: PM Press, 2018), 33–38.

Gossip becomes a means of resistance when women disclose their salaries or discuss how they use public toilets that are obviously not built for them; when they start talking about evictions, apartment hunting, preemptive purchasing rights, and the nationalization of housing because their neighbors complain they will soon no longer be able to afford the rents.

fem_arc +Diāna Lucas-Drogan

Gossip is work on relationships, and the neighborhood space SP*TI is a site for this work in the neighborhood of Rollberg. Community is created at the table, while cooking, working, making music, and in workshops regularly held as part of the public program accompanying the installation *GOSSIP*.

The embroidery circle is a camouflage, between the aestheticization of a historical image of the woman as reserved and quietly busy and an emancipatory craft. As a legitimate meeting place for women to improve their craft and thus excuse their absence from family duties, the embroidery circle grew into a community of solidarity. What may seem like an old-fashioned leisure activity to us today was once part of a woman's basic education and an important aspect of her often isolated unpaid work at home. The meetings, which took place in small groups, enabled the development of social bonds and opened up a space for exchange—for joint "gossip" with breaks and listening. Generating entire patterns from individual lines takes time, during which you also let your eyes wander to the embroidery frame next to you and see how it is evolving and what is being tried out there. Embroidery is a practice based on solidarity: it thrives on listening, looking, and learning from each other. By constantly working with the needle and thread, embroidery leaves room for silence and allows dialogues to remain open. This way of connecting with the material and those present while being considerate makes embroidery a tool for connecting with each other. The embroidery circle builds a space of caring for shared learning.

TEXT
Diana Lucas-Drogan

All photos: © Duygu Atceken.

PROGRAM (GOSSIP):
Exhibition, workshop, discursive program
TEAM (GOSSIP):
Océane Vé-Réveillac, Amelie Schindler, Insa Streit, Lara Stöhlmacher, Lucía Gauchat Schulte, Aslı Varol, Ana Rodriguez Bisbicus; Noumissa Sidibé, Sofía Ribas, Reem Alfahad, Fernande Njonkou Njanjo, Teresa Hoffmann; workshop “Gossip and Subversive Embroidery” with Diana Lucas-Drogan
LOCATION: Berlin
YEAR: since 2021

The architect, spatial planner, and map artist Diana Lucas-Drogan at the workshop “Gossip and Subversive Embroidery” on reappropriating embroidery as a feminist practice. Comparable to the conceptual history of gossip, embroidery underwent similar devaluation in modern history and, as a woman’s activity, was subordinated to other art forms.

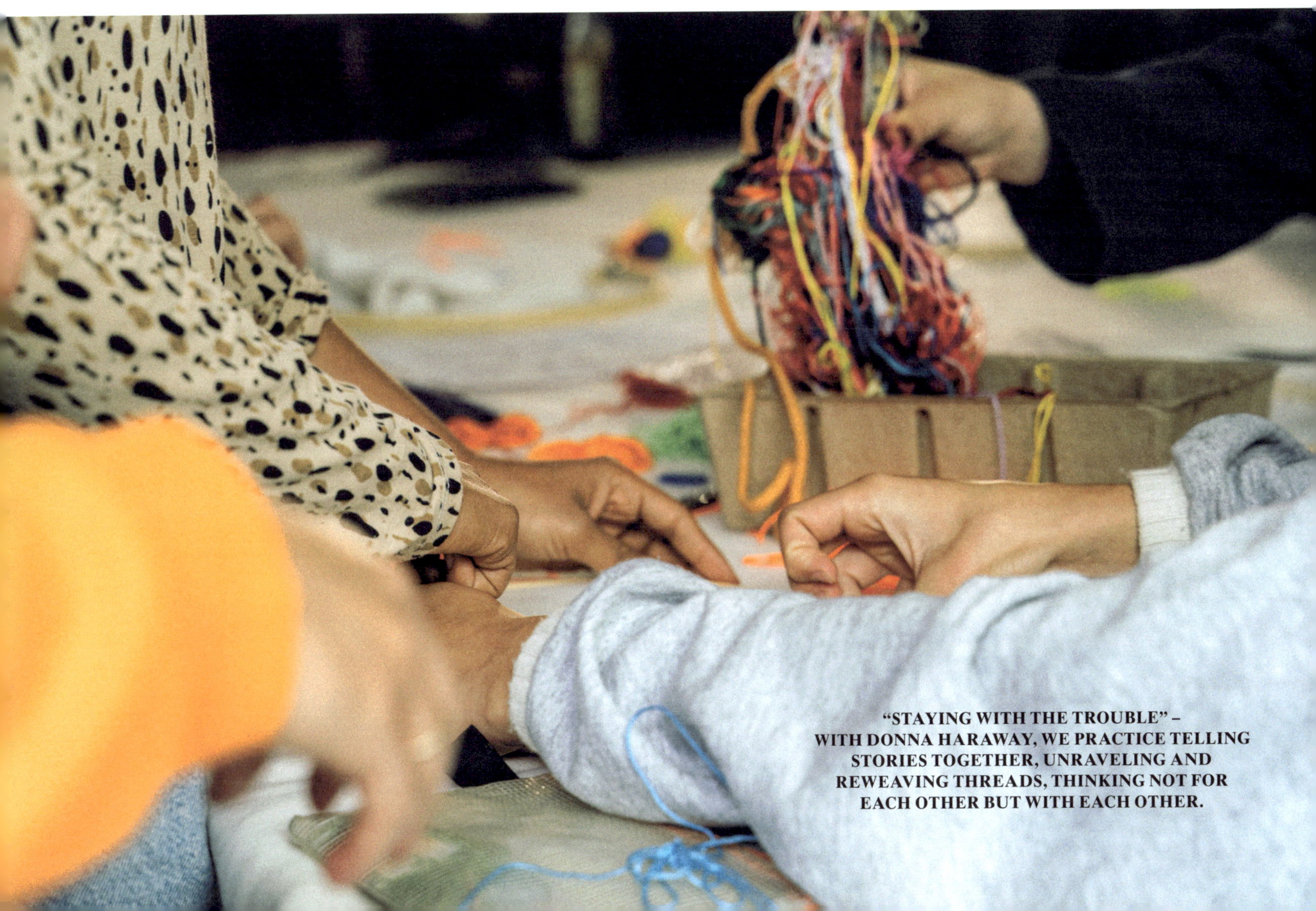

“STAYING WITH THE TROUBLE” – WITH DONNA HARAWAY, WE PRACTICE TELLING STORIES TOGETHER, UNRAVELING AND REWEAVING THREADS, THINKING NOT FOR EACH OTHER BUT WITH EACH OTHER.

Matri-Archi(tecture)

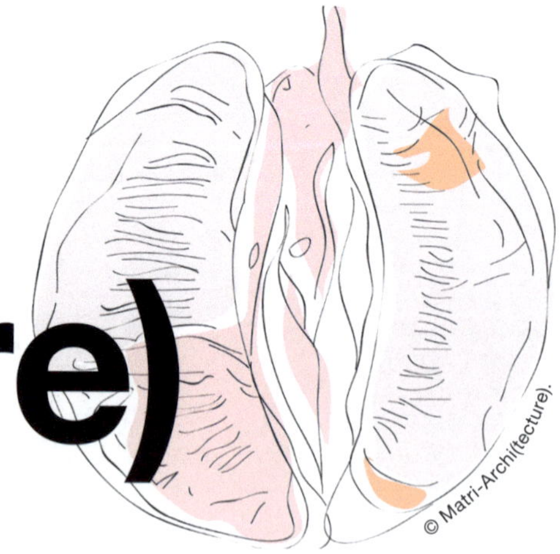

TEAM: Khensani de Klerk, Solange Mbanefo, Tapiwa Manase, Tshego Mako, Aude Tollo
LOCATIONS: Basel / Cape Town
FOUNDED: 2018

Matri-Archi(tecture) is a transversally networked intersectional collective working from Basel and Cape Town for the visibility of Black architects and designers of African and multiethnic origin. The collaborative online database *Matri-Archives* gathers information about these underrepresented protagonists, revealing their contributions to architectural history and their achievements in both academic and non-academic contexts. Matri-Archi(tecture) also works with like-minded practitioners to expand the definition of (architectural) knowledge with respect to the specific cultural context and traditions of narration and documentation. In doing so, they are not only pursuing their goal of challenging the canon but also building on this work to develop contemporary formats for architectural education. In addition to their design practice, this involves various text forms, podcasts, and exhibitions. The activist approach taken by Matri-Archi(tecture) focuses on broadening (educational) access to architecture, including theory and practice. It takes its work beyond the exclusionary mechanisms of private and public universities in Central Europe and North America and back into cities on the African continent.

MATRI-ARCHIVES: A digital atlas of collaborative geographies

In the digital ecosystem, participation, information exchange, and networking no longer require a physical presence in one place but are based primarily on internet access. The Matri-Archives digital atlas takes advantage of this, blurring geographical boundaries. It is constantly in flux and not subject to fixed categories. The references gathered in this archive critique the static nature of the architectural canon as it exists in academia to this day in order to give due credit to those overlooked in traditional architectural education. In doing so, the Matri-Archives reveal histories and imaginaries that reflect an intersectional, built environment and make it tangible as lived space.

WEAVING CONSTELLATIONS OF IDENTITY

Weaving Constellations of Identity is Matri-Archi(tecture)'s contribution to the exhibition *Here We Are! Women in Design 1900–Today*, on view from September 2021 until March 2022 at Vitra Design Museum in Weil am Rhein. For this piece, the collective spoke with Lesley Lokko, Alafuro Sikoki-Coleman, Philiswa Lila, Sandra Obiago Mbanefo, and Danielle Noelle Dreier-Harris—five esteemed Black African designers and practitioners—about their careers. Foregrounding emotional experiences, the collective translated the women's different experiences into video works and the haptic format of a tapestry. The recorded stories reveal meandering biographies marked by turning points and thresholds of varying intensity. The tapestry is more than just a design object, telling of subjective experiences and an expanded understanding of narrative patterns transferred into the fabric. Emotions such as joy, passion, and vulnerability are color-coded in the tapestry's weaving process, executed by Basel textile designers and coordinated by Solange Mbanefo. The biographical videos also show how these emotions are a driver and source of creative work. The focus on experiential horizons instead of functionalist thinking about form aims to motivate and inspire other designers who still have their professional paths before them. **GS**

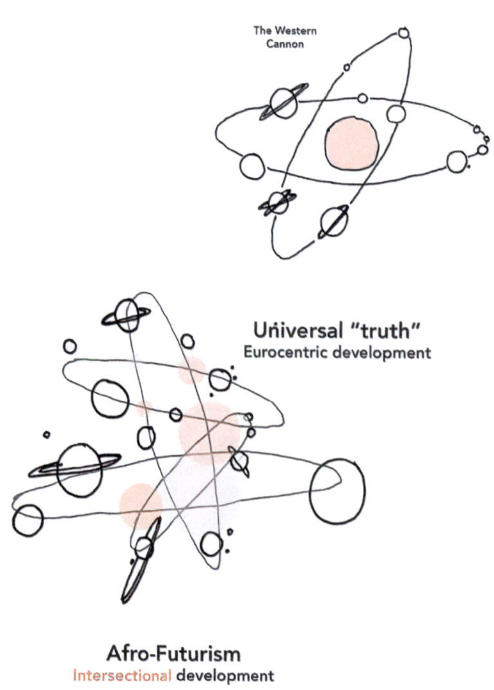

"Afro-futurism is not what we commonly (mis)perceive as the notion of 'futuristic' black science fiction. [...] It is an ever-present projection [...] of possible futures beyond the realms of the existing world we occupy today. Afro-futurism is far from a representation of purely fictional adventures. It is a way of thinking and an imagination that speaks beyond the 'naturalized western' objective universal rules of law [...] and transcends the systemic obstacles set in place by white supremacy."
From: Khensani de Klerk, Matri-Archi(tecture), *Afro-Futurism (Space is the Place) | Afro-Futurism: An Approach to African Development* (2017). © Matri-Archi(tecture), accessed September 1, 2022, www.matri-archi.ch/essays/afro-futurism-space-is-the-place-afro-futurism-an-approach-to-african-development.

Matri-Archi(tecture) translated narratives about the careers of the Black architects Lesley Lokko, Alafuro Sikoki-Coleman, Philiswa Lila, Sandra Obiago Mbanefo, and Danielle Noelle Dreier-Harris into a rug design. Emotional states associated with the respective career turning points are assigned a color code.
Poster: Matri-Archi(tecture). © Khensani de Klerk and Solange Mbanefo.

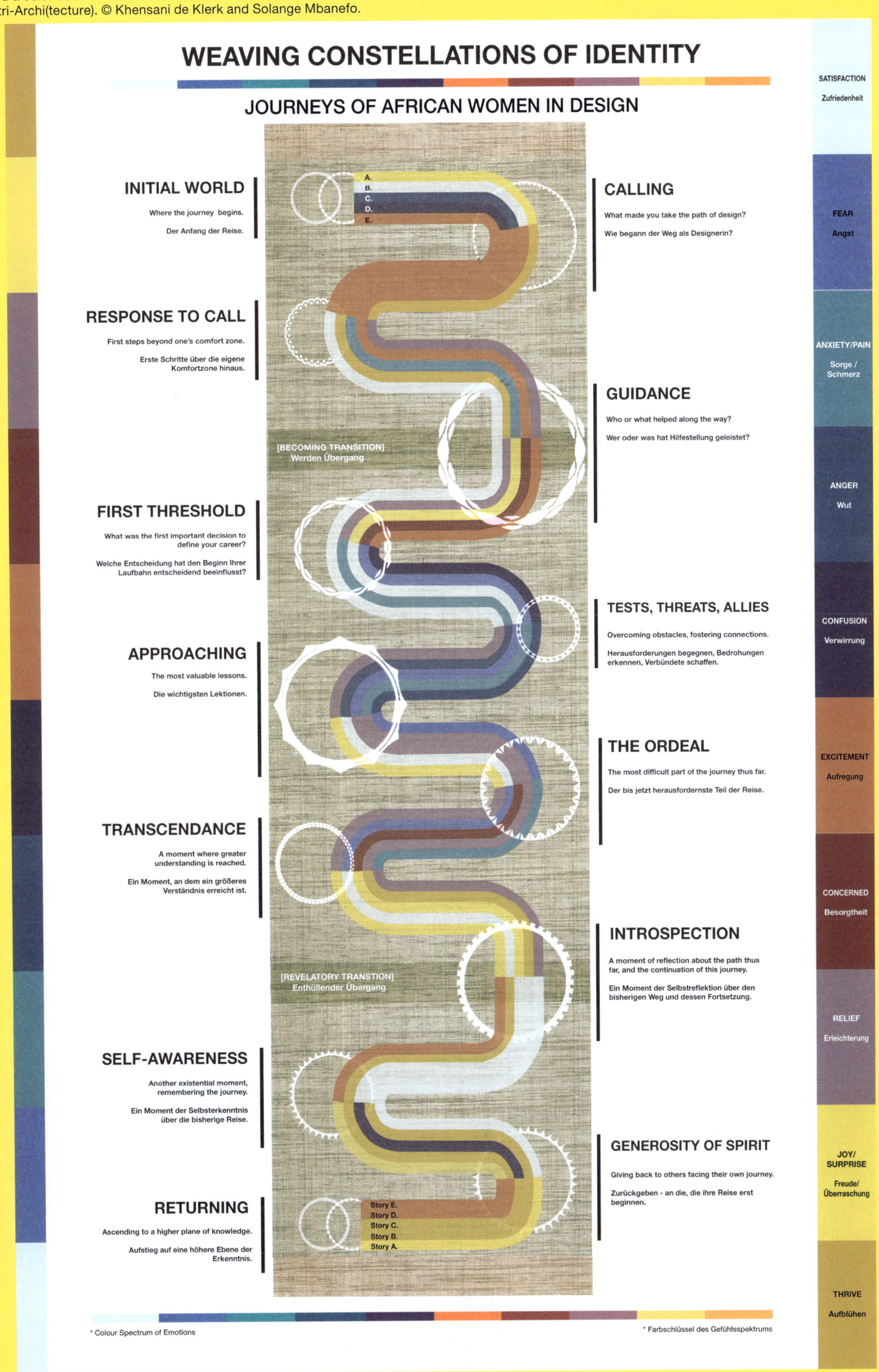

Weaving Constellations of Identity, 2021, exhibition view, *Here We Are! Women in Design 1900–Today*, Vitra Design Museum, Weil am Rhein 2021.
© Matri-Archi(tecture): Khensani de Klerk and Solange Mbanefo.

Video still.
Videography: Katharina Halser, Jonas Conklin.

Details from the tapestry produced for the exhibition.
© Matri-Archi(tecture).

ARTISTIC DIRECTION: Matri-Archi(tecture) – Khensani de Klerk and Solange Mbanefo
DIRECTOR OF CRAFT PRODUCTION: Danielle Noelle Dreier-Harris
TAPESTRY CRAFT PRODUCTION: Anita Vrolijk, Mirjam Spoolder, June Bicker, Salomé Dreier, Fátima-Frida Salum Said, Anna Cordasco, Kira Herrman, Leonie Wienandts, Hannah Strøem, Solange Mbanefo, Khensani de Klerk
COORDINATOR AND SUPERVISION OF TAPESTRY PRODUCTION: Solange Mbanefo
SOUNDSCAPE PRODUCTION: Khensani de Klerk
VIDEOGRAPHY: Katharina Halser, Jonas Conklin
TRANSCRIPTION: Khensani de Klerk, Tapiwa Manase

Practice

Office Hours

© Office Hours.

TEXT
Esther M. Choi

Office Hours is a socially engaged initiative that facilitates the sharing of worldmaking knowledge among practitioners who identify as Black, Indigenous, and People of Color (BIPOC). Our programming is rooted in intersectional justice and aims to increase representation, democratize access to knowledge, and encourage self-determination for BIPOC creative practitioners. Addressing topics such as starting an architecture practice, becoming an urban designer, and strategies for community organizing, we aim to highlight creative methodologies that aspire to imagine and shape the world according to values rooted in emancipation, accountability, and interdependence. Since 2020, our 32+ sessions have been attended by over 2,000 people of the global majority based in 14+ countries.

At Office Hours, we invite speakers whose practices acknowledge and combat interlocking forms of oppression and whose own layered identities intersect across categorizations of race, ethnicity, class, gender identification, sexuality, disability, age, and immigration status. Embracing intersectionality, we encourage our speakers to engage in open discussions about the ways that their overlapping social identities have shaped their professional experiences and insights. By addressing and embracing the textures of personal lived experiences—especially the challenges BIPOC folx have faced as a result of white supremacy and other axes of domination— we believe in the power of sharing strategies with others who find themselves navigating the unequal and uneven terrain of our professional lives and our world. Each session offers attendees a path or set of techniques to encourage agency and self-determination. All attendees turn their cameras on for our events—technology and accessibility permitting—and arrive accountable to the group dynamic. Sessions are recorded for our archives but not posted publicly.

Our group mentoring format allows us to practice the values of multi-racial and multi-ethnic solidarity, empathy, and generosity—rather than the tenets of singularity, extraction, and competition—as powerful social tools for living and working together with a shared sense of responsibility.

Attendees are active participants in shaping our sessions. In this way, the dialogical framework of this ongoing and ever-changing experiment is rooted in the relationships of our community members and their mutual empowerment.

Office Hours is steeped in the tradition of oral storytelling common among BIPOC communities and operates according to a maxim based on disability and BIPOC empowerment: "nothing about us without us." We believe an equitable ecosystem for cultural practice begins with us. We regard Office Hours as an ongoing experiment in sociability, ethics, and etiquette—one that enables us to practice and observe the political and emancipatory implications of listening, empathy, and, in the words of Anna Deavere Smith, a "radical hospitality." The project's premise is that holding ourselves accountable to the standards we seek to cultivate in the world is the first step.

www.office-hours.design

Intersectional Justice and Visibility

Black Females in Architecture
*2018
in London

© Black Females in Architecture.

is an international network led by Akua Danso, Neba Sere, and Selasi Setufe that works to increase the visibility of Black and Black mixed-heritage women in the architecture industry and other built environment fields. BFA actively addresses issues of intersectional inequality and the lack of diversity in architecture. The network provides a platform for members to exchange ideas, share knowledge, and benefit from advice, guidance, access to personal networks, and the expertise of other members. Through various event formats, including lectures, workshops, and regular meetups in both digital and physical formats, BFA offers Black and Black mixed-heritage women a space to discuss current issues and develop collaborative projects. **MAK**

www.blackfemarc.com

Part W
*2018
in London

PART W

© Part W.

is an action group of women architects, designers, and spatial planners founded by Zoë Berman to fight intersectional discrimination in the building industry. Its first campaign, *The Alternative List* (2019), targeted the lack of recognition of women and ethnically diverse people in architecture through juried award structures like the RIBA Royal Gold Medal. To draw attention to the fact that this award had been given only once to a woman and never to a Black person in its 170-year history, Part W initiated a crowdsourced list of 169 influential women in architecture with diverse backgrounds. The debate had an impact: in 2020, the Royal Institute of British Architects awarded the medal to Yvonne Farrell and Shelley McNamara, and in 2021 to Sir David Adjaye. **MAK**

www.part-w.com

depatriarchise design & Futuress
*2017/2020
in Basel

© Futuress / depatriarchise design.

are two collaborating nonprofit research platforms working at the juncture of (intersectional) feminism, design, and policy. In their multifaceted investigative and activist practice, they explore the complicity of design in the reproduction of systems of injustice through different outreach formats, such as publications, workshops, and exhibitions. Their online directory feministcurricula.org, published in 2021, maps and documents educational initiatives in design that employ feminist pedagogy to explore alternative ways of learning, teaching, and practicing design. This ever-growing compilation of courses, workshops, and programs includes assignments, projects, reading lists, and strategies that facilitate collaboration among designers, students, teachers, and researchers. **MAK**

www.feministcurricula.org

Sound Advice
*2020
in London

© Sound Advice / Joel Antoine-Wilkinson.

is a nonprofit platform founded by Pooja Agrawal and Joseph Henry that fights spatial inequality and discrimination in the architecture industry. *Now You Know* was published in 2021 and features contributions from 60 architects and urbanists of color. The book came together during the Covid-19 pandemic, which was associated with a disproportionately higher mortality rate and vulnerability among people of color. The collection of poems, interviews, and essays testifies to the structural racism embedded in the built environment, from housing and mobility infrastructure to access to clean air and public (green) space. *Now You Know* presents perspectives from a variety of marginalized, emancipatory positions and calls for new approaches to the design of cities, spaces, institutions, and societies. **MAK**

www.instagram.com/sound_x_advice

After the murder of George Floyd and the global Black Lives Matter protests it sparked in June 2020, the statue of Edward Colston was toppled and sunk in Bristol Harbour. In the weeks after the incident, the vacant pedestal was occupied by various artistic interventions, including Marc Quinn's *A Surge of Power (Jen Reid)*, 2020. The work depicts the anti-colonial activist Jen Reid raising her arm in a Black Power salute.
Photo: Harry Pugsley. © action press.

When Statues Fall

TEXT
Paul B. Preciado

Statues of colonizers are falling.

The autumn of the patriarch has arrived. Jean-Baptiste Colbert, the French minister of state from 1661 to 1683 and chief architect, together with his son, of the *Code Noir* (the laws governing slavery in France's imperial outposts),[01] awakens covered in paint; Francis Scott Key, enslaver and author of "The Star-Spangled Banner," is pulled to the ground; British human trafficker Edward Colston ends up at the bottom of the River Avon; Christopher Columbus is decapitated; Leopold II of Belgium and his noble steed are ignominiously defaced; King Louis XVI has his hand snapped off; J. Marion Sims, the gynecologist who performed surgical experiments without anesthesia on enslaved women, vanishes; the word *RACISTA* is scrawled on the pedestal of Franciscan missionary Junípero Serra ... Believers in national and republican iconophilia on both the right and the left are up in arms: *The police should come and protect these statues.* The very same police who beat and mutilate the racialized, sexualized living bodies of protesters and migrants in the streets—let them now come protect these stone and metal bodies. Perhaps that is ultimately the purpose of any police force: to protect monuments to power. In his first solemn statement on the issue, on June 14, President Emmanuel Macron warns that France "will not take down statues."[02] He seems to have forgotten the first law of democratic gravity: All statues fall down sooner or later. As W. G. Sebald reminds us, "monuments that represent the power some wield over others paradoxically contain in their violent and grandiloquent style the root of their own destruction."[03] The iconoclastic gesture's supremacy over any sculptural governmental decree is hidden but determinant. And the bigger the statue, the better the wreckage.

But why all the commotion over a few pounds of stone and metal? What is a statue when it is situated in a space deemed "public"? And what is it that falls when a statue falls?

The statues that have been attacked by decolonial activists are monumentalized representations of human bodies, sometimes accompanied by animal bodies, especially horses, and on occasion oxen, dogs, bears, geese, cats, or even elephants or camels. Such statues surround us, incarnating a kind of sculptural biopolitics. It is necessary to acknowledge the performative force of giving shape to one body and not another—representing it in victory or defeat, armed or unarmed, on horseback or on foot, clothed or nude, as a simple bust or from head to toe—and embedding it in the space of the city with durable materials that defy erosion and change. "Wrought works that imitate nature with the objective of extolling and elevating somebody's actions" (as officially defined by the Real Academia Española), statues are ghosts of the past, petrified in order to arouse adoration and respect, reverence and fear, exaltation and obedience. They are oversize collective ex-votos, prostheses of historical memory that memorialize the lives of those deemed important, that preserve the bodies that deserve to be "statuefied."

THE PATRIARCHAL-COLONIAL CITY EMBODIED

What has been placed in doubt in recent months by protests against racist police violence and by the attacks on statues is the bourgeois fiction that "public space" is neutral and egalitarian. The streets do not belong to us, nor have they ever. Neither do the bodies that matter, those that warrant "statuefication." In patriarchal societies of colonial heritage, "public space," in fact, does not exist. As David Harvey has argued, space generally called public is highly hierarchical and commercialized. Urbanist Itziar González Virós points out that the street is not a public space but an administrative one, regulated and policed by municipal and state authorities. In short, what has until now been called public space is in reality a space segmented by lines of class, race, sex, sexuality, and disability, where only the white, male, heterosexual, abled, and national body may circulate as a full-fledged subject. Migrant, nonwhite, female or effeminate, nonheterosexual, functionally diverse bodies are constantly subjected to various forms of restriction, violence, exclusion, surveillance, ghettoization, and death. These modes of governance operate in very different ways, through architectural divisions, urban barriers, institutional confinements, and military, police, and political controls. Of all these techniques, perhaps the "softest" and most aestheticized (and yet still brutal) is the production of a monumental marker, which inscribes a dominant cultural narrative in urban space through the sculptural reproduction of some bodies—and not others.

The power of statues derives precisely from the fact that they are representations of human bodies, figures that look like (or do not look like) us, that we can (or cannot) compare ourselves to, however strange their scale or attire. Any one of us could, theoretically, be a statue. But for this to happen, it is essential that your body "matter."[04] In fact, we know that although the faces of modern statues really are likenesses (if typically aggrandized) of the people represented, the bodies are often those of the working poor, including sex workers, who were used as models. Their bodies were copied and at the same time erased to serve as the foundation for faces that mattered and were worthy of eulogizing. That's why all of these statues are a lie. They do not represent the bodies of specific individuals, but rather the normative political body; they stand for the values of virility, racial purity, wealth, and power, affirm the victory of the patriarchal-colonial discourse that commissions and installs them and occludes undesirable narratives. There is no statue that depicts Colbert jerking off as he looks at a map of Africa, or of Brother Junípero or Colston sexually assaulting indigenous or Black men, women, or children.

All statues are a lie. All statues are made to one day be toppled.

In the modern patriarchal city of colonial heritage, the normative monumentalized bodies of statues collectively articulate an aesthetic of domination that produces identification and distancing, cohesion and social exclusion. "Public" sculptures do not represent the people; rather, they construct them. Not only do they instantiate a pure, national body, they also establish an ideal of colonial, sexual citizenry. We collectively inhabit an iconic landscape that is saturated with signs of power endorsed by historical and epic narratives and aestheticized and naturalized to the extent that we are no longer able to perceive their cognitive violence. This is why some people claim that Barcelona's statue of Columbus, for example, not only is beautiful (!?) but "belongs to" the city's landscape. Nevertheless, a Catalan or a migrant walking by will not see the statue in the same way a Castilian does; a racialized person and a white person are not questioned in the same manner by a sculpture of Brother Junípero; an assigned female does not see the huge number of nude female statues in parks or gardens, facing numerous militarized male bodies bearing swords or guns, in the same way as someone who has been raised as a man. Stated differently, this ubiquitous corporeal public praise of the values of white, masculine, and heterosexual supremacy makes the modern city a patriarchal-colonial amusement park, a kind of Westworld[05] populated by eerily motionless avatars of domination, belonging, and recognition—or submission, exclusion, and erasure. That's why all statues must fall.

On the occasion of Juneteenth, the annual commemoration of the liberation of African Americans from slavery held on June 19, the statue of Albert Pike in Washington, DC, was toppled and set on fire by demonstrators. The protest lasted until the early hours of June 20, 2020.
Photo: Maya Alleruzzo. © picture alliance.

In summer 2017, women from Black Youth Project 100 protested against a statue in Central Park, New York, depicting the gynecologist J. Marion Sims, who performed medical experiments on enslaved Black women without anesthesia. The statue was removed from the park in April 2018 and relocated to a cemetery elsewhere in the city, to be re-erected near Sims's gravesite with added historical information.
Photo: Eduardo Munoz. © picture alliance.

During the global Black Lives Matter protests in June 2020, paint was poured on the statue of Jean-Baptiste Colbert in front of the French Parliament building in Paris.
Photo: Thibault Camus. © picture alliance.

How statues fall

Judging by the forces that destabilize them, statues fall for three reasons: decline, removal (from above), and toppling (from below). In the first case, the statues become meaningless objects: They are forgotten and left to erode until they are disfigured; they become faceless stones; they are worn out and not repaired—even the name on the plaque may fade or be covered by mold or ivy.

In the second case, they are pompously dislodged by government decree: a grandiose gesture via heavy machinery that usually signals a regime change. The de-Sovietization processes in the former Eastern Bloc involved hundreds of demolitions of this type. Often, these procedures were intended to convince the public that radical change was indeed under way. In Ukraine in 2015, Communist monuments were destroyed in the morning, and almost that same afternoon new heroes took their places. It is more productive when, instead of a simple substitution, symbols from the past are maintained but reread in a critical manner. For example, in the Ukrainian city of Yuzhne, the artist Alexander Milov transformed a sculpture of Lenin into one of Darth Vader and wrote on an accompanying plaque: "To the father of our nation, from its grateful children and stepchildren."

The third case is the most unpredictable and politically the most interesting. With ropes, hammers, picks, shovels, bags, paper, paint, flowers, and any other implements or techniques available, statues are collectively transformed, disfigured, partially dismantled or dismembered, or brought down completely in an unauthorized, unofficial, and usually illegal manner. The French Revolution; the anticlerical, anarchist movement before and during the Spanish Civil War; and the ongoing global uprisings against racism are a few examples of the kind of upheaval that galvanizes waves of this most dramatic form of "falling."

The removal of statues "from above" that Preciado describes finds cinematic expression in *The Gaze of Ulysses* (1995), directed by Theo Angelopoulos. During his wanderings through the Balkan countries, the protagonist "A" repeatedly encounters the "grandiose gesture via heavy machinery" described by Preciado, through which monuments are removed as a sign of political upheaval.
From *The Gaze of Ulysses* (1995), directed by Theo Angelopoulos, distributed by trigon-film. © trigon-film.org.

DE-PETRIFYING URBAN GRAMMAR

The most recent attacks on statues supplement preexisting graffiti, including the thousands of feminist, queer, and trans tags that have gradually covered cities in recent years. All of these phenomena are, to borrow Umberto Eco's phrase, forms of "semiological guerilla warfare"[06]: They question dominant discourses around racial, sexual, and gender privilege through means at once rhetorical and physical. The current campaign targets the material manifestations of cultural grammar in the city. It aims to rupture the false coherence of patriarchal-colonial reason's semiotic framework, to open closed discourses, and to return meanings that have been reified—literally "petrified"—to the public arena, extracting them from the sacralization of power so that they can be collectively reconsidered. When a statue falls, it opens a possible space of resignification[07] in power's dense and saturated landscape.

That's why all statues must fall.

There's a tectonic analogy between the toppling of statues that have served as Western civilization's cultural emblems and the necessary dismantling of the patriarchal-colonial infrastructure of capitalist modernity. In the same way in which we talk about the restitution of works stolen during colonization from their countries of origin, we have now begun to focus on an equally necessary process, which could be called the destitution of public symbols commemorating colonial reason. If restitution involves the physical displacement of stolen objects—that is, their return from Europe and North America to former colonies—then "destitution" is about setting in motion practices for the cognitive resignification of history. Contrary to the opinion of "universalists" (who, of course, are not universalists at all but seek to protect the dominant culture and white supremacy), the actions of those who tear down statues cannot be an anachronistic sin against the intelligibility of history because history is always and by definition "anachronistic"; rather, the iconoclasts are challenging *a* history and, by extension, contesting the idea that the past is ever merely intelligible, as opposed to constructed and reconstructed. The sculptures of Colbert and Columbus have always been anachronistic; to use Robert Smithson's beautiful words, they have always been "ruins in reverse."[08] Columbus was first installed in Barcelona in 1888 and Colbert in Paris in 1830. We are meant to grant these effigies the status of relics, to honor them as physical links to the past, but in fact they have nothing to do with the 15th and 17th centuries, just as the famous clock in Shakespeare's *Julius Caesar* has nothing to do with classical antiquity.

Processes of antipatriarchal and anticolonial subjectivation merge with these practices of destitution and resignification. The question is not whether statues should fall, but rather whether public authorities and cultural elites want to participate in overturning them or would prefer that those demanding justice remain silent subalterns so they can maintain their petrified privileges.[09]

This process of material resignification of urban space generates chaos but also political joy and eventually critical justice. A revolution is not just a supplanting of modes of government but also a collapse of modes of representation, a jolt to the semiotic universe, a reordering of bodies and voices. It is important that these moments of intervention, critique, and destitution not be criminalized but rather welcomed as gestures of the political subjectivation of those who have been and still are objectified by the techniques of patriarchal and colonial government. One characteristic of a radical democracy is its capacity to understand the critical reinterpretation of its own history as a source of creativity and collective emancipation, instead of hastening to homogenize voices and contain dissidence.

For a Monument to Modern Global Necropolitics

When statues are toppled, it is as if a collective force has grabbed hold of the clock of history and sped up its hands. Right now, the hands of the clock are spinning. Unfortunately for nationalist iconophiles, patriarchal and colonial statues have either fallen, are falling, or will fall. Now the question is what to do with the remains of Colbert and Columbus, Napoleon and Josephine, Key and Jefferson Davis.

One could, for example, replace the statue of Columbus at the foot of La Rambla in Barcelona with the sculpture *Not Dressed for Conquering / HC 04 Transport*, 2011–, by Austrian artist Ines Doujak, which some say depicts the former king of Spain Juan Carlos I in a sexual embrace with the anticolonial Bolivian activist Domitila Barrios de Chúngara and Walter Benjamin's proverbial wolf of fascism.[10] But perhaps this would be too much of a tourist attraction, and Barcelona needs not only decolonization but also detouristification. A better option would be to ditch Columbus and leave an empty space that invites public debate and critique and offers an unobstructed view of the horizon, so that the main thoroughfare of Barcelona opens to the Mediterranean: a gesture of hospitality rather than one of conquest.

Iconoclasm is as prone to failure as crash diets: Three statues are removed today, and a dozen more appear tomorrow. We need a slow and deep iconoclasm that is not just a preface to a replacement of figures. All monumental statues that commemorate patriarchal-colonial modernity would have to be taken down—absolutely all of them: the political, military, and ecclesiastical figures that compose the majority as well as the human traffickers, the doctors and scientists who espoused race theory, the solemn rapists and eminent *génocidaires*, and, not least, the writers and artists who produced the language and representations of power. To console iconophiles unsettled by the fate of their idols, all these statues—from Colbert to Columbus, San Martín de Porres to Brother Junípero, Leopold II to Colston, Davis to Sims, and so on—could be used to create the Monument to Modern Global Necropolitics. While we're at it, let's also get rid of the sculptures housed in nongovernmental spaces, the dozens of Francos and Mussolinis gathering dust in the museums of "historical memory."

Let the museums remain empty and the pedestals bare. Let nothing be installed upon them. It is necessary to leave room for utopia regardless of whether it ever arrives. It is necessary to make room for living bodies. Less metal and more voice, less stone and more flesh.

All, absolutely all, of the dismounted statues should be relocated to the same place and, rather than elevated, made to stand on the ground, side by side, about six feet apart, as if maintaining social distance to protect themselves from viral contamination—violence, terror, and hate are more infectious than any virus. Visitors could walk among them in that silent Mausoleum of Modern Historical Terror, touch them, get to know them, look them in the eye, perhaps one day forgive them. As for statues that have been decapitated (such operations are hardly new; for example, in Fort-de-France, Martinique, the

During the de-communization of Ukraine, numerous statues of Lenin were threatened with removal. In the port city of Odessa, an intervention by the Ukrainian artist Alexander Milov transformed the bronze statue into Darth Vader from the film *Star Wars* by adding the iconic mask and cape. According to Milov, Lenin can be easily exhumed by "grateful or not-so-grateful descendants" if needed. © Niels Ackermann / Lundi13.

The photo was part of the *Looking for Lenin* series by Niels Ackermann and Sébastien Gobert, published as a book by FUEL Publishing in London in 2017.

Inés Doujak, *Not Dressed for Conquering / HC 04 Transport*, 2011–, installation view, MACBA, Museo d'Art Contemporani de Barcelona. © Markus Wörgötter.

acephalic Empress Josephine was on display from 1991, when her head was removed by activists denouncing her involvement in Napoleon's restoration of slavery, until this past July, when the statue was destroyed completely), the disarticulated body parts could be recovered, and the figures that have been broken into pieces intermingled with the bodies that are still intact. Within public space as well as within the unconscious, a fragment can sometimes be more powerful than a complete object, just as an absence can be more meaningful than a presence.

We could debate the best site for this gigantic recycled Monument to Modern Global Necropolitics. One option would be to install the statues in the main square of the city of Burgos, Spain, a few steps away from the Casa del Cordón, where Columbus, it is said, signed the agreement with the Catholic monarchs to set out on his transatlantic journey. They could be placed at the Port of Liverpool, or in the Place de la Concorde in Paris, or in front of the Bourse Maritime in Bordeaux, France, or in the gardens of the Royal Palace of Brussels … There is no shortage of appropriate places, but none would be big enough to accommodate them all. So maybe the best place to put them is on a line that precisely delineates the borders of Europe and the United States, as defined today by their respective governments. That Punctured Wall of Infamy would replace the barriers and ditches, walls and fences, border-police stations and customs offices. All those statues, situated a few feet apart from one another, would remain there, signaling that the territories currently defined as Europe and the US are the results of their practices and discourses of violence. And there they would stand, history's last borders, reminding us of where we came from, until, one day, they fell—pushed over by the wind, jostled by passersby (who would no longer have to be called migrants), dissolved by the rain.

In the meantime, while the toppled and relocated statues melt away, let's use the empty pedestals left behind in all cities as performative platforms that other, living bodies can stand atop. We do not suffer from a forgetting of normative history but from a systematic erasure of the history of oppression and resistance. We do not need any more statues. Let's not ask for marble or metal to fill those pedestals. Let's climb up on them and tell our own stories of survival and liberation.

This text first appeared in *Artforum International* 59, no. 3 (December 2020). With kind permission from Paul B. Preciado.

In the series *Post(-Colonial) Cards*, WAI Think Tank unmasks romantic depictions of occupied landscapes and the violence of erasure inherent in them. By directly referencing iconic avant-garde works (such as Krutikov's *Floating City*, El Lissitzky's *Tribune*, and Malevich's *Architectons*), the studio depicts archetypes intended to memorialize or invent new iconographic, political, and ideological symbols as part of postcolonial narrative architectural projects: a stage for postcolonial plays, camps for ideological monuments, modernist hotels, globes and javelins, aviaries and floating fortresses. The series exemplifies the studio's efforts to establish anti-racism in the practice and teaching of architecture. The studio takes a similar approach with its works *Post-Novis, A Manual of Anti-Racist Architecture Education*, and *Six Buildings on an Island*.

01 Editors' note: The *Code Noir* was in force from 1685 to 1848. The decision made after the French Revolution to abolish slavery in all French colonies was never implemented, and the *Code Noir* was explicitly reaffirmed under Napoleon.
02 Michel Rose, Sudip Kar-Gupta, "Macron Says France Won't Remove Statues, Erase History," *Reuters*, June 14, 2020, accessed September 1, 2022, www.reuters.com/article/us-health-coronavirus-france-macron-stat-idUSKBN23L0QP.
03 W. G. Sebald, "Between History and Natural History," *Orbis Litterarum* 37, no. 4 (Winter 1982), 345–66.
04 Judith Butler, *Bodies That Matter: On the Discursive Limits of "Sex"* (New York, NY: Routledge, 1993).
05 *Westworld* is a neo-western television series from the United States, first broadcast in October 2016 on the US cable channel HBO, set in a fictional theme park populated with android "hosts." The sole purpose of the hosts is to satisfy all the desires of the guests, including those who are sexually abusive or violent, raising new questions of morality in virtual space.
06 Umberto Eco, "Towards a Semiological Guerilla Warfare," in *Travels in Hyperreality*, trans. W. Weaver (San Diego, CA: Harvest Books, 1990), 135–44.
07 The concept of resignification goes back to Judith Butler's first work, *Gender Trouble: Feminism and the Subversion of Identity* (New York, NY: Routledge, 1990). It refers to the (re)appropriation of a derogatory term into a positive self-designation, such as with the word "queer." Inherent in performative acts of reoccupation and (re)appropriation is an emancipatory moment that aims to change power relations.
08 Robert Smithson, *Project Space: Ruins in Reverse*, exhibited at Tate Britain, London, March 1 to June 24, 2013, accessed September 1, 2022, www.tate.org.uk/whats-on/tate-modern/exhibitionseries/project-space/project-space-ruins-reverse.
09 See Gayatri Spivak, "Can the subaltern speak?" in *Marxism and the Interpretation of Culture*, eds. Cary Nelson and Lawrence Grossberg (Urbana, IL: University of Illinois Press, 1988), 271–313.
10 The sculpture was the subject of official censorship in 2015 at the exhibition *La bestia y el soberano/La bèstia i el sobirà* at Museu d'Art Contemporani in Barcelona due to its references to colonial history and the body of the king.

Fanon on Colonial Space

TEXT
Samia Henni

Histories, theories, and practices of architecture and urbanism are intimately intertwined with processes of colonialization and the mechanisms of what Frantz Omar Fanon (1925–1961), psychiatrist, political philosopher, and anticolonial activist from the French colony of Martinique (today a French Department), called "the Manichaean world."[01] This modern world could only come about through violent activities of war, occupation, exploitation, dispossession, destruction, and construction. Since the 15th century, European administrators, architects, and planners, serving both civil and military purposes, have been actively participating in constructing empires and framing their representations.[02] These professionals were commissioned to imagine and design various infrastructures, public buildings, and private settlements across the multiple territories of the empires under which they operated, including the British, Dutch, French, German, Italian, Ottoman, Portuguese, Russian, and Spanish empires. The richness of colonized spaces across the world has been instrumental in exploiting capital and resources and implementing an uneven distribution of power.[03] To this end, the making of spaces in the colonizer world cannot be understood without the making of spaces in the colonized world. These rapports must be studied and theorized together: both along and against the grain.[04]

According to Fanon, "the colonial world is a Manichean world"[05]—a world that is segregated into compartments and characterized by a strict division between the colonizer and colonized people. He argued that, for the colonizer, "the town belonging to the colonized people, or at least the native town, the Negro village, the Medina, the reservation, is a place of ill fame, peopled by men of evil repute."[06] Among the manifold reasons for the association of colonized people—and their spaces—with "ill fame" and "evil repute" is the invention of the *self* and thereby of the *other*. A colonized "other" that the colonizer "self" deemed inferior and, therefore, destined to be subjugated and dominated by the colonizer "self," but without becoming the "self." This international division, self-assigned supremacy, and racial segregation are at the heart of the Manichean mechanism and the resulting systemic violence.

For Fanon, violence is both a human (political) and a medical (scientific) notion. He identified at least three categories of violence: offensive colonial violence, defensive anticolonial violence, and violence in the international context, opening up possibilities for constructive reconsiderations of world orders, spaces, and assumptions. His ambition was to scrutinize the "them-or-us" or "the other-or-the self" dichotomy of both the colonial world and the Cold War—including the threat of nuclear war—and to map the complex nuances that the colonizer might have, consciously or unconsciously, censored, distorted, or obliterated.[07] The division between the "self" and the "other" as well as the representation of the "other" is a human construct.[08] It is contingent on the person or institution that establishes, evaluates, judges, and qualifies another person or space in relation to the "self," the norm, the normative. However, colonial regimes have propagated these constructs and disseminated their misconceptions among European populations since the beginning of the first wave of colonization and the transatlantic slave trade through, among others, Universal, International, and Colonial Exhibitions. Here, children, women, and men from the colonies, protectorates, overseas territories, and departments were locked up in cages and put on display. These "living exhibits" and the establishment of Human Zoos, also called Ethnological Expositions, promulgated racist, discriminatory constructs, some of which still exist to this day.[09]

FRANTZ FANON, *DIE VERDAMMTEN DIESER ERDE*, 1969; FRENCH ORIGINAL: *LES DAMNÉS DE LA TERRE* (1961); ENGLISH TRANSLATION: *THE WRETCHED OF THE EARTH* (1963). COURTESY ROWOHLT VERLAG.

In the colonies, however, the production of the colonial space entailed the destruction of existing spaces and buildings and, thereby, the imposition of certain norms of forms of living, commuting, and governing.[10] Whether it was called the "civilizing mission" in the context of colonization or "development" and "investment" in today's context of globalization, these spatial practices reinforce a particular world order/disorder.[11] As Fanon argued, the primary encounter between the colonizer and the colonized people and their spaces was marked by violence. Fanon contended: "Violence in its practice is totalizing and national. As a result, it harbors in its depths the elimination of regionalism and tribalism."[12] Architectural examples of this elimination can be found in various geographies, including Africa, Asia, Australia, Canada, and the Americas. These places are marked by the genocide of the native people, along with the destruction of their habitat and the imposition of imported forms, norms, and construction materials from England, France, Netherlands, Portugal, Spain, and other European countries. In analyzing the exclusionary relationship between the colonizer and the colonized space, Fanon argued, "No conciliation is possible, for of the two terms, one is superfluous."[13] The spatial organization of colonialization indicates that inequality and difference, segregation, and imposition are integral parts of the Manichean dualism.

Fanon's critique of the colonial space and its representation provides an ethic of decolonial reason, which incites us to reflect on the ongoing cartographies of the so-called "postcolonial" or "global" that often echo the colonial world order of dispossession—including the extraction, exploitation, and transportation of capital and resources, as well as the circulation of forms that do not respond to specific environmental and socioeconomic conditions.[14] This tendency should be challenged together with the widely accepted architectural taxonomies, such as formal/informal settlements, modern/traditional architecture, private/public spaces, and other well-known categories that also belong to the Manichaean world Fanon meticulously analyzed and critiqued.

Fanon's arguments reveal existing racist positions and violent spatial conditions that public institutions have generated and are tolerating or, in some cases, are trying to overcome. These situations are to be understood transnationally, connecting the construction of spaces in the metropolitan centers of colonizing regimes with the construction and destruction of the spaces in the formerly colonized countries. Such a multiscale view is informed by anticolonial, abolitionist, indigenous, Black, queer, feminist, and other traditions of associating antiracism with aspirations for independence, freedom, liberation, and justice.

Fanon's pathology (political and scientific) of colonial ideologies and anticolonial struggles incites an intersectional approach to architectural practices—including historicizing, theorizing, and curating architecture—that considers multiple aspects of space-making, such as race, class, religion, gender, resources, climate, and violence.

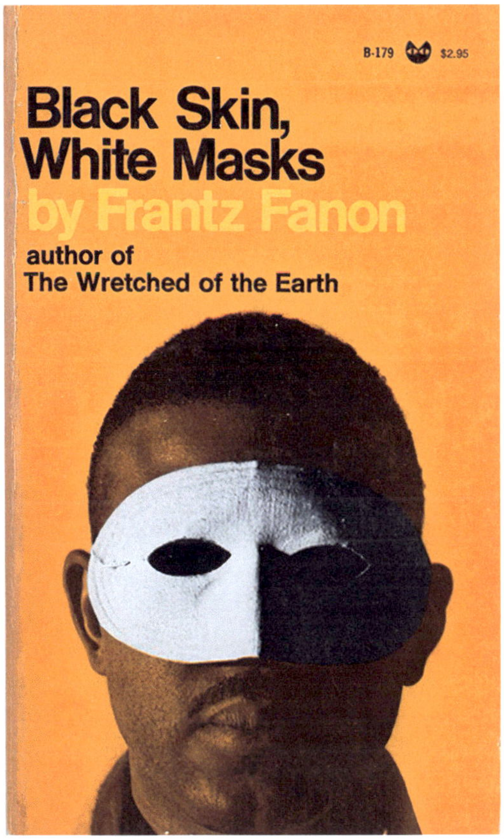

Frantz Fanon, *Black Skin, White Masks*, 1967.
© Grove Press.

01 Frantz Fanon analyzed his theories on the Manichean system in four books: *Peau Noire, Masques Blancs* (1952) (Engl.: *Black Skin, White Masks*, 2008); *L'An V de la Révolution Algérienne* (1959) (Engl.: *A Dying Colonialism*, 1967); *Les Damnés de la Terre* (1961) (Engl.: *The Wretched of the Earth*, 2004); and *Pour la Révolution Africaine*, published posthumusly in 1964 (Engl.: *Toward the African Revolution*). He also wrote numerous articles in professional journals and revolutionary newspapers, such as the Algerian *El Moudjahid*. The publication of previously unseen works in *Écrits sur l'aliénation et la liberté* (2015) (Engl.: *Alienation and Freedom*, 2018) concludes Fanon's anticolonial engagement and decolonialization efforts.

02 Samia Henni, "Colonial Ramifications," *e-flux Architecture*, History/Theory, gta Institute, ETH Zurich, accessed September 1, 2022, https://www.e-flux.com/architecture/history-theory/225180/colonial-ramifications/.

03 See Frederick Cooper, *Colonialism in Question: Theory, Knowledge, History* (Berkeley, CA: University of California Press, 2005).

04 See Ann Laura Stoler, *Along the Archival Grain: Epistemic Anxieties and Colonial Common Sense* (Princeton, NJ: Princeton University Press, 2009).

05 Frantz Fanon, *The Wretched of the Earth*, trans. Richard Philcox (New York: Grove Press, 2004), 41.

06 Ibid., 39.

07 On Fanon's definitions of violence, see "Concerning Violence" and "Violence in the International Context," in Fanon, *The Wretched of the Earth* (see note 5), 35–106. Fanon's approach to violence and its effects is informed by the violence of the colonial world that he experienced and attempted to cure. Sometimes his work has been taken out of context and he was unfairly accused of inciting violence. However, Fanon argued that violence is the "natural state" of colonial rule and that the colonial space is maintained through violence.

08 See also Franz Fanon, *Black Skin, White Masks* (1961), trans. Markmann Charles Lam (London: Pluto Press, 2008); Edward W. Said, *Orientalism* (London: Routledge & Kegan Paul, 1978); Athena Athanasiou and Judith Butler, *Dispossession: The Performative in the Political the Performative in the Political* (Cambridge: Polity, 2013); Achille Mbembe, *Critique of Black Reason* (Durham, NC: Duke University Press, 2017); Walter Mignolo, *Local Histories/Global Designs Coloniality, Subaltern Knowledges, and Border Thinking* (Princeton, NJ: Princeton University Press, 2012).

09 See also Pascal Blanchard and Musée du quai Branly, *Human Zoos: The Invention of the Savage* (Arles: Actes Sud, 2011); Lucy Michael and Samantha Schulz, *Unsettling Whiteness* (Oxford: Inter-Disciplinary Press, 2014).

10 See also Paul Rabinow, *French Modern: Norms and Forms of the Social Environment* (Chicago, IL: University of Chicago Press, 1989); Nezar AlSayyad, ed., *Forms of Dominance: On the Architecture and Urbanism of the Colonial Enterprise* (Aldershot, VT: Avebury, 1992); Itohan Osayimwese, *Colonialism and Modern Architecture in Germany* (Pittsburgh, PA: University of Pittsburgh Press, 2017); Samia Henni, *Architecture of Counterrevolution: The French Army in Northern Algeria* (Zurich: gta Verlag, 2017).

11 See also Samia Henni, "The Colonial Order of Things," in *Archithese Reader: Critical Positions in Search of Postmodernity*, 1971–1976, eds. Gabrielle Schaad and Torsten Lange (Zurich: Triest Verlag für Architektur, forthcoming).

12 Fanon, *The Wretched of the Earth* (see note 5), 51.

13 Ibid., 39.

14 See also Arjun Appadurai, *Modernity at Large Cultural Dimensions of Globalization* (Minneapolis, MN: University of Minnesota Press, 1996); Samia Henni, "Anticolonial Remedies: From Colonization to Globalization," *Perspecta 53: Onus*, eds. Caroline Acheatel, et al. (2020): 193–203; Walter Mignolo, *Globalization and the Decolonial Option* (Abingdon: Routledge, 2010).

A Letter to Audre Lorde

Audre Lorde, *Sister Outsider*, 2007. © Crossing Press.

TEXT
Afaina de Jong

Dear Audre,

Although you are no longer with us on earth, I am writing to you because your writing has had a profound impact on me and my work. With your life's work, you laid the foundation for intersectional feminist thinking. In doing so, you encouraged me to develop a feminist practice that advocates for a more just and equitable society on a social and spatial level by allowing for differences.

In general, when I talk as an architect about the necessity for intersectional feminist thinking, it is often directly linked to the undeniable need to improve the position (and representation) of women in this male-dominated profession. But for me, the issues you raise in your writings remain indispensable for architectural thinking itself, more than 40 years later.

In spring 2021, I was invited by the collective Claiming*Spaces, based at Vienna University of Technology, to develop and teach a design studio as their first visiting professor. I wanted the studio to be a space free from the usual rules, guidelines, or solutions that the students would be familiar with through their previous studies. Hence the name: *A Space of Freedom*. In the first half of the semester, we read and analyzed five essays from your book *Sister Outsider*, including "The Uses of Anger: Women Responding to Racism" (1981), "The Uses of the Erotic: Eroticism as Power" (1978), and "The Transformation of Silence into Language and Action" (1978). Your writing helped the students articulate their individual experiences in architectural education and practice—frustration, anger, and abuse. But your writings also offered inspiration, gave us a language, and helped our understanding and analysis of social injustices. More importantly, they also opened up new possibilities for action. With their newfound insights, the students formulated their own proposals for spatial intervention, all of which, in their own way, aimed to make themselves heard, embrace difference, see the erotic as "a source of power and information,"[01] or use anger as a source of creativity, because, as you write, this is not about blame(ing) but about "genuine change,"[02] because "guilt and defensiveness are bricks in a wall against which we all flounder; they serve none of our futures."[03] In your essay "The Transformation of Silence into Language and Action," you ask an important question: "Perhaps for some of you here today, I am the face of one of your fears. Because I am woman, because I am Black, because I am lesbian, because I am myself—a Black woman warrior poet doing my work—come to ask you, are you doing yours?"[04] We must relate this question to ourselves as architects at this crucial moment in history. After all, architecture as a practice, with its myriad theories and buildings, is undeniably enmeshed in structures of inequality, oppression, and exploitation. Are we, as architects, doing the work? Are we saying what needs to be said, or do we (in your words) betray ourselves by our silence and make ourselves complicit?

Your work gives us a way to understand our position in society. No, we are not all the same; our experiences are different because they are shaped by privilege or oppression. And yes, we can design for difference and abandon the standardization of the Modular Man. But in order to do so, we need to advance our vocabulary. As you say: "What are the words you do not yet have?"[05] By adding words like "ally," "asexual," "femmephobia," "mansplaining," or "cisnormativity" to the architectural discourse, it will also become easier to name certain grievances and power asymmetries. And if words are followed by actions, my hope is that the architectural design language will also change so that we can spatially implement equality, freedom, and a non-exploitative relationship with people and the environment.

The potential of architecture to explore the layers of languages and modes of expression or even to create new architecture through new words is extremely exciting. But none of this will be possible if the same old tools, the same old canon, and the same old teaching methods continue to be used. In your essay, "The Master's Tools Will Never Dismantle the Master's House," you write: "What does it mean when the tools of a racist patriarchy are used to examine the fruits of that same patriarchy? It means that only the most narrow perimeters of change are possible and allowable."[06] This also applies to the often privileged way architects view the world. When coupled with design paradigms in which architects have learned to see themselves as the only ones with the ability to design, this privileged position is highly problematic.

Women, people of color, people who identify as queer, and indigenous people are still being asked to explain their existence and needs, even to justify them. The idea you put forth, that this is an old and primary mechanism of a system to occupy the time and effort of oppressed people, again influenced my thinking profoundly. The alternative you describe is "to make common cause with those others identified as outside the structures in order to define and seek a world in which we can all flourish."[07] In my contribution, *The Multiplicity of Other*, to the Dutch Pavilion at the 2021 Venice Architecture Biennale, I explored marginalized knowledge, practices, and values that are not part of the dominant paradigm in spatial planning and have been for the most part ignored by the architecture canon. Today, these seem all the more important for driving structural transformations in architectural practice that are urgently needed. This also applies considerably to your work.

Your writings urge us to explore those values, methods, knowledge, practices, and vocabularies of architecture and move them from the margins to the center to transform the largely exploitative dynamic into feminist, anti-racist, and non-exploitative forms of coexistence.

And for that, I thank you.
Afaina de Jong

Afaina de Jong, *The Multiplicity of Other*, 2021. Contribution for the Dutch Pavilion at the 17th Architecture Bienniale in Venice. Photo: CXCasulo. Courtesy CXCasulo / Afaina de Jong.

"The Master's Tools Will Never Dismantle the Master's House."

01 Audre Lorde, "Uses of the Erotic: The Erotic as Power," in *Sister Outsider: Essays and Speeches by Audre Lorde* [1984], revised edition (Berkeley, CA: Crossing Press, 2007), 53.
02 Ibid., 59.
03 Audre Lorde, "The Uses of Anger: Women Responding to Racism," in *Sister Outsider* (see note 1), 124.
04 Audre Lorde, "The Transformation of Silence into Language and Action," in *Sister Outsider* (see note 1), 41–42.
05 Ibid., 41.
06 Audre Lorde, "The Master's Tools Will Never Dismantle the Master's House," in *Sister Outsider* (see note 1), 111.
07 Ibid., 112.

Decarbonize, Decolonialize, Deinstitutionalize

Born in Scotland and raised in Ghana, after studying and teaching in various institutions in the UK and USA, in 2015 LESLEY LOKKO established the Graduate School of Architecture (GSA) at the University of Johannesburg, the first dedicated, post-graduate-only architecture school in Africa. In 2020, after resigning as dean of the Bernard and Anne Spitzer School of Architecture in New York, she moved back to Ghana and established the African Futures Institute (AFI), a pan-African, post-graduate school of architecture and public events platform located in Accra. She recently spoke with TOM EMERSON, who, together with Stephanie Macdonald, has led 6a architects in London since 2001. Emerson has also been a professor at the Department of Architecture of ETH Zurich since 2010 and its dean since 2021. In their conversation, Lokko and Emerson discuss the necessity of decolonializing, decarbonizing, and deinstitutionalizing architectural education. The conversation was moderated by Tonderai Koschke and Sarah Maafi (TU Munich).

TONDERAI KOSCHKE AND SARAH MAAFI: Lesley, you recently founded the African Futures Institute (AFI), a pan-African post-graduate school of architecture in Accra. What inspired you to establish this institute in Ghana, and how does the AFI differ from architecture schools in the Global North?

LESLEY LOKKO: Let me start by saying that I was very lucky to have had the opportunity to study architecture at The Bartlett School in London. In the 1990s, The Bartlett was a very confident school. That confidence meant that the school could be very generous in terms of what it took in and what it gave back to students. You could come in with almost anything—any idea, any obsession—and the school was robust and generous enough to take it. This relationship between confidence and generosity has always stayed with me. My later experiences teaching in various other institutions were very different. Twenty years later, when I was developing the curriculum for the newly established Graduate School of Architecture (GSA) in Johannesburg, a well-known South African academic said to me, "I need to tell you that you're being incredibly irresponsible." When I asked why, she said, "What you have to understand is that Black students need jobs. They don't need to be taught to dream." In that moment, I understood the clash between imagination, creativity, and confidence on the one hand and a very pragmatic economic argument on the other, which to me seemed incredibly racist. For this reason, when setting up GSA and later the AFI, I decided to reverse this argument and put confidence, creativity, and generosity at the forefront of the agenda.

The name African Futures Institute was chosen very carefully: "African" because the institute aims to be postnational; it is not only about Ghana; it is about the relationships at play within Africa, the African Diaspora, and the aspirations of Africa as a whole. "Futures" because the institute is future-facing; we are the world's youngest continent; the average age here is below 20 years, which is about half the average age in Europe, and so we're passionately interested in what the next generation of African students is going to do. "Institute," as opposed to school, because for me, the curriculum is only one aspect of an educational institution—beyond the curriculum is a whole infrastructure of culture that extends beyond and around the school, and that has almost nothing to do with the academic program.

TK/SM: The AFI is explicitly trying to recruit post-graduate students from the African diaspora around the world. In this sense, you set a clear goal of trying to overcome racial inequalities, but how is the AFI tackling other divisions, for example, gender and class?

LL: The big difference between Ghana and the rest of the world is that race is not the foremost paradigm of discrimination. Everybody is Black here, so people don't see one another through the lens of *Blackness*, per se. EDI [equity, diversity, and inclusion] policies here don't mean quite the same thing. In the postcolonial world, categories like "Third World" and "First World," or "Global North" and "Global South" play a very important role. At the moment, the AFI offers an entirely free program, which is primarily how we address the issue of class inequality. We can afford to do so because I have been lucky enough to attract some fairly generous seed funding. Many philanthropists and philanthropic institutions, particularly in the Global North, would like to see the AFI succeed, so for the moment, we're blessed in that the question of how to finance the institute is not at the top of the agenda. In the long term, however, the model I would like to follow is the one set up by Dr. Margaret Nkrumah—one of our patrons and the founder of the SOS-Hermann Gmeiner International College in Tema, Ghana. A percentage of students with means pay fees that subsidize students without means. That's the pragmatic answer to your question.

But the other issue that, for me, is very important is to look at gender, race, and class struggles as creative issues. Enabling students to think about *how* these paradigms affect, infiltrate, and influence their work is really important. I think of the curriculum simply as the vehicle that allows students to reach the maximum of their imaginative capacity. In South Africa, where the cultural paradigm is much closer to that of the Global North, we often talk only of political or economic equality, but I have always been much more interested in the idea of creative equality. If students feel

Local architects spoke about their unrealized projects in the AFI lecture series *The Ones That Got Away.* © African Futures Institute, Design: Fred Swart.

The *Case Study Talks* at AFI featured speakers Kofi Essel-Appiah, Ruth-Anne Richardson, Joe Osae-Addo, Nat Amarteifio, Allotey Bruce Konuah, Joseph Hayford, Kofi Akakpo, Baerbel Mueller, and Juergen Strohmeyer.

empowered to investigate these issues, not as a result of policy, but as a result of their own interests and obsessions, often the outcome is highly political, but it's not the only lens through which work can be seen, understood, and appreciated. The AFI is a post-graduate institute for a reason: it's a school that is about developing a discourse rather than obtaining a certificate. When we put together programs that deal with issues such as sexuality and space, or poverty and space, rather than preface them by saying that this is an inherently "good" thing to study, we are more interested in what emerges, often unexpectedly, out of the conversation. This is a much more productive strategy because the conversation is driven by the students' curiosity rather than by an agenda set by the institution. This is what I mean by generosity.

TK/SM: Tom, let's return to the Global North, where racial inequality is a more compelling issue. How do students of color enter ETH Zurich? And what outreach strategies does ETH engage in, if any? Is there a consciousness of wanting to attract more students of color?

TOM EMERSON: The context here at ETH is very different. If the African Futures Institute is postnational, then one has to remember ETH is a founding institution of the Swiss Federation. The curriculum here plays a very important role in the governance structure of the institution, as well as in its operations, outputs, traditions, etc. Even by Global North standards, ETH is a privileged institution, both financially and academically. ETH is mainly state-funded and, therefore, very accessible to Swiss students. It would be wrong to say that fees are negligible, but they're low. Also, ETH, different from most leading schools of architecture like The Bartlett or Harvard Graduate School of Design, is non-selective: anyone who finishes an academic secondary school can sign up. Students of color come in through the same door like everybody else because the institution guarantees equal opportunities in terms of access. The reality is that ETH students tend to conform to what we expect an architect in the Global North to be. They are mainly white, not exclusively, but mainly. As far as I know, ETH doesn't do any outreach. If there is any selection, it precedes university by many years through the *Gymnasium* or vocational paths in secondary school. If you go to *Gymnasium*, your route almost inevitably leads to a university like happens during the course. If you have 300 students starting the first year, that number will likely go down to 200 by the second year. This is largely a process of self-selection, in the sense that relatively few students fail, but quite a few choose to quit during the first year. As they move through the five-year bachelor's and master's programs, students become more homogenous. Interestingly, while doing a little research in preparation for this conversation, I discovered that ETH does not keep diversity records. I have a certain amount of anecdotal awareness of who our students are but no data, which in itself is the best answer to your question.

TK/SM: This is exemplary of the institution's rootedness in its 19th-century liberal polytechnic tradition. Do you see ETH as advocating for a revision of the curriculum today?

TE: At the moment, there is a whole set of curricular reforms at work. I would say they are probably arriving slightly late compared to other institutions, but there are very dynamic reforms in place. Some of them are student-led. In some cases, the students have galvanized their voices collectively and applied pressure for curricular reforms. There have been challenges to the canon, like in many schools of architecture, with particular complaints arising from not contextualizing prominent works of Modernism in the rather dark biographies of their authors. Other initiatives are more structural, like challenging the very notion of the crit as a pedagogical instrument. Some other changes are coming from teaching staff. Quite important changes, for example, were initiated by Charlotte Malterre-Barthes, among others, in 2014, when the Parity Group emerged from grassroots activism within the department, committed to improving gender equality and diversity at the school and in the profession. The group is now becoming more and more institutionalized and exchanges directly with the executive board as well as the grassroots community. Every six or seven years, there is a peer evaluation by external colleagues who recommend that the department use its privileged position to engage beyond the Global North. However, this has to be weighed in relation to domestic responsibilities. ETH is funded by Swiss taxpayers and must address Swiss society at large.

The architecture department is very big, compared to UK schools at least. If you take The Bartlett, the Architectural Association, and the architecture department of London Metropolitan University all together, they are not as big as the department at ETH. It is a very big institutional apparatus with deep-rooted traditions and a very stable structure. Reform is slow, but once it happens, it is less reversible. I sometimes wish it could move quicker, but at the same time, I appreciate a certain degree of stability because it protects it from being buffeted by trends, which, ultimately, I believe is the strength of ETH.

TK/SM: Lesley, We don't want to move too much into a duality of the slow-moving beast ETH versus the young and agile AFI, but we were wondering if you think that AFI has more agency when it comes to addressing incumbent political issues precisely because it is so new. For example, you advertise AFI as having a decarbonized curriculum, an issue we need to act on really fast, perhaps faster than a bureaucratic institution like ETH ever could. Do any such considerations shape your vision for the curriculum?

LL: My experiences as director of the Graduate School of Architecture in Johannesburg and dean of the Bernard and Anne Spitzer School of Architecture in New York both took place against the backdrop of extreme change. In South Africa, the student protests of 2015 and 2016 almost shut down the universities, and the protests that broke out after the killing of George Floyd in 2020 opened the lid on a lot of issues that, particularly in the United States, simply were not being addressed. My reaction to both situations was to seize the moment. Being in the eye of the storm is often the right moment to push for maximum change. The strategy worked in South Africa, but it backfired spectacularly in the United States, so much so that in the end, I chose to resign. These two experiences were foundational in developing the curriculum of AFI. Social, racial, and environmental justice—however laterally we might define those terms—are now at the forefront of students' minds.

Besides the two enormous categories of decarbonization and decolonialization, there's a third "de" that I would like to bring to the fore: deinstitutionalization. Institutions have to have the courage to examine their protocols, many of which also depend on things like the context, the size of the school, the size of the academic board, etc. For example, in Johannesburg, for years, I was the only full-time faculty member. Although the workload was crippling, at least I didn't have to negotiate every single proposed change with a committee. In New York, it was exactly the opposite—I sometimes felt as though committees were simply the places where good ideas went to die. It is a very fine line between vision and viability, and, as I learned in New York, most institutions are built to withstand change. That's their nature.

TK/SM: So far, we mainly discussed how institutions are affected by the social and political changes happening around them, but what about the reverse? How can we address broader structural issues in society from within the institution? And what can we do to prevent responsibility for change being shouldered solely by those affected by the structural disadvantages?

LL: There's a saying: "the ruling classes do not commit suicide." In other words, power generally doesn't give itself up voluntarily. It has to be forced, in one way or another, to change. This is not to say that Black students will have to make those changes alone. The impetus for change comes from everybody. If you want change, you have to be the change that you seek. At the University of Johannesburg, Vice Chancellor Tshilidzi Marwala used to say to me, "You say you want change, but when I look around, I see the same old academics, the same old practitioners. Where are these African academics that you are talking about? Where are these Black architects that you want to bring in?" I used to say, "They're not here; you're right. But it's not our job to go out and *find* them; we have to make them. That's the job." I see the institution as part of a much longer trajectory. Keeping an eye on the timescale is very important because we are in the trenches right now, but we may only begin to see the changes we want in a generation's time. On the other hand, if we *don't* start now, in 50 years, we will be talking about the same things.

TE: I like how you define institutions as instruments invented to resist change. It's almost like introducing a new character: you have the people within the institution—students, staff, etc.—who put together the curriculum and take part in research and teaching, and then there is the institution, with its governance structure and those that we are accountable to, which essentially is the executive board, the president and, eventually, the government. This new character, the institution, is a very complex one. It can be infuriating, but it can also be protective. The good thing is that it is very robust. This is why I feel quite excited about the changes that are happening and about the new energy that is coming from the students. People can assemble themselves in all sorts of different configurations and apply a lot of pressure, but it's not going to break.

LL: Yes, I think this is a very important point because, as you know, with that robustness also come resources. Producing the skills requires resources. If you're completely under-resourced, you face a whole set of different criteria. At the AFI, I'm both the person who sets the vision and the person who goes out to buy petrol to put in the generator when the power goes off (and the power goes off quite often here). It's not a sustainable model. Maybe our creative task should be to find new models of cooperation that bring together the stronger attributes of both institutions—ETH and the AFI—in ways that we haven't thought of before. At the moment, I receive 300 emails every day from people wanting to do something together. Most of the time, what they want to do is very vague, but what *is* clear is that there is an appetite to build partnerships across barriers, which was not there five years ago. Something is emerging that is postnational or even post-international.

TE: I think you touched on a key point here: the potential for cooperation. Cooperation has given us access to certain opportunities and resources that are much more than just financial. At ETH, things like decarbonizing the curriculum will encounter little resistance. It is an issued shared by all departments and the ETH as a whole. But decolonialization is a much more complicated story here because, even if there is a lot of energy that is moving in that direction, in Switzerland, decolonization is not understood like in other places. Switzerland was only indirectly colonial. The topic here is not present as elsewhere. For example, I am in London right now, where in the last two years, people have really turned up the volume on issues of postcolonialism—in the streets, in the press, on television. Here you don't have to walk very far to see the spoils of the empire. It's embedded in the place, it's in the neighborhood, it's in the bricks around me. Here you can make decolonization a very tangible, very visible architectural subject, whereas, in Switzerland, it's much harder to find evidence of the empire in the built environment. This makes it a very complex task to give it agency in the architecture curriculum.

LL: Returning to the killing of George Floyd, on the surface, it was just a series of circumstances: somebody choking, video footage going viral on social media, etc. But suddenly, a 300-year-old question was out in the open: What is the relationship between a society that prides itself on a myth of meritocracy and its daily reality of oppression? The cat was out of the bag. The problem was visible to everyone. One of the lasting effects that came out of all the discussions and protests was a deeper and wider understanding of what we mean by "structural." Whether structural psychologies, structural trauma, structural racism, or structural inequality, whatever—suddenly everybody was talking about "structure." For me, this was an incredibly interesting opportunity because in architecture schools, at all levels, we teach students how to think about structures. Here, all of a sudden, there was something very specific to architectural education that people could grasp. I saw an opportunity to get students to think about structure in terms of the theory and technology of *structures* as well as in terms of the underlying structures in society. For example, apartheid could not have happened without the complicity of the architecture profession. In South Africa, an entire society had been carved up along racial lines, and it was done *spatially.*

The past two years with Covid-19 have been really hard—the introspection, the isolation—but I think this is really a genuine moment of change. Issues of identity and understandings of gender are much more complex and multifaceted than before. Institutional identity is also becoming understood differently: the kind of identitarian tribalism that institutions have always been immersed into when they mimic nation-state tribalism by saying, "We are the ETH, we are the Bartlett, we are the GSD," I think that this model is disintegrating. The 30-something generation knows it instinctively. We, the 50- and 60-somethings, have a task now: to figure out how to take this new dynamism and work with it productively inside the spheres of power we occupy.

TE: This task also concerns how the discipline and the profession are changing. In the Global North, there is huge anxiety about what is happening to architecture as a profession. Over the past 20 years, architects have handed over responsibility for how the environment is designed to contractors, suppliers, specialists, politicians, project managers, etc. As a result, the architect has become a more and more marginal figure that has been pushed into a niche like the "heritage expert" or the "visualization expert," which depoliticizes the profession as responsibility for the built environment is being eroded. Academia responded with a kind of educational countercurrent, whose aim is to reinforce the role of the architect as a generalist; someone who is educated in the humanist tradition to be able to address societal questions and bring them into a disciplinary form by producing space. That's a really interesting outcome because, on the one hand, it strengthens the traditional role of the architect in an almost reactionary way, but on the other, it tries to confront and resist the forces that want to break the profession down in order to seize control over space production. Reinforcing the idea that space production is a discipline in its own right could prevent division into different specialisms that no longer have agency against larger forces, particularly against the market. These existential questions play a very important part in the conversation: Who are the architects? What are they going to be doing? What sort of agency do they have when AI is banging on the door and Google and Facebook are coming in with their own idea for the future of the profession? There is a sort of technological and political overlay that globally is going to play out very differently.

LL: Yes, how the profession is seen in different places is a key element. For example, in universities in West Africa, every single teaching staff by law has to have a PhD. For me, this decision comes from a place of deep insecurity. It shows that the political, economic, and cultural paradigm in which we operate is a very insecure one. This is also usually when the demagogues appear—not just the *religious* demagogues; I'm talking about the *institutional* demagogues, those who use this kind of law to bolster a very weak internal self. Over the past 30 years, I've become more and more aware of architects as being chronically insecure, partly because, as you say, so many others have picked over the bones. But in places that are less stable, conversely, you are also less afraid of change because there is less at stake. You know, change is something that you either embrace and work with, or you resist. When we talk about the future of the profession, I am not sure yet which one would lead to a better outcome.

TK/SM: How much do we need for established institutions to legitimize our actions and drive change?

LL: Very much, unfortunately. But *if* the institution wants to change, *if* it wants genuine diversity, inclusion, and equality, it also has to make the mechanisms possible to recognize it. I cannot sit at another diversity committee meeting. I *can't*. Because in the end, what we are doing at these meetings, most of the time, is *performing* diversity and equality, but we're not *being* it. I think this is a very tough challenge for institutions because you have to give up something in order to give somebody else a seat at the table, and who wants to give up privilege?

TE: Yes, that is the bombshell: Who is going to give up power? It is not in the DNA of powerful, established institutions. I think that is something that a very large part of the academic community is aware of but is ill-equipped to discuss in a public forum. So, what I have to do now is to take Lesley's last statement and carry it around. And maybe, at some point, we will be able to talk about it with more fluency.

LL: Yes, but also, a very important thing to say here is that the words "give up" are not just about ceding power. To "give up" sometimes means merely "to share" or "to make more space." Too often, people understand "giving up" only in terms of loss, but most of the time, it is also about winning something. It's not about being de facto "diverse." It's a balancing act—too much diversity and disruption can lead to chaos, but too much homogeneity leads to stasis. If you have too much similar expertise, you can also lose vision.

TEAM:
Guest editors: Torsten Lange and Gabrielle Schaad with Tonderai Koschke and Sarah Maafi;
ARCH+: Mirko Gatti, Melissa Makele.

The *Black Atlantic Speaker Series* at AFI in 2021 featured Olalekan Jeyifous, J. Yolande Daniels, Ibrahim Mahama, Kibwe Tavares, and Felecia Davis.
© African Futures Institute. Design: Fred Swart.

Practice

Serpentine Pavilion 2021

Counterspace Studio

The Four Aces Club in Hackney, demolished in 2007 despite protests, was among the first venues in London to play Black music, starting in the 1960s. This building was one of the many references for the pavilion design by Counterspace. © Alan Denney, 1984.

At first glance, the building appears massive but is actually a lightweight construction. It is made of plywood elements treated with microcement and supported by a recycled steel structure.
© Counterspace. Photo: Iwan Baan.

Stories of communality are diverse, as are the spaces of resistance and security of migrant and intercultural communities. With this in mind, Counterspace Studio designed the 20th Serpentine Pavilion. The Johannesburg-based architecture practice was founded in 2015 by Sumayya Vally. Vally spent four months in London for the project, finding traces of diasporic and cross-cultural communities in informal gathering places threatened by erasure and oblivion. These references were integrated into the architecture of the pavilion. The integration was more than metaphorical: for the first time in the history of the Serpentine Pavilion, building fragments were taken beyond the site in Kensington Gardens and installed in partner organizations whose work inspired its design. These fragments support the everyday operations of these organizations and can be used both individually and collectively.

The generous absorption of extended contexts is reflected in the main building: its form is the result of architectural abstractions that translate the shapes of London into the pavilion structure at various scales of intimacy. The Serpentine Pavilion is a gathering place in the best sense of the word; unlike what is often the case, it brings together the stories and memories of London in a way that only a multi-perspective understanding of architecture and community can accommodate. In its fragmented monumentality, the building mirrors the city and, in turn, becomes a part of it. **MUK**

One of the Serpentine Pavilion fragments installed at various locations throughout London; this one is in the Becontree Forever Arts and Culture Hub at Valence Library.
© Counterspace. Photo: George Darrell.

When experienced close-up, the pavilion gives the impression of a stage set whose diverse elements contribute to a sense of intensity. © Counterspace. Photo: Iwan Baan.

Essay

And We Do Not Inhabit Single-Issue Spaces[01]

Why We Need Intersectional Knowledge Production and a Culture of Memory in Architecture

TEXT
Niloufar Tajeri

Installation by Pınar Öğrenci for her film *Gurbet Is a Home Now* in the exhibition *Porous City – Thresholds in Urbanity* at Kunstraum Kreuzberg / Bethanien, Berlin 2020.

Exhibition photo: L. Fiorio; historical photography in the video installation by Eric Tschernow.

The political struggle over architecture and planning in Berlin, which lasted from the 1968 exhibition *Diagnose zum Bauen in West-Berlin* (Diagnosis for Construction in West Berlin)[02] to the International Building Exhibition Berlin 1984/87 (IBA Alt/Neu), brought about a paradigm shift within the city and presented demands for greater (social) sustainability and spatial justice. However, the movement also contained an internal struggle. Important figures within "feminist planning discourse" in West Germany in the late 1970s[03] organized to demand that "women's living conditions and women's interests be taken into account in planning and building."[04] These women included Kerstin Dörhöfer, Ulla Terlinden, and Myra Warhaftig. Their criticism focused on architecture and planning which was "gender unjust" (*geschlechter-ungerecht*), in other words, which discriminated against women.[05] In doing so, they succeeded in making their demands heard during preparations for the IBA 1984/87, calling for greater participation by female architects and planners, and for "IBA projects to more strongly consider programmatic aspects of gender sensitive planning."[06] It is well known that this pressure resulted in the IBA seeking to recruit more women in architecture and planning positions. Moreover, there was another substantial achievement: the IBA Alt (*alt* = old, for existing buildings) incorporated ideas of participation, in other words, greater openness to and participation by residents. Nonetheless, many other perspectives, needs, problems, aspirations, and hopes were entirely absent from discourse at that time and have only been made visible in recent years. This was because the feminist planning discourse had emerged from the critique of power articulated by the second women's rights movement but reduced this critique to the single aspect of gender injustice. Recent feminist works with an intersectional approach have made clear that the critique of power must reflect other forms of social oppression, including racism and racialization, as well as discrimination based on economic status, sexual orientation, religious affiliation, etc.[07] These more recent analyses can be understood as an appeal to add much-needed complexity to critical discourse. At the same time, they offer a chance to understand justice in architecture and spatial planning as involving more than the needs of white, educated middle-class people, regardless of their gender.

Film stills from *Gurbet Is a Home Now*, 2020. © Pınar Öğrenci.

Esra Akcan, an architecture historian and author of the 2018 book *Open Architecture: Migration, Citizenship, and the Urban Renewal of Berlin-Kreuzberg by IBA 1984/87*, and Pınar Öğrenci, an architect and artist who directed the 2020 film *Gurbet Artık Bir Ev (Gurbet Is a Home Now)*, both highlight the experiences and memories of migrantized tenants of buildings in the IBA Alt in their work. In doing so, they enable multilayered, nonlinear reflection on the history of the IBA, including its ruptures, contradictions, and continuities. They draw attention to those who experienced the IBA Alt as migrantized users and raise questions that remain unresolved: How can participation function if some people are not ascribed political belonging according to the nationally prescribed notion of citizenship? How can spaces be planned with justice when there is an unfair planning process and planners regard their users as a social problem? If the same system privileges some and disadvantages others, how can we communicate on a basis of equality, and how can we make collective decisions? How can we guarantee security for everyone when some in the group can never feel safe? What about migrantized workers who experience sexism as well as racism and classism? Their experience of sexism is qualitatively different from that of white academic feminists, because it is intertwined with other forms of discrimination.[08] Do they actually have a right to the city if they—remaining invisible themselves—are represented by white feminist "advocate-planners"?[09] The answer is no, and these questions are all the more problematic since migrantized workers were by no means a minority in the areas of Kreuzberg subject to the planning process.

Researching and processing memories and experiences that were previously absent and marginalized in our collective memory is not simply something "nice to have." It is an urgent necessity. As the Black German literary and cultural scholar Peggy Piesche explains: "Collective memories that do not belong to the mainstream [...] necessarily

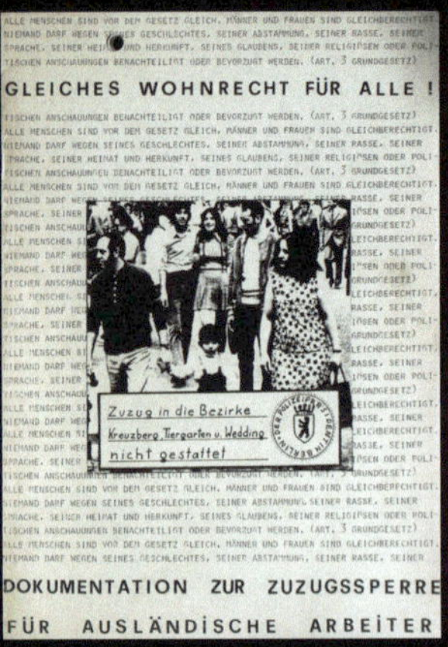

January 1, 1975: West Berlin imposes a ban on foreigners moving to the districts of Kreuzberg, Tiergarten, and Wedding. At this time, the foreign population of these areas was more than 12 percent. Migrants would only receive a residence permit if they could prove they were renting an apartment outside these districts. The restriction referred to § 2 [1] of the Federal Aliens Act (1965): "Foreign nationals and stateless people do not have a relation of mutual obligation with rights and obligations. In regard to these people, the state acts from considerations of expediency, based on its political goals." The ban was not lifted until 1990.
Ezra Akcan private archive.
Reproduced courtesy of Esra Akcan.

Film still from *Gurbet Is a Home Now*, 2020.
© Pınar Öğrenci, Cihan Arın: aerial photo of Kreuzberg, 1980.

Film still from *Gurbet Is a Home Now*, 2020.
Ezra Akcan private archive.
Reproduced courtesy of Esra Akcan.

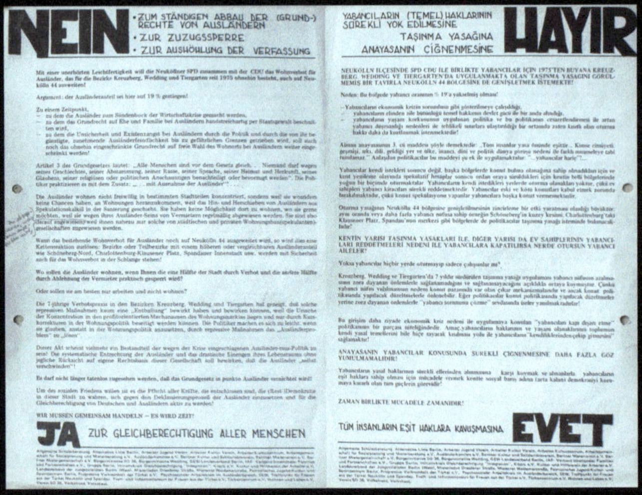

Flyer in German and Turkish, mobilizing opposition against the immigration ban and the "ongoing dismantling of foreigners' [basic] rights," mid-1970s. Ezra Akcan private archive. Reproduced courtesy of Esra Akcan.

Interior of an old building at Naunynstrasse 62, designated for renovation as part of the sensitive urban renewal scheme, February 1983. Photo: STERN GmbH. Source: FHXB Friedrichshain-Kreuzberg Museum.

Film still from *Gurbet Is a Home Now*, 2020.
© Pınar Öğrenci. Photo: S.T.E.R.N. GmbH.
Source: FHXB Friedrichshain-Kreuzberg Museum.

bring up different memories, different questions, and perhaps different answers, especially at a time of profound social change."[10] Piesche goes on to explain that an intersectional culture of remembrance creates a space in which to reflect on collective memories. This is a process in which "similar as well as different experiences" can be empathetically shared, essential to imagining a possible "collective future."[11] What is broken up by this is the idea of a single, supposedly correct, hegemonic history that unites some (majority society) and excludes others (marginalized). What emerges are complicated, contradictory, interwoven stories. These stories testify to the many other realities, analyses, and ideas that shape the present, and which can be the starting point for creating a shared, more just future for everyone.

The Trinidadian communist Claudia Jones first described the phenomenon of multiple discrimination as long ago as 1949. The liberation of the "triple oppressed" Black woman, she wrote, was a horizon of liberation for all women: "the triply-oppressed status of [Black] women is a barometer of the status of all women, and that the fight for the full, economic, political and social equality of the [Black] woman is in the vital self-interest of white workers, in the vital interest of the fight to realize equality for all women."[12]

By its nature, capitalism is crisis. This can be seen in various forms: climate catastrophe, displacement and distribution struggles within our cities, and racism and forced migration around the world. Given this, our answers and approaches must be developed in a way that is intersectional and critically anti-racist. Anti-racist because many problems are structurally racist and more strongly affect Black people, Indigenous people, and people of color (BIPOC). Intersectional because inequalities are intertwined between sexism, racism, and classism.[13]

This also applies to the disciplines of architecture and spatial planning. In neighborhoods shaped and formed by migrants, such as the Neukölln district of Berlin, people who are migrantized, racialized, and/or poor are known to be more strongly affected by displacement.[14] At the same time, this part of the city is undergoing major structural change driven by designated redevelopment areas, modernization measures, and the redesign of parks, streets, and squares, as well as by densification and new construction. This structural disadvantage is a direct consequence of urban planning actions. Nonetheless, neither urban planning nor architectural practice have approaches that would allow them to reflect on this disadvantage, let alone find practical solutions to it. Even today, white professional normative perspectives continue to ignore specific forms of discrimination against racialized and marginalized groups.[15] Instead, these groups—usually regarded simply as "others"—are seen as a problem to be spatially rectified or disciplined, intermixed or integrated.[16] This attitude remains firmly anchored in the 20th century. It can only be dismantled by producing intersectional memory practices and new forms of knowledge based on the critique of racism.

The work of Esra Akcan offers a new account of the planning history of the IBA Alt, tracing the perspectives and memories of migrantized tenants and planners alongside critical feminist planners. Thus, Akcan's book addresses the role of the architect and activist Cihan Arın in the IBA. Arın was one of only four architects of Turkish origin on the IBA team and was responsible for related aerial photos. Arın had the far-sightedness to reflect on how different kinds of disadvantage were intertwined. His particular focus was on the economic status and migrantized status—today we might speak of "racialization"—of tenants in the IBA planning process, in the context of the project's sensitive urban renewal and improvements to living conditions. Arın was involved in the Initiativkreis Gleichberechtigung Integration (Equal Rights Integration Initiative), which developed a series of urban planning and architectural strategies for migrant tenants in Kreuzberg. These strategies included avoiding major rent increases, with modernization carried out in close consultation with tenants, considering their financial circumstances. Demolition would take place only if and when unavoidable, and with tenants' approval. Apartment applications were only to be conducted in collaboration with tenants' associations interested in the rights of migrantized people and those suffering discrimination on the housing market.[17] In Pınar Öğrenci's film, the director speaks to Arın about the insecurity and distrust experienced by tenants at the time, which prompted him—rather than undertake standard planning work—to establish a tenants' rights consultancy in the context of the IBA Alt. In 1984 as now, displacement was an issue; for migrants, displacement could also mean displacement from the country. For example, Klaus Franke, then the West Berlin Senator (minister) for Construction, a member of the conservative party of Christian Democrats, said this: "We want to integrate [foreigners] if they want. [...] Whoever comes to Germany should feel like the Germans here. [...] But of course, we also offer incentives for foreigners, especially for Turks, to return to their homeland, as part of our general policy on foreigners. We also help everyone who really wants to move out of their old life circumstances and reorient themselves in their efforts to leave Kreuzberg."[18]

Attempts by individual actors like Arın—himself affected by structural racism—to approach migrantized workers are still relevant today, but they must be considered within this wider context. In the film, Akcan also interviews Heide Moldenhauer, an architect who planned the renovation of neglected building blocks as part of the IBA Alt "cautious urban renewal" program (*Behutsame Stadterneuerung*) under Hardt-Waltherr Hämer. Specifically responsible for blocks 76 and 78, Moldenhauer was one of seven women among the 69 signatories of the *Aktion 507* manifesto launched at the Technical University of Berlin and published as part of the 1968 exhibition *Diagnosis for Building in West Berlin*.[19] Many prominent signatories would later go on to do exactly what they had criticized in the manifesto, especially in the context of IBA Neu projects: a combination of opaque, profit-driven collusion between politicians, architects, and the construction industry, with a lack of participation by users and others affected. This enabled such architects and planners to enjoy correspondingly smooth and successful careers, developing buildings celebrated in architectural circles. Their cultural and social capital helped them to prominence within architectural historiography. This contrasts with Moldenhauer's invisibility in the history of architecture, which is largely structured according to criteria that favor male architects, as well as Western forms of thought and action.

Beginning in 1981, alongside her planning work for IBA Alt, Moldenhauer maintained close contact with residents, many of them first-generation contract workers from Turkey. She helped to organize participatory projects, self-help activities, new public art, exhibitions, and events, documenting the entire process in photographs.[20] The images she captured are impressive, atmospheric visualizations of residential and other urban spaces at that time. Their focus on people, especially migrantized women and children, make them striking and highly unusual.

By rediscovering Moldenhauer's photographs and making them accessible to the public, Esra Akcan and Pınar Öğrenci are at last giving these people visibility and a history. As a woman, Heide Moldenhauer also experienced discrimination, something which has until now excluded her from architectural historiography. However, we do still find her name in reports, her contribution is documented, and her pictures are protected by copyright in the Berlin State Archive. In other words, her voice has been handed down. This does not apply to the women with whom Moldenhauer worked closely to renovate the apartments and houses. They have been rendered completely invisible, thanks to the triple discrimination they suffered: as women, as racialized people, and as workers.

In her study Esra Akcan clarifies that Moldenhauer did not look down on Turkish women as victims nor regard their husbands as perpetrators. She did not patronize them with suggestions that they should integrate or assimilate, still a hegemonic demand today, which conceives of social coexistence as an authoritarian process rather than a dialogic one.[21] On the contrary, she repeatedly emphasized something she and the women had in common: the oppression visited on women by patriarchal society. In 1984, along with her translator Necla—only her first name is recorded—Moldenhauer organized an exhibition at SO36 addressing questions of discrimination against women. The exhibition focused on the concerns of female architects but also those of the migrantized workers with whom Moldenhauer and Necla had worked during the renovation process. However, the disparity in representation here is striking. Good intentions alone cannot eliminate discrimination, despite the positive role of individuals like Moldenhauer. We thus urgently need to talk about intersectionality and structural racism. Similarities do exist in terms of the oppression of women. But there are also differences when this first discrimination is further reinforced by other phenomena, such as racism and classism. Why is it that we do not know Necla's family name, even though as a translator she had a key role in the planning process? Why do we not know all the women who were involved in the planning as users of the spaces in question? In Moldenhauer's images—on which she retains copyright—these women are depicted in their private living spaces, going about their everyday lives. But they were never allowed to have a say in how these images were published or archived. Ultimately, Moldenhauer remains the author, and she alone can decide whether we get to see these pictures in order to better understand these women's stories and histories. The women (still) have no say in negotiating their own presence/absence, visibility/invisibility. Why is Kreuzberg, once dominated by a migrantized, working-class population, now mostly white and middle-class? Despite the best of intentions, structural racism—including displacement, one of its spatial consequences—cannot be eliminated if social conditions are not negotiated in an intersectional way.

Nor was it possible to overcome the paternalism of the IBA Alt, which regarded people as a "social project." In her film, Pınar Öğrenci brings together the voices of critical Turkish intellectuals and poets of the time, as well as the sounds and music of the left-wing, politicized Turkish community in Kreuzberg, and conducts interviews with the few witnesses still alive. Lale Özdemir, a resident of the neighborhood, sums up the colonial aspect of well-intentioned planning that nonetheless incorporates structural discrimination. Based on her memory of participatory processes and the various planning rounds, she says: "I think they probably saw us as a social project."

Had it not been for Moldenhauer, who took the initiative to actively listen to the women, aware of their common oppression; had it not been for Esra Akcan, who in her book addressed the IBA 1984/87 from a migrant perspective; and had it not been for Pınar Öğrenci, who addressed these issues in her film and located the few witnesses who remain from the migrantized population, I would not be addressing intersectionality in spatial displacement and structural racism in planning and architectural historiography today. Questions from that era remain relevant, unresolved, and fraught with conflict. It is time to face up to these questions. It is time to redefine strategies, possibilities, and ways of producing space, remaking them in ways that are socially equitable and based on solidarity. A first step would be for more people to address the subject from an intersectional perspective, dealing differently with both past and present to reshape both space and the future.

Interior of apartments in IBA blocks 76/78 and 81, renovated under the direction of Heide Moldenhauer and Cihan Arın, as part of the IBA Alt (old) sensitive urban renewal scheme. © Esra Akcan, Berlin, 2009–2016.

01 The title of this essay alludes to a key statement by the Black author and poet Audre Lorde about intersectionality as a multidimensional political and social struggle, and extends it to include questions of space and spatial justice. See Audre Lorde, "Learning from the 60s," in *Sister Outsider: Essays and Speeches* (Trumansburg, NY: Crossing Press, 1984), 134–44, 138: "There is no such thing as a single-issue struggle, because we do not live single-issue lives."

02 Aktion 507, eds., *Manifest: Diagnose zum Bauen in West-Berlin – Materialien zur Diskussion* (Berlin: Druck Rump, 1968).

03 Sabina Riss, "'Frauengerechte' Modellwohnprojekte der 1990er Jahre: Die versuchte Einflussnahme von Frauen als Auftraggeberinnen auf den österreichischen geförderten Wohnungsbau," dissertation, Technische Universität Vienna, 2016, 52.

04 Kerstin Dörhöfer, "Raumplanung für Frauen: Theoretische Positionen und praktische Konzepte in Deutschland," *PERSPEKTIVEN* 1/2 (1994): 19–23, 20, quoted in Riss 2016 (see note 3), 55.

05 Marianne Rodenstein, "Gruppe 'Frauen, Steine Erde': Frauen-Räume-Architektur-Umwelt," in *Schlüsselwerke der Geschlechterforschung*, eds. Martina Löw and Bettina Mathes (Berlin: VS Verlag für Sozialwissenschaften, 2011), 135–47, 135.

06 In 1981, some 300 experts from architecture and spatial planning, along with representatives from interest groups were invited to a large preparatory meeting for the IBA 1984/87. Not a single woman was among them. Seven feminist architects and planners stormed the event, staging a go-in and making seven notable speeches. They demanded, among other things, greater participation by women in the planning of the IBA. The activists self-deprecatingly referred to their go-in as a "faux pas." The same year, they went on to found FOPA (Feminist Organization of Planners and Architects).

07 In her 1949 essay "We Seek Full Equality for Women" (see note 12), the Trinidadian communist Claudia Jones first described the triple discrimination of Black women workers as the "triply-oppressed status of [Black] women." In the late 1980s, the lawyer Kimberlé Crenshaw took this as a reference point, coining the term "intersectionality" to describe entangled and interdependent forms of discrimination.

08 This structural difference can be illustrated by a typical example: that of management positions in architectural offices and universities. While white women from academic backgrounds are represented there, white women from a working class milieu are rare, and migrant women from a working class milieu even more so.

09 Riss, "Frauengerechte' Modellwohnprojekte" (see note 3), 66.

10 Peggy Piesche, ed., *Labor 89: Intersektionale Bewegungsgeschichte*n aus West und Ost* (Berlin: Verlag Yilmaz-Günay, 2019), 7.

11 Ibid., 7f.

12 Claudia Jones, "We Seek Full Equality for Women" [1949], republished online in *Viewpoint Magazine* in 2015, accessed August 16, 2022, viewpointmag.com/2015/02/21/we-seek-full-equality-for-women. In the original text, Jones uses the term "Negro," which is replaced here with the term "Black" since this terminology is preferred today by those affected.

13 See Encarnación Gutiérrez Rodríguez, Pinar Tuzcu, "Wege zum Migrantischen Feminismus," in *Migrantischer Feminismus in der Frauen:bewegung in Deutschland (1985–2000)*, eds. Encarnación Gutiérrez Rodríguez and Pinar Tuzcu (Münster: assemblage, 2021), 13f. The authors point out that figures within migrant feminism in Germany had already recognized the principle of intersectionality in the 1980s and 1990s, but these principles remained largely invisible within narratives of feminism.

14 See the paper by Defne Kadıoğlu Polat, "'Now the German comes': The ethnic effect of gentrification in Berlin (2018)," *Ethnicities* 20/1 (2020): 155–76. "Together with an increased influx of new residents and tourists after German reunification, competition for housing in Berlin has grown to be one of the biggest concerns for politicians, civil society, and locals […]. As argued above, Turkish immigrants and their descendants are disproportionally affected due to their multiple disadvantages. Moreover, in the case of Berlin, they have historically tended to cluster in the central areas, which are now the first to gentrify."

15 See Irene Cheng, Charles L. Davis II, and Mabel O. Wilson, eds., *Race and Modern Architecture: A Critical History from the Enlightenment to the Present* (Pittsburgh: U. Pittsburgh Press, 2020). The editors of this anthology explore the history of architecture and the production of knowledge in modern architecture and planning, showing that the subject of racism was avoided while also reproduced in the production of knowledge. In this way, racism was woven into the epistemic premises and fundamentals of modern architecture and production of space.

16 See Vassilis S. Tsianos, "Urbane Paniken: Zur Entstehung des antimuslimischen Urbanismus," in *Wer MACHT Demo_kratie: Kritische Beiträge zu Migration und Machtverhältnissen*, eds. Duygu Gürsel, Zülfukar Çetin, and Allmende e.V. (Münster: assemblage, 2013), 28ff.

17 See Esra Akcan, *Open Architecture: Migration, Citizenship and the Urban Renewal of Berlin-Kreuzberg by IBA 1984/87* (Basel: Birkhäuser, 2018), 218ff.

18 "Interview mit dem Berliner Bausenator [Klaus] Franke," *Der Architekt* 10 (October 1984): 445–47, 447.

19 Aktion 507, *Manifest* (see note 2).

20 Akcan, *Open Architecture* (see note 17), 233.

21 Ibid., 234f.

Feminist Architectural Histories of Migration

TEXT
Anooradha Iyer Siddiqi,
Rachel Lee

"Since 2015, there has been an upsurge in scholarly interventions that engage with migration and exile. The 'crisis' perceived in Europe has impacted European traditions of architectural history, architecture culture, and discourse. Thus, the writing on architecture and the built environment resulting from this turn has tended to focus on contemporary displacement related to cities, landscapes, and social fabric in Europe. These have broadly drawn from a Eurocentric perspective of border transgression, rather than taken migration as an ontological condition, to be understood from the migrant's perspective."

Anooradha Iyer Siddiqi and Rachel Lee, "On Margins: Feminist Architectural Histories of Migration," 2019[01]

Feminist Architectural Histories of Migration is a multi-sited, ongoing project with a collection of works that takes migration as its core concept and historical event to better understand feminist thought, work, and narrative in a spatial, material, and aesthetic field. The project labors in concert with a growing body of initiatives to write feminist histories of modern architecture through collaborative and intersectional historiographic practices. These redistribute power, co-produce solidarity, and reassess objects and methods that have been turned to with regularity in architectural history.

The contributions in *Feminist Architectural Histories of Migration* build on two arguments: first, that the dynamic of a situated and re-situated perspective[02] is foundational to feminist histories of architecture, and second, that feminist approaches destabilize presumptions of historical fixity. Narratives, perspectives, and practices based on these arguments have emerged from acts and experiences of migration performed individually or collectively, moving into and out of geographies of control and subjugation, beyond gender or gender framings, across lifeworlds.

Writing feminist architectural histories of migration demands the recovery of hidden figures and clandestine spaces. It calls for seeing the bodies of laborers within the grid of authorship, acknowledging the spatial practices of occupation by activists or prisoners, engaging the obscured work of teachers, researchers, and writers, studying material environments built by migrants, and naming homemakers and others whose designated use of architecture endowed it.

Feminist Architectural Histories of Migration is hosted on three open-access platforms: *Architecture Beyond Europe, Canadian Centre for Architecture*, and *Aggregate*, where we examine migration, respectively, through "margins," "diffractions," and "collaborations."[03] We have placed texts within three platforms as a gesture to the conceptual multiplicities of migration; this scaffold is intended to establish instabilities and shifting frameworks as the base theoretical principle, which, perhaps paradoxically, offers a different kind of anchoring.

Migration and mobility, as well as their converse conditions of restriction and confinement, call for collaborations. *Feminist Architectural Histories of Migration* asks how such collaborations created, unsettled, and enacted forms of power through enclosure, solidarity, labor, exile, embodiment, and care. The authors in these collections engage in collaborative methods, following migrants and engaging in physical and conceptual migrations. These movements acknowledge architecture only as a work by many hands, and its historical recovery only as a process of collaboration, material and theoretical.

01 Anooradha Iyer Siddiqi and Rachel Lee, "On Margins: Feminist Architectural Histories of Migration," *ABE Journal: Architecture beyond Europe* 16 (2019), accessed September 1, 2022, journals.openedition.org/abe/7126.

02 The "situated perspective" refers to Donna Haraway's concept of "situated knowledge," which challenges assumptions of objectivity, universality, and the neutrality of knowledge and promotes an understanding of knowledge as historically and culturally specific, tied to context and location. It follows that there is also no universal knowledge, but only partial, diverse forms of knowledge ("knowledges"). See also Donna Haraway, "Situated Knowledge: The Science Question in Feminism and the Privilege of a Partial Perspective," in *Simians, Cyborgs, and Women: The Reinvention of Nature* (New York, NY: Routledge, 1991), 183–201.

03 See *Architecture Beyond Europe* 16 (2019), accessed September 1, 2022, journals.openedition.org/abe/7126; Canadian Centre for Architecture (CCA), accessed September 1, 2022, www.cca.qc.ca/en/articles/issues/30/of-migration/81045/on-diffractions-feminist-architectural-histories-of-migration; Aggregate, accessed September 1, 2022, we-aggregate.org/project/on-collaborations-feminist-architectural-histories-of-migration.

Som City, Cape Town. Photo: Huda Tayob, 2014.

Black Markets
Transnational Architectures of Care

TEXT
Huda Tayob

Huda Tayob explores, through ethnographic research and studies of oral history, the largely multistory arcades of Cape Town, South Africa, as spaces of refugee inhabitation. These spaces are located in urban margins yet perform the circulation of transnational spatial stories, practices, people, and goods. In tracing the emergence and relationship of similar sites from Cape Town to Nairobi and Minneapolis, she argues for recognizing these as "Black markets," drawing on AbdouMaliq Simone's framing of Black urbanism[01] to frame the local specificities of racialized urbanism and locate these spaces within broader landscapes of forced migration, informal global trade, and transnational networks of care established and maintained by female labor.

Drawing is a central process for an architect. The drawings shown here from the project *Black Markets* follow architectural conventions in order to elucidate subaltern spaces[02]—a practice of care. The various markets and individual stalls are located in Bellstat Junction, a "Somali mall" in Cape Town, South Africa, run by refugee women. Although questions around refugees and migration are often situated at the scale of the nation state, through these drawings, the focus moves to the spaces of work, home, and shelter where daily life is negotiated.

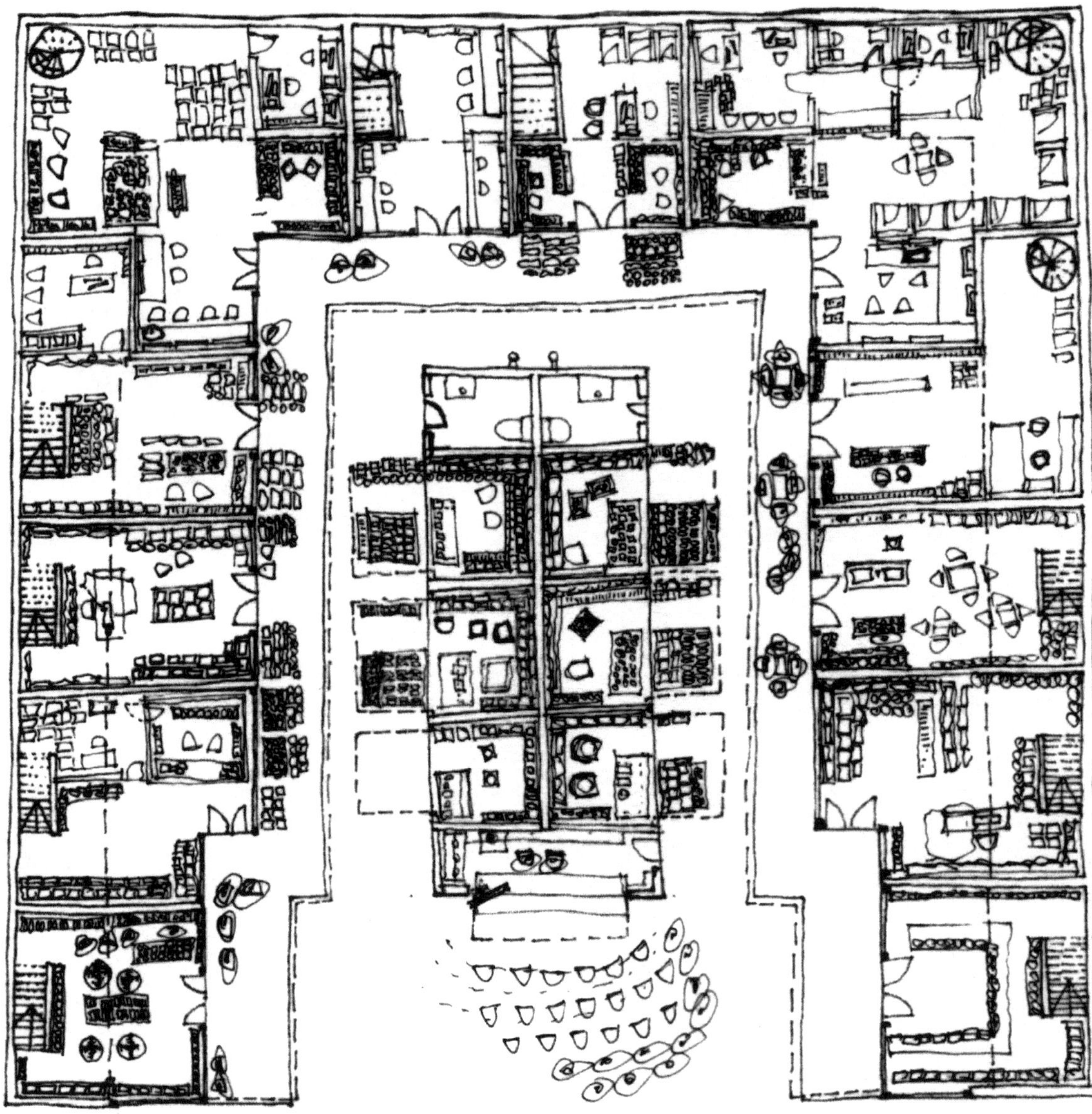

Bellstat Junction, a Somali mall in Cape Town.
All drawings: Huda Tayob, 2014–2015.

These drawings and re-drawings map my encounter with these markets. They were made over the course of a year, in response to conversations on site. Drawing within the markets led to numerous discussions and questions about my research with the owner-inhabitants of the markets, and became a way of actively speaking to each other.[03]

My adoption of the architectural conventions of plan and section stems from my training as an architect. Yet rather than precise measurements with a legal weight, the drawings are based on estimates and approximations to create a "contingent," ongoing "living archive" (Stuart Hall) of these interiors.[04] The detail corresponds to repeated visits and a slow recognition of what was important for those who live and make these interior spaces. The drawings therefore depict the density of occupation along with goods sold, furniture, and crockery—in other words, everyday objects not always included in architectural drawings, yet rendered in the very same drawing conventions that would otherwise overlook spaces like these, treating them as invisible. Drawing these markets asks us to consider them as spaces worthy of being drawn. In contrast to the emphasis often placed on the improvisatory nature of spaces for informal trade, these forms of representation point to the very real existence of physical built forms, and to the concrete spatial and material affordances of what may be glossed over as ad hoc. These drawings express in everyday details how forcibly displaced people assemble new spatial nodes as a way of overcoming formal exclusion.

These drawings are central to reading complex architectures of care. They present a manifestation of that which is not reducible or exhausted by mechanisms of control,

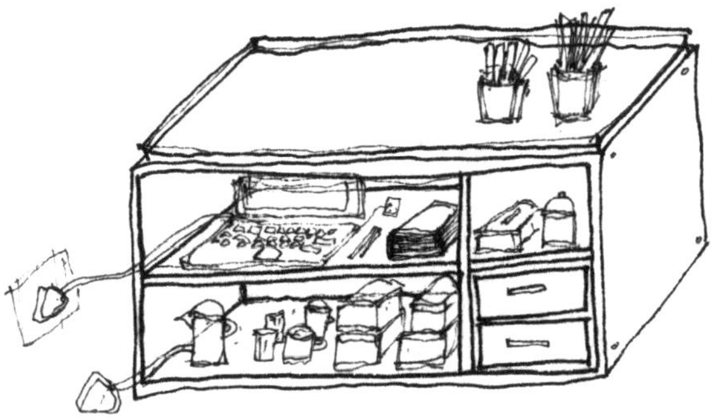

Fatima's shop, Bellstat Junction, Cape Town.

offering a marginal or counter-archive of affective but overlooked sites.[05] Writing and drawing these Somali malls as architectures becomes a means of acknowledging the ways that people make livable lives. The drawings, in turn, are traces of these lives, and a recognition of the daily practices of refusing the status quo and building a set of intimate spaces. These sites therefore operate at the unstable locus of precarity and possibility, offering both a record of the past and a tracing for the future.

This text appeared online in a slightly different version in Of Migration *on the open-access platform curated by Anooradha Iyer Siddiqi and Rachel Lee,* On Diffractions: Feminist Architectural Histories of Migration *at the Canadian Centre for Architecture (CCA). With kind permission from the author and CCA.*

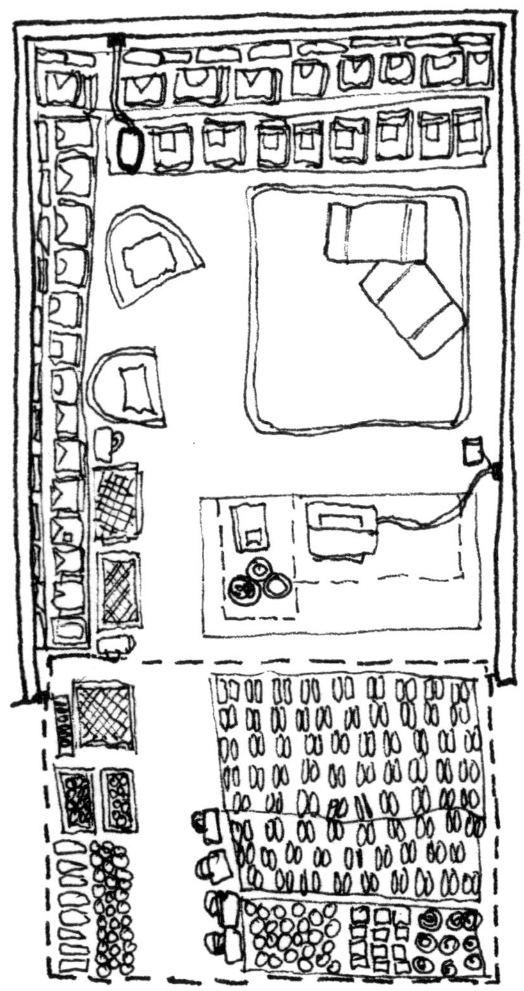

01 See AbdouMaliq Simone, "Reclaiming Black Urbanism: Inventive Methods for Engaging Urban Fields from Dakar to Jakarta," in *City Life from Jakarta to Dakar: Movements at the Crossroads* (New York, NY: Routledge, 2009); AbdouMaliq Simone, "Urbanity and Generic Blackness," in "City of Potentialities: Race, Violence and Invention," special issue, *Theory, Culture & Society*, 2016, accessed September 1, 2022, www.abdoumaliqsimone.com/files/116353251.pdf.

02 On the concept of the subaltern in postcolonial discourse, see Gayatri Spivak, "Can the subaltern speak?" in *Marxism and the Interpretation of Culture*, eds. Cary Nelson and Lawrence Grossberg (Urbana, IL: University of Illinois Press, 1988), 271–313.

03 On the practice of drawing as communication medium, see John Berger, *Bento's Sketchbook* (London: Verso, 2015).

04 See Stuart Hall: "Constituting an Archive," *Third Text* 15, no. 54 (March 2001): 89–92.

05 On the notion of margins, see bell hooks, "Choosing the Margin as a Space of Radical Openness," in *Yearning: Race, Gender, and Cultural Politics* (Boston, MA: South End Press, 1990), 145–53.

Intervention

HIKMA

atelier masōmī, Studio Chahar

The mudbrick mosque had become too small and was in a poor state of repair. The initial plan was to replace it with a larger concrete building. However, architects Yasaman Esmaili and Mariam Issoufou Kamara suggested retaining the existing building while also constructing a new building out of mudbrick. Formwork and reinforcement similar in method to cast-in-place concrete were used for repairs to the faces and edges of the walls.

All photos: © James Wang. All drawings: © atelier masōmī, Studio Chahar

The Republic of Niger gained independence from France in 1960. The former colonial power left behind a vulnerable state that experienced several military coups and attempted coups in the following decades. Today the landlocked West African country has the world's youngest population and is in a process of political stabilization. A major commitment to actively bringing about change is required in Niger, which has been especially hard hit by crises, including terrorist attacks, epidemics, and the climate catastrophe. A new generation of architects and planners, in search of new creative perspectives, is taking on this task. Two architectural offices, atelier masōmī, led by Mariam Issoufou Kamara, and Studio Chahar, led by Yasaman Esmaili, were initially commissioned to construct a new mosque in the small town of Dandaji, the hometown of then-president Mahamadou Issoufou. Instead, the two offices joined forces to convince local authorities to preserve the old mosque and develop the area into a cultural and educational complex.

For both architects, women's public access to secular and religious education was essential since, without this, women's social and spatial lives are restricted to domestic spaces from an early age. The project's name refers to the Bayt al-Hikma (House of Wisdom), founded in Baghdad in the ninth century, a kind of academy that possessed what was at the time the world's most extensive library. Muslim scholars

Indoor temperatures are regulated by the buildings' thermal mass and natural ventilation through openings in the facade. The blue-painted steel shutters can be opened and closed by hand, making electric ventilation and cooling unnecessary.

USE (AREA):
Mosque, two cleansing stations, apartment for the imam of the mosque, library, classrooms, reading and study areas, garden (5,238 m^2)
DESIGN TEAM:
Yasaman Esmaili, Mariam Issoufou Kamara
CLIENT:
Entreprise Salou Alpha et Fils
LOCATION: Dandaji
YEAR: 2015–2018

Compressed earth blocks were used for the construction of the new mosque. They require less maintenance than the adobe of the old mosque, but share its characteristic aesthetics and thermal qualities.

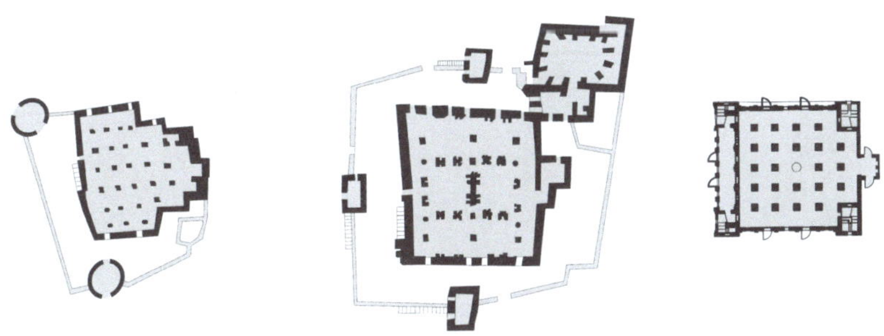

The design was based on a typological study of various Muslim sacred buildings in the precolonial Hausa states.

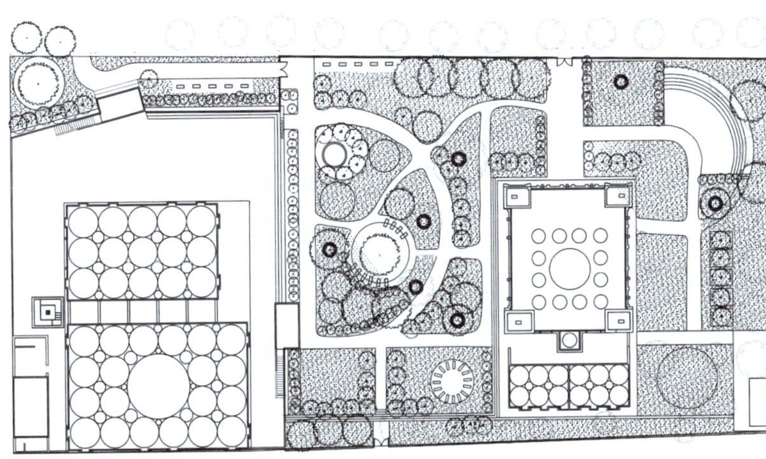

The mosque premises create a comfortable microclimate in an otherwise arid part of western Niger. Native vegetation keeps open spaces cool. As well as providing shade, these plants can last longer in periods of drought. Drip irrigation and a reservoir supply the plants with water.

The underground cistern saves rain, which falls during the few wet months of the year.

It is expensive to use glass in this region, so it was deliberately not used in either of the buildings. The contemporary dome construction draws on local traditions for both its form and building methods.

The two prayer rooms can be used in parallel by men and women, depending on demand and time of day. The larger of the two is usually reserved for men.

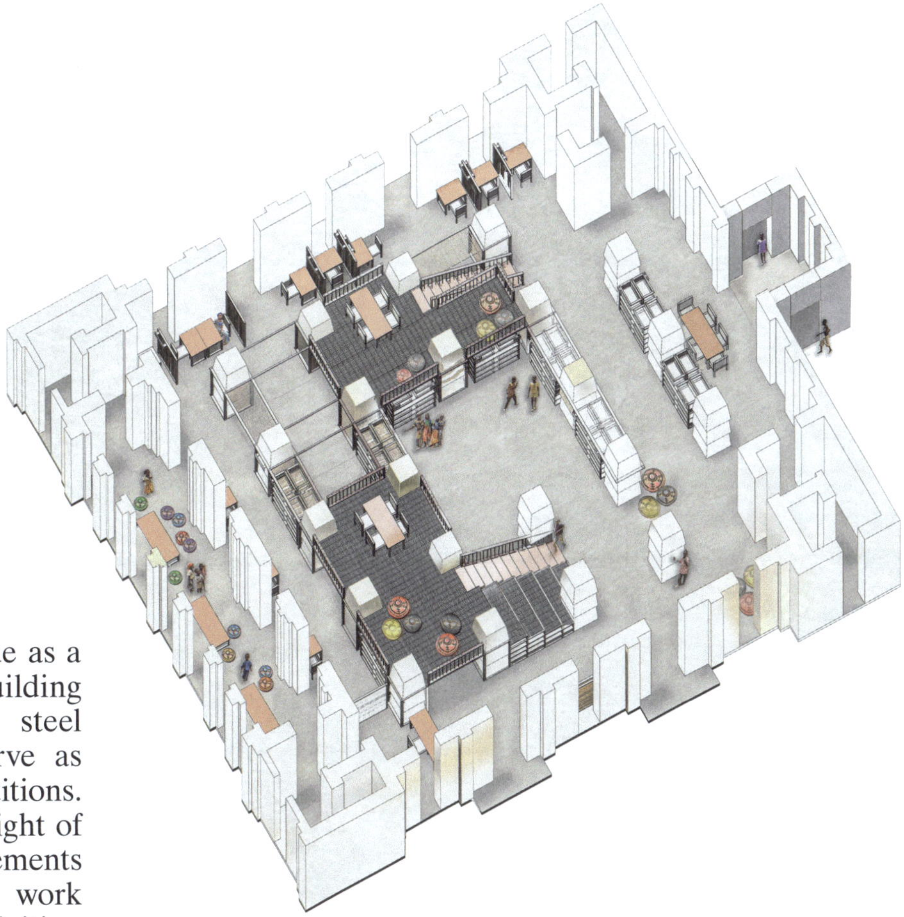

To remodel the old mosque as a library, the mudbrick building was strengthened with steel reinforcements, which serve as both bookshelves and partitions. As well as bearing the weight of the mezzanine, the steel elements define various zones for work and group activities.

Intervention

there translated ancient Greek, Latin, and other source texts, making a vital contribution to the transmission of knowledge. The Hikma complex in Dandaji regards itself as particularly bound to this heritage, not least since Niger has the world's lowest literacy rate, with few years spent in school on average.

With the involvement of local women's groups and village elders, the architects developed an overall concept for the complex. In addition to constructing a new mosque, their plan envisaged the restoration and conversion of the old mosque. Until this point, the mosque had categorically excluded women in both its principles and spatial layout. Now the library conversion moved women and young people to the center of the teaching areas as members of the community. The new mosque offers additional prayer rooms and ritual facilities for women.

Their approach is based on a method known as "memory as a blueprint," which uses ethnographic observation as its primary design tool. The new building took precolonial sacred buildings of the Hausa states as a typological model,[01] rather than the classic Middle Eastern mosque. Characteristics of this Hausa architecture include the division of space into separate volumes, using varied paths of circulation and ritualized threshold spaces. The design of the Hikma complex exhibits these characteristics, including cleansing stations, informal paths, and differently formulated interior and exterior spaces. The spacious complex comprises two buildings and an outdoor prayer space, offering opportunities for contemplative retreat, including Friday prayer meetings and the Eid festivals.

Care, or better, designing for care, is expressed through social programs and respectful interaction between Muslim and secular visitors, but also in the way ecologically sustainable design prompts mindful use of local building resources. Clay bricks from the local laterite soils were used for the building's shell and vault. This improves climatic conditions inside the building and also allows significant cost savings compared to cement brick. The successful combination of old and new buildings, religious and secular teachings, and traditional values and progressive ideals forms an ensemble. The creation of a visual identity is thus also largely due to the wealth of experience within local craft guilds. Their close collaboration with the design team offered access to expertise passed down through generations. By maintaining and expanding existing structures and by drawing on local knowledge, Mariam Issoufou Kamara and Yasaman Esmaili look to question colonial thought and design patterns to create forward-looking, resilient architecture that takes social, ecological, and cultural traditions and responsibilities into account. **FG**

01 The Hausa states were an association of city-states in what is now northern Nigeria and central Niger. It is likely that they existed since the Middle Ages, and they persisted in the form of recognized traditional states, even after their territory had been forcibly and arbitrarily divided by colonial powers.

The minaret provides a visual endpoint for the central axis that connects the two buildings.

The new mosque has a decentralized structure with several access options and an independent ritual infrastructure. This enables men and women to use the mosque in parallel at prayer times. The central passage separates the two prayer rooms, but it becomes the connecting element at ceremonies and festivals.

The Women's House is situated atop a ridge where several footpaths cross. © Thomas Noceto.

Women's House

Building Beyond Borders, BC Architects & Studies

USE (AREA): Women's shelter; work, study, and meeting place for women (130 m²)
DESIGN TEAM: Participants in the Hasselt University postgraduate program Building Beyond Borders: John Silvertand, Hannah Van Breen, Arnaud Goossens, Auranne Leray, Margot Lambrechts, Eline Hoftiezer, Tinne Beirinckx, Kjell Keymolen, Aurora Fanti, Sofie Van den Velde, Jolien Bosmans, Martina Petrosino, Giulia Ventre, Emily Haest, Miki Z, Biniam Hailu, Alice Chang, Dany Depuydt
LOCAL COLLABORATION TEAM: Women from Association des Femmes d'Ouled Merzoug; Abdelaziz Agoram, Mohamed Oualla, Abdelhadi Arifi, Abdelkbir Sayah, Bouchaib Darai, Hassiz Kassimi, Abde Sadak Agoram, Mehdi El Finti, Allal El Finti, Abdelkarim Kassimi, Abdelwahid El Finti, Rachid Esmali
CLIENT: Association des Femmes d'Ouled Merzoug (AFOM)
LOCATION: Ouled Merzoug, Morocco
YEAR: 2019

Villages in rural Morocco are often occupied only by women and children for much of the year since many men are forced to migrate to the cities in search of work. Women play a central role in ensuring their families' survival, and they have thus begun to organize associations to strengthen women's autonomy and develop mutual support. In Ouled Merzoug, a village in the rural province of Ouarzazate, south of the High Atlas, a new community space was created for and with one such local women's organization. Its aim is to support women in their local economic activities and as a place for meeting and learning.

The Women's House at Ouled Merzoug was designed and built by villagers along with students from the Department of Art and Architecture at Hasselt University as part of Building Beyond Borders (BBB), a two-year postgraduate program bringing together students and experts to research regional materials and construction methods and examine the potential of regenerative and distributive planning and construction processes. The program takes a global, integrative understanding of architecture as a starting point to learn from local people and collaboratively develop hybrid, low-tech solutions. In 2018, students first examined the subject in theoretical terms, analyzing and mapping local conditions in Morocco to develop design specifics. Then a workshop was held on site with village residents, followed by the building of the Women's House in 2019. This was BBB's first implemented

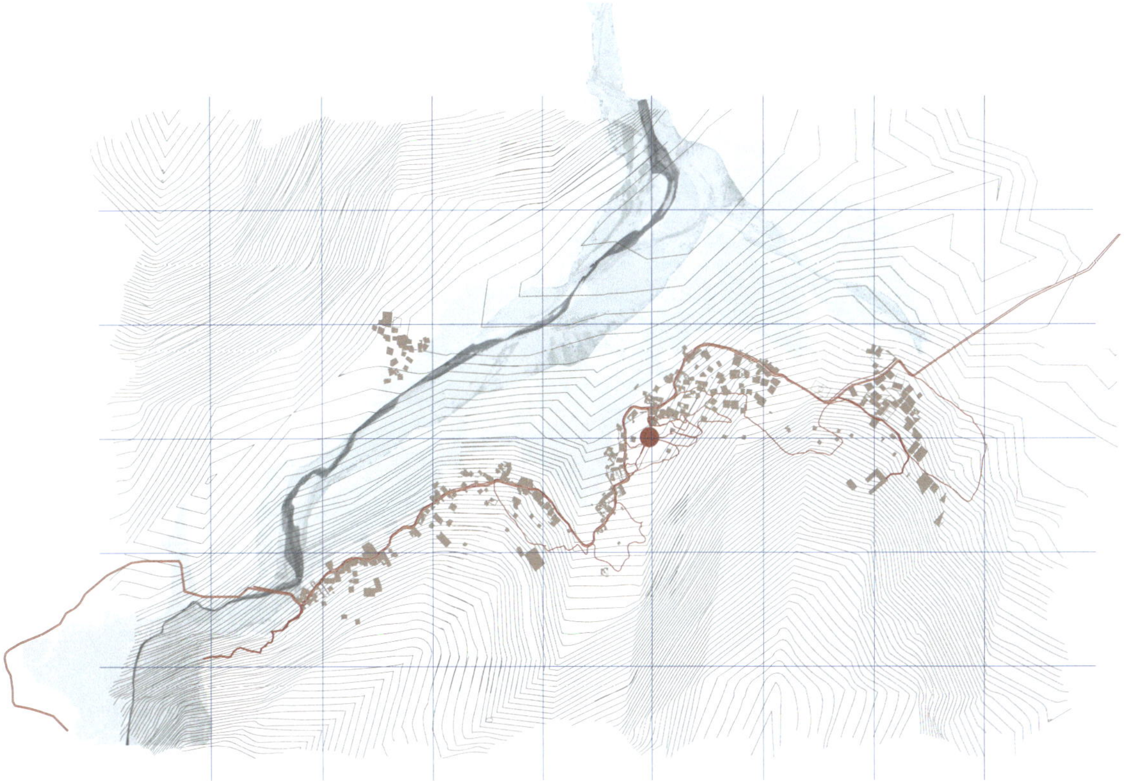

Ouled Merzoug site plan.
© Building Beyond Borders.

Village women were involved in the process, from the design phase to implementation. During construction, they prepared reeds for the ceilings and used rammed earth to build the foundations of the terraces.
© Tinne Beirinckx.

Granite stones from the surrounding hills were used for the outer walls. One small team specialized in choosing appropriate stones while another provided masons with a supply of *teng,* a mortar made of clay and straw.
© Thomas Noceto.

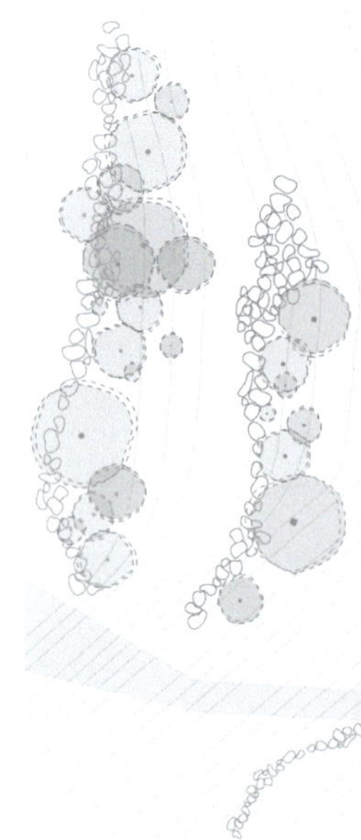

project, carried out in cooperation with BC Architects & Studies from Brussels, which had built a kindergarten in the village three years earlier using a similar process.

The Women's House site belongs to the recently founded Association des Femmes d'Ouled Merzoug (AFOM) and is located at a key location in the village where several informal footpaths cross. These include shortcuts from the village center to the cemetery and the religious square, as well as from the soccer field to the primary school via the kindergarten. The new building, built on the crest of a hill, consists of two spaces meeting at an angle, incorporating height differences created by the slope. The two wings form a courtyard, which holds the main entrance area, the most public part of the Women's House. One part of the building houses the *atelier des femmes,* a workshop space used for spinning and weaving and teaching those activities. The other section contains the *boulangerie commune,* a communal bakery where people eat, bake, and sell together. Both parts of the building consist of a functional space with an enclosed garden at the front. Wall openings create visual

© John Silvertand.

© Thomas Noceto.

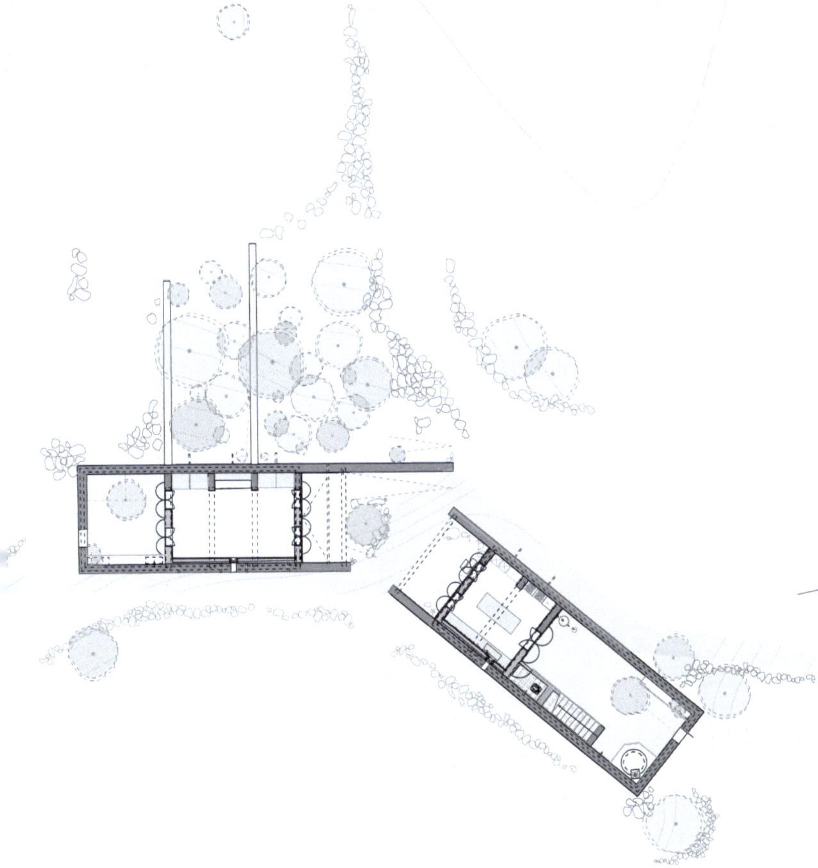

Floor plan and section.
© Building Beyond Borders.

The *boulangerie commune* hosts communal baking and eating. The piston-furnace oven in the enclosed garden was designed and built in collaboration with a local oven specialist, while the kitchen fixtures were crafted from eucalyptus wood by local carpenters.

connections between the two parts of the building and the parts of the village beside them. The garden courtyards contain facilities to help with the activities carried out in the main spaces: a bread oven and a large sink for washing and dyeing wool, respectively.

As with the previous project by BC Architects & Studies, the building was created in close cooperation with skilled local craftspeople. Outer walls are made from granite stones quarried in the surrounding hills; the roof span was based on the length of the longest eucalyptus beams available at the local market. Interior walls are made from adobe, faced with a mixture of clay, river sand, lime, and straw. Villagers carried out most of the work on the interior; local carpenters made doors and fixtures, a local potter made lamps and pottery, and village women wove the curtains and built the oven. A forest garden was planted in the ravine next to the hill. Not only does this provide a new public space for people and a habitat for various animals, it also helps reduce soil erosion. **VK**

View from the courtyard to the entrance of the *atelier des femmes.* © Thomas Noceto.

In the *atelier des femmes,* a large loom is used to weave and spin. Wool can be washed and dyed in the garden courtyard. © Thomas Noceto.

The dramatic landscape is enhanced by including views from the courtyard created by the two parts of the building, as well as views from the walled courtyards. © Cinzia Romanin.

Concreto Rosa

TEAM: Raquel Batista, Fernanda Dantas, Geisa Garibaldi, Jéssica Lage, Emmily Leandro, Fernanda Paixão, Lidiane Sá, Ester Viana
LOCATION: Rio de Janeiro
YEAR: 2015

Geisa Garibaldi, the founder of Concreto Rosa (far right), with four members of the team. © Concreto Rosa.

Entrepreneurship is a tool for emancipation. This is the view of Concreto Rosa, a business founded in 2015 by Geisa Garibaldi in Rio de Janeiro. Not only does the collective undertake renovations, construction, and repairs, it also serves to build and promote solidarity networks and support political activism for intersectional feminism and LGBTQ+ rights in Brazil. The initiative comprises a team of mainly Black women trained in architecture, civil engineering, electrical engineering, hydraulics, and masonry.

For Concreto Rosa, architecture embodies a collective experience and a practice that leads to greater spatial justice. The focus is on small-scale repair, installations, maintenance, and remodeling work in homes, commissioned mainly by women from both affluent and disadvantaged areas in Rio de Janeiro. Projects are documented in before-and-after videos and images and shared on Concreto Rosa's social media channels, where they are featured alongside videos about Black consciousness and Black feminist thought.

Starting out, Concreto Rosa had no working capital or modern equipment—a tool bag was all Garibaldi had. At that time, informal employment in Brazil accounted for over 45 percent of the total labor force. The ruling Workers' Party (PT) set out to expand the formalization of the labor force, reduce poverty, and take measures to promote women's employment and entrepreneurship. Results of these concrete efforts were noticeable in the construction industry, where women's participation increased dramatically. The empowerment and positioning of women in a male-dominated labor market has always been a topic of concern for Garibaldi. She became known for grassroots actions against discriminatory and patriarchal practices in architecture and construction. With Concreto Rosa, Garibaldi reminds us that we architects and critics must also leave the ivory tower and challenge the dynamics of authority within the architectural discourse as well as the built and urban space. **DOS**

Based in Rio de Janeiro, the collective Concreto Rosa uses social media channels like Instagram to spread the word about their practice, which involves repair, maintenance, and renovation work in private homes. © Concreto Rosa.

Essay

Maintenance and Visibility

For a Critical Theory of Architecture and Care Work

TEXT
Elke Krasny

July 25, 2021. It is very early this Sunday morning, in a summer defined by the living conditions during the global Covid-19 pandemic. Hardly any people are on the street. The museums and galleries of the Kunstareal museum complex in Munich will only open in a few hours. As expected, large crowds visited on the weekend. Overnight, the spacious, manicured green spaces became a sea of bottles, cans, and cardboard boxes. During the pandemic, revelers have used large open spaces, like those around these prominent cultural buildings, as temporary party zones. Early next morning, they are gone, and their garbage must be taken care of by someone else—a fact that those enjoying their carefree amusements likely gave little thought. It is taken for granted that someone will come to clean up after them. I start taking photos of all the trash scattered across the lawn.

Three people appear in the lens of my cell phone camera. They move about the stone slabs of the plaza in front of the Pinakothek der Moderne and on the lawn, bending down, picking up the garbage, and putting it into the large bags they thought to bring. Two of the three cleaning workers are men; one is a woman. One of the men, who has a history of migration to Germany through his immediate or distant family, approaches me. He asks me to forward my photos to the museum management because he is sure they have no idea what it looks like here on Sunday morning. I ask him if he does the cleaning for the museum, and in answer, he points to the logo-like inscription on his white polo shirt. He indicates the company he is on duty for only by gesture, without saying its name. He tells us that it is only since Covid-19 that it has become so problematic with partying and that it looks terrible every weekend. He stresses that they have to start cleaning up early and be much faster than before Corona so that everything is ready before people start lining up to enter the Pinakothek der Moderne. Probably the waiting visitors will not give a thought to the fact that there must have been someone who ensured that the waiting area in front of the museum was in perfect condition as expected. As is usually the case, or actually always the case, care work—like cleaning public urban spaces in this case—only attracts attention when it is omitted, when there is something to find fault with. The fact that it took place unnoticed, on the other hand, is considered normal. Caring for the uninterrupted restoration and renewal of normalcy is simply overlooked. Such work remains below the threshold of public visibility, even though it is often performed in plain sight in urban spaces.

This text is intended as a contribution to the development of a critical theory of architecture and care work, a constellation that is deeply enmeshed in the reproduction of relations of injustice. The above scene in Munich serves as a key to analyzing the standards and values that shape the relationship between system maintenance and visibility. With the support of feminist imagination, the findings can pave the way for other future-oriented practices.

An analysis of the relations of injustice characterizing architecture and care work must start by observing the prevailing everyday relations. This leads to the following fundamental questions: For whom and why does the built space perform care, and how? How can built space be understood as a support system providing built care work that people rely on in their day-to-day lives? Who will do the daily care work needed so that architecture can perform these supporting tasks well? Who washes, cleans, and nurtures? Who takes care of maintenance and repair? Who helps to ensure that architecture is understood more as support and less as representation? Architects and architectural researchers rarely answer questions like these. To create the conditions for a different future, architecture as representation and its economies of production must be fundamentally rethought; only then can the relationship between architecture and care work be organized differently.

THE SCALE OF JUSTICE IN ARCHITECTURE

A critical theory on architecture and care work, like any other critical theory worthy of the name, must start from concrete realities. Through analysis, it can contribute to changes enacting social and environmental justice that challenge the world-dominating system of labor exploitation and resource extractivism. Gender inequities are part of the intersectionally spatialized, sociomaterial, ecomaterial, and biopolitical relations of injustice, shaped by various historical and local conditions. Nevertheless, these forms of injustice are based on the fact that differences—whether between human beings, nonhuman beings, or matter—are used to derive hierarchies and scales of value that give rise to systemic disadvantages. As long as they determine how we coexist in the world, architecture will be complicit in the creation of unjust relations. Through the way architecture builds on such differences, systemic disadvantages manifest in built, lived, and everyday space.

As a spatial discipline, architecture is known to be committed to scale. On the one hand, the built scale of architecture can be seen as a neutrality that objectifies space. It is assumed that there is no need to distinguish between the bodies of human and nonhuman beings and the environment inside and with architecture. On the other hand, the real effects of architecture show that the reasons for applying different, i.e., non-neutral, non-neutralizing scales do not serve the fight against injustice resulting from disadvantage due to differences, but rather economic considerations and political motivations. For example, buildings are constructed differently for those with financial means and those without. Spaces designated for care work are valued differently than spaces for other functions. In designing spaces that are not for care, little thought is given to how care-intensive they will be in the future, and how well they will enable those who care for them to carry out this task and recover from it. What scale does architecture live up to? What would it, and will it, entail to redesign the scale of justice in architecture?

Building system maintenance

From the long-term perspective of history, architecture can be understood as a permanently built system; it serves to maintain the system in both a physical/material and a representative/symbolic sense. Whether feudal, colonial, socialist, capitalist, or neoliberal, the system is built with architecture and advanced both economically and symbolically. Between that, at the juncture of economy and symbolism forged by architecture, political power unfolds at both the level of state-supporting political representation and the (micro)political effects on the organization, order, and control of human and nonhuman bodies and resources. Architectural historians can analyze the enmeshment of political power, notions of social order, and resource extraction based on a building's style, typology, and materials—granted they have the appropriate methodological tools and interest in critical social research. But such approaches are still the exception in architectural research. Many architecture schools continue to focus strongly on issues of style and typology—without considering how they are related to materials, resources, and bodies to understand how architecture is not only part of prevailing systems and relations of injustice but also their built expression.

By using the tools of research to understand architecture as a history of built injustice in social, economic, and ecological terms, we can also show what changes are needed in built architectural practice to develop and implement new scales that do not make the built environment complicit in maintaining systems of injustice and perpetuating unjust local and global relations. The latter are built on profit maximization, financialization, and resource extractivism, which increasingly lead not only to the destruction of nature, nonhuman life, and so-called non-living matter but also to an unlivable and unaffordable life for humans.

CARE WORK IS ESSENTIAL FOR LIFE

Living beings depend on care work. To ensure their survival and existence, they must be cared and provided for. Care work maintains the system, as the pandemic has made abundantly clear. In this context, too, scales can be used to critically analyze the modes of action and real effects of architecture on the body and the environment. Can care work be based on a seemingly neutral, objectifiable scale that applies equally to the bodies of all human and nonhuman beings? After all, they all have very different care needs. They also have very different opportunities, capacities, knowledge, resources, and infrastructures to care for themselves, others, and the environment. There are as many ways of existing as there are ways of caring. Some of these are based on choice, though many do not have the freedom to engage in self-determined care work. Many receive insufficient care and attention or none at all—not to mention the issue of preventative care. For many people, care work means exhaustion, exploitation, stress, and high costs. The worse the possibilities to care for oneself and others, the worse the living conditions and chances of survival. As stated above, a scale that is considered neutral and objectifiable negates real existing differences between bodies and their necessities and needs, leading to cruel violations. The values and systems derived from the idea of the white man as the measure of all things have long determined our coexistence. Feminist and critical race theories have highlighted the brutal effects of detaching the idea of the subject from real living bodies. The impact of these historical formations can still be felt today and are primarily responsible for the increasing impossibility of the future.

ARCHITECTURE PERFORMS CARE WORK

Neither the canon of architectural history nor established architectural theories have yet to consider architecture as care work. The same is true the other way around. Neither political, constitutional, or philosophical considerations of care work, nor their accompanying social theories, whether historical or contemporary, have considered and examined architecture as care work. Architecture performs care work, for example, by protecting people from the effects of the environment and the inclemencies of weather. It ensures that people have a home. Having a home is a prerequisite for existential and everyday processes like sleeping, preparing food, eating, personal hygiene, and washing clothes. But it also has many more functions, which not only fulfill physical needs but also have affective, emotional, intellectual, intimate, sexual, social, or convivial dimensions. I propose to conceive of this provision of functions as care work through architecture.

Care work is generally seen as an activity that performs supportive actions between human beings, between human and nonhuman beings, but also between humans and things and between humans and matter. The notion of architecture as care work entails conceiving architecture as a built space for action, as a long-term and permanent support system. The carer, in this case, is not a human being who cares for other people and things or who self-cares, but the architecture, the built.

This theoretical convergence of architecture and care work makes architecture recognizable as built care work. Human beings can better survive and lead a better life the better they are supported and can care for themselves. While architecture should be understood as built care work, there are nevertheless fundamental differences between architecture and what is conventionally considered care work in terms of the scales that apply to their respective social, economic, and political significance, value, and organization.

SYSTEM MAINTENANCE AND VISIBILITY

For a critical understanding of architecture and care work, a critical reading of the concepts of system maintenance and visibility is essential. These two concepts encompass unquestioned norms and values that shape the deep structures of society and politics, and harbor relations of injustice, violence, and power. The ideas handed down and articulated within them are at odds with transformative justice and the construction of futurity.

Systems are large-scale organizational entities addressing a whole and interacting with its parts. In this context, they are economic, social, and political systems that shape the coexistence of human and nonhuman beings within the built environment. The following systems are of particular interest for architecture and care work: the nation-state, the globalized economic order based on exploitation and profit maximization, and resource extractivism based on human exceptionalism, which exploits and destroys the Earth as a storehouse of raw materials. Architecture helps build these systems and is deeply involved in their maintenance. Moreover, architecture is always visible and in every political and economic system it deals with the spatial organization of everything directly affecting human bodies, their living conditions, and the upkeep of their health and well-being. This includes global housing production but also food supply and healthcare. Whether and how these systems produce just or unjust conditions always depends on how the system's individual parts interact, how they are organized, and which value scales are used to measure the specific political, economic, social, and cultural significance of the different parts of the system. The real existing differences in the ways that human and nonhuman beings coexist are determined by this organization of meaning, to which architecture contributes significantly. If the system is to change, the organization of meanings that sets the scales architecture produces and spatializes must become radically different. An architecture that actively contributes to preserving the habitability of planet Earth and sets standards against gendered, racialized, and classist discrimination will have to build up care work differently in order to repair the future.

As the scene at the Kunstareal in Munich described at the beginning of this text shows, the maintenance of public space is, on the one hand, dependent on care work and, on the other hand, withdrawn from the public eye as far as possible in terms of both space and time. This invisibility corresponds to the prevailing value scales. Care work is an interruption, disrupting the visible representational function of architecture and culture. We must ask: What kind of architectural or cultural understanding does care work disturb?

The architecture of representational cultural buildings articulates and maintains the symbolic significance of the respective system. However, museums not only serve this representative visualization through the public display of exhibits but also take care of their storage and protection, ensuring their continued existence and the stock of artifacts and objects. In this case, we can observe a clear, spatially structured division of functions and a hierarchization inherent in the system and embodied by the architecture. Architectural methods are used to render visible those museum spaces where artifacts are displayed, which are comprehended as being significant for the nation-state by political theory and as public spaces by social theory. Architectural methods are used to render invisible those museum spaces mainly dedicated to the care of the exhibits, their storage, conservation, preservation, and continued existence. In the representative hierarchy of space, showing is above storing; presenting is above protecting. But the latter is the prerequisite for the former. The storage and protection of objects in collections and depots enables them to become exhibits in the exhibition spaces. As shown by the museum building example, architecture assumes the task of spatialized system maintenance by strategically separating the space into areas that are visible and invisible to the public. System maintenance is both the symbolic and powerful representation of the system and the provision of all the infrastructure and labor necessary for its maintenance so that the visible representation can occur at all. While the latter is conventionally associated with system maintenance, the former, the representational function, is usually not. Critical theorizing of architecture and care work therefore requires overcoming this unquestioned assumption through a new research perspective, in which the meanings and values of system maintenance do not follow the division between visible and invisible implied by the spatial organization.

The multifaceted liberation movements in the second half of the 20th century—including anti-colonial and decolonial struggles, feminist struggles, and struggles by sexual minorities, workers, and dissidents against authoritarian political regimes—have made the museum, with its function of preserving the representative system, a highly contested institution. On the one hand, artifacts that have entered the collections of Europe's museums through looting, dispossession, and other forms of illicit acquisition are being reclaimed by people in formerly colonized places. On the other hand, women, queer people, people of color, blue-collar workers, and many other groups that have been marginalized by collection policies and exhibition strategies are demanding the inclusion of their cultural achievements in museums. Reproductive labor—including unpaid and low-paid housework, cleaning activities, garbage collection, services in trade and tourism, body-related services such as beauty, hairdressing, and nail salons, transportation services, and healthcare and eldercare services—does not produce artifacts in the strict sense. The lack of collectible objects in reproductive labor excludes it from the logics of collecting and exhibiting followed by the representational regime of cultural hegemony embodied by museums. Architecture, which clearly leads to object-like products, has historically always been part of the logic of production. A new critical theory of architecture in its relation to care work must not only assume that architecture provides for system maintenance and human life support, thereby making it dependent on constant care work such as cleaning, care, repair, and maintenance. It must also focus on how architecture builds hegemonic scales of value committed to the imperatives of production and visibility.

This is where the imagination of feminist futures must step in. If museums and other cultural institutions want to continue representing cultural values, they must be the first to reorganize the relations between system preservation and visibility and put it into practice. What would happen if architects and planners developed architecture and care work in concert with those who carry out the everyday care work, including those who maintain the architecture? What if, in the future, museums and cultural institutions treated daily care not as exploitative, invisible labor but as a self-evident part of the use of public spaces—organized and carried out jointly by all who frequent these spaces? Then these architectures and the culture they represent would be truly representative of a system well worth preserving.

Maintenance Art

Mierle Laderman Ukeles

Mierle Laderman Ukeles, *Washing / Tracks / Maintenance: Inside*, July 22, 1973, performance at the Wadsworth Atheneum Museum of Art, Hartford, part of the *Maintenance Art Performances* series, 1973–1974.

In 1969, when she was 30 years old, shortly after the birth of her first child, Mierle Laderman Ukeles published the *MANIFESTO FOR MAINTENANCE ART*.[01] Facing the social expectations placed on her as an artist and young mother, Ukeles called the traditional role of women as providers into question, while emphasizing the particular "life-sustaining" value of everyday housekeeping and maintenance work, which is largely done by women.

"I am an artist. I am a woman. I am a wife. I am a mother (random order). I do a hell of a lot of washing, cleaning, cooking, renewing, supporting, preserving, etc. Also (up to now separately) I 'do' Art."

Ukeles's manifesto expresses her decision to no longer keep (her) art separate from the sphere of everyday housework, which is often carried out invisibly. Instead, she presents "maintenance," "servicing," "preservation," and "care" as creative strategies and artistic activities in themselves: *"My working will be the work."*

In the early 1970s, Ukeles cleaned museums and galleries as an artistic performance. In her later works, her concept of maintenance expanded further, now also including "social maintenance" and public systems of care. For *Touch Sanitation* (1977–1980), she visited every one of New York's 8,500 public sanitation workers at their workplace, personally thanking them with the words, "Thank you for keeping New York City alive."

A pioneer of Social Practice Art, since early in her career Ukeles has pointed the way toward artistic practices that could radically question modern conceptions of aesthetic autonomy, pressure to innovate, and the economic compulsion to "create something new." Her work introduces feminist ideas of care, repair, ecosystem, and circular economy into her art. These ideas are none the less valid today. With new urgency, the Covid-19 pandemic has demonstrated just how "systemically relevant" the care professions and care infrastructure really are, necessary for all our survival.

At the beginning of the second wave of the coronavirus in September 2020—40 years after *Touch Sanitation*—Ukeles's text was again displayed on over 2,000 digital screens in the city's subway stations and in Times Square: "Dear Service Worker, 'Thank you for keeping NYC alive!' for → forever …" **MAK**

01 Mierle Laderman Ukeles, ***MANIFESTO FOR MAINTENANCE ART, 1969!***, September 30, 1969, accessed August 16, 2022, feldmangallery.com/exhibition/manifesto-for-maintenance-art-1969.

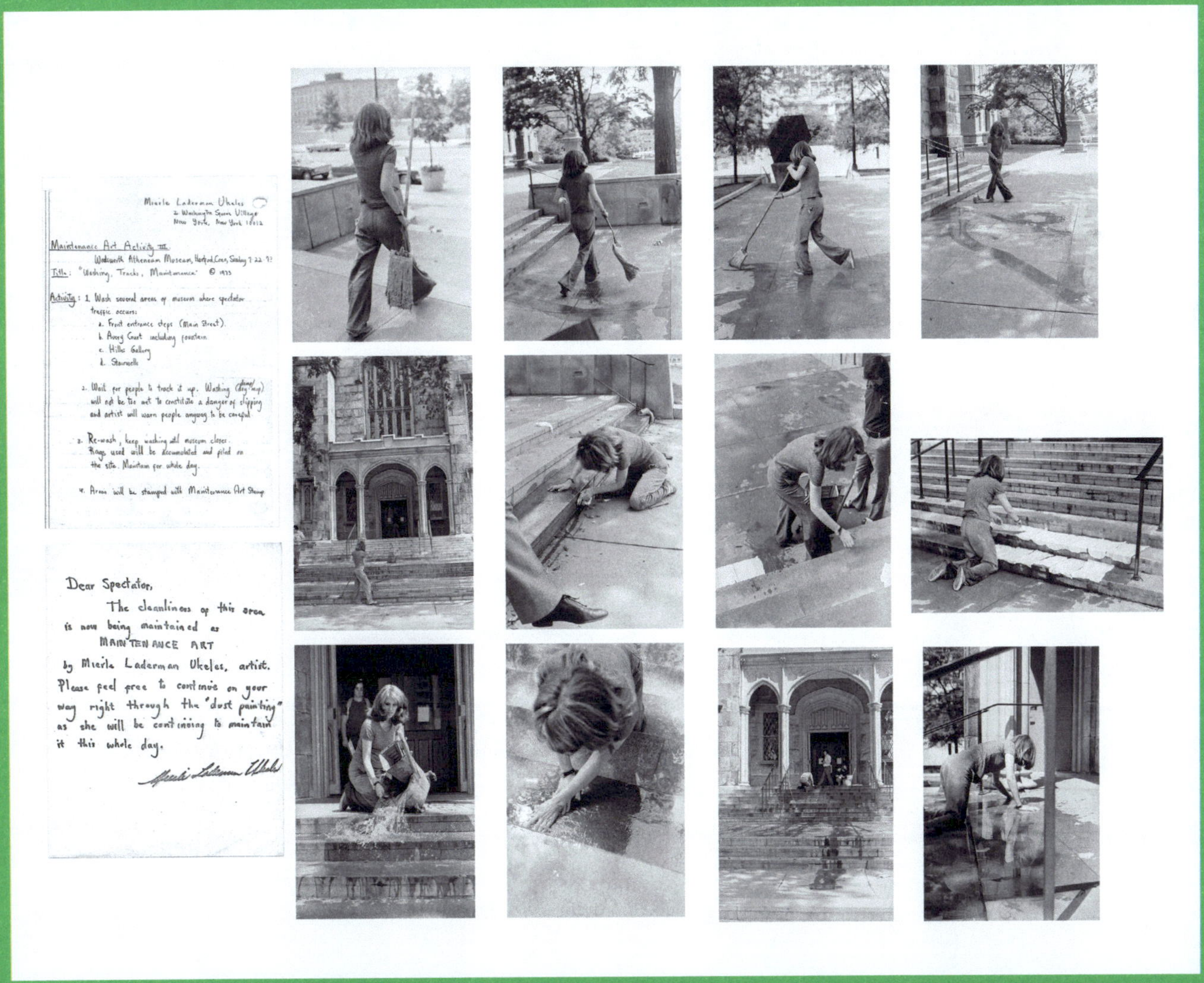

Mierle Laderman Ukeles, *Washing / Tracks / Maintenance: Outside*, 1973, performance at the Wadsworth Atheneum Museum of Art, Hartford, part of the *Maintenance Art Performances* series, 1973–1974.

Dimensions of Repair

TEXT
Irene Cheng

Kader Attia, *Chaos + Repair = Universe*, 2014. Sculpture made of mirrors and metal wire, installation view, *Sacrifice and Harmony*, MMK, Frankfurt, 2016.
Courtesy Kader Attia and Galleria Continua.
Photo: MMK Museum für Moderne Kunst Frankfurt / Axel Schneider.

First published in *Log* in the Winter/Spring 2020 issue, the conversation between Mabel Wilson and Bryony Roberts on the theme of "radical repair" was prescient in a number of ways. Looking back over a year later, the discussion anticipates subsequent, and ongoing, conversations about racial justice ignited by George Floyd's murder by police officers in May 2020, as well as a global pandemic that has killed over six million people worldwide (and counting) while laying bare various inequalities. Amid these dual crises, the theme of repair remains particularly urgent: How do we repair a world that seems irreparably broken? We cannot go back to the way things were, yet we also cannot ignore, much less escape, the past. As Wilson puts it in the interview, she is not "interested in restoration—to return [...] to the thing that it was" but instead wants to explore "actions of radical repair that recognize the transformation of time and the violent acts that have produced disruption and social divisions."

Discussions of repair are of the moment but also, as Wilson hints in the interview, draw on decades of thought among scholars and activists in a number of spheres, from critical race theory to law to feminist thought to ecology to media and technology studies. The potential forms of repair raised by these various approaches vary widely, encompassing psychological, legal, monetary, environmental, and artistic means. Below I sketch a few ways that the theme of repair has been addressed by others before concluding with an example of Wilson's own recent work.

Beyond reparation?

Within the context of the United States, the idea of making amends for slavery through reparations—usually defined as compensation for losses sustained or enabled by the state or private actors—is not a new idea. As Ta-Nehisi Coates points out in his oft-referenced 2014 essay "The Case for Reparations," there were instances of enslaved Africans successfully suing for monetary compensation as early as 1783.[01] In the 20th century, the argument for reparations has periodically resurfaced in the national conversation, only to founder repeatedly on seemingly practical quandaries—who should pay, who is entitled to receive payment—as well as entrenched resistance among conservatives. Thus, the history of reparations is the "history of a nonevent," a history marked by "belatedness and insufficiency."[02]

From another perspective, several radical Black scholars have mounted compelling arguments about the inadequacy of reparations. Stephen Best and Saidiya Hartman have written incisively about the impossibility of fully redressing the losses engendered by racial slavery and its aftermath. Any legal remedy is inevitably too narrow, any payment inadequate:

"If what has been done cannot be undone, then the forms of legal and social compensation available are less a matter of wiping the slate clean than of embracing the limited scope of the possible in face of the irreparable, and calling attention to the incommensurability between pain and compensation. How does one compensate for centuries of violence that have as their consequence the impossibility of restoring a prior existence, of giving back what was taken, of repairing what was broken?"[03]

For Best and Hartman, the central issue is not monetary compensation—an objective that they note remains ensconced within the liberal paradigm of individual rights and property—but the recognition that slavery's violence is ongoing, that freedom and abolition are "unfinished projects." Rather than concentrating on "what happened then" or "what is owed because of what happened then," they argue for grappling with the "contemporary predicament of freedom, with the melancholy recognition of foreseeable futures still tethered to this past"[04] while seeking out forms of political aspiration that "are illegible because they are so wildly utopian and derelict to capitalism."[05] In other words, a myopic focus on reparation risks obscuring more radical forms of redress and repair.

Similar critiques of the inadequacies of "reparations politics" have been discussed within the field of international human rights. Valentina Rozas-Krause, drawing on the work of scholars such as Roy L. Brooks and John C. Torpey, observes, regarding the pervasiveness of memorials to commemorate historical wrongs in Europe, that "apologies are meant to ease the pain of an injustice and to repair the victims"[06] while transforming remorse into national reconciliation. Yet often, such apologies "slip into an empty rhetoric of reconciliation in the face of persistent injustices." For this reason, some who are wronged have refused to grant absolution on the grounds that forgiveness leads to forgetting. For survivors of wartime and other atrocities, the refusal of a too-constrained form of repair is a political statement.

“How does one compensate for centuries of violence that have as their consequence the impossibility of restoring a prior existence, of giving back what was taken, of repairing what was broken?”
– STEPHEN BEST AND SAIDIYA HARTMAN

Kader Attia, ***The Repair from Occident to Extra-Occidental Cultures***, **2012, installation view,** ***The Museum of Emotion***, **Hayward Gallery, London 2019. The multimedia installation includes books and wooden busts that Kader Attia created in collaboration with traditional artisans in Senegal, based on archival photographs of wounded soldiers from the First World War. It also includes marble busts the artist had hewn by marble sculptors in Carrara, Italy, based on ethnographic studies from the late 19th century.**
The Repair from Occident to Extra-Occidental Cultures **was commissioned for dOCUMENTA (13) and was produced with the support of Kader Attia, Galleria Continua, Galerie Nagel Draxler, and Galerie Krinzinger. Additional support was provided by Fondation Nationale des Arts Graphiques et Plastiques, France.**
Photo: Thierry Bal.

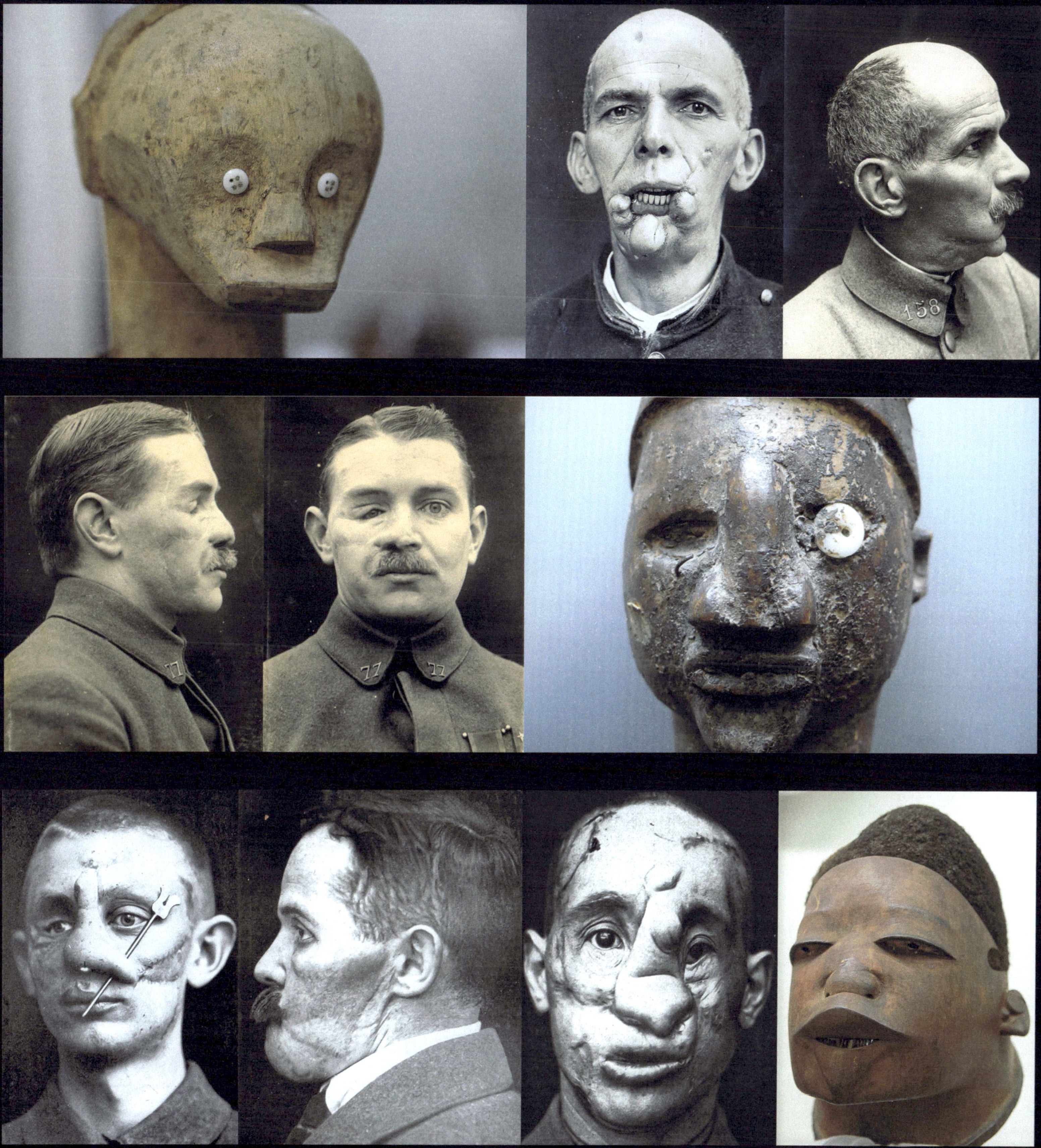

Kader Attia, *The Repair*, 2012. Diptych of slide projections, details.
The projection juxtaposes archival photographs of wounded soldiers from the First World War with images of objects, sculptures, and people from different cultures in former colonies that bear visible traces of repair.
Courtesy Kader Attia, Collection Marguliés, Collection Centre Georges Pompidou, private collection, and Galleria Continua. Photos: Musée du Service de Santé des Armées, Paris, and Martin Monestier, MARKK, Hamburg.

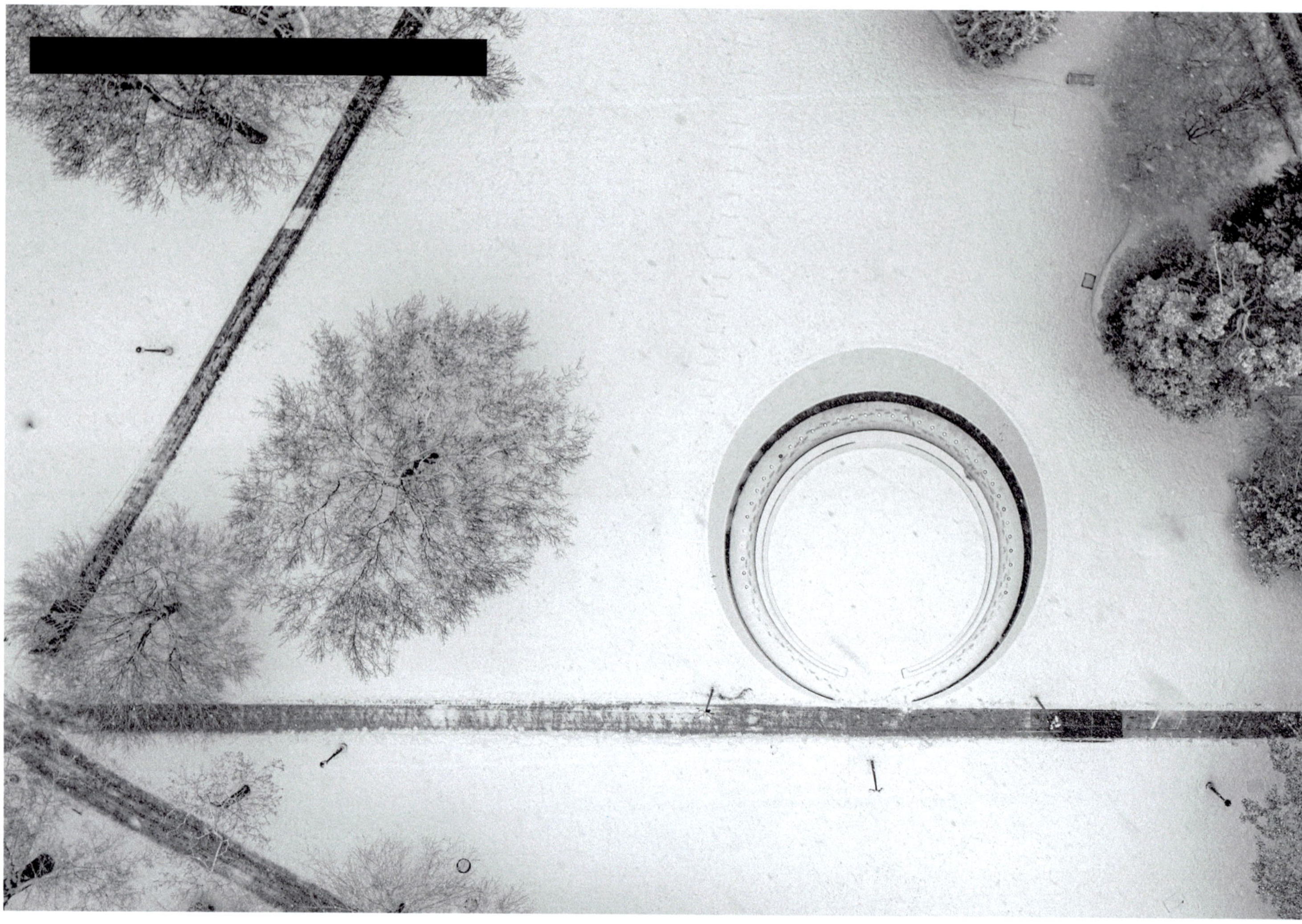

The Memorial to Enslaved Workers, located on the University of Virginia campus in Charlottesville, was designed in 2020 by Höweler + Yoon Architecture in collaboration with Mabel O. Wilson, Frank Dukes, Gregg Bleam, and Eto Otitigbe. © Sanjay Suchak.

1. Gathering circle.
2. Inner ring: Timeline and water table; liberation and libation.
3. Inner wall: Engraved names and memory marks; honoring the enslaved.
4. Outer wall: Eyes of Isabella Gibbons; remembering the enslaved.
Courtesy Höweler + Yoon Architecture.

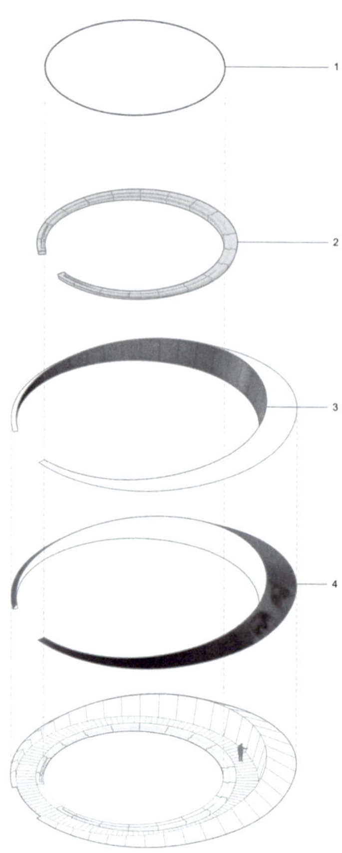

**Engraved on the interior wall of the granite ring are names of the estimated 4,000 enslaved persons who worked at the University of Virginia between 1817 and 1865. "Memory marks" represent those whose names were not listed in the records.
Courtesy Höweler + Yoon Architecture.**

“The task of repair, at once impossible and imperative, calls for new techniques of discovering, revealing, and writing the past, as well as for linking history to actions that call forth a different future.”

REVALUING REPAIR AS CARE WORK

While several critical race theorists and human rights scholars have pointed to the limitations of reparations-as-repair, a more expansive concept of repair has drawn support from other quarters. Since the 1960s, many feminist scholars have argued for the importance of repair—defined as everyday acts of mending, fixing, maintenance, and domestic and reproductive labor. These acts of repair can be linked to the feminist elaboration of an ethics of care that is relational and intersubjective. More broadly, the revalorization of care work calls attention to the many forms of unwaged labor carried out primarily by women, as well as the low-paid labor of cleaning, maintenance, childcare, and elder care disproportionately undertaken (in the US context) by immigrant women and women of color.

Drawing on these ideas, artists and architects have turned their attention to the unheralded work of maintenance, beginning with Mierle Laderman Ukeles's pioneering of the term “maintenance art” to describe art practices that “flush [...] up to consciousness” everyday acts of care such as “washing, cleaning, cooking, renewing, supporting, preserving.”[07] Hilary Sample's book *Maintenance Architecture* similarly uncovers the workers and technologies engaged in the upkeep and repair of buildings and cities.[08]

Ideas about repair have permeated ecology, with many environmentalists advocating for the extension of a feminist ethics of care, with its intersubjective orientation, to nonhuman others, landscapes, and ecological communities. Indigenous epistemologies emphasizing stewardship and care for the land have also contributed to the emergence of reparative environmental practices and philosophies. As with critical race theorists, a number of environmental thinkers have emphasized the impossibility of repair, understood as the restoration of a landscape to a pre-disturbed state. Instead, it is argued, repair must be conceived as a rebuilding of relationships to enable survival and even flourishing within an irretrievably damaged world.

Similarly, a number of scholars of media and technology studies, including Steven J. Jackson and Shannon Mattern, have identified repair as an essential practice for a “broken world”—a world characterized not by “progress and advance, novelty and invention” but by “risk and uncertainty, growth and decay, and fragmentation, dissolution, and breakdown.”[09] As Jackson points out, the implications for thinking about technology include a profound shift in values. Rather than idealizing innovation and the new, we must begin to appreciate “the subtle arts of repair by which rich and robust lives are sustained against the weight of centrifugal odds.”[10] It is an admonition applicable to all fields in which a view of modernity as technologically driven advancement has traditionally reigned, including architecture.

Memory as radical repair

These strands of thought form part of the context, the weave, into which Mabel O. Wilson's recent work enters. As she explains in the interview with Bryony Roberts, themes of repair have threaded through her work, including a recent studio she taught at Columbia University. Wilson cites as an influence Kader Attia, an Algerian-French artist whose work has explored radical practices and ideas of repair. In *The Repair from Occident to Extra-Occidental Cultures* (2012), for example, Attia juxtaposes photographs of surgically reconstructed yet still visibly mutilated faces of World War I veterans with artifacts from former colonies in Africa that have been mended by local artisans—often in ways that highlight their refurbishment (for example, an African sculpture with eyes replaced with European buttons). Eschewing the ideal of repair as seamless restoration to a prior state of being whole, Attia's work proposes a practice of repair that acknowledges damage while embracing appropriation, assemblage, and improvisation.

Similarly, Wilson's architectural and scholarly work has often simultaneously called attention to historical wrongs while seeking forms of redress that are explicitly unfinished, bridging historical research with contemporary design and activism. For the Memorial to Enslaved Laborers at the University of Virginia (UVA, 2020), on which she collaborated with Höweler + Yoon Architecture, Wilson worked with researchers to uncover records of the 4,000 enslaved people who are believed to have worked and lived at the university between 1817 and 1865. Of these, the names of 587 individuals have been recovered, and another 311 appear in archival records, but their names are unknown. The designers memorialize these 4,000 souls in the form of linear gashes engraved in a circular granite wall: some of the marks are augmented with first and last names, others bear only first names, still others feature descriptions such as “woodcutter” or “sister,” while the majority lack any specific identifying trait. In this way, the memorial lays bare what has been lost and what was denied: names, identities, personhood, citizenship. It also remains an incomplete record, comprising an opening rather than a closing.

Acknowledgment of the brutality and the loss created by slavery and its aftermath is a necessary task, but it is not enough, for “what has been done cannot be undone,” as Best and Hartman put it. In the meantime—a time they call the “interval between the no longer and the not yet, between the destruction of the old world and the awaited hour of deliverance”[11]—memorials such as the one at UVA might be understood as attempts to repair, to mend, to forge new relations, in a badly broken world. Such acts of repair cannot absolve the institution but are part of the ongoing work of historical revision and redress. As Wilson writes, “We're going to have to survive somehow. We're going to have to make some way of being human in the world intellectually, in the mind, and also in the body, materially. So the optimist in me believes that to do that we're just going to have to make do and rework what we have.” The task of repair, at once impossible and imperative, calls for new techniques of discovering, revealing, and writing the past, as well as for linking history to actions that call forth a different future.

01 Ta-Nehisi Coates, “The Case for Reparations,” *The Atlantic*, June 2014, accessed September 1, 2022, www.theatlantic.com/magazine/archive/2014/06/the-case-for-reparations/361631.
02 Stephen Best and Saidiya Hartman, “Fugitive Justice,” *Representations* 92, no. 1 (Fall 2005): 1–15, 4.
03 Ibid., 1–2.
04 Ibid., 5.
05 Ibid., 9.
06 Valentina Rozas-Krause, “Memorials and the Cult of Apology,” *e-flux Architecture*, September 2020, accessed September 1, 2022, www.e-flux.com/architecture/monument/349760/memorials-and-the-cult-of-apology.
07 Mierle Laderman Ukeles, *Manifesto for Maintenance Art*, 1969.
08 Hilary Sample, *Maintenance Architecture* (Cambridge, MA: MIT Press, 2016).
09 Steven J. Jackson, “Rethinking Repair,” in *Media Technologies: Essays on Communication, Materiality, and Society*, eds. Tarleton Gillespie, Pablo J. Boczkowski, and Kirsten A. Foot (Cambridge, MA: MIT Press, 2014), 221–39, 221.
10 Ibid., 222.
11 Best and Hartman, “Fugitive Justice” (see note 2), 3.

Torkwase Dyson, *Plantationocene*, from the series *1919: Black Water*, 2019, installation view Arthur Ross Architecture Gallery, Columbia GSAPP, New York, 2019. Acrylic, graphite, brass, wood, ink on canvas; diameter: 250 cm. In her work, the artist Torkwase Dyson addresses the legacy of slavery and the African diaspora in the United States. She is interested in how (Black) bodies perceive space, architecture, and the city. Courtesy Arthur Ross Architecture Gallery, Columbia GSAPP. Photo: Nicholas Knight.

Radical Repair

Mabel O. Wilson in conversation with Bryony Roberts

BRYONY ROBERTS: The catalogue for Torkwase Dyson's show *1919: Black Water*, which opened at Columbia's Arthur Ross Architecture Gallery in September, includes a great conversation between you and the artist. You talked about the importance of decolonizing the tools of creation and listed some as "the book, the argument, the essay, and the memorial." This was after a longer conversation about decolonizing form. Could you talk more about how you approach decolonizing these tools in your own practice, as someone who makes books, forms, and arguments?

MABEL O. WILSON: Well the root problem is decolonizing knowledge. There is a Peruvian sociologist who recently died, Aníbal Quijano, who said we have to decolonize the episteme. The Western body of knowledge that everyone takes for granted as universal actually isn't. It has multiple histories and origins, and there are other bodies of knowledge—ways of knowing and naming and understanding subjectivity in the world—that are not Western at all. They were not necessarily centered on the individual, on the human body, on the subjectivity of liberalism. Even in the so-called West—Europe or pre-Europe—there were other ways of being in the world.

But the trick about the Western episteme, and you see this meticulously analyzed in Foucault's writings, is that it becomes universal. That's its trick. It absorbs all other bodies of knowledge and posits that there's only one body of knowledge and one way of being in the world. Architecture is part and parcel of that—it's the Western practice of building. I've come to the realization that the art of building is part of the formation of the Western episteme.

We can see how other cultures built—the Incans, the Chinese dynasties, Māori tribespeople—in ways that weren't necessarily the Western methods of architecture. I'm talking about conceptualization and modalities of representation, like drawing, that rely on paper, ink, and geometric projection. Europeans did not invent geometry per se but borrowed concepts from ancient Greece and Islam. These tools were combined into a discourse and a discipline of architecture, which solidified by the 18th century. In the 19th century, architecture was a body of knowledge that was institutionalized within both a profession and modern universities. This all emerged alongside colonialism, which fueled the wealth of Europe and enabled the construction of museums, theaters, and government buildings. Architecture's function was, in part, to house the modern nation-state and modern liberal society.

So those tools are what we inherit. That's what we teach. That's what we practice. But they have a very particular history.

BR: So, how do you think about your own process of writing, researching, and designing?

MW: I found early on, when I kept trying to explore Black neighborhoods, spaces, and histories, that the language, tools, and techniques of architecture were completely inadequate because they're not made to register and give meaning to those things. So, I was constantly developing new techniques, hybridizing them, turning things inside out, questioning, and renaming in order to begin to even record those spaces and imagine what those spaces could be. I looked at literature, art, and other creative ways that people have done work on these subjects and then tried to translate them into architecture.

BR: Torkwase Dyson describes "Black compositional thought" as a way of improvising spaces and objects of liberation in an oppressive system. That resonates with what you describe in your book *Negro Building* and also with what you and I researched in our project *Marching On*. But alongside these ways of appropriating and manipulating a found system, there are recent moments of visible institution building, like the National Museum of African American History and Culture, which in some ways takes on the monumentality of the colonial system. Do you see the improvisational techniques as being replaced by institution building or as a means of creating alternative kinds of institutions?

MW: I think that there are two trajectories. One is Afro-pessimism, which argues that the Enlightenment project, including its institutions, is bankrupt given the contradiction of the presence of freedom alongside slavery, so there has never been a place for people of color to find liberation within it. We're never going to survive in that system. And I think they're right. But I'm more aligned with the optimistic position that we're going to have to survive somehow. We're going to have to make some way of being human in the world intellectually, in the mind, and also in the body, materially. So the optimist in me believes that to do that we're just going to have to make do and rework what we have. That's why I think challenging and changing institutions is important, and the new African American museum is the perfect example, because it took 100 years to come into fruition. Different generations kept trying and trying again. It didn't happen overnight. That was primarily because the archive was never meant to collect the culture of Black peoples because the belief was that if you were African or of African descent, you had no history.

That's what Kant argued, Hegel expanded, and European intellectuals debated, and the concept spread. So, often there's little Black history in the institutional archives. The Smithsonian collected almost nothing of Black people from its founding in the mid-19th century. The project of the African American museum was not only to build a museum but also to build a collection. They had to make an archive of Black life in America because there wasn't one. So institutionally, it's a really radical proposition.

BR: So is it useful to work with the normative conventions of institutions to gain a place in a canon? Or is it important to just create new methods and new forums that don't follow those rules?

MW: I think you can do both. At some point, there are certain things—concepts, practices, or methods—that are just going to be exhausted, and you have to leave them behind. But there are also ways of working with what exists. For the Smithsonian to take on a project to build a Black museum, particularly at this moment of such division, was a radical act. And now the museum is in a position to help a lot of other institutions, smaller Black museums, and to transform other Smithsonian museums as well. So it is impactful.

BR: You've talked about how the institution of architecture has served as an instrument of oppression. For example, at the University of Virginia, Thomas Jefferson used elevational changes in section to obscure slave labor. Can you expand on that?

MW: An article could be written about Jefferson and the way he uses the section to hide what he knows to be a disavowal of his fundamental Enlightenment values. With Monticello, he develops all the dependencies below ground. The best signifier of that is the dining room's dumbwaiter. The enslaved waiter remained unseen because he would just place the bottle on the dumbwaiter and pull it up. The other bodies in the intimate spaces of the main house were kept at bay or kept outside.

Jefferson did the same thing at the University of Virginia. All of the areas where the enslaved people worked were below the pavilions or in the gardens that everyone thinks were formal gardens but were actually work yards. Those areas weren't meant to be seen. If you did happen to walk through that zone, your eye was delighted by the serpentine walls, right? So the aesthetic beauty of the brick wall shields the brutal labor of the enslaved just on the other side.

BR: A lot of your work is to bring history into the present and to wrestle with stories that weren't fully told or weren't recorded. I'm wondering how you work with someone else's personal history or the reconstruction of someone else's memory. How do you approach telling stories of people who are not here and can no longer speak for themselves?

MW: Part of it is personal—not knowing my family history, for instance, and trying to understand why that information was unknown. I've been piecing it together through genealogical research over the years, which has been fascinating. I had a white friend in college who said once, I can trace my family back to 12th-century France.

Torkwase Dyson, ***1919: Black Water***, **2019, installation view, Arthur Ross Architecture Gallery, Columbia GSAPP, New York, 2019.**
In *1919: Black Water*, Dyson addresses the murder of the Black teenager Eugene Williams in 1919, who unwittingly crossed the unmarked boundary between the Black and white beaches at Lake Michigan in Chicago on a self-made raft. Here, the motif of the raft stands metaphorically for how Black people navigate and transform spaces shaped by white society.
All images on this double-page spread courtesy Arthur Ross Architecture Gallery, Columbia GSAPP.
Photos: Nicholas Knight.

Torkwase Dyson, *Place, Raft and Drift*, from the series *1919: Black Water*, 2019, installation view, Arthur Ross Architecture Gallery, Columbia GSAPP, New York, 2019. Acrylic, graphite, wood, ink on canvas, 152 × 178 cm.

Torkwase Dyson describes "Black compositional thought" as a way of improvising spaces and objects of liberation in an oppressive system.

Torkwase Dyson, *Pilot*, from the series *1919: Black Water*, 2019, installation view, Arthur Ross Architecture Gallery, Columbia GSAPP, New York, 2019. Acrylic, graphite, brass, string, wood, ink on canvas, 183 × 244 cm.

> "We aren't interested in restoration—to return
> we are asking students to engage in actions of
> recognize the transformation of time and the
> disruption and social divisions."
>
> – MABEL O. WILSON

He had the evidence to show a famous poet in his family lineage. By contrast, I didn't know much about my family before my grandparents. Black folks just don't talk about those painful histories. So I've always been curious.

When I studied architecture as an undergraduate, I learned canonical history, primarily European history, but I sort of felt like an outsider—not seeing myself in these narratives. Why should I care about the Villa Lante, for example, which is absolutely beautiful and its proportions are perfect, but in the end the heritage of the Italian aristocracy was somewhat meaningless to me. Now, of course, I find it utterly fascinating through its social history, its connection to the development of mercantile capitalism in Italy, and what it means to own land outside the city. But that's not how architectural history was being taught at the time—as a social history.

The first opportunity that I had to consider Black history and architecture was in a studio as an undergrad at UVA. We had a site named Oregon Hill in Richmond, Virginia, next to a very famous cemetery with a large pyramid that was a Civil War monument to the 18,000 Confederate soldiers buried there. On the cemetery's other side was a Black community, in the Randolph neighborhood. I was interested in the Black community too, so I just expanded my site across the cemetery and into Randolph. That move in my project engaged the racialized spatial politics and histories of Richmond.

When I came to Columbia's GSAPP to do my master's degree, I was interested in probing these questions. My final project looked at race head-on through the lens of a single-family suburban house. I examined how the history and spaces of the house had been racialized by covenants and redlining. Levittown's exclusivity—no Blacks or Jews—was produced by those restrictions. So my project unpacked the racial exclusions buried in suburban domestic spaces and construction. Aunt Jemima, after all, still lurks in the kitchen cabinet![01]

In my project, I was extremely interested in how history and, more specifically, methods of drawing can dissect and transform the meaning of architectural representation and architectural history. That became a long-term project, one that has nonetheless been challenging because studying race, racialization, and racism in the disciplines of architecture and architectural history has made people uncomfortable.

Currently, I'm wrapping up a collection of essays with Irene Cheng and Charles Davis called *Race and Modern Architecture: A Critical History from the Enlightenment to the Present*, and, in a way, it's the project that I really wanted to undertake as my dissertation. But now, instead of just my voice, it's 18 voices that explore race as part and parcel of the formation of modernity and modernism.

BR: Who are some of the people now, both in writing history and in design practices, who are inspiring to you?

MW: I think the work of Charles Davis, my coeditor, is really timely and thorough. It's been great working and thinking with him about how the racial shapes modern bodies of knowledge. Darell Fields did a lot of the early work that was really impactful, and Irene Cheng's work is also brilliant and probing important histories. We have some great people in the book: Dianne Harris, who wrote an important history titled *Little White Houses*, which explored how architecture helped build the whiteness of American suburbia in the 1950s; Mark Crinson's scholarship on imperialism and the racial made important strides; Reinhold Martin, my colleague from Columbia, who has been thinking through the implications of racial difference in his work on American universities. We want the book to serve as a primer that can be foundational to future research. We want our proposition to be debated.

But I also look at artists like Torkwase, who explores Blackness through space and the language of architecture. This semester my studio is framed by concepts from the artist Kader Attia, who posits radical repair through reappropriating and transforming modernist architecture.

BR: Your work with Columbia's Global Africa Lab also opens up other modes of representing these histories. Can you talk about that?

MW: Along with my codirector Mario Gooden, we've been developing data spatialization techniques to look at complex landscapes, like postapartheid Johannesburg, to ask if it's really no longer divided. In some ways, it is unified. People move more freely. But in other ways, economic inequalities and racial stratification remain embedded. Working with data spatialization has helped us show that despite media images representing the city as world-class, neoliberalism and globalization are nonetheless reproducing precisely the same inequalities as apartheid.

BR: How do you work with these representational tools in a studio context? How do you transition from analysis into the design process?

MW: In terms of pedagogy, I've always found it helpful to show how representational techniques have their histories and their

the thing that it was—but instead
ical repair that
ent acts that have produced

limits. You have to understand what the tools actually produce so that you can use them to produce not what you already know but new knowledge—new ways of working.

To spatialize data we used Rhino for the last six years, with software plugins developed by Carson Smuts, a researcher in the Global Africa Lab, to scrape and spatialize data from social media feeds like Twitter. We used it to trace how people move through and occupy the city. These types of mappings prompted a radical rethinking of the tools and techniques. But also, these tools and techniques document the transformation of cities over time, animating daily life as well as history in the making.

For my current advanced studio at Columbia's GSAPP, we're looking at the theme of repair and reparations. Students have worked on an object of radical repair, where they take two objects and try to use one to repair the other. We've looked at the artist Jan Vormann, who patches stone and brick walls around the world with LEGO bricks. It produces this playful but also incongruent landscape attentive to the everyday. We've also been interested in the artist Yeesookyung, who breaks apart beautiful ceramic vases and then reconstructs them in these crazy monstrous ways with gold adhesive.

The studio asks: What would those techniques produce when you start to think about repair at the urban scale? My students examined the Cross Bronx Expressway, which forms a gash in those Bronx neighborhoods. So what would a protocol of repair do for the inequalities that are rampant in the South Bronx, how do we give them a stronger voice in the public sphere of the city? We aren't interested in restoration—to return it to the thing that it was—but instead we are asking students to engage in actions of radical repair that recognize the transformation of time and the violent acts that have produced disruption and social divisions.

BR: How do you see the agency of design in the face of this historical violence? What might the design of radical repair look like?

MW: We need to delve into all aspects of architecture's frameworks—its historical formation, its tools of representation, its academic structure, and its professional organization. All of these facets of the discipline emerge from the Western episteme and are thus just as entangled with the racial, racialization, race, and its legacy as they are with capitalism, another parallel modern formation. When it comes to radical repair, I like to rework Audre Lorde's declaration on power and institutions in the form a question: Can the master's tools dismantle the master's house?

This interview was originally published in Log48: Expanding Modes of Practice *(April 2020). With kind permission from* Log / *Anyone Corporation.*

01 Editors' note: Aunt Jemima was a popular US brand for breakfast products such as syrup and pancake mixes, whose trademark until 2020 was the image of a stereotypical smiling Black woman. In 2020, the brand owner announced that the brand name would be discontinued; and in 2021 the brand was renamed Pearl Milling Company.

On Intersectional Architecture

What significance could intersectional feminist discourse have for architecture? Can it point the way to an architecture free of discrimination and the democratic design of space? These and other questions were discussed in a non-hierarchical, open email correspondence by guest editors *Torsten Lange, Charlotte Malterre-Barthes, Daniela Ortiz dos Santos,* and *Gabrielle Schaad* with the architects *Menna Agha,* founder of the architecture and research platform Project Unsettled; *Adam Caruso,* partner of the architecture firm Caruso St John Architects in London/Zurich; *Tei Carpenter,* founder of the design studio Agency-Agency in New York; and *Carla Juaçaba,* founder of Carla Juaçaba Studio in Rio de Janeiro.

On Monday, July 5, 2021, at 10:04 a.m. Charlotte Malterre-Barthes wrote:

Dear Menna, dear Adam, dear Carla, dear Tei,

Against the backdrop of past institutional failures to undo all forms of discrimination in architecture, how can practices (in a holistic sense) deconstruct relations of power and combat the obstructive forces that still shape architectural discourse? How do feminism and queerness inform your own practice and pedagogy—is there an example you can share from your own contextualized experience that illustrates that? What potentials do you see for future practices in engaging with intersectional and queer-feminist transformation—from norms to office policies, from design decisions to material choices, both at the office and in the curricula—perhaps illustrated with a project you pursue. Please note that, in looking for practical examples, I do not mean the conventional theory-practice split—the dichotomy between those who build and those who don't—that still pervades contemporary architectural culture.

We very much look forward to your thoughts!

Warmly,

Charlotte with Torsten, Gabrielle, Daniela

ON MONDAY, JULY 5, 2021, AT 03:27 P.M. CARLA JUAÇABA WROTE:

Dear Charlotte, Torsten, Gabrielle, Daniela,

I believe in a democratic space design, which not only brings together all social differences but gender differences as well. Where everyone shares the same ground, on the same level. So, we can re-learn from Shakespeare's universal and marginal theater, from Peter Brook's redesign of theatrical spaces, from Lina Bo Bardi's free space of Museu de Arte de São Paulo (MASP), and from the collective ground floor of the indigenous *oca* house.

We need to identify and avoid illustrious and hierarchical spaces and redefine a "horizontal ground" where one can feel a sense of communion again.

Warm regards,

Carla

ON SATURDAY, JULY 10, 2021, AT 03:53 A.M. MENNA AGHA WROTE:

Dear all,

I agree with Carla's call for plurality, and for a space that recognizes and works for social and gender differences, although I pause at recognizing Shakespeare, or anything, as Universal.

And I wish to add the pressing need for a space to recognize pluriversality: to recognize the different cosmogenies and fields of meaning, and, respect their spatial performance. So on that note, I believe the discussion around the theory-practice split would be meaningful only if we first stop gaslighting ourselves by subscribing to a singular Western understanding of what is "to build." The use of "build" that relies on utilitarian ethics erases all the ways in which people in different fields of meaning entail to building; fields in which what we call "theory and practice" are mutually inclusive.

Looking forward to reading your response.

Best,

Menna

On Thursday, July 15, 2021, at 5:39 a.m. Adam Caruso wrote:

Dear all,

For a long time I believed that architecture and building were inexorably connected, and that their increasing separation, starting in the 1970s, was unfortunate. I tried to build and to write, and felt that the relationship between my teaching and my practice was a productive one. In the last decade this apparent balance is threatened by the ever more impressive, and scary, triumphs of capitalism and the quickening path towards environmental disaster.

I used to say that architecture meant building, now I think it probably means not building.

Architecture is fundamentally a positive action, you do not need architecture to make things bad, that happens by itself.

So what do I teach my students now, and what should I write and build about? I have tried to answer these questions, with a lot of guidance from others, by re-framing who makes architecture and why. This necessarily involves challenging the white, male "canon" of architecture, and searching for the ways in which previously hidden agents have in fact always contributed to how we think about and develop the built environment. This involves the rediscovery of suppressed voices from the past, like the protagonists of Dolores Hayden's

The Grand Domestic Revolution, it also means instrumentalizing the work and ideas of pioneers like Martha Rosler so that architecture includes a richer and more diverse set of voices and ideas. With these adjustments our discipline suddenly becomes more open and inclusive, and one discovers themes and actions that can positively engage with the challenges that confront us today.

Best regards,

Adam

ON MONDAY, JULY 19, 2021, AT 4:43 P.M. TEI CARPENTER WROTE:

Good morning All,

Undoing the assumptions of architecture as building and the meaning of "to build," as both Adam and Menna outline, is critical to develop an approach that encounters the complicity of architecture within deep systemic inequity and the climate crisis. For me, it is an act of both unlearning and relearning from my own education to consider more inclusively who makes architecture. It also means supporting mentoring initiatives that open up the possibility of shepherding a more diverse body of young people into the discipline.

To understand whether an act of design means building is to also ask to whom is the design directed and how to be resourceful with material interventions. As I think about audience and to whom a design is directed, I have recently been nourished by work outside of the discipline, including political theory from Jane Bennett looking at lively things and matter and Jack Halberstam's approach to wildness, both of which offer ideas about how to transgress and unsettle known subjects.

Best wishes,

Tei

On Tuesday, September 14, 2021, at 9:53 p.m. Charlotte Malterre-Barthes wrote:

Dear all,

When Menna talks about a "western understanding of what is 'to build'" and following your reckoning of an architecture that could be "not building," how does this tangibly translate for you, in your work as architect? Could you point at examples (yours or by others) that pave the way toward these ecofeminist future practices?

We would like to recollect the idea of "democratic space design" that you have brought and link it with Tei's question on "who makes architecture." In referring to democratic space design, Carla gave us specific examples of four buildings (Shakespeare, Brooks, Bo Bardi, and *oca*)—all of them designed to act as performative spaces—in order to suggest that architecture goes beyond building. While we, architects, like to see ourselves as enablers, "democratic" design seem little practiced yet. How would you negotiate this friction, in practice?

Warmly,

Charlotte, Daniela, Gabrielle, Torsten

On Thursday, September 16, 2021, at 10:09 a.m. Adam Caruso wrote:

Dear Charlotte,

I can only respond from the position of a Western architect who has done some building in the past, and has come to the conclusion that the time for new building within late-capitalist economies has now come to an end. My understanding of other, non-Western architectural practice is inexcusably slight, but drawing on narratives like that of Yasmeen Lari in Pakistan, suggests that there exist alternative practices that are more intellectually economical and materially fleet of foot, where reuse and new, interim, and permanent all contribute equally to what architecture can be.

Adam

ON MONDAY, SEPTEMBER 27, 2021, AT 5:21 P.M. CARLA JUAÇABA WROTE:

Dear Charlotte,

As Karl Marx says, "design is a tool of domination and control" if it is treated like that. And it's been treated like that, we must be conscientious of that. I agree with Tei about "unlearn and relearn," and consequently rethink how to teach.

If it is such a powerful tool, one should use it with less naivety, and understand it as a tool for coexistence—this is already a new design.

Warmest,

Carla

ON THURSDAY, OCTOBER 14, 2021, AT 10:24 A.M. TEI CARPENTER WROTE:

Good morning All,

Thank you for the discussion.

Thinking around architecture beyond building suggests expanding a straightforward idea of building with methods and processes outside of a static, permanent, autonomous understanding of it. I think an example such as the Ise-jingū in Japan offers a potential direction to consider. It's an ancient Shinto shrine and as part of a festival that takes place every 20 years, the grand shrine and other parts of the complex are symbolically dismantled and reconstructed. Through this continual renewal of the buildings, the knowledge of craft and skills are passed down across generations, embodying a notion of cultural resonance and continuity tied to the architecture. At the same time, the act of building is tied to a ritual which suffuses the architecture with an awareness of the passage of time, material life, labor, and maintenance.

Best wishes,

Tei

ON THURSDAY, OCTOBER 28, 2021, AT 06:52 A.M. MENNA AGHA WROTE:

Thank you, Tei, for mentioning the Ise-jingū shrine, as an example that opens up our discussion to possibilities of an otherwise. And reminds us that building/construction/architecture as they stand, in a Western field of meaning, has been defined by the exclusion of what is otherwise, by defining what is worthy of becoming, and by erasing others. Notions like informality stand as an example of such exclusion and architecture's—in its canon—complicity in epistemicide.

As we—spatial practitioners—recognize this, we open the door for abolitionist politics that seeks to stop building/construction/architecture and start thinking about places/spaces of the otherwise. Places/spaces that are constituted by their performance.

Best,

Menna

Contributors

Menna Agha
is an architect and assistant professor for design and spatial justice at Carleton University in Ottawa, Canada. She is a third-generation displaced Fadicha Nubian, a legacy that ushers her research interests in race, gender, space, and territory. Her published articles include "Nubia Still Exists: The Utility of the Nostalgic Space" (2019), "The Non-Work of the Unimportant: The Shadow Economy of Nubian Women in Displacement Villages" (2019), and "Liminal Publics, Marginal Resistance" (2017).

The Architecture Lobby
is an internationally operating organization of architectural workers based in New York, founded in 2013. It campaigns for the public and material recognition of architectural achievement within the discipline. A central concern are the precarious working conditions experienced by those working in architecture.

atelier masōmī
was founded in 2014 in Niamey, Niger, by Mariam Issoufou Kamara. As an architecture firm, it works primarily on public housing, commercial buildings, and urban planning projects, usually based on intensive field studies. Atelier masōmī prioritizes the careful, deliberate, and material integration of buildings into their sociocultural contexts and the consideration of cultural and climatic conditions. The Hikma Community Complex won the 2017 Gold LafargeHolcim Award for Africa and the Middle East, and the 2018 Silver Global LafargeHolcim Award for Sustainable Architecture. Since 2023, Kamara is a professor at the Department of Architecture at ETH Zurich.

BC Architects & Studies
was founded in Brussels in 2009. It is an architecture firm (BC Architects), an experimental educational lab (BC Studies), and a cooperative for recycled building materials (BC Materials). The team of around 20 people develops bioregional, circular, and inclusive low-tech architectures, sharing their experiences through teaching activities at the KU Leuven and the Hasselt University. Thus far, the projects have principally been conducted in Europe and Africa.

Katarina Bonnevier
(born 1970) is an artist, architect, researcher, and founding member of MYCKET collaboration, with whom she currently runs the artistic research project *Troll Perceptions in the Heartlands*. Bonnevier's work uses perspectives of gender to address the connections between architecture, aesthetics, and power. Her dissertation *Behind Straight Curtains: Towards a Queer Feminist Theory of Architecture*, completed at the KTH Royal Institute of Technology in Stockholm, was published by Axl Books in 2007.

Büro Juliane Greb
was founded in Ghent in 2005 by Juliane Greb (born 1985). In 2017, Petter Krag (born 1978) joined as an additional partner. The practice has carried out most of its building and design work in Germany and Belgium, shaped by an anti-exclusive outlook that finds expression in various scales and uses. Greb teaches at the University of Antwerp and the TU Delft. Juliane Greb and Petter Krag are both co-curators of the German Pavilion at the 18th Architecture Biennale (2023) in Venice.

Brady Burroughs
(born 1970) is active both as a writer and teacher of architecture, preferring experimental methods and the transmission of critical ideas outside academic contexts. She is the co-author and editor of *Ahmed for Architecture Students* (2019) and the author of *Architectural Flirtations: A Love Storey* (2016). She completed her doctorate in Critical Studies of Architecture at the KTH Royal Institute of Technology in Stockholm, where she is currently in charge of second-year teaching.

Tei Carpenter
(born 1982) founded the architecture and design studio Agency—Agency in New York in 2014. Carpenter's design projects and research engages architecture, infrastructure, and everyday rituals. She has taught at the Columbia GSAPP, Brown University, and the University of Toronto. She has been honored as a winner of the 2021 League Prize by the Architectural League of New York and the 2018 New Practices New York Prize by the American Institute of Architects.

Adam Caruso
(born 1962), along with Peter St John, founded the architectural firm Caruso St John Architects in 1990. The practice has offices in London and Zurich and has built throughout Europe, undertaking projects that range in scale from major urban developments and cultural projects to intricate interventions in complex historic settings. Caruso St John won the RIBA Stirling Prize in 2016 for the Newport Street Gallery and represented Britain at the 2018 Venice Architecture Biennale. Adam Caruso has been a professor of Architecture and Construction at the ETH Zurich since 2011.

Matilde Cassani
(born 1980) studied architecture at the Politecnico di Milano and architecture and urban culture at the CCCB and the UPC in Barcelona. Her work explores the spatial implications of cultural pluralism in contemporary western cities. She participated in Manifesta 12 in Palermo in 2018, the Chicago Architecture Biennial in 2017, and the Oslo Architecture Triennial in 2016. Cassani currently teaches at the Politecnico di Milano, the Domus Academy in Milan, and the Architectural Association in London.

Studio Chahar
was founded by Yasaman Esmaili in Tehran in 2017. Studio Chahar is a nomadic, research-driven architectural design studio focused on community-based design, design equity and innovation in the context of global practice. Studio Chahar's projects have been recognized with several awards including the 2017 Gold LafargeHolcim Award for Africa and Middle East, and the 2018 Silver Global LafargeHolcim Award for Sustainable Architecture.

Lilian Chee
(born 1971) is an associate professor at the Department of Architecture, National University of Singapore, where she co-leads the Research by Design Cluster. Her research connects embodied experience and affective evidence with architectural representation, affect theory, feminist politics, and creative practice methods. Her award-winning film collaboration *03-FLATS* (2014) has been screened at numerous festivals and exhibitions. Current books are *Architecture and Affect* (2022), *Remote Practices* (2022, co-edited with Matthew Mindrup), and *Art in Public Space* (2022).

Irene Cheng
is an architectural historian, critic, and associate professor of Architecture at the California College of the Arts in San Francisco. She is co-editor of *Race and Modern Architecture: A Critical History from the Enlightenment to the Present* (2020) and *The State of Architecture at the Beginning of the 21st Century* (2004). Her current book project is entitled *The Shape of Utopia: The Architecture of Radical Reform in Nineteenth-Century America*.

Esther Choi
is a Canadian multidisciplinary artist and architectural historian whose artwork, writing, and scholarship investigate how concepts of nature and notions of the human have shaped and been shaped by world-making practices. She is also interested in the intersections between representation and dialogical aesthetics. Her critical essays have appeared in publications, including *Artforum*, *e-flux Architecture*, and *Art Papers*. She is co-editor of *Architecture is All Over* (2017) and *Architecture at the Edge of Everything Else* (2010). Choi is an Adjunct Associate Professor at the Cooper Union and a Lecturer at the University of Pennsylvania.

Beatriz Colomina
(born 1952) is an architectural historian and theorist. She has been a professor of History and Theory at the Princeton University School of Architecture since 1988, where she was a founder of the program in Media and Modernity and continues to direct graduate and doctoral studies. Her published works include *X-Ray Architecture* (2019), *Are We Human? Notes on an Archeology of Design* (2016), *The Century of the Bed* (2015), *Manifesto Architecture: The Ghost of Mies* (2014), *Clip/Stamp/Fold: The Radical Architecture of Little Magazines 196X–197X* (2010), *Domesticity at War* (2007), *Privacy and Publicity: Modern Architecture as Mass Media* (1994), and *Sexuality and Space* (1992).

Concreto Rosa
is a Rio de Janeiro-based practice founded by Geisa Garibaldi. Concreto Rosa's collaborators are mostly Black women holding professional diplomas as bricklayers, architects, and electrical, hydraulic, and civil engineers. Their work coordinates across complex systems of making, design, transportation, reparation, and care, while enduring social, racial, gender, and even geographical biases that characterize the Brazilian society where they operate.

Counterspace Studio
is an architectural practice founded in Johannesburg in 2015 and led by Sumayya Vally. The studio's work focuses on the triad of inclusion, diversity, and the future, addressing these through research-based, interdisciplinary projects, which include architecture, community-based work, exhibitions, interventions, urban research, and design.

Afaina de Jong
is an architect. In 2005, she founded the architectural studio AFARAI in Amsterdam, which seeks to overcome the limits of traditional architectural practice through intersectional and interdisciplinary investigations of the city. Integrating design, theory, and research, AFARAI sees itself as a feminist practice that drives change on social and spatial issues while taking issues of difference into account. De Jong is the director of the MA program in Contextual Design at the Design Academy Eindhoven. In 2021, she worked with Debra Solomon on the Dutch Pavilion at the Venice Architecture Biennale.

Yvonne P. Doderer
(born 1959) is an architect and artist and has a doctorate in political science. She is currently a professor for gender and cultural studies at the University of Applied Sciences in Düsseldorf and runs the Office for Transdisciplinary Research and Cultural Production, based in Stuttgart. Her recent books include *Glänzende Städte: Geschlechter- und andere Verhältnisse in Stadtentwürfen für das 21. Jahrhundert* (2016) and *Rote Rosen statt Zerstörung: Frauen im Widerstand gegen Stuttgart 21* (2013).

Edit Collective
is a feminist design collective founded in London in 2018, which works to address prejudices and hierarchies in the built environment. The collective understands design to be a vehicle for promoting equality, which should be present in the design process as well as the designed object. In 2021, Edit was responsible for the exhibition architecture at the Barbican Centre in London and produced an alternative catalogue for the retrospective *How We Live Now: Reimagining Spaces with Matrix Feminist Design Co-operative*. In 2019, the collective participated in the Oslo Architecture Triennale.

Tom Emerson
(born 1970) co-founded 6a architects with Stephanie Macdonald in London in 2001. 6a designs buildings and landscapes for the arts and education. Alongside practice, Emerson is a professor of architecture and dean of the Department of Architecture at ETH Zurich, where he leads a studio exploring the relationship between making, landscape, and ecology. Books include *Never Modern* (2014), *6a architects 2010-17* (El Croquis, 2018) and a series of atlases on *Forst* (2012), *Galway* (2013), *Glasgow* (2016), and *Pachacamac, Peru* (2021).

Silvia Federici
(born 1942) is a feminist activist, author, and professor emeritus at Hofstra University in New York. She was a co-founder of the International Feminist Collective, which launched the "Wages for Housework" campaign in the 1970s. She has written books and articles on feminist and Marxist theory, social history, and education. Her publications include *Beyond the Periphery of the Skin: Rethinking, Remaking, and Reclaiming the Body in Contemporary Capitalism* (2020), *Re-Enchanting the World: Feminism and the Politics of the Commons* (2018), *Revolution at Point Zero: Housework, Reproduction, and Feminist Struggle* (2012), and *Caliban and the Witch: Women, the Body and Primal Accumulation* (2004).

fem_arc
is a group of women architects in Berlin who have been working together on projects from an intersectional feminist perspective since 2018. The collective's members are Océane Vé-Réveillac, Amelie Schindler, Insa Streit, Lara Stöhlmacher, Lucía Gauchat Schulte, Aslı Varol, and Ana Rodriguez Bisbicus.
In formats including lectures, workshops, podcasts, and audio and video works, fem_arc critically examines power structures in space, as well as the intersection of individual experiences of discrimination associated with gender, race, economic status, ability, queerness, and religion, among others.

Hélène Frichot
(born 1970) is a professor of Architecture and Philosophy and director of the Bachelor of Design program at the University of Melbourne. Her research fosters creative practice methodologies and develops concept-tools and theories that draw on feminist new materialism, the posthumanities, environmental humanities, and affect theory.
Her recent publications include *Dirty Theory: Troubling Architecture* (2019), *Creative Ecologies: Theorizing the Practice of Architecture* (2018), and *How to Make Yourself a Feminist Design Power Tool* (2016).

Ignacio G. Galán
studied architecture at the ETSA Madrid, the Delft University of Technology, and the Harvard GSD. He received his doctorate in architectural history and theory from Princeton University. Located at the intersection of architecture, politics, and media, his research focuses on nationalism, colonialism, and the displacement of population groups in the 20th and 21st centuries. He leads the architecture practice igg - office for architecture in New York and is an assistant professor at the Department of Architecture at Barnard and Columbia College.

Samia Henni
(born 1980) is a theoretician and historian of the built, destroyed, and imagined environments. An assistant professor at Cornell University, she held the Albert Hirschman chair at the IméRA in Marseille in 2021–22 and was a visiting professor at the University of Zurich in 2021. She is the editor of *gta papers 2: War Zones* (2018) and the author of *Architecture of Counterrevolution: The French Army in Northern Algeria* (2017). In 2020, she participated in Manifesta 13 in Marseille. Between 2017 and 2019, her exhibition *Discreet Violence: Architecture and the French War in Algeria* toured worldwide.

Kristina Herresthal
(born 1978) is an architect and architecture writer. After studying at the TU Berlin and the Mackintosh School of Architecture in Glasgow, she worked at various architectural firms in Vienna, New York, and Berlin, including Georg Reinberg and Grüntuch Ernst Architects. She worked in a scholarly and editorial capacity for the German *Shrinking Cities* project and *ARCH+*, among others, and writes regularly for various architecture publications. Together with Lisa Kristin Kadel, she founded the architecture practice Linie Architektur, which she now heads in partnership with Magnus Creutzfeldt as Linie Creutzfeldt Architekten in Berlin.

Carla Juaçaba
founded the architecture firm of the same name in Rio de Janeiro in 2000, undertaking primarily cultural and private projects. She won the first edition of the international prize ArcVision Women and Architecture 2013 in Italy, and the first prize of AREA Architectural Review Emerging Architecture Award 2018. In 2018, Juaçaba's project *Ballast* formed part of the main exhibition at the Venice Architecture Biennale, where she also designed one of the ten chapels in the Vatican Pavilion. Juaçaba lives in London and teaches at the Academy of Architecture in Mendrisio, Switzerland.

Tonderai Koschke
is an exchange student at the Harvard Graduate School of Arts and Sciences and is also pursuing an MA degree in architecture at the TU Munich. She previously worked at Boltshauser Architects in Zurich and Architangle in Berlin and has undertaken research into Zimbabwe's colonial heritage for the *Architecture and Politics in Africa* project at SOAS in London. She also works outside an academic context and is a co-founder of the pan-African association Isusu Ffena.

Elke Krasny
(born 1965) is a professor at the Academy of Fine Arts Vienna. Her research and curatorial work addresses social and ecological justice in the contexts of architecture, urbanism, art, reproductive labor, transnational feminisms, and the politics of memory. In 2019, she co-edited *Critical Care: Architecture and Urbanism for a Broken Planet* with Angelika Fitz. She is currently working on the book *Living with an Infected Planet: Covid-19 Feminism and the Global Frontline of Care.*

Lacol
is a cooperative of architects founded in Barcelona in 2009, which creates community infrastructures for sustainable living spaces. It regards these infrastructures as a key instrument in bringing about environmental and social change through architecture, cooperativism, and participation. Lacol's current members are Arnau Andrés, Eliseu Arrufat, Ari Artigas, Carles Baiges, Anna Clemente, Lali Daví, Cristina Gamboa, Ernest Garriga, Mirko Gegundez, Laura Lluch, Lluc Hernàndez, Pol Massoni, Jordi Miró, and Núria Vila.

Torsten Lange
(born 1979) is a lecturer in cultural and architectural history at the Lucerne University of Applied Sciences and Arts. He studied architecture and the history and theory of architecture at the Bauhaus University in Weimar and the Bartlett School of Architecture in London, where he received his doctorate in 2015. His work centers on historical research into the production conditions of the built environment in late socialism and on the spatial practices of queer subcultures. In addition to his own scholarly essays, he co-developed *Architectural Historiography and Fourth Wave Feminism*, a special issue of the open access journal *Architectural Histories* (2020), and co-edited

Contributors

Re-Framing Identities: Architecture's Turn to History, 1970–1990 (2017).

Rachel Lee
is an assistant professor at the Department of the History of Architecture and Urban Planning at the TU Delft and an associate researcher in the METROMOD research project affiliated with the LMU Munich. Her work examines the history of colonial and postcolonial architecture and urbanism at the intersection of migration and exile, transnational practice, cultural heritage, mobility, and gender, particularly in South Asia and East Africa. She is currently a Mellon Fellow for the research project *Centring Africa: Postcolonial Perspectives on Architecture* at the Canadian Center for Architecture.

Lesley Lokko
(born 1964) is the founder and director of the African Futures Institute (AFI) in Accra, Ghana, an independent postgraduate school of architecture and public events platform. She is the editor of *White Papers, Black Marks: Race, Culture, Architecture* (University of Minnesota Press, 2000) and the editor-in-chief of *FOLIO: Journal of Contemporary African Architecture*. She is a founding member of the LSE—UN Habitat Council on Urban Initiatives and a trustee of the London-based Architecture Foundation. She was a Visiting Professor at the Bartlett School of Architecture and is the curator of the 18th Architecture Biennale (2023) in Venice.

Diana Lucas-Drogan
is a freelance planner and mapping artist. Her work is extra-disciplinary, working with conceptual and material formats, with a focus on feminist and intersectional methods in planning and critical spatial production. She is a member of the metroZones collective and a founder of the independent magazine *Stadtseiten*. She teaches at the TU Braunschweig.

Sarah Maafi
is an architecture student at the TU Munich and a fellow of the Oskar von Miller Forum. She is the recipient of the 2021 RIBAJ/Future Architects essay prize. Along with Tonderai Koschke, she runs the MA course on postcolonial traces and continuities in German cities at the TU Munich. Her work has been published in *RIBA Journal*, *Architects Journal*, and *Involved Magazine*, among others.

Mona Mahall & Aslı Serbest
have worked together in space, image, sound, and text since 2007, operating at the juncture of architecture and art. They have participated in a variety of projects, including exhibitions at the Venice Architecture Biennale, the Ural Biennial in Yekaterinburg, and the Storefront for Art and Architecture in New York. They are the editors of *Junk Jet* magazine and curated the 7th Sinop Biennial in Turkey in 2019. Serbest is a professor of Temporary Structures at the University of the Arts Bremen. Mahall is a professor of Architecture and Art at the HafenCity University Hamburg.

Melissa Angela Alemaz Makele
(born 1989) is an editor at ARCH+. She studied architecture, art history, and philosophy at the Karlsruhe Institute of Technology and as a visiting student at the Karlsruhe University of Arts and Design. Since graduating, she has worked for Atelier Bow-Wow in Japan, among others. She is co-curator of the German Pavilion at the 18th Architecture Biennale (2023) in Venice.

Charlotte Malterre-Barthes
is an architect, urban designer, and assistant professor at the Swiss Federal Institute of Technology Lausanne. Most recently assistant professor at the Harvard Graduate School of Design, Malterre-Barthes' interests are related to urgent aspects of contemporary urbanization, material extraction, climate emergency, and ecological/social justice. In 2020, she started the initiative "A Global Moratorium on New Construction," interrogating current development protocols. Malterre-Barthes holds a doctoral degree from the Swiss Federal Institute of Technology Zurich on the political economy of commodities in the built environment. She is a founding member of the activist networks Parity Group and Parity Front.

Matri-Archi(tecture)
is an intersectional collective directed by Khensani de Klerk and Solange Mbanefo that brings African womxn of color together for the empowerment and development of African cities, within the realm of spatial education. Matri-Archi(tecture) produces knowledge that constantly aims at catalyzing and fostering dialogue while encouraging consciousness in spatiality, bringing to the forefront the need for an Intersectional Space.

Elli Mosayebi
(born 1977) is a professor of design and architecture at the ETH Zurich and, together with Ron Edelaar and Christian Inderbitzin, heads the architecture office Edelaar Mosayebi Inderbitzin in Zurich. Her work and research focus on social and ecological change in living practices. In 2021, along with ETH students, she created the walk-in installation *Klanghemd* for the multi-day public event *FrauMünsterhof21*, which marked the 50th anniversary of women's suffrage in Switzerland.

Iván L. Munuera
is a critic, curator, and historian of architecture and art based in New York. His work addresses the relationship between culture, technology, and politics, as well as bodily practices within modernity. Since 2015 he has worked at the Princeton University, where he is writing a dissertation on the architecture of HIV/AIDS. His writing has appeared in publications including *Log*, *Perspecta*, *The Architect's Newspaper*, and *El País*. He also produced the podcasts *Bauhauswelle 2018* for the Floating ~~University~~ in Berlin and *Chromanoids* for the 2017 Seoul Biennial of Architecture and Urbanism and the 2016 Istanbul Design Biennial.

MYCKET Collaboration
is an intersectional art, design, and architecture collective founded in Stockholm in 2012 by Mariana Alves Silva, Katarina Bonnevier, and Thérèse Kristiansson. Its artistic research projects are often done in collaboration with other participants and include theater productions, the design of public spaces, exhibitions, performances, text and theory production, and lectures.

Anh-Linh Ngo
(born 1974) is an architect, author, and the co-publisher and editor-in-chief of ARCH+. He co-founded the international initiative projekt bauhaus (2015–19), which critically examined the Bauhaus's ideas. From 2010 to 2016, he was a member of the Art Advisory Board at the Institute für Auslandsbeziehungen (ifa), for which he co-curated the touring exhibition *Post-Oil City* (2009) and *An Atlas of Commoning – Places of Collective Production* (2018). In 2021–22, he co-curated the exhibition *Cohabitation* in Berlin. He is a member of the advisory board of the Goethe-Institut and a member of the board of trustees of the Akademie Schloss Solitude and the IBA 2027 StadtRegion Stuttgart. He has been a member of the Academy of Arts in Berlin since 2022. He is co-curator of *The Great Repair* and the German Pavilion at the 18th Architecture Biennale (2023) in Venice.

Office for Political Innovation
is an architectural practice founded by Andrés Jaque in 2003, which works at the intersection of design, research, and critical environmental practices. Based in New York and Madrid, the Office for Political Innovation develops its projects in different scales and mediums and aims to promote inclusivity within the built environment. In 2016, the Office for Political Innovation was awarded the Austrian Friedrich Kiesler Prize for Architecture and the Arts. In 2014, it received the Silver Lion for the best research project at the Venice Architecture Biennale.

Daniela Ortiz dos Santos
is an assistant professor at the Goethe University in Frankfurt, where she is also the academic coordinator of the Center for Critical Studies in Architecture (CCSA) and a member of the GRADE Center Gender at the Cornelia Goethe Center for Women's and Gender Studies (CGC). She studied architecture in Rio de Janeiro and Buenos Aires and received her doctorate from the ETH Zurich. Through her research, teaching, and curatorial work, she aims to develop alternatives to dominant narratives within architecture history and historiography. She is co-editor of *Bauhaus Clouds: Challenges to the Nebula of Architectural Histories and Archives* (in preparation) and the author of the essay "Invisible Files in Visible Institutions: Notes on Max Cetto's Papers" (2020).

Mary Pepchinski
(born 1955) is an author and architectural historian based in Berlin. She is co-editor of *Ideological Equals: Women Architects in Socialist Europe 1945–1989* (2016, with Mariann Simon) and *Women Architects and Politics: Intersections between Gender, Power Structures and Architecture in the Long 20th Century* (with Christina Budde) and co-curated the exhibition *Frau Architekt* (2017/18) at the German Architecture Museum (DAM) in

Frankfurt. She taught at the TU Graz, the TU Berlin, the University of Applied Sciences in Dresden, and the University of Applied Sciences in Mainz. She was a professor of Architecture and Society at the TU Dresden until 2021.

Paul B. Preciado
(born 1970) is a writer, philosopher, curator, and a leading voice in the field of gender and body politics. Among other projects, he curated the public programs of documenta 14 in Kassel and Athens in 2017 and the Taiwanese pavilion of the Venice Art Biennale in 2019. He was director of the Independent Studies Program at MACBA in Barcelona and taught philosophy of the body and transfeminist theory at the University of Paris VIII-Saint Denis and New York University. His books include *Can the Monster Speak?* (2021), *An Apartment on Uranus* (2020), *Pornotopia* (2014), *Testo Junkie* (2013), and *Countersexual Manifesto* (2002).

Anna Puigjaner
(born 1980) holds a doctorate in architecture and is co-founder of the architectural office MAIO, which uses new spatial structures to break up normative architectures. Puigjaner researches alternative forms of housing and living that can offer improvements to unbalanced social structures. She teaches at the Graduate School of Architecture, Planning and Preservation, Columbia University, having previously taught at the Royal College of Art in London and the Barcelona School of Architecture ETSAB/ETSAV. In 2016, she was awarded the Harvard GSD Wheelwright Prize for her research project *Kitchenless City*. Since 2023 she is professor for architecture and care at ETH Zurich.

Jane Rendell
(born 1967) is a professor of Critical Spatial Practice at the Bartlett School of Architecture in London. Her books, which include *The Architecture of Psychoanalysis* (2017), *Site-Writing: The Architecture of Art Criticism* (2010), and *Art & Architecture* (2006), introduced the concepts of "critical spatial practice" and "site-writing." She is co-editor of *Critical Architecture* (2007) and *Gender Space Architecture* (1999) and curates the websites sitereadingwritingquarterly.co.uk and practisingethics.org.

Joel Sanders
is the professor-in-practice and former director of Post-Professional Studies at the Yale School of Architecture. He is the co-author of *Groundwork: Between Landscape and Architecture* (2011) and editor of *STUD: Architectures of Masculinity* (1996). In 1989, Sanders founded the New York-based architecture studio JSA, which since 2018 has included the think tank MIXdesign.

Gabrielle Schaad
(born 1982) is a postdoctorate researcher at TU Munich and a research associate at the Zurich University of the Arts. She was awarded her doctorate from the ETH Zurich, where her dissertation examined the promises and pitfalls of technological optimism and body concepts in Japanese post-war art and architecture. Her research focuses on images of space and the body in transcultural art and design practices since the 1960s, as well as collective initiatives and the spatialization of power and gender relations. Her monograph *Shizuko Yoshikawa* was published in 2018. She is co-editor of the 2022 *gta papers: Care & Architecture* and the anthology *archithese reader: Critical Positions in Search of Postmodernity, 1971–1976*.

Anooradha Iyer Siddiqi
is an assistant professor at Barnard College in New York, where she heads the Insurgent Domesticities working group at the Center for the Study of Social Difference. Her publication *Architecture of Migration: The Dadaab Refugee Camps and Humanitarian Settlement*, analyzes the history, spatial politics, visual rhetoric, and iconography of the Dadaab refugee camps of northeastern Kenya, presenting them as an epistemological starting point for the African and Islamic world.

Summacumfemmer
is an architectural practice founded by Anne Femmer and Florian Summa in Leipzig in 2015. It regards its buildings and designs as research investigations into topics including experimental (co-)habitation, construction at the nexus of economy and ambition, and pressing questions of form, design, and expression. Their approach, involving simultaneous research and design, is also characteristic of the architects' teaching. They were guest professors for Integral Architecture at the TU Graz and currently hold a guest professorship at the Berlin University of the Arts. Anne Femmer and Florian Summa are both co-curators of the German Pavilion at the 18th Architecture Biennale (2023) in Venice.

Niloufar Tajeri
(born 1980) is an architect, architectural theorist, and activist. She taught at the Institute for History and Theory of Architecture and the City (GTAS) at the TU Braunschweig and is currently completing a doctorate at TU Berlin on structural racism and colonialism in urban planning processes, based on the example of a planned large-scale project in Berlin. She is co-editor of *Nights of the Dispossessed: Riots Unbound* (2021) and *Small Interventions: New Living in Post-War Modernism* (2016). She was a fellow at Akademie Schloss Solitude and is a founding member of the Hermannplatz Initiative in Berlin.

Huda Tayob
is a senior lecturer at the University of Cape Town and is currently a Mellon Fellow for the research project *Centring Africa: Postcolonial Perspectives on Architecture* at the Canadian Center for Architecture. Her work addresses minority, migrant, and subaltern architectures and investigates the potential of literature as a reaction to archival gaps in architectural research. Along with Suzanne Hall and Thandi Loewenson, Tayob runs the open access curriculum racespacearchitecture.org, and with Bongani Kona curates the podcast series and online exhibition *Archive of Forgetfulness*.

Inés Toscano
(born 1989) is a doctoral student in the Department of Theory and History of Modern Architecture at the Bauhaus University in Weimar. In her research and on the website couplingstactic.com, Toscano critically maps architect couples who live and work together. She is writing her dissertation, *Couplings' Tactic: A Study of Intimate-Creative Labor Strategies in Architecture*. Since 2018, she has engaged in proactive intersectional feminist pedagogy in the context of her teaching at the Anhalt University of Applied Sciences and the Bauhaus University in Weimar.

Mierle Laderman Ukeles
(born 1939) is an artist based in New York and considered the founder of Maintenance Art. In 2016, a major retrospective dedicated to her work was held at the Queens Museum, New York. Between 2013 and 2015, the traveling exhibition *Maintenance Art Works 1969–1980* was hosted by various institutions around the world, including the Konsthall C in Stockholm; the Institute of Modern Art in Brisbane, Australia; the Arnolfini Center for Contemporary Arts in Bristol, UK; and the Grazer Kunstverein in Graz, Austria. She is represented by the Ronald Feldman Gallery in New York.

Ariane Wiegner
(born 1978) is an architect who is active in practice, research, and teaching. She studied architecture in Berlin and via a DAAD scholarship in the United States and gained professional experience at Steven Holl Architects, Shrinking Cities II, Barkow Leibinger, and David Chipperfield Architects, among others. In 2018, she co-founded the practice Kirchberger & Wiegner Rohde in Berlin. She has taught and conducted research in Tokyo, Berlin, and Arizona.

Mabel O. Wilson
(born 1963) is an architect and scholar and runs the interdisciplinary office Studio&. She is the Nancy and George Rupp Professor of Architecture, Planning and Preservation, professor of African American and African Diasporic Studies, and director of the Institute for Research in African American Studies at Columbia University. Wilson is the author of *Begin with the Past: Building the National Museum of African American History and Culture* (2016) and *Negro Building: Black Americans in the World of Fairs and Museums* (2012), and is currently working on the book *Building Race and Nation*, about the influence of slavery and dispossession on American civic architecture. In 2020, she co-edited the anthology *Race and Modern Architecture*.

Xcessive Aesthetics
is an all-female interdisciplinary design collective founded in London in 2019. It grew from the idea of exploring data and digital technologies through spatial design in order to recognize the hidden potential of new technologies and convey them in works of art that are easily accessible and playfully designed. These take the form of installations, talks, and workshops.

Imprint

©Mona Mahall/Aslı Serbest

ARCH+
Journal for Architecture and Urbanism

PUBLISHERS
ARCH+/Spector Books

ARCH+ PUBLISHERS
Nikolaus Kuhnert, Anh-Linh Ngo

ADVISORY BOARD
Arno Brandlhuber, Beatriz Colomina, Philipp Oswalt, Stephan Trüby, Georg Vrachliotis, Mark Wigley, Karin Wilhelm

EDITOR-IN-CHIEF
Anh-Linh Ngo*

MANAGING DIRECTOR
Arno Löbbecke

EDITORIAL TEAM
Nora Dünser*, Mirko Gatti*, Franziska Gödicke*, Christian Hiller, Felix Hofmann, Max Kaldenhoff (creative direction)*, Sascha Kellermann, Markus Krieger*, Melissa Makele* (project leader), Alex Nehmer, Jakob Walter

GUEST EDITORS
Torsten Lange*, Charlotte Malterre-Barthes*, Daniela Ortiz dos Santos*, Gabrielle Schaad*

MANAGING EDITOR
Nora Dünser*

STO-SCHOLARSHIP
Paul Barth*, Vera Krimmer*, Daniel Kuhnert*, Anna-Maria Mayerhofer*, Victor Lortie*, Lukas Meyer

*Editorial team for this publication, which is based on the German issue ARCH+ 246: *Zeitgenössische feministische Raumpraxis* (December 2021)

ART DIRECTION
Mike Meiré

DESIGN
Charlotte Cassel, Christopher Tröster, Meiré und Meiré

TYPESETTING
André van Rueth, Daniel Vandré, Stan Hema

PROJECT MANAGEMENT STAN HEMA
Niki Moreira

COPY EDITOR
Alisa Kotmair

TRANSLATIONS
Brían Hanrahan (pp. 42–43, 80–97, 120–125, 132–135, 168–173, 178–189, 196–197, 212–215),
Alisa Kotmair (pp. 1–6, 10–17, 34–35, 54–55, 68–79, 98–107, 126–131, 136–145, 166–167, 192–195)

PROOFREADING
James Copeland

PREPRESS
max-color, Berlin

PRINTING
Medialis Offsetdruck GmbH, Berlin

HEAD OF RESEARCH & EXHIBITION PROJECTS
Christian Hiller

HEAD OF EVENTS
Sascha Kellermann

HEAD OF COMMUNICATIONS & MARKETING
Barbara Schindler

HEAD OF ORGANIZATION
Elke Doppelbauer

ASSISTANT
Friederike Kiko

AMBASSADORS
Martin Luce, Christine Rüb

ARCH+ Verlag GmbH
Friedrichstraße 23a
10969 Berlin, Germany
Phone: +49 30 340 467 19
verlag@archplus.net
Managing Directors:
Nikolaus Kuhnert, Anh-Linh Ngo
ARCH+ gGmbH (non-profit organization)
ggmbh@archplus.net
Managing Director: Arno Löbbecke

ADVERTISING
anzeigen@archplus.net
archplus.net/en/mediakit

DONATION ACCOUNT
GLS Bank
IBAN: DE47 4306 0967 1229 2768 01
BIC: GENODEM1GLS
archplus.net/en/nonprofit

DIRECT ORDERS
of ARCH+ English editions:
archplus.net/en/shop/english-publications

SUBSCRIPTIONS
Only German issues:
archplus.net/en/subscriptions

DISTRIBUTION
Spector Books
Harkortstraße 10
04107 Leipzig
www.spectorbooks.com

Germany, Austria: GVA, Gemeinsame Verlagsauslieferung Göttingen GmbH & Co. KG, www.gva-verlage.de
Switzerland: AVA Verlagsauslieferung AG, www.ava.ch
France, Belgium: Interart Paris, www.interart.fr
UK: Central Books Ltd, www.centralbooks.com
USA, Canada, Central and South America, Africa: ARTBOOK/D.A.P., www.artbook.com
South Korea: The Book Society, www.thebooksociety.org
Japan: twelvebooks, www.twelve-books.com
Australia, New Zealand: Perimeter Distribution, www.perimeter-distribution.com

Bibliographic information published by the German National Library: The German National Library lists this publication in the Deutsche Nationalbibliografie; detailed bibliographic data is available online at dnb.dnb.de.
Library of Congress Control Number: 2020937306
ISBN 978-3-95905-701-1 (Spector Books)
ISBN 978-3-931435-76-9 (ARCH+)

First edition: 2023
Printed in Germany

This publication is supported by

swiss arts council prohelvetia

Harvard University Graduate School of Design